CHANGING THE SUBJECT

NEXT WAVE: NEW DIRECTIONS
IN WOMEN'S STUDIES
A series edited by
Inderpal Grewal, Caren Kaplan,
and Robyn Wiegman

CHANGING THE SUBJECT

FEMINIST AND QUEER POLITICS IN NEOLIBERAL INDIA

Srila Roy

DUKE UNIVERSITY PRESS
Durham and London 2022

Designed by A. Mattson Gallagher
Typeset in Garamond Premier Pro and Helvetica Neue
by Westchester Publishing Services

Library of Congress Cataloging-in-Publication Data
Names: Roy, Srila, author.
Title: Changing the subject : feminist and queer politics
in neoliberal India / Srila Roy.
Other titles: Next wave (Duke University Press)
Description: Durham : Duke University Press, 2022. |
Series: Next wave | Includes bibliographical references and index.
Identifiers: LCCN 2021059681 (print) | LCCN 2021059682 (ebook) |
ISBN 9781478016243 (hardcover) | ISBN 9781478018889
(paperback) | ISBN 9781478023517 (ebook)
Subjects: LCSH: Feminism—India. | Women in development—
India. | Neoliberalism—India. | Non-governmental
organizations—India. | Women—India—Economic conditions—
21st century. | Gay rights—India. | Queer theory. | BISAC: SOCIAL
SCIENCE / Women's Studies | HISTORY / Asia / South / General
Classification: LCC HQ1240.5.I4 R69 2022 (print) |
LCC HQ1240.5.I4 (ebook) | DDC 305.420954—dc23/
eng/20220307
LC record available at https://lccn.loc.gov/2021059681
LC ebook record available at https://lccn.loc.gov/2021059682

Cover art: Upasana A, *Untitled*, 2020. Digital artwork,
21 × 23 inches. Courtesy of the artist.

CHANGING THE SUBJECT

FEMINIST AND QUEER POLITICS IN NEOLIBERAL INDIA

Srila Roy

DUKE UNIVERSITY PRESS
Durham and London 2022

© 2022 DUKE UNIVERSITY PRESS
All rights reserved
Designed by A. Mattson Gallagher
Typeset in Garamond Premier Pro and Helvetica Neue
by Westchester Publishing Services

Library of Congress Cataloging-in-Publication Data
Names: Roy, Srila, author.
Title: Changing the subject : feminist and queer politics
in neoliberal India / Srila Roy.
Other titles: Next wave (Duke University Press)
Description: Durham : Duke University Press, 2022. |
Series: Next wave | Includes bibliographical references and index.
Identifiers: LCCN 2021059681 (print) | LCCN 2021059682 (ebook) |
ISBN 9781478016243 (hardcover) | ISBN 9781478018889
(paperback) | ISBN 9781478023517 (ebook)
Subjects: LCSH: Feminism—India. | Women in development—
India. | Neoliberalism—India. | Non-governmental
organizations—India. | Women—India—Economic conditions—
21st century. | Gay rights—India. | Queer theory. | BISAC: SOCIAL
SCIENCE / Women's Studies | HISTORY / Asia / South / General
Classification: LCC HQ1240.5.I4 R69 2022 (print) |
LCC HQ1240.5.I4 (ebook) | DDC 305.420954—dc23/
eng/20220307
LC record available at https://lccn.loc.gov/2021059681
LC ebook record available at https://lccn.loc.gov/2021059682

Cover art: Upasana A, *Untitled*, 2020. Digital artwork,
21 × 23 inches. Courtesy of the artist.

To Mira and Salomé
My cannonballs and unicorns
And to Alf
Who is the whole of the moon

CONTENTS

ABBREVIATIONS

AIDWA	All India Democratic Women's Association
AWM	Autonomous Women's Movement
BJP	Bharatiya Janata Party
CAA	Citizenship Amendment Act
CALERI	Campaign for Lesbian Rights
CPM	Communist Party of India (Marxist)
FTM	female-to-male
ITPA	Immoral Traffic (Prevention) Act
IWM	Indian women's movement
JU	Jadavpur University
MFI	microfinance institution
MTF	male-to-female
NALSA	National Legal Services Authority
NGO	nongovernmental organization
NRC	National Register of Citizens
PBGMS	Paschim Banga Ganatantrik Mahila Samiti
SC	Scheduled Caste
SFE	Sappho for Equality
SHG	self-help group
SRS	sex reassignment surgery
UN	United Nations
VG	Vigil Group

ABBREVIATIONS

AIDWA	All India Democratic Women's Association
AWM	Autonomous Women's Movement
BJP	Bharatiya Janata Party
CAA	Citizenship Amendment Act
CALERI	Campaign for Lesbian Rights
CPM	Communist Party of India (Marxist)
FTM	female-to-male
ITPA	Immoral Traffic (Prevention) Act
IWM	Indian women's movement
JU	Jadavpur University
MFI	microfinance institution
MTF	male-to-female
NALSA	National Legal Services Authority
NGO	nongovernmental organization
NRC	National Register of Citizens
PBGMS	Paschim Banga Ganatantrik Mahila Samiti
SC	Scheduled Caste
SFE	Sappho for Equality
SHG	self-help group
SRS	sex reassignment surgery
UN	United Nations
VG	Vigil Group

Feminist histories are histories of the difficulty of that we, *a history of those who have had to fight to be part of a feminist collective, or even had to fight against a feminist collective in order to take up a feminist cause.*

Sara Ahmed, *Living a Feminist Life*, 2017

This is a book about feminism and feminist subjects. It is about how feminist subjects are made—and make themselves—in a time and place not considered amenable to the production of such subjects. Our times are marked by extraordinary forms of oppression and abjection—toward gendered, racialized, and sexualized bodies in particular. The scale of gender and sexual violence, victimization, and inequality leaves one breathless, unable to fathom its cessation or undoing. The Global South has historically functioned to provide the evidence to confirm this sorry state of affairs. It has provided a readily available site for external intervention, in supplying the raw material—the objects and others—and the moral certitude for an interventionist epistemology and politics located outside its boundaries but enacted in its name. It has served less as a site of feminist struggle in its own right than of the making of feminist subjects elsewhere.

Considerable energy has gone into debunking these assumptions—that feminism originates in the West and spreads as what Sara Ahmed (2017, 4) calls an "imperial gift" to the non-West, which is, in turn, the home of other women who fortify the agency of white Western women as feminists. We now have stories of being a feminist and of living a feminist life in very many places in the world, in struggles with very many patriarchies. We have our own stories, but we also have our own unique postcolonial burdens when it comes to "telling feminist stories" (Hemmings 2011). Our stories have undertaken two tasks at once: of speaking back to local patriarchs who have dismissed our feminist struggles as derivative of Western ones and of undermining the forms of cultural and historical othering that have fundamentally shaped white Western feminisms. We, too, were making history, we have had to say—to establish ourselves as subjects worthy of national citizenship and belonging, on the one hand, and as agential, feminist subjects, on the other—while simultaneously bringing questions of sexual and gender difference to their limit in favor of what some would call intersectionality. And yet, the loudest feminist voices continue to belong to white feminists in the northern metropole, whose power derives from their capacity to exclude and to appropriate, for the sake of foregrounding not "me, too" but in fact, "me, not you" (Phipps 2020, 3).

Part of the centering of this *me*—even in accounts critical of this very move—is not only the exclusion of other feminist voices and histories but also their inevitable flattening into an essentialized and homogeneous mass. Given that *our*—as opposed to *their*—feminisms have been constituted through an unavoidable dialogue with the West and the nation-state, we have ended up speaking as if in one voice, with the *we* of our stories constituting a perfect foil to the *me* of white Western feminisms at scales both global and local. But who is this *we*? Or, to put it differently, who is the subject of our feminisms? If it has become possible to imagine feminist politics and futures without having to posit an essentialized subject—implicitly white and Western—then how sustainable is it to think of feminist subjects *elsewhere* in singular, uniform, uncontested, and internally undivided terms? If anything, the category of *woman* has proved even less sustainable in the rest of the world, where gender has continually fractured in intersection with other categories of identity and difference. Yet the feminist stories that have proved most audible have proceeded on the basis of a given, stable *we*, affording less space to the histories of struggle that have led to its fragile and contested constitution, as Ahmed (2017) reminds us. It has proved still harder to tell a story of internal differences and power relations—of what is residual and emergent—within our feminisms (Williams 1977). To restore feminist subjects outside the West to their rightful position—as autonomous, knowing, and willful agents—they must be worthy not merely of recognition but also of judgment and critique.

I found feminism when it appeared deeply fractured. In the early 2000s, when I took my first ever gender studies courses as a recently arrived Indian graduate student in the United Kingdom, feminist stories were infused with feelings of loss. I read the work of northern feminists bemoaning the institutionalization of feminism—in the very women's studies programs that were under siege in British universities. Away from home for the first time, I discovered—in a dislocation that Mary John finds conducive to the study of home—the "historical field of feminism in India" (1996, 122). Indian feminists were also engaged in a difficult internal debate about the limits of those ideals, categories, and subjects—of a *we*—that had constituted the foundations of their worlds and selves.

The tenor of these troubles did not come as a surprise to me. I had come of age in the 1990s in India, when caste- and religion-based cleavages were felt in transformative ways, even if not fully understood by young, privileged, and sheltered middle-class, upper-caste, metropolitan Indians like myself. When the city of Bombay, where I lived, was engulfed in flames after the demolition of the Babri Masjid (followed by a spate of coordinated bomb blasts across the city), I knew that the affects of a previous era—captured in state-sponsored slogans like "unity in diversity" (*anekta mein ekta*)—had long passed.[1] It was this past that Indian feminists mourned the loss of, and with it the certainty of their own political aspirations to speak on behalf of *all* Indian women, while attempting, at the same time, to self-reflexively tell a story of the past and how it had gone wrong: how was it possible that the feminist *we* had turned out to be nothing more than a mere fiction?

These were affects I both could and could not partake of. While these feminists, of a certain generation, were mourning the passing of feminism, Indian women and queers from subsequent generations were discovering feminism for the first time. Some were encountering feminist literature and politics at universities, and others in some of the newer spaces that a global-ized India offered, such as nongovernmental organizations (NGOs). When I first began to think seriously about the questions that would inform this book, I turned quite naturally to NGOs. Indeed, I often thought that had I not obtained funding for a PhD program and a subsequent stable job in a fast-imploding academic labor market, I might well have ended up in an NGO working on women's or sexual rights. It was obvious to me that these were spaces of feminist learning and doing (not unlike the classroom); yet, in generationally motivated stories, they were written off as depoliticized spaces productive only of "Nine-to-Five Feminists" (Menon 2004, 242n31).

Notwithstanding this emergent generational divide, there was much in common across distinct generations of Indian feminists. After all, "we" occupied the related spaces of professionalized academia and activism, not merely out of a shared ideological and political commitment but also because of our social backgrounds. The unnamed intimacies of class and caste enabled middle-class and upper-caste (*savarna*) Indian women to take advantage of the "mobilities of education" that came postindependence and to later capitalize upon new globalized opportunities and become part of a growing international class of global elites (John 1996, 10). Unlike those in more lucrative and ethically dubious corporate jobs, we—activists and academics—never lost sight of the poor. What perhaps endured most, as Indian feminism was both lost and recalibrated at the hands of new feminist subjects, was a distinctly postcolonial mode of "speaking for" in which middle-class and upper-caste feminists took upon themselves the mantle of representing the interests of others. Feminism endured as an imperial gift in the postcolony, handed down from one generation of a privileged *we* to the next.

Feminism's pasts and others haunt the millennial feminist sites and subjects of this book, including those minority feminists who were no longer spoken for but instead spoke for themselves. Even as they powerfully interrupted the we of Indian feminism, they could not escape its class, caste, and metrocentric biases, or the ethics and politics of "saving" others—of all genders and sexualities. I am able to mobilize this critique by bringing into the fray the voice and agency of those individuals and groups that have been at the receiving end of imperial and metropolitan feminist aspirations. But as I attempt to restore subalterns as millennial feminist subjects in their own right, I remain mired in the pitfalls, even the violence, intrinsic to such projects of recovery, which only reinforce historical processes of objectification and othering (Spivak 1988).

The critiques offered in this book around activist or "NGO-ized" feminisms are well directed at academic feminists who have historically benefited from both: the subaltern's silence and (mediated) voice. But even in our conjoint failings, *we* are not equal. I have, on occasion, felt relief in my inability to do any real damage—given my limited capacity to effect any real change in this world—but NGO workers or activists who take on this responsibility are also more vulnerable for it. They are implicated in circuits of neocolonial funding in ways that academic critique can damage while leaving the imperial benefactor—and the individual academic—unharmed. And they can also feel betrayed when they hear the academic telling a different tale of their reported truths, rooted in an assumed *we* of feminist sisterhood and solidarity.

Finally, the *we* that constitutes class and caste belonging is also lived in complex and ambivalent ways, contra the assumptions of a homogenizing imperial gaze. If this book is filled with feminism's ghosts, then it is equally populated by those I call, after Nirmal Puwar (2004), space invaders, who enter spaces not meant for them. In globalized and digitalized India, millennials are space invaders in not always obvious ways—they might have names that identify them as being upper caste but struggle to speak fluent English, and they might have consumer capacity but the "wrong" taste and so end up closeted in the wrong closet. Closets can offer comfort and safety from several registers of judgment and failing.

While researching this book, I failed at the only project I was socialized for—namely, heteronormative conjugality. Notwithstanding an education at prestigious schools and colleges in India, I was raised in anticipation of marriage in ways that are typical of the anglicized Bengali *bhadralok* (respectable) milieu I inhabit. I fulfilled these aspirations well—through a long-term relationship, a marriage, and motherhood—until I no longer did. Within a year, I found myself on unfamiliar ground: I moved from one country to another, endured a traumatic childbirth, was confronted with the end of a decade-long relationship with the father of my children, and became involved in a protracted custody battle. Such ruptures with heteropatriarchy are not easily folded into dominant caste, "cultured" Bengali families for whom they have less to do with custom or religion than with maintaining status and respectability (see Sen 2018). I often chose the comfort of passing than revelation. I also think I was embarrassed at my own failing, at being dumped so spectacularly. And this sense of embarrassment was enough to cast me, in my own eyes, as a bad feminist.

These are feelings that also haunt the subject(s) of the pages that follow, even if obliquely. They permeate some of the intense and intimate negotiations with norms and normativities that readers will encounter— negotiations that pervaded my own attachment to and rejection of heteropatriarchal norms, as well as Indian feminists' desires for a *we* rooted in a reified secular political past. Even as the individuals and communities at the heart of this book attempted to live in ways that transgressed the burdens of heterosexuality, patriarchal control, or even the seductions of consumer capitalism, they were all caught within it. After all, we are all caught, no matter how free. Who is there to judge us?

ACKNOWLEDGMENTS

This project and book have spanned a decade of my life. Through many a transformation intimately felt but universally known—migration, motherhood, and a global pandemic—it has distracted me while also being my crutch. I am so very glad that this project always returned me to India, and to those individuals and communities there deeply committed to social justice and increasingly firefighting on all fronts. It is to them, and especially those activists and organizers affiliated with Sappho for Equality and Janam, that I owe the biggest thanks.

When I first started this research—as a pilot study on the Indian women's movement—I met several activists and academics across India. There are far too many individuals and organizations to name, and even as the book developed differently, those initial conversations shaped its overall direction. As with my first book, this research would not have been possible without the generosity, patience, and acuity of Kolkata's feminist lifeworld. Besides those who appear in this ethnography, there are many more to thank who gave to this project their time, reflections, and resources: Anirban Das, Anchita Ghatak, Jasmeen Patheja, Sutapa Patra, Kavita Punjabi, Mira Roy, Rukmini Sen, and Samita Sen. Anchitadi made many things possible in the field which would not otherwise have been possible. Even as she might not agree with everything in this book, she has been key to my appreciation of the complexities of Indian feminism.

This book began its life at the University of Nottingham, where I worked as a lecturer in sociology. It was generously supported by the university, a British Academy Small Grant, and colleagues and friends there. The wider community of UK-based feminist scholars inspired the formulation of early questions. Warm thanks to Kristin Aune, Jonathan Dean, Sara de Jong, Catherine Eschle, Clare Hemmings, Amal Treacher Kabesh, Bice Maiguashca,

Maria do mar Pereira, Aimie Purser, and my forever Warwick friends, Maud Perrier and Elisabeth Simbürger.

When I moved to the University of the Witwatersrand, I entered an unusually vibrant academic culture in the intense and complicated city of Johannesburg. The appetite for intellectual life at Wits is a rare thing and nourished my thinking when I needed it most. Field trips to India and various other research costs—from availing precious research assistance to luxurious writing retreats—were made possible by the university's Friedel Sellschop Award, its humanities faculty, and, beyond Wits, a grant jointly given by the National Institute for the Humanities and Social Sciences, South Africa and the Indian Council of Social Science Research, and a grant from the Andrew W. Mellon Foundation (grant number 41600691).

Many colleagues and friends—even those who are no longer at Wits or in Johannesburg (but will always be part of it)—took an interest in my research and supported it in distinct ways: Keith Breckenridge, Brett Bowman, Sharad Chari, Jackie Dugard, Debjyoti Ghosh, Pamila Gupta, Keval Harie, Mehita Iqani, Dilip Menon, Joel Quirk, Stephen Sparks, Ahmed Veriava, Becky Walker, and Eric Worby; and writing and reading buddies Cathi Albertyn, Elsje Bonthuys, Barbara Buntman, Catherine Burns, Sarah Charlton, Natasha Erlank, Shireen Hassim, Tessa Hochfeld, Isabel Hofmeyr, Caroline Jeannerat, Nafisa Essop Sheik, and Alison Todes. For all things Governing Intimacies—a project that has materially and intellectually supported this book—my thanks to Caio Simões de Araújo and Yurisha Pillay. Without Yurisha's exceptional competence, my steering of development studies at Wits would have left little time for anything else, let alone write this book.

The Department of Sociology at Wits has always been supportive and accommodating of my research needs. Thanks to Ingrid Chunilall, Jacklyn Cock, Ran Greenstein, Sam Kariuki, Sedzani Malada, Sarah Mosoetsa, Lorena Nunez Carrasco, Ben Scully, Michelle Williams, and, beyond, to Mucha Musemwa and Garth Stevens. Shireen Ally and Zimitri Erasmus were some of the first to witness "data" becoming something more, and this book would not have gotten off the ground without their encouragement and enthusiasm. I owe special thanks to Nicky Falkof, Bridget Kenny, and Sarah Nuttall, who not only read my words (often on incredibly short notice) but assured me of those words' meaning and worth. Their brilliant ideas, sage advice, and good humor kept me grounded when the writing and publishing of this book felt too much.

I am also indebted to those who read individual chapters of the manuscript and whose astute comments both challenged and inspired me: Swethaa

Ballakrishnen, Pratiksha Baxi, Rachel Berger, Sayan Bhattacharya, Trent Brown, Rohit Dasgupta, Debanuj Dasgupta, Amanda Gilberston, Tanya Jakimow, Stephen Legg, Kenneth Bo Nielsen, Sangeeta Ray, Debarati Sen, Nafisa Essop Sheik, Millie Thayer, and old friend and fierce editor Kaavya Asoka. Rajeswari Sunder Rajan's interest in this book and my scholarship more generally has always been a gift.

Srimati Basu, Inderpal Grewal, and Raka Ray came together to read a first full draft of the manuscript just as the world shut down. Notwithstanding these extraordinary circumstances, they engaged my work in ways that shaped this final product but also modeled what collegiality and mentorship ought to look like in our profession. Additional thanks to Inderpal for being such a supportive editor of such a stellar book series at Duke University Press.

I am grateful for the diverse communities I have to think with; these are colleagues and comrades who, without even necessarily engaging the concerns of this project, have inspired me with their own: Anjali Arondekar, Brinda Bose, Raewyn Connell, Aniruddha Dutta, Radhika Gajjala, Sahana Ghosh, Shalini Grover, Yasmin Gunaratnam, Ravinder Kaur, Ananya Jahanara Kabir, Dolly Kikon, Prabha Kotiswaran, Kavita Krishnan, Atreyee Majumder, Deepak Mehta, Nivedita Menon, Deepti Misri, Trish Mitra-Kahn, Kathryn Moeller, Nirmal Puwar, Padmini Ray Murray, Richa Nagar, Shilpa Phadke, Kalpana Ram, Atreyee Sen, Svati P. Shah, Dina Siddiqui, Subir Sinha, Carole Spary, Ajantha Subramanian, Nandini Sundar, Ashwini Tambe, and Rashmi Varma. The interest and generosity of Gayatri Chakravorty Spivak, since the publication of my first book, has been a privilege.

I have been lucky to present this research to rich audiences across the world. I would like to acknowledge the graciousness of my hosts at two institutions, in particular: Amanda Gilberston at the Australia India Institute in Melbourne; and Carmen Geha, Sara Mourad, and Kathryn Maude at the American University of Beirut. In both places, colleagues went out of the way to read and support my work, and I hope I can do the same for them.

The academic community on Twitter has turned out to be an unexpected site of solidarity and support. For their generous contributions to my thinking on contemporary Indian feminism (and genuine forms of assistance), my thanks go to Sohni Chakrabarti, Arpita Chakraborty, Proma Ray Chaudhury, Shraddha Chatterjee, Sohini Chattopadhyay, and Dyuti. I have also learned much from the various postgraduate students I have supervised at Wits, and I thank them for making the labor of feminist teaching such a pleasurable one. My co-editors at the journal *Feminist Theory* have long constituted a source of inspiration, comradeship, and collegiality.

As editor, Caroline Jeannerat cannot be thanked enough for the care that she takes with one's words and the worlds they are struggling to conjure. Thanks are also owed to Meghan Drury, who made sharp and timely interventions into this manuscript as it journeyed through its rounds of peer review.

I have also lucked out with research assistance. Upasana Agarwal offered sustained support in Kolkata, and I learned much from our discussions on feminist and queer politics. While Debarati Sarkar's primary role on this project was to transcribe and translate the interview data, her energy, ideas, and enthusiasm offered it much, much more. Getting to know her and her scholarship has been one of the unexpected rewards of this research.

From the start, Elizabeth Ault at Duke University Press has pushed my thinking in the right direction. Besides being consistent and kind, she sourced the best readers for this manuscript—one anonymous and the other, Naisargi Dave, as revealed. Their reviews were extraordinarily rich, insightful, and generative, and this book is vastly improved because of the contributions made by the editor and reviewers. Ishan Tankha is owed more than thanks for allowing me, once again, to generously use his photograph to say what text alone cannot say. In the final stages of publishing this book, writing fellowships at the Johannesburg Institute for Advanced Studies and the Rockefeller Foundation's Bellagio Center renewed my energy.

My final thanks are reserved for my families—those inherited, chosen, and built. Stephen Legg is that academic friend who will roll his eyes at you for asking the same question about governmentality for the hundredth time but will still answer it. His friendship has never felt far, especially when I have most needed it. Julia O'Connell Davidson has held my hand tight through many a roller coaster ride and ensured that I felt loved and held whether I was on it or off it. And even as she has read little of this book, many of my ideas—and much of my person—are shaped in and by her light. Jessica Breakey has nourished me and this book in very direct ways, from child- and dog-minding to offering sharp ideas and urgent research assistance to never letting me forget life beyond the book. Wherever she might be in the world, Jessica will be my home in Johannesburg. For two decades now, Disha Mullick's friendship has inspired me to think harder and to write better. This project began in her image, and even as she might not see herself in it, I hope I have done some justice to the messiness of the world that she has made me see.

This project and book owe much to my family in India. My sister, Mishta Roy, has always inspired and cheered me on and, together with my brother-in-law, Anirudh Moudgal, and my terrific niece, Mohini Roy Moudgal, is a source of unconditional love. My parents, Debashis and Reeti Roy, are by now well acquainted with the specific demands of academic life; they have grown accustomed to asking "And how is the book coming along?," worrying when I worry, and celebrating my wins. Those wins, if any, are also because of their love, support, and teaching.

In Johannesburg, as a recently divorced single parent of two small babies, I would not have been able to hold down a job—let alone write anything—without the competence and care of Thembi Ndlovu. Through many house moves and shifting (and difficult) domestic situations, Thembi's work made my work possible. My children, Mira and Salomé, will be most delighted to see this book in the world, being forever the first to ask, "Have you finished your book?," "Are they going to publish your book?," and "When will they publish your book?" I hope one day they might even read this book and remain committed to transforming a patriarchal society into a feminist one. It is hard to adequately thank Alf Gunvald Nilsen for the gift of our life together. Besides all the material ways in which Alf made it possible for me to write this book—by taking care of the children and pets, the house and garden, and by keeping me fit and fed—he also read multiple iterations of its arguments, gave only the smartest comments, and lifted me up when I felt lost. He is all of my world, and I am so grateful.

Introduction
Changing the Subject
of Indian Feminism

When mass protests around the gang rape and murder of Jyoti Singh Pandey erupted in Delhi toward the end of 2012, I watched from afar with amazement. I saw how this singular yet all too routine event—the rape and murder of a young woman—brought thousands of ordinary, mostly young, and mostly middle-class urban protestors onto the streets in India's capital and across the nation. So unprecedented were their numbers and force that in Delhi, at least, the police resorted to tear gas and water cannons to disperse furious crowds. I watched the event travel and engage global publics; feminists in South Africa, where I had recently arrived, asked when they would have their "Delhi moment." And with feminists back home I struggled to make sense of this seemingly new feminist consciousness and energy.[1]

It was only a few years ago that I had started researching the terrain of Indian feminist activism, and yet it already felt like a different moment. Across major cities, I met academics, activists, those working in gender and sexual rights nongovernmental organizations (NGOs), and constitutive of distinct generations of Indian feminists. Those who saw themselves as belonging to something called the Indian women's movement (IWM) shared a common diagnosis of the present.[2] As a feminist lawyer who had been politically active since the 1980s told me, "the space for spontaneous, voluntary activism—of being an activist lawyer, for example—has gone. Radical discourse has gone. But the disparity between activists has increased because those at the grass roots remain unpaid and those working in NGOs lead a comfortable life because they are funded." A feminist academic, involved in similar movement circles in Delhi, explained the underlying logic behind such claims: "In India, there was always a strong sense of keeping funded and nonfunded activism and politics separate.... [T]o make a distinction between funded and autonomous politics, to raise the question of responsibility, accountability, and who comes into the movement." With India's economic liberalization making it far easier to obtain transnational funds for social development work, this distinction mattered less than how funding was perceived to orient feminist priorities toward the agendas and imperatives of the state, the market, and international development. It challenges nothing, said an older feminist, who worked in publishing, as a way of explaining the consequent depoliticization of the IWM.[3]

Unlike feminists of this generation who were professionals in a range of sectors—from law to academia to journalism and publishing—and contributed to the movement outside of their work hours, a subsequent generation of women were fully employed by or even heading their own funded feminist organizations. For these women—who were said to have come into the movement through NGOs and not through activism—it was obvious that affectively charged proclamations of the political present concealed more than they revealed. "Funding—the taking or not taking of money from external sources—is articulated, if not explicitly, as a moral issue," said a younger feminist, the director of a Mumbai-based women's rights NGO. The more strident critiques of funded politics and "NGO-ization" also came, she argued, from places of privilege: "The issue about funding is also about women's work." Many like her, who saw themselves as straddling movement and NGO spaces, defended the need for institutional and financial support on multiple grounds: the sustainability and continuity of activism ("What kind of institution are you building? How will you give anything to young people coming in?"); the question of livelihoods and pay ("What is wrong with providing women good salaries to sustain themselves independently?"); the notion of feminist consciousness-raising ("We have glimpsed feminism within these organizations"); and the unexpected expansion of the remit of gender struggle ("The queer movement is also a product of this context"). Yet these defenses were haunted by the ghost of a "real" feminist; as an NGO worker in Bangalore remarked, "There is a definite sense that you have to measure up to some things to be called a real feminist."

An initial motivation for writing this book was to participate in this defensive logic by showing that accounts of contemporary feminisms as being co-opted, depoliticized, and lost were grossly inadequate. As generationally motivated narratives they told us more about nostalgia for a revolutionary past than they did about a rapidly transforming landscape of gender and sexual rights under conditions of global neoliberalism. By declaring feminist struggles as co-opted and depoliticized—a thing of the past—they were also unable to make room for futurity. After all, few anticipated the kind of mass upsurge that took place around gender justice on the streets of Delhi in 2012. These protests overwhelmingly comprised young millennials whom many had dismissed as apolitical ("Young women are not joining the movement"), but, at times, it was hard to tell if they were feminist at all. If anything, they seemed to represent a still newer generation whose calls for the death penalty and castration of rapists suggested "the failure of several decades of feminism in this country" (Tellis 2012).

In a short period of time, then, I knew that the counter to nostalgia did not lie in defensive appraisals of the present that lent to celebratory affects. Ambivalence and contradiction marked the responses of those who understood the need for institutionalization, with a feminist organizer involved in both funded and nonfunded women's groups in Kolkata stressing, "there is a huge political shift once you become fully dependent on funding." From the carceral feminism of the ordinary millennial to the critical dispositions of the NGO-ized activist, these conversations laid bare the contradictions of feminist politics across the Global North and Global South. Above all, they suggested how feminist struggles were caught between being free or autonomous on the one hand and beholden or co-opted on the other. If in a previous generation, Indian feminists were reliant on forms of professional security to sustain their activism (equally emanating from the privileges of class and caste), a subsequent generation was insisting on but also wary of the risks of institutionalization. Across these generational divides were collective pledges to remain critical and resistant, yet few could claim to be entirely free of messy entanglements. As one queer feminist I interviewed in Delhi said to me, "You let loose an idea that is beyond your control. Everything gets co-opted."

This book locates itself in this struggle between being autonomous and being co-opted. More specifically, it concerns the present state of feminism in India through distinct forms of feminist and queer feminist activism that emerged and evolved in the eastern region of West Bengal since the 1990s.[4] A watershed decade in independent India, the 1990s coincided with the opening of the economy and the introduction of neoliberal economic reforms. Liberalization not only had far-reaching political and social effects—by advancing privatization and creating new patterns of wealth and inequality—but also reconfigured the terrain of existing social movements, like the women's movement, while giving rise and legitimacy to new sites of struggle around sexual rights. It was in this conjuncture that internal contradictions within the IWM became explicit, with worries that its mainstreaming, in governmental and nongovernmental practices, amounted to nothing more than co-optation.

Changing the Subject shows that there is more to this story than co-optation and the polarizing stances of despair or defensiveness. It uses the current conjuncture—"postliberalization"—to trace longer and wider shifts in the logics and techniques of governing a range of gendered, classed, and sexualized subjects, especially in the Global South. Queer feminist governmentalities, as I call them, reveal a deep and dynamic historic architecture, which while entangled in global neoliberalism, is not reducible to it. In their explicit orientation toward changing the self, these governmentalities also constitute the conditions for making new subjects and selves. The interplay between techniques of governance and techniques of self-making is at the heart of this book, which offers a new way of knowing feminism, its practices, logics, subjects, and others. Feminism, I suggest, is shaped by governing forces while governing and shaping the conduct of individuals and groups, providing the tools to craft a new kind of self and way of life. As a conduct of conduct in the broadest possible sense *and* as a technology for remaking the self, feminism is thus always already co-opted while being a creative and transformative force in the world. It is this productive tension that this book inhabits, animated by hope in feminism's life- and world-making capacities.

I first began to map changes to the IWM, owing to India's liberalization, in 2009. Since then, the project developed around two self-identified feminist organizations located in West Bengal, a location that was rich in regional specificity. Originating in the 1990s, both organizations emerged as major players in the region's feminist field, being part of influential local, regional, national, and transnational networks for women's and sexual rights. Sappho for Equality (SFE), a queer feminist organization, had a history that mirrored a previous generation of autonomous Indian feminisms: beginning as a small support group of middle-class and metropolitan cisgender lesbian women, it became a fully funded NGO in ways that transformed activism, expanded geographies of intervention, and integrated marginalized queer activists into projects of governance on behalf of a range of queer subjects and communities. Unlike this trajectory of beginning in an autonomous mode and undergoing NGO-ization, Janam (its name has been changed to preserve anonymity) was representative of those "post-Beijing" NGOs that fused neoliberal development strategies (e.g., microfinance) with discourses of women's agency, rights, and empowerment. While both organizations had offices in the state's capital city of Kolkata (formerly Calcutta, though always Kolkata to its residents), SFE was solidly urban and middle-class, while Janam worked with the peri-urban and rural constituents of the surrounding southern belts. My entry into this field was facilitated by my familiarity with the region (the site of my first book) and fluency in the local language of Bengali, details of which I will return to at the end of this introduction.

Governmentality, Neoliberalism, Others

The two organizations, SFE and Janam, form key nodes of what in this book I call queer feminist governmentality to reference an assemblage of discourses, practices, and techniques aimed at empowering subaltern subjects of the Global South along the axes of gender and sexuality.[5] I trace changes in activist governance—changes that, in turn, changed the self—that were entangled in but not reducible to global neoliberalism. Thus, while this book maps queer feminist governmentalities at the point of intersection with neoliberal logics and techniques as they manifested in India, it insists—alongside critical scholarship to which my thinking is indebted—that neoliberalism is no singular, pure, or unchanging formation.[6]

In understanding neoliberalism not as politico-economic structure but as a migrating governmental logic in the Foucauldian sense of governmentality, Carla Freeman (2014, 18) emphasizes (after Ong 2006) how it "can be adapted and melded within specific conditions, through specific cultural forms, in time and space." Analyses of this sort showed how, in the Global South, neoliberalism was not a vernacularized version of the global dominant or in opposition to local culture. It did not enter an empty, unmarked space, and neither did it invent things from scratch. It is, in fact, neoliberalism's tenacious capacity to appropriate—rather than simply co-opt—what exists and make it do different, distinct work that posed the specific kinds of ideological and political challenges that we face—namely, the increased inability to draw clear dividing lines between different and even oppositional political projects (including neoliberalism and feminism; see Calkin 2017; Fraser 2009; McRobbie 2009; and Rottenberg 2018). To put it simply, neoliberalism looks very different in different parts of the world, which should go some way to reduce "its density and totalizing weight—and the analytical and political breathlessness that such weight induces" (Clarke 2008, 145).

A key manifestation of neoliberal transformation was scalar in how governance expanded beyond the state and implicated nonstate entities and actors in techniques of government otherwise associated with the state, such that the state shrank but government grew (Ferguson 2011, 63; Ferguson and

Gupta 2002). In these changing state and civil society relations, where state functions of governance and development shifted to nonstate or nongovernmental arenas, NGOs mattered. Whether actively collaborating with the state or acting in state-like ways, NGOs exuded forms of governmentality and sovereignty.[7] An understanding of neoliberal governance as permeating the social not only complicates the dichotomous—and affectively loaded—ways in which divides between states and nonstate actors are produced but also assumptions that the one (the state) co-opts the other (NGOs). Throughout this book, I show the material transformations to activism in processes of NGO-ization, evident in its scalar expansion, from the local to the transnational; its professionalization and institutionalization; its imbrication in biopolitical fields of managing population groups; and its promotion of certain selves and modalities of working on the self in new arts and techniques of government.

And yet, activism was a deeply productive terrain of regulation, discipline, and creative self-formation that was not reducible to the dynamics of NGO-ization alone or to transnational neoliberal compulsions. Both SFE and Janam employed a range of governmental techniques, some of which were obviously neoliberal (like microcredit), while others attempted to queer neoliberal logics and practices, but all showed neoliberalism's ability to adapt and repurpose—that is, to retool—what exists to new effect (see Von Schnitzler 2016). Both organizations relied, for instance, on forms of consciousness-raising that were a product of mixed and complex genealogies, from the local Left to transnational development and human rights discourses. These concrete instances of neoliberalism's entanglement with others also revealed important continuities in a range of contrasting ideological projects—feminist and queer, the Left and neoliberalism—that in turn informed the distinct motivations and workings of organizations that were similar but also distinct from each other. The targets of their emancipatory imaginations and interventions (girls, women, lesbians, and transpersons) displayed an amenability, or a "readiness," to be governed that one could trace to their being subject to successive, multiple—but not always successful—projects of governance and rule.[8] It is, in fact, the proclivity toward reappropriation and resignification that leaves hegemonic projects—like neoliberal development—vulnerable to disruption, destabilization, and even failure. Subaltern politics have historically flourished in these cracks and fissures.[9]

It should be obvious that neoliberalism was not only experienced differently in specific locales—where it was overlaid by other techniques and logics

of regulation—but that it also evoked a plurality of times. This is a claim that is obvious but also hard to make given the temporal—and affective—stakes in producing the global neoliberal through a register of difference and discontinuity. Liberalized India signaled a break with a third world past and the arrival, on the world stage, of a modernized and globalized "brand new nation" (Kaur 2020). In these linear progressivist temporalities, women's and gay rights served to contrast one India, "new and modern," from another, "old and backward," as was manifest in international media reportage of the rape and murder of Jyoti Singh Pandey (Roychowdhury 2013, 282). In critical feminist scholarship, in contrast, liberalization and globalization and their consequential processes for the IWM (like institutionalization and NGO-ization) marked not progress but co-optation, depoliticization, and decline.[10]

Against narratives of progress or loss, I found in the feminisms of the present the coexistence of multiple times, to surprising affect. While queer politics was predictably attached to futurity, it also felt backward in echoing with "older" modes of governing subaltern subjects in the Global South.[11] These forms of millennial feminism, as I call them, were haunted by feminisms past—by the terms of political intelligibility and the kinds of authentic subjects that these had served to institutionalize and normalize. If anything, activists turned to the past in more explicit, even defensive ways in the face of threats of co-optation in the present. They remained locked in the horizon of political possibility made available in a previous, preliberalization era, if from only a few years earlier. The historical and cultural lineages they most relied on were also quintessentially local, and I show how it was regional idioms of feminist politics that accrued activists the greatest forms of legitimacy and value. Hauntings of this kind complicate easy assessments of the present as succeeding the past or the global as decimating the local; they did not have uniformly transgressive or nonnormative effects, either. There are indeed multiple hauntings and ghostly figures at play in the queer and nonqueer feminist sites I explore in this book, but with messier and more ambivalent effects than seductive readings of feminist and lesbian hauntings might make room for.[12]

If the sites of this book evoke a past, then they equally gesture toward an authoritarian future that has now come to pass. While the time of my research was saturated with concerns around global neoliberalism, the time of the writing of this book has reoriented us toward authoritarian regimes and spectacular state violence against Black, Dalit, and Muslim lives.[13] But these are scarcely separate times, in ways that a neoliberal nationalist India especially demonstrates. Hindu nationalism has worked in tandem with neoliberalism; it has successfully fused neoliberal accumulation strategies with religious majoritarianism to build legitimacy (Kaur 2020; Nilsen 2020).

Be it liberalization, global neoliberalism, or right-wing Hindu nationalism, the challenges that grip the present are fundamentally plural and can hardly be explained in terms of any one factor. Mary John has consistently uncovered the multiple political traditions that inform the IWM to show how accounts of the co-optation of an autonomous women's movement can flatten its entanglements in processes both historical and ongoing, local and transnational, close to and away from power (John 2009, 46; see also John 1999, 2002). John's plea for richer narratives of the recent developments in the IWM is one that I hope to furnish. By situating feminism at the convergence of neoliberal governmentality and its others—as a governmentality in its own right—I discern shifts, big and small, in relations and rationalities of power, and their effects on society and selves. While these effects may be disciplinary and normalizing in ways that are consonant with state governmentalities, they are also transformative in ways that might surprise us.

Even as such an approach has its advantages—especially for making sense of a heterogeneous present (see, for instance, Walters 2012)—it is not without its limits or problems. After all, governmentality has become yet another totalizing way to speak about power, leaving little room for considering its limits (see Death 2016). I prefer to think of governmentality in a straightforwardly Foucauldian sense: never as describing a state of sheer domination, oppression, or constraint—as we tend to think and feel about power—but as a highly generative, mobile, and reversible set of relations and techniques through which a self is both governed and governs itself. This is what makes a governmentality approach both overwhelming and unique: how it encompasses the governance of the self by external forces *and* the government of the self by the self, or everything from the state's techniques of governing populations to the micropolitics of the self. The specific focus on the interplay of technologies of governance and technologies of the self enables questions—not only around how one is governed but how one let's oneself be governed—that cannot be posed within totalizing analytics of power and domination. At the heart of the kind of NGO and activist governmentality this book considers is the constitution of new forms of self, enabling insights into feminism as a site of governance and power that contains within itself the capacity for ethical self-making and resistance.

Self-Government

The feminist and queer governmentalities that I consider in this book were defined, most fundamentally, by their subject-producing nature. From the services they provided (counseling, advocacy, training, and income generation) to the tools and techniques they employed (consciousness-raising, sensitization, awareness-raising, self-help, and peer support) the two organizations sought to transform the individual through specific forms of labor performed by the self on the self. Such interventions dovetailed with the kinds of assumptions and practices that were paradigmatic of millennial development on the one hand and neoliberal feminism on the other, besides showing their convergence upon distinct sites.

Who were the addressees of such interventions? My interlocutors in this book were ambiguously positioned, as both target group and activist in SFE and as agent and beneficiary of development in Janam. I am less interested in carving out a space to assess impact on beneficiaries and choose to stay instead with an ambiguous set of subject positions that these governmental practices produced. As advocates of specific humanitarian and development goals, my interlocutors were active instruments of queer feminist governmentality, incited to empower the self for governing—empowering—others. They saw themselves as being in the business of doing good and of saving the less fortunate, and they erected divides between themselves, "those who will to empower," and the object of this will (Cruikshank 1999, 125). Yet the emancipatory pedagogies and tools on offer were as much about governing, (re)orienting and caring for the self as they were about caring for or empowering others.[14] This enabled a central claim of this book: if feminism can be thought of as a form of (neoliberal) governmentality, it can also be considered a project of self-government and transformation.

Indeed, one of the unique aspects of neoliberalism is how it informs entirely new ways of relating to the self and constitutes new kinds of subjects and subjectivities (W. Brown 2015; Foucault 2008; Lorenzini 2018; Oksala 2013; Rose 1999). Feminists insist that the kind of subject most amenable to neoliberal subjectification is feminine. In other words, women are ideal neoliberal subjects, incited—to a much greater degree than men—to self-regulate, self-discipline, self-manage, and self-transform (see Gill and Scharff 2011; McRobbie 2009; Rottenberg 2018; and Scharff 2014). While northern feminists arrived at these conclusions in charting the rise and dominance of neoliberal subjectivities in popular culture and the media, southern feminists uncovered the racialized, and not just gendered, nature of "homo œconomicus" (Foucault 2008) as manifest in good governance agendas and corporatized development initiatives (Hickel 2014; Koffman and Gill 2013; Li 2007; Moeller 2018; Rankin 2001; Wilson 2015). In South Asia, critical feminist ethnographies honed our attention on how neoliberal development, through technologies of self-empowerment, self-help, enterprise, and responsibilization, emerged a robust terrain of changing subjectivities and making selves (see Jakimow 2015; Madhok 2012; D. Sen 2017; and Sharma 2008).

While these observations drove my interest in the making of a new, neoliberal self, they also cautioned against certain tendencies. In much critical feminist commentary, neoliberalism appears to hail gendered and sexualized subjects in much the same ways, such that a neoliberal feminism appears aspirational and promissory to all, everywhere.[15] Subjects in the Global South fare particularly poorly in such analyses, which end up producing younger, urban, and class-privileged women as mimetic of a neoliberal feminist subject in the Global North, and rural working-class women as curiously passive, a perfect foil to the excessive agency that neoliberalism endows them with. In contrast, the literature that explores a plurality of subjects, ways of making the self and concrete lives under neoliberalism—especially in postcolonial locales—remains limited, as does our capacity to imagine subjective orientations toward neoliberal environments in diverse, nuanced, and even resistant ways.[16] Even as a neoliberal ethics of entrepreneurialism has indeed globalized, Carla Freeman (2014, 4) reminds us that "the kind of subject being mobilised, the nature of the labour they are performing, the feelings rallied and produced within this supple and unstable system, and the meanings these affects hold cannot be assumed to be consistent." Neoliberal governmentality's heightened hailing of a gendered and racialized self—especially in places "less inclined towards thinking reflexively about selves"—offers, in fact, a unique opportunity to trace how modern power forms the self, without lapsing into the grip of disciplinary control (C. Freeman 2014, 4).[17]

Across the divides of class and caste, the urban and the rural, the local and the translocal, queer activists and development workers engaged not just in new acts, tastes, and relations but also in experiments in becoming different people. Self-government took the form of embodied and aesthetic practices—what others have called self-styling, self-fashioning, or self-making—and also an increased, more intense awareness and consciousness of the self and of social norms and their normalizing imperatives.[18] In their explicit orientation toward changing the self, activist and NGO governmentalities folded into personal projects of self-transformation (even as these bore the imprint of wider social and cultural forces). They offered not a set of rules or norms to be followed but sites and resources for self-making through which individuals could rework and reimagine the self and even exercise some choice with respect to what it means to be a certain person and live a certain life.

While this idea of choice might signal, for some, the entry through the back door of disciplinary power, it offered me other possibilities, especially as a way of moving beyond the tired debate around power and resistance that has long dominated feminist theorizing. Even as I was adamant that self-government was more than an imprint of governmentalities, I was equally skeptical of easy proclamations of resistance and agency (concepts also conflated with one another; see Mahmood 2005). The technologies of feminist and queer self-making I encountered in the field were, in any case, not amenable to such readings. They did not straightforwardly map onto the aspirations of activists and development practitioners for resistance, agency, or even antinormativity; on the contrary, self-making stabilized some norms while disrupting others, remaining firmly entangled in power. The relationship that one had to oneself, however free and empowering, was ultimately rooted in, and even reliant upon, a wider field and force of government.[19]

Given that neoliberalism entails a new way of governing the self, subjectivity is, however, a crucial site of struggle, for constituting ways of relating to oneself that might be an alternative to mainstream technologies (Lorenzini 2018).[20] In challenging the norms that constitute the self, one is also challenging the materials and conditions through which that self is constituted, or the wider social and political forces which exist in oneself. Self-transformation thus implies social transformation.[21]

Such proposals are not helpful to Indian feminists who have tended to regard the self as an inadequate site of real resistance and have fixed their gaze instead on the possibilities of collective identity and struggle alone.[22] A queer feminist I spoke to in Delhi back in 2009 claimed that the IWM was, in fact, haunted by these dynamics: "The main problem of the women's movement is that so much of [it] works for the *other*, that even though it's within the category of woman, the focus is on that oppressed woman *out there* who is not you. . . . If you hear the language of the movement, the word *us* is not used at all." She added, "What is energizing about queer activism is that the people who are engaged with it have something at stake."

It was such reflections that drew me toward questions and practices of queer and feminist self-making, especially in historical and regional settings saturated with political attachments to the other and not the self (and the prioritization of the collective over the individual). India's liberalization appeared an especially thick terrain of new subjects and selves, with fresh stakes and potential impacts on both the self and the world. Indeed, one of the central paradoxes that Indian feminists had to contend with was that while the IWM felt depoliticized, and even undone, in forms of institution-alization and transnationalism, successive generations of Indian women and sexual minorities assumed the front line of struggles against ever-expanding sexual violence and deepening state authoritarianism. New selves existed in a tenuous relationship to a neoliberal governmentality in whose crevices they had emerged, but also to world-making projects and possibilities. In other words, the relationship between governmentality and the self does not offer any straight line from the micropolitics of the self to wider political transfor-mation.[23] In this book, I resist the urge to turn too quickly toward collective possibilities, staying instead at the scale of the individual, not only to mark the limits of government's reach and power but also to ask whether the self could constitute the locus of a new kind of governmentality and politics.

Indian Feminism and Its Subjects: Before and after Liberalization

Colonial and nationalist governmentalities, and postcolonial developmen-talities, shaped the contours of the IWM, the origins of which are usually traced to nineteenth-century social reform efforts and the anticolonial struggle. While this was a remarkable period for the advance of Indian women—through changes to education, conjugality, and women's rights—it also pegged gender and sexuality to nation, culture, and nationalisms in fundamental and enduring ways. Even when only a small section of elite upper-caste Hindu women emerged as potentially rights bearing, these new subjectivities were overwritten by patriarchal concerns—and contests—over tradition, culture, and nation (P. Chatterjee 1989; Kapur 2005; Sangari and Vaid 1989; Sarkar 2001; S. Sen 2000). The woman's question was inseparable from the making of the nation, but also inseparable from the homosexual or, indeed, the lesbian question.[24] As Paola Bacchetta notes, "Lesbians may be constructed . . . as threats to, not embodiments of, heteronormative national culture; as dishonoring heterosexual male citizen-subjects because not ap-propriated by them; in *xenophobic, lesbophobic* terms, as originating outside the nation and as antinational" (2002, 951–52, emphasis in the original). The "nationalist resolution of the women's question," as Partha Chatterjee (1989) famously put it, thus produced a foundational incommensurability between being Indian and being lesbian, one that would only be open to resolution at a much later time and, even then, only in incomplete ways (see Dave 2012).

The postindependence IWM—which came into its own as one of the new social movements in the 1970s—operated within the terms of political intelligibility formed in the colonial-nationalist moment (Omvedt 1993; Ray and Katzenstein 2005). It demanded rights and development from the postcolonial state on behalf of Indian women, construed as lacking in agency but also as singular and nonintersectional; *woman* was unmarked by caste, community, and sexuality in ways that made feminism "a form of identity politics" (Madhok 2010, 225). It was not until the arrival of a catalytic report in 1971 that Indian feminists were forced to confront the limits of the postcolonial Indian state.[25] The autonomous feminists of the 1970s and 1980s—middle-class, upper-caste, urban, educated, professional women of a leftist bent—threw their energies into filling the gap between state potential and its realization, turning their attention to poor women who had emerged as the worst off by all accounts.[26] A split between a feminist self, comprising middle-class metropolitan women, and its object of investigation and reform—poor, rural women at the grass roots, or "out there," to recall what one of my interlocutors suggested—helped to establish the cultural authenticity and local legitimacy of an otherwise elite, Western, and alien social movement (John 1996). The IWM's ability to speak on behalf of the poor, the "backward," and the morally virtuous (but not sexually desiring) yielded tangible, even profitable, outcomes with the influx of foreign aid, under economic liberalization (Dave 2012). At the convergence of distinct governmentalities—colonial, nationalist, and neoliberal—was the figure of the subaltern woman, who emerged as the preeminent subject of Indian feminism and afforded generations of activists the right to speak on behalf of those rendered reified and spectral.[27]

Liberalization was understood as disrupting nationalist frames and transforming the discursive contexts in which issues like gender and sexuality were raised, framed, and fought for. Neoliberal economic reforms were inaugurated—stealthily and unevenly (R. Jenkins 1999)—from 1991 onward as a response to the fiscal crisis of the Indian state and the contradictions of state-managed development. It was fast recognized as a thoroughly elite project, serving elite interests and reinforcing elite status, as a response to democratizing drives from below (Hansen 1999; Jaffrelot 2003). In addition, liberalization came to be associated with the rise of the right-wing Hindu nationalist Bharatiya Janata Party (BJP) as a political force to be reckoned with. This process reached its apogee under the regime of Prime Minister Narendra Modi (since 2014), which was far more aggressively supportive of corporate and capitalist interests than the earlier BJP government of Atal Vihari Vajpayee (1999–2004) and also more openly antidemocratic and authoritarian, especially toward religious minorities and vulnerable caste groups.

Constituting a watershed moment for Indian feminists, liberalization reconfigured the material and normative terrain of their struggles away from the episteme of the nation-state (John 2014). Feminists were directly implicated in the expansion of state logic and governance on the one hand and in the proliferation of global development and humanitarian agendas on the other. They entered into unprecedented collaborations with the state and became new actors in global donor networks and markets of social movement and humanitarian intervention. Feminist-inspired state institutions and reformed laws around sexual violence emerged just as new organizational forms, such as NGOs, came into play. These NGOs fundamentally transformed the organizing of Indian feminism from the autonomous feminist formations of the 1970s—which, though small, departed to the IWM its public visibility and legacy—to more structured and professionalized organizations, constituting "a move out of movement mode," as one of the older feminists I initially met described it.

Even as I document these changes to the terrain of feminist mobilizing in liberalized India in chapter 1, I point to their paradoxical implications—namely, how India's economic liberalization not only signaled the co-optation and depoliticization of struggles around gender and sexuality but also amplified their visibility and vitalization in unexpected ways. If the IWM was considered testament to the former trend, then the emergence of a new terrain of activism around sexuality—comprising sex worker and queer politics—embodied the other (see Lakkimsetti 2020; Menon 2009; Mokkil 2019; and Vijayakumar 2021). The 1990s coincided with the global fight against HIV/AIDS, catalyzing organizing around sexuality and offering—for the first time—concrete material support to sexual subalterns themselves. These included groups that were also historically marginalized by the elite, Hindu, and heteronormative lineages of Indian feminism; a sexually conversative mainstream IWM had not always made space for the recognition and agency of sex workers, for instance (see Kotiswaran 2011;

and Menon 2007a). The Mandal-Masjid years,[28] as a critical period in the 1990s came to be known, forced feminists to confront their own major-itarianism, which was highly amenable to a growing upper-caste Hindu nationalism. It also raised a more fundamental question: Who is the subject of feminist politics?[29]

If liberalization transformed the terrain of existing struggles while giving rise to new ones, then it also saw a proliferation of millennial subjects, em-bodiments of neoliberal self-making. The new middle classes—comprising disproportionately those who were also upper-caste and Hindu—were at the heart of "India Shining," the name of the BJP's 2004 election campaign and ubiquitous metaphor of the successes and failures of liberalization. Even as it made up less than a quarter of the population (Jodkha and Prakash 2016), it was this class that came to represent a major shift in national culture—from ideologies of state-led development and consumer moderation to rampant consumption and entrepreneurialism—besides emerging as both a beneficiary and a proponent of economic liberalism and the BJP's political illiberalism (Fernandes and Heller 2006; see also Baviskar and Ray 2015; Deshpande 2003; Kaur 2020; and Mazzarella 2005). Gender and sexuality were key to the consolidation of the transnationality and modernity of the "new" middle class, ensuring it was "appropriately Indian" (Radhakrishnan 2011; see also Donner 2008; Fernandes 2000; Oza 2006; Thapan 2004; and, on similar dynamics across South Asia, Hussein 2017). They also constituted the grounds for a domestic reconfiguration of a "Brahmanical Hindutva" and bolstered the legitimacy of the Hindu Right under Modi, which as-sumed a specific form of gender and sexual governance (Rege 1998, 43; see also Baxi 2019).

The neoliberal conjuncture afforded unprecedented queer possibilities. The market, for instance, recognized that Indian queers enhanced the global attractiveness of "Brand India" and offered some inclusion well before the Indian state did (Boyce and Dutta 2013; Shahani 2017; Sircar 2017; Sir-car and Jain 2017a). The market did not recognize all queers, however, and while some (cisgender middle-class metropolitan gay men and even women) were interpellated as "model capitalist subjects," others (histori-cally marginalized and stigmatized transgender communities) lobbied the state on the basis of their "backwardness," an available site from which to demand redistributive measures (Rao 2020b, 25). These dynamics, which were pronounced in the run-up to and the afterlife of the decriminalization of homosexuality, showed the different temporalities at work among queers at the same time and place.

In the chapters that follow, we meet several of those whom Ritty Lukose (2009) has called "liberalization's children," from lower-middle-class urban queer activists to rural lower-caste development workers. We are perhaps more used to encountering such groups in distinct, even incommensurate ethnographic worlds, associated with either consumption and pleasure on the one hand and with poverty and development on the other, in ways that also exaggerate their apartness from each other (Chandra and Majumder 2013; Jalais 2010). While the middle-class queer activists of this book fit seamlessly into narratives of modernity, fashion, and youth consumption, rural development workers who are of the same generation fall outside it. They are not the imagined modern girls of liberalized and globalized India—a narrow construct that hails the middle-class, upper-caste, English-speaking cosmopolitan self and marginalizes those from lower-class, lower-caste, and nonmetropolitan backgrounds (Lukose 2009). Instead this book establishes rural women not only as "liberalization's children in their own right" but as millennial feminists (Lukose 2009, 7). It also nuances the new Indian middle classes of a liberalized and globalized India by showing their diversity and heterogeneity. The queer feminists I met not only hailed from a range of social backgrounds but also inhabited blanket categories of "middle classness" in messy ways, which revealed the historic and regional work that class performed in this context.[30] Whether from the middle class, the lower middle class, or at the margins of class privilege, the individuals that constitute the core of the book took up the NGO-ized subjectivities, relations, and aspirations on offer to fulfill desires for personal autonomy, mobility, and modernity, even as these were realizable in highly partial, precarious, and exclusionary ways.

Millennial West Bengal: Settings and Methods

Kolkata and its peri-urban fringes are the sites of this book, shaped by affectively charged and historically enduring imaginaries that make up a "West Bengal exceptionalism."[31] Crumbling urban infrastructure, a haunting colonial cityscape, left-wing intellectualism, and *adda* (chat) and *cha* (tea) have always been part of Kolkata's uniqueness. They are what make it different from, and even an alternative to, the hypercapitalist modernity represented by other major Indian cities. If the "rumor of Calcutta" (Hutnyk 1996) made the city attractive to white hippie tourists and saviors alike, then this rumor was also part of what Ananya Roy (2003, 9) has called the "self-orientalization" that the Bengali communists excelled in. The city's marginalization acted as the perfect foil to their investment in a vision of plentiful and utopian Bengali rurality, "the fiction of a *Sonar Bangla*," or a Golden Bengal (Ananya Roy 2003, 24).[32] These were also gendered constructs, with the city being the domain of the *bhadralok*, the upper-caste, middle-class Bengali gentleman, and the village standing for, in nationalist, communist, and postcommunist rhetoric alike, the motherland (see Nielsen 2018).[33] Both the city (the "rumor of Calcutta") and the village ("the fiction of a *Sonar Bangla*") lent to assumptions of exceptionalism (Ananya Roy 2003, 24).

The region was also marked by a history of left-wing dominance, represented by the thirty-four-year rule of the Left Front government, one that exceeded the electoral success of comparable communist parties in democratic contexts. Evaluations of its long reign, which ended in 2011, were consistent. Most agreed that the Left Front's major rural reform policies, such as decentralized governance and the redistribution of agricultural land, were of benefit to the middle peasantry, who became a new rural elite, but excluded the majority of the rural poor and kept structures of poverty intact.[34] Untouched by land reforms, the rural poor flocked to the city, as domestic servants and day laborers in highly gendered patterns of "distress migration" that took place throughout the 1980s and early 1990s (Ananya Roy 2003). Even as Kolkata's fortunes had steadily declined since independence and partition, the communists showed little interest in urban revival. They were eventually left with no choice but to turn to urban development, in the face of stagnant agricultural growth and a new liberalized economy where Indian states could no longer rely on central assistance but had to compete to attract foreign investment. The Left Front embarked on a "New Communism," one that was "for the new millennium, a communism as comfortable with global capital as with sons of the soil" (Ananya Roy 2003, 10). It undertook projects to clean up or "beautify" the city by forcibly removing street hawkers and squatters and erecting middle-class housing developments that displaced the poor. Such forms of appropriation and dispossession came to a head in the violent clashes that took place between the government and resistant forces around planned industrial developments in Nandigram and Singur, iconic sites of India's new land wars (S. Majumder 2018; Nielsen 2018).

These events were considered instrumental in bringing about the electoral defeat of the Left and the rise to power of the opposition party, the Trinamool Congress, under the leadership of Mamata Banerjee. An upper-caste, lower-middle-class woman with little social capital and often dismissed as a mere populist, Banerjee represented a major shift in the genteel and middle-class—*bhadralok*—politics of the Communist Party of India (Marxist), or CPM (see Nielsen 2016). She brought caste and religion back into the political fray, in contrast to the upper-caste, "secular" communists who had subordinated caste to class and refused to take religion seriously.[35] Unlike the southern part of the country, with its history of resisting upper-caste hegemony, and the north, with its strong Dalit Bahujan political parties representing the interests of Dalits and the lower castes, West Bengal never witnessed any comparable "silent revolution" (Jaffrelot 2003).[36] And even as it did not face communal violence, not since its own bloody partition history, West Bengal's Muslims were marginalized under Left Front rule.[37] Postcommunist West Bengal created ripe conditions for the entry of the BJP, an otherwise nonplayer in regional politics (Basu and Das 2019; Daniyal 2019; Mukherjee 2019). More so than ever before, the new millennium belied any claims toward Bengali exceptionalism.

As it was for caste and religion, the communist and postcommunist record on gender was uneven at best. The gendered patterns of rural-to-urban migration that Ananya Roy (2003) found confirmed how little the Left Front's land reforms had done to shift existing gender imbalances in rural areas (A. Basu 1992; Da Costa 2010). Its other major claim to success—decentralization through the restructuring of the panchayat system of local governance—also did little to enhance women's political representation at this scale (A. Basu 1992). And notwithstanding the Left's emphasis on women's economic empowerment—to "stand on one's own two feet," as the slogan went—West Bengal had absurdly low workforce participation among women (Goswami 2019). The region also did poorly when it came to social indicators in comparison to the rest of the country; it lagged behind the national average on women's literacy, and had some of the highest rates of child marriage in the country, which were still higher among Muslims and Scheduled Caste groups (Sanyal 2014; Sen and Sengupta 2012). Neoliberal development schemes like cash transfers, introduced by the Trinamool Congress to promote women's education and curb child marriage, reinforced hegemonic gendered norms that they intended to subvert (Ray Chaudhury 2020). And while some middle-class women were able to take advantage of the newer professional opportunities on offer, such as in the technology and service industries, women across all classes were hardly optimistic of neoliberal change in West Bengal (Donner 2008; Ganguly-Scrase 2003).

The region's nineteenth- and twentieth-century legacies of nationalism, social reform, and left-wing hegemony—which informed distinct and highly gendered projects of governance and rule—might have made it a fertile ground for the birthing of feminist ideals, radical women's movements, and robust political representation. Available scholarship has revealed the opposite to be true (A. Basu 1992; R. Ray 1999; Sinha Roy 2011; S. Roy 2012b; Sarkar 1991). Raka Ray's (1999) foundational mapping of Kolkata's "fields of protests" showed how left-wing hegemony prevented the flourishing of more explicitly feminist currents, whether affiliated with the party or autonomous in relation to it; indeed, Bengali political culture was positively hostile to feminism. The women's wing of the Left bore absolute allegiance to the party, epitomized in its negotiation of a major gang rape case that implicated party members in the early 1990s (Da Costa 2010; Sarkar 1991). The Trinamool Congress's record on gender and sexual rights fared not much better.[38] The institutional cultures of both major political parties—as well as the BJP, which started making inroads in the region in later years—revealed a limiting milieu for advancing women's rights and for enabling their political participation. Major trade unions like the Centre of Indian Trade Unions and the Indian National Trinamool Trade Union Congress, which mobilized women workers, also tended to reflect their parent organizations rather than act independently (see P. Ray 2019).[39]

Nonparty and nonfunded, "autonomous" women's group proved less radical than comparable ones elsewhere in the country given their entanglement in leftist ideologies, from which they claimed autonomy (see R. Ray 1999). The region had, however, a long and robust history of women's participation in people's struggles (both communist-led struggles and those breaking away from the organized Left); women activists were invariably spoken for by male leadership in these spaces, however (Nielsen 2018; Sinha Roy 2011; S. Roy 2012c). It was one such key radical Left movement that gave me the story for my first book (S. Roy 2012c).[40] Many of these leftist women joined autonomous feminist groups in the 1970s and 1980s, and it was their biographies that organically led me from an exploration of leftist selves to forms of feminist self-making. Women's groups that asserted their autonomy from left-wing groups were gradually replaced by NGOs, to which the Left Front was initially hostile.[41] Both Ananya Roy (2003) and Raka Ray (1999) have wondered what NGOs would bring to millennial Kolkata, with Ray speculating whether they would "create an alternative political culture, one that perhaps will offer more space for a diversity of interests and voices" (1999, 166). At the start of the millennium, Nivedita Menon (2004, 222) declared that Ray's optimism was misplaced as NGOs were "driven by the compulsions of funding." This book takes off where Ray's ends; indeed, her study was the principal source of my initial interest

Figure I.1 Maitree poster. Photo by the author.

in a transformed terrain of feminist activism, caught between a sense of possibility and closure. While it was obvious that much had changed in the field that Ray had uncovered (of which NGO-ization was a key maker), much also remained the same. Leftist pedagogies and "structures of feeling" did not merely haunt NGO spaces and selves, but I also encountered the actual bodies of the Left as consultants and professionals in Kolkata's NGO sector (Williams 1977). Kolkata-based NGOs were part of Maitree (Friendship), a conglomerate of local women's groups and activists that lobbied the state on women's issues and constituted a feminist counterpublic in the gentleman's city. Maitree represented both dents in left-wing hegemony and its durability as it accommodated newer and queerer concerns—around sex work and LGBTQ rights—but in conditional ways.

Finally, new neoliberal and NGO governmentalities implicated the growth and rise of sexuality politics in the region, best represented by sex worker and LGBTQ activism. Millennial Kolkata emerged as a prominent site of sex worker organizing that, even though rooted in HIV/AIDS prevention work, developed its own direction and agency, in alliance with local feminist and labor organizing.[42] When it came to LGBTQ politics, the city was the site of informal collectives from the late 1980s onward, and this fed into subsequent forms of more visible and interventionist queer organizing; the first Pride walk in the country is said to have taken place in Kolkata in 1999. Given that early forms of support were dominated by middle-class gay men and that the activism around HIV/AIDS—a crucial prehistory to the queer movement in India—focused on female sex workers and men who had sex with men, it was surprising that Kolkata became home to one of the few organizations for queer women in the area and even in the country. Queer feminist politics grew there, as elsewhere in the country, in a complex relationship of dependence and solidarity with women's groups. And even as the Left (and a leftist feminism) was not conducive to the flourishing of LGBTQ politics, a leftist milieu accommodated and did not violently repress—as did right-wing forces elsewhere in the country—more radical political articulations. These regional differences were obvious when trouble erupted in 1998 around what came to be known as India's first lesbian film, *Fire*, a critical event in queer feminist politics at national and regional scales.[43]

Sappho, the support group that preceded SFE, emerged out of the "*Fire* moment" and changed considerably during my research, going from Sappho, a support group, to SFE, the NGO. This trajectory made possible certain kinds of insights at particular times. In general, data collection for this project was contingent on the structure, membership, and changing life courses of the two organizations that constitute its core. With SFE, my main method of enquiry was the interview, shifting from more informal, conversational interviews in the early days to more formal ones in later years. While in an earlier time I would casually interview members in the neat residential flat in which the organization was housed, in later years I would meet a single individual—a project leader, for instance—at a "reception" area (also in a private home). Alongside interviews, I attended and observed some planning meetings and the Thursday meetings open to all SFE members (which I had signed up to become). I also met key respondents—over a period of time—within the organization's space or outside it, such as in a coffee shop of their choosing. The coffee shop was not an unimportant site for openly queer women, and it paved the way, in easy and extended conversations, for rich accounts of self-fashioning. The changing fortunes of SFE mirrored wider changes to queer culture, sociality, and activism in the city, and I gained valuable insights into the significance of these changes from those lesbian and transgender activists who emerged on the scene in later years and outside SFE.[44]

With Janam, my main method was that of participant observation. Again, the organization's distinct character and unusual degree of openness—in comparison to other NGOs—determined the choice of method and data obtained. While Janam was housed in an office (in a cluster of residential flats), the life of the organization stretched well beyond these walls, especially through its microfinance institution (MFI), which spanned across fifty villages. The office space was reminiscent of NGOs elsewhere (see, for example, Thayer 2010): it was crowded with busy staff members and housed women who were engaged in production activities on-site. While I conducted formal interviews with staff members at the office, my interactions with grassroots development workers—who became core to my learning and interest—were mobile and multi-sited. I went where they went, which included regular field visits and training sessions on and off the NGO's premises. I took notes on their interactions with self-help groups (SHGs) and with each other, reserving more individual questions for our travel together (often a combination of bus, rickshaw, and foot travel) or when the workers were on lunch breaks. These women formed a strong friendship group and my presence and company on a range of sites and activities enabled the development of meaningful relationships with at least some of them. But whatever degree of closeness might have manifested between us—helped by subjective changes, such as my entry into parenthood, and material ones, like new mobile technologies that enabled us to stay in touch from afar—was undercut by fundamental locational, class, and caste-based differences. In addition to the intense periods of time I spent with this group of women, I observed a range of activities that made up Janam's everyday goings-on, including meetings for the MFI, SHG meetings, regular outreach events that took place in various villages, and protest action in Kolkata and in villages in which Janam participated.

I developed very different relationships not only with the two organizations but with their distinct constituents. It is fair to say that my relationship with Janam was of a closer nature, so much so that I shared with its founder some—critical—publications emerging from the research (processes of writing and sharing that felt troubling given a shared sense of solidarity). In this book, I present still sharper critiques based on my observation and interactions with those employees who were most precariously positioned in the organizational hierarchy and to whom I felt the greatest sense of commitment. It is primarily to protect and honor their courage of critique that I decided to anonymize not just individuals but the organization itself. In the case of SFE, while members' names are anonymized, I have retained the organization's name; given its distinct character, anonymity would be meaningless. I also felt that SFE had a strong enough public profile and standing for the more critical observations made in this book, as voiced by some of its own members who were not vulnerable in the same way as subaltern women were (but have nevertheless been given a pseudonym). These critical claims might well have been facilitated by members' appreciation of me as an outsider, an unusual position to occupy given the intimate nature of most queer ethnographies (see, for example, Dave 2012).[45] Whether articulated by an insider or outsider, queer feminist critiques of feminist spaces and movements can constitute sources of hurt and conflict; we need, as I point out in this book's conclusion, practices of critique as care, not least because of the shrinking spaces and colossal costs of critique and dissent in India today.

An Overview of the Book

The chapters that follow locate feminist interventions and subjects across specific translocal sites of governance, affective economies of loss and aspiration, and entangled and enduring techniques of making gendered, racialized, and sexualized subjects in the Global South. Chapter 1 charts Indian feminism's entanglement in a range of convergent governmentalities, to hone in on a central paradox of the neoliberal moment—namely, its enabling of both the co-optation and intersectional expansion of gender and sexual rights. I trace how the state and law, development, the urban, and the digital have constituted fields of possibility for limiting and expanding queer feminist political horizons in ways that anxieties around neoliberal co-optation do not fully capture. Against the affective and analytical optics of a metrocentric neoliberal feminism that served to re-center northern trends and frame newer and younger feminist interventions in southern locales in derivative ways, I foreground specific feminist histories, geographies, and referents that newer activists have drawn on and departed from.

Chapter 2 traces the story of SFE—and its origins in the support group, Sappho—in ways that were inseparable from the trajectory of India's globalization and neoliberalism but also shaped by the affective weight of past feminisms that produced a backward-looking queer feminist politics. I trace activist beginnings in the need for the support and safety of lesbian women to the closure of the support group, premised on the opening of new spaces for queer sociality and support, especially in urban and digital milieus. The changed conditions that made activism possible—globalization, NGO-ization, new digital technologies, and the urban economy—created new regimes of normalization and regulation, in which older forms of inclusion and exclusion endured and made subaltern lesbians, in particular, amenable to metrocentric and class-privileged—but also anticapitalist—political futures.

Chapter 3 presents queerness as a way of making life and the self in Kolkata, set against the accelerating temporalities of gay normalization, generational differences, and a queer political logic of "no going back." These constitute the conditions of a shifting horizon of possibility for queer people living in the city. Younger members of SFE were some of the first to occupy the spatiotemporal register of being out of the closet. In engaging a range of technologies of the queer self—somatic, aesthetic, and epistemic—I show how queer visibility does not equate with livability, and how young queers engage social norms in complex and fundamentally intersectional ways. For those located at the intersection of marginalized identities, queer self-making fashions new possibilities—revealing, for instance, some of the queer ways in which caste identities are inhabited in liberalized India.

In turning to feminist governmentality, chapter 4 offers an account of a richly layered terrain of "developing" subaltern women, shaped through the legacies of regional feminisms, the developmentalist state, the local Left, and global efforts to render neoliberal development commensurate with women's rights. My argument in chapter 4 is especially important in showing how neoliberal development interventions—like microfinance—were more continuous with other governmental logics, powers, and technologies, which they repurposed to new effect. Subjects of neoliberal government and development were, I show toward the end of the chapter, not passive; they offered not necessarily resistance but the demand to be governed differently. In turning to the subaltern subject who occupied a spectral position in metrocentric queer feminist imaginaries, chapter 4 shows how she constituted their material and not merely imaginative possibilities and limits and, in refusing the offer of rescue and rehabilitation, even propelled them to failure.

In exemplifying the irresolvable tensions of neoliberal feminist governmentality, it is the rural woman, as agent and not beneficiary of development, who most represents feminist failure and its ambivalent gifts. In chapter 5, I provide a fuller account of the subjectivities of those rural development workers who were brought into Janam's fold as volunteers rather than employees and who persisted despite a cruel kind of attachment to this feminist lifeworld. I show how they shaped the self in creative and wayward ways and turned, in both public and private, to conduct the self according to one's own norms. Their acts of embracing joy—in unproductive fun, new forms of conjugality, and middle-class and metropolitan consumptive pleasures—fundamentally shift our imagination of what millennial Indian feminism can look like and be in the current neoliberal conjuncture.

The book's conclusion returns to the politics of telling feminist stories on and from the Global South. I recap the stories told in this book while also telling other, unfolding stories of feminist self- and life-making in times of unprecedented crisis. The historical present requires sharper forms of critique than those afforded by co-optation, but also care to sustain precarious queer feminist futures. I conclude by asking what it might mean to offer critique as a cultivated practice of care in ways to further expand rather than foreclose the transformatory potential of the kinds of feminist queer political practice that this book explores.

1
Indian Feminism in the New Millennium
Co-optation, Entanglement, Intersection

Co-optation can be a charge that hopes to produce retrospectively a prior vision or subject of a feminism that does not have the long historical and intimate connections with other institutions and movements.

Inderpal Grewal, interviewed by Srila Roy, "The Positive Side of Co-optation?," 2017

Entanglement ... is an idea which signals largely unexplored terrains of mutuality, wrought from a common temporality of past, present and future; one which points away from a time of resistance towards a more ambivalent moment.

Sarah Nuttall, *Entanglement*, 2009

This book is located in a changing landscape of queer feminist politics in India, in a period in which these changes—and their meaning and significance—emerged as serious sources of questioning, even contest, among those activists and scholars who occupied this terrain. Even as I take as my point of departure the watershed decade of economic liberalization, much changed in the ensuing decades, given the ascendancy of the Hindu Right to electoral power and cultural common sense. The Hindu Right's deepening authoritarianism also provoked unexpected forms of popular struggles, to which I turn in this book's conclusion. Unlike this "time of resistance," liberalization appeared to be "a more ambivalent time" (Nuttall 2009, 11). At the heart of this ambivalence was a central paradox: (neo)liberalization enabled greater visibility to sexual and gender struggles but also entailed their dilution or depoliticization. We see this paradoxical double move occurring at a number of sites—state and law, development, urban, and digital—where queer feminist demands were incorporated, as opposed to being outright rejected, with uneven effects. In ways that made these contradictions most evident, the same historical conjuncture that produced anxieties around the co-optation and loss of feminism forced upon Indian feminists a more intersectional lens and even dissolved the normative subject of the Indian women's movement (IWM). While *co-optation* captured feelings of ambivalence and loss, *intersectionality* revealed such feelings to be misplaced, in making clear that the subjects and practices of feminism had never existed outside their messy entanglement with power.

Inderpal Grewal—whose words open this chapter—insists on the inadequacy of descriptors like *complicity* and *co-optation* to address the complexities in which contemporary feminism lies. What feminists lament as co-optation can be understood, instead, as the conditions for the emergence of specific types of feminist politics. Feminist subjects in the postcolony were made through markers of class and caste majoritarianism that, together with racialized and metrocentric legacies of empire, "produced a certain kind of feminism in relation to other women" (Grewal, quoted in S. Roy 2017b, 259).[1] Seen from the perspective of these long, entangled, and enduring histories, feminism has always been intersectional, "but what that intersection *is* is different" (Grewal, quoted in S. Roy 2017b, 259, emphasis in the original).

Sarah Nuttall (2009), in making sense of newly emergent presents in postapartheid South Africa, turns to entanglement to contend with the intricate connections between the past and the present and between here and elsewhere. Multiple forces produce the kind of intimacy and apartness—the complicated tangles—that Nuttall observes. Entanglement, with its emphasis on relationality and connection, is indeed common to activist attempts to address the complexity of the social, even as it can have paralyzing effects. A way of moving beyond this impasse is to fully reckon with the exclusions that are intrinsic to activism, even as some exclusions might appear to be natural.[2] These thoughts on entanglement—and on what comes after entanglement (Giraud 2019)—are especially useful for acknowledging two things at once: how the neoliberal present is "seamed through" multiple times and spaces, and how these shape Indian feminism and its relations, often of inequality and exclusion, to others (Nuttall 2009, 154).

In showing queer feminism's entanglement in state and law, international development, NGOs, and the transnational, neoliberal, and digital, this chapter foregrounds the tensions, instabilities, and contradictions of the postliberalization moment in ways that enabled both the co-optation and intersectional expansion of feminist (especially queer, Dalit) politics. As we see toward the end of this discussion, the affective and analytical optics of neoliberal feminism served to re-center northern trends and frame newer and younger feminist interventions in southern locales in derivative ways.

And yet, queer feminist subjects in liberalized India had specific feminist histories, geographies, and referents to draw on and depart from.

In this book as a whole, but especially in this chapter, it is important to be mindful of the ways in which all feminist stories are marked by absences and erasures; we have bigger and smaller stories (Sukthankar 2012; see also Hemmings 2011). Throughout this chapter, I show how debates around Indian feminism privilege certain dimensions and gloss over others, in ways that naturalize particular epistemes with strong affective currents and implications. Co-optation is itself a powerful mode of structuring knowledge, feelings, and modes of intervention around what ails feminism today.[3] My (partial) story of the paradoxical possibilities of the neoliberal moment offers modes of knowing and feeling that are alternatives to co-optation; they act as an antidote to our "bad feelings," without, however, the promise of making us feel better (Love 2007, 158).

Queer Entanglements in State and Law:
Frictions and Solidarities

Our political journey, charted through our demands for an acknowledgement of our sexual difference and also our lived experiences that were gendered, brought us closer to the women's movement in Kolkata and took us away from the larger gay movement.

Ranjita Biswas, Sumita Beethi, and Subhagata Ghosh, "Maneuvering Feminisms through LGBTQ Movements in India," 2019

During the course of my research, the Delhi High Court struck down Section 377 of the Indian Penal Code, effectively decriminalizing homosexuality among consenting adults, only for the highest Indian court to reinstate it in a judgment in 2013.[4] The Indian courts' shifting stance on Section 377 exemplified the constitutive role of state and law in institutionalizing heteronormativity and homophobia.[5] The nationwide and immensely popular campaign around same-sex love made the removal of the law a key symbol for queer recognition and sexual citizenship. Legal activism around Section 377, which was catalyzed by HIV/AIDS prevention imperatives and evolved into a broad-based coalition of LGBTQ, feminist, and human rights activists, came to stand in for the Indian queer movement itself.[6] But it was not without its contradictions or tensions, constituting a terrain of feminist, queer, and trans friction. The eventual decriminalization of homosexuality in 2018 evoked mixed feelings. Notwithstanding this landmark in the global history of LGBTQ rights—as well as a sea change in domestic perceptions of same-sex sexuality—the judgment was seen as fulfilling the horizon of expectation and aspiration of primarily urban, upper-caste, cisgender gay men (Rao 2020b, 7).[7] Many of the queer feminist activists I came to know through my research received the news with ambivalence, if not cynicism.

No women had been convicted under Section 377, and not a single case of sex between women had even reached the Indian courts (see Bhaskaran 2004).[8] Queer feminist activists were, unsurprisingly, skeptical about prioritizing a campaign to repeal Section 377. The presence or absence of the law meant little for lesbian women beyond the symbolic, they argued. Given the law's obsession with penetrative sex, lesbians were, in fact, "invisible to phallocentric sodomy law" (Dave 2012, 170).

They were not invisible on the register of the law alone. The HIV/AIDS crisis fundamentally recast the terrain of sexual politics in India, offering unprecedented scope to marginalized and even criminalized population groups to transform their "risky selves" into legitimate claims-making subjects (Vijayakumar 2021; see also Lakkimsetti 2020). Unlike female sex workers and gay men, however, Indian lesbians were not found to be "at risk," and thus this limited their visibility to the state (and to transnational donors). The political economy of managing the HIV/AIDS crisis deepened friction between emergent lesbian activism and a gay male community: "To lesbian collectives, the state seemed politically out of reach; to the organizations serving gay men, kothis, and MSM [men who have sex with men], HIV provided a reason to feel beyond the punitive practices of the state" (Dave 2012, 175).[9]

Ambivalence toward legal reform and alienation from HIV/AIDS turned lesbian activists away from gay struggles and toward the IWM, a natural ally, "since lesbianism was for them, first and foremost, a women's issue," writes Shraddha Chatterjee of lesbian activists in the 1990s (Chatterjee 2018, 15).[10] The IWM, however, provided them with only conditional acceptance and inclusion: they treated lesbianism as a private, not political, matter and thus remained uncomfortable with sexuality and desire constituting nodes of public organizing. The Sappho for Equality (SFE) activists quoted at the start of this section noted how their inclusion into a local women's movement, represented by the Kolkata feminist network, Maitree, was, by virtue of being simply another women's rights organization, representing women who were discriminated against and victimized. One Delhi-based queer activist I interviewed in 2009 put such forms of conditional solidarity in stronger terms: "There was no linkage between gender and sexuality except in relation to violence." But even feminist framings of violence had their limits; the IWM

operated with a hierarchy of violence in which certain forms of violence—
"dowry deaths, domestic violence and poverty"—ranked high and contributed to "the trivialization of lesbian issues" (Banerjea et al. 2019, 18–19).
Ultimately, when the controversy around the film *Fire* erupted, groups that
sprang into action, like the Campaign for Lesbian Rights (CALERI)—and,
later, Sappho—made a decisive break from gay groups *and* women's rights
organizing.[11]

If women's groups deemed sexuality a private matter, then so did the legal
campaign to repeal Section 377 of the Indian Penal Code. A major bone of
contention around the legal battle was its reliance on liberal and bourgeois
notions of privacy—to argue for sexual rights on the basis of the right to
privacy.[12] While this move left untouched the state's capacity to regulate and
criminalize sex—and reinforced a divide between forms of good private sex
and bad public sex (Sircar 2017)—it was also counterproductive to feminist
struggles aimed at dismantling the public-private divide itself. Feminists had
long argued that women's historical marginalization was contingent on their
relegation to the private, a domain that liberal law had been instrumental
in constituting and not just regulating. The kind of unceasing violence and
atrocity that queer women had to contend with emanated, moreover, from
the home, the very realm that a nationwide queer movement was attempting
to secure outside the reach of the law. Even as privacy claims also criminalized
gay men's public sex, the contradictions between the lived experiences and
needs of queer men and queer women could not have been starker.

While queer women were invisible to the law, subaltern sexual groups
were hypervisible and especially vulnerable to the state's carceral capacities. *Hijras* and *kothis* were disproportionately targeted by the police, who
mobilized a whole host of laws, from antitrafficking regulations to the
criminalization of vagrancy, to police them.[13] The public-private split thus
recriminalized subaltern sexual minorities (not only *hijras* but also female
sex workers) and left them unprotected from the abuse of state power. In
demanding and ultimately gaining state recognition of love as a private
good, queer legal activism served the modernist aspirations of the globalized,
neoliberal, and nationalist state. The simultaneous removal of an archaic
colonial law and the production of a new class of rights-bearing, respectable, and consumptive homosexual citizens announced India's arrival into
Western modernity.[14]

If the homosexual was constituted as a figure of modernity, then the
transgender subject—specifically, the *hijra*—was relegated to tradition.

Rahul Rao (2020b) shows the backward temporality that underpinned the transgender demand for state recognition and affirmative action through recourse to constitutional protections offered to "backward" classes.[15] Not only did the Indian court recognize transgender rights—in response to a petition filed by the National Legal Services Authority (NALSA)[16]—only four months after it denied recognition to same-sex sexuality, but it did so on the basis of ascribing caste status to transgenderism. The Transgender Persons (Protection of Rights) Act that was eventually passed in 2019 fell far below expectations, however: it ensnared individuals in the bureaucratic, overtly medicalized, and transphobic webs of screening committees and surgical interventions and was firmly rejected by trans activists and communities (Dutta 2014; Lakkimsetti 2020).

As a final point, let me turn to queer feminist alliances that worked against transgender inclusion and more intersectional queer feminist futures. A long-standing debate on gender neutrality in the Indian rape law not only pitted queer positions against feminist ones but also aligned queer and nonqueer feminists against gay and transgender ones. While the latter argued for recognition of the vulnerability to rape and sexual assault of *all* and not just those assigned as female at birth—especially as a way of addressing high levels of violence against *hijras*—the former fought for retaining a gender-specific law. Indian feminists were traditionally averse to widening the category of the victim of gender-based violence in their understanding of the distinctly gendered nature of such violence (Agnes 2002). Both queer and nonqueer feminists also feared misuse of the law, except that queer activists additionally worried that their first instance of visibility to the state and law would be a negative one (with Section 377 still in place).[17] Even as they had consciously broken away from mainstream feminist attachments to sexual injury and female victimization—which the IWM had served to naturalize—queer feminists appeared deeply attached to categories of male aggressor and female victim.

At the end of this discussion on queer entanglements with the Indian state and law, we see that the state impacted sexual minorities differently and that they, in turn, engaged the state in contradictory ways. Feminists, queers, and sexual subalterns did not always ally with one another as they marched forward; they also felt backward in their reiteration of normative ways of engaging the state and law. The queer feminist activism at stake in this book constitutes a locus of these distinct and entangled trajectories of queer and feminist organizing.

Developing Women: Co-optation and Resistance

Development has long constituted a site for considering shifting state and so-ciety relations, transforming governmentalities, and reconfiguring subaltern struggles. It has proved especially productive for changing the subject that is woman and, belatedly, other genders and sexualities.[18] With neoliberalism, development was perceived as an especially rich site of co-optation given its historic borrowing from critical pedagogies and social movements, but in ways that could diffuse or even derail their resistant and transformatory potential. The governmentalities of the developmentalist, neoliberal, and increasingly authoritarian state were not, however, comprehended so easily through co-optation/resistance binaries. Here I map the restructuring of development under neoliberalism (what some have called the "neoliberal turn within development"; Madhok 2010, 234) at scales both domestic and transnational, before turning, as a final point, to the gendered governance of the regime of Prime Minister Narendra Modi. These entanglements speak of longer, layered histories of governing, developing, and empowering women that come to bear upon the present.

As development became a core nationalist project in independent India, offering a decisive break from a colonial past, the fate of women became bound up in its trajectory and legitimacy (John 1999; Madhok 2012; Rai 2002). The 1974 state-commissioned *Towards Equality* report, which emerged as a "founding text" for the IWM (John 2009, 48), provided in-disputable evidence that, as a population group, women were lagging behind men on nearly each and every developmental indicator, notwithstanding elaborate steps toward formal equality enshrined in the Indian constitution. Internal pressure from autonomous women's groups led to the state becom-ing more receptive to feminist demands at a time of growing transnational emphasis on women in international development—evident, for instance, in the first United Nations (UN) Decade for Women. There were concrete institutional manifestations of this receptivity—for instance, in the inclu-sion of women's development into the Indian state's five-year plans and the reservation of seats for women at different levels of India's polity, from local government to national parliament.

Influential initiatives of the 1980s and 1990s—the Women's Develop-ment Program and Mahila Samakhya—constituted a unique partnership between the state and Indian feminists. They signaled an important shift in feminist-state relations, from being antagonistic to cautiously collabora-tive (Madhok 2012; A. Sharma 2008; S. Sharma 2011). These hybrid state and nonstate projects were markers of shifts occurring at other scales and with implications beyond the national. Third world and antiracist feminists had labored hard to establish subaltern women in the Global South as disempowered but not powerless. They provided evidence of their agency to counter pervasive assumptions of the passivity and victimization of third world women at the hands of tradition, culture, and poverty (Batliwala 2007; Kabeer 1994; Wilson 2015). While initiatives like Mahila Samakhya appeared to be responsive to these transnational feminist currents and even other counterhegemonic third world projects (like Paulo Freire's liberation theology; see A. Sharma 2008), they were also shaped by market-driven neoliberal ideas of women's empowerment. At the very moment at which the Indian state's welfare capacities were undone under the burdens of structural adjustment and market spaces opened and expanded under economic liberalization, the end of welfare came to be recast as empowerment (A. Sharma 2008, xvi).

At the heart of this neoliberal resignification of empowerment—from its leftist, feminist, and even Gandhian roots to neoliberal ideas around self-help and self-governance—was the gendered subaltern, whose industrious, enterprising, and altruistic nature proved to be especially amenable to the realization of neoliberal development ambitions. In an instance of what Nancy Fraser (2009) has called the "cunning of history," feminist arguments against women's victimization nurtured the neoliberal fetishization of individual agency and empowerment, at the cost of structural analysis, critique, or intervention. Ideas around women's agency were also racialized in ways that sharply recalled what Chandra Mohanty designated, some thirty years ago, as "Third World difference" (Wilson 2015). A queer feminist activist told me in 2009 that microcredit was "the newest construction of the good woman, who saves regularly for the development of the family and not for herself." She termed microcredit as "the most dangerous trend in the realm of gender and development," even as some feminist NGOs were trying to "straddle microcredit and women's empowerment and rights."

Indeed, microcredit schemes proliferated just as "states abandoned macro-structural efforts to fight poverty, efforts that small-scale lending cannot possibly replace" (Fraser 2013, 222). There is now considerable evidence to show microfinance institutions' debilitating and not merely benign effects, such as ever-expanding debt traps (what Julia Elyachar [2005] calls "empowerment debt"); increased burdens of loan repayment; limited control over loans; and new forms of surveillance, discipline, and punishment that intensify patriarchal control over women borrowers, their primary targets

(Karim 2011; K. Krishnan 2020; Nirantar Trust 2015; Rankin 2010; Ananya Roy 2010; Sen and Majumder 2015; see also my discussion in chapter 4). The queer feminist activist I quoted in the previous paragraph reflected on how pro-woman or even feminist NGOs were transforming into microfinance institutions and "burdening poor marginalized communities they are working with."

Microfinance, a phenomenon that rapidly rose in tandem with liberalization, informs the site of feminist developmentality that I consider in this book. Equally, this site resonates with the rising trend of philanthrocapitalism, centered on the unique potential of the adolescent girl of the Global South. The adolescent girl of Nike's Girl Effect campaign was, for instance, both subject of enormous risk—not to corporate exploitation but to cultural threats of marriage, motherhood, and the lack of education—and of immense and unique potential; she was both an "at-risk" girl and a "can-do" girl (Harris 2004). Education was key to the transformation of at-risk to can-do girls, for unleashing a chain of positive effects, from preventing early marriage, to controlling fertility, to freeing up hidden entrepreneurial capacities and producing enterprising neoliberal subjects (Khoja-Moolji 2018; Koffman and Gill 2013). Projects like the Girl Effect campaign thus furthered the policy consensus on poor women's education and empowerment that emerged in the 1990s as a way of easing the pain of the devastating effects of structural adjustment programs in the Global South (Moeller 2018).

As ideas around third world women's agency and empowerment gained traction in transnational development practice, women's adverse incorporation into the political economy of neoliberalism left them more precarious than ever. Some of the distinctly gendered fallouts of India's economic liberalization included a reduction in women's workforce participation, a fall in wages for both regularly and casually employed women workers, a falling availability of jobs, an increase in the gender pay gap, and the elimination—especially in state government positions—of permanent jobs, with an overall move toward increased casualization and precarity.[19] Women were exclusively positioned to pick up the fallout of state withdrawal from key areas of welfare provision like education and health.

Statist or NGO-run projects increasingly sought gendered labor to run; subaltern women were no longer the mere objects of development initiatives but also its agents, responsible for the provision of tangible material goods like education, health services, and nutrition and, increasingly, nonmaterial ones like knowledge, sensitization, peer support, and intangible empowerment (A. Gupta 2001; Jakimow 2013; K. Jenkins 2009). Primarily poor, lower-caste women were paid a small honorarium or stipend—but never a salary—in ways that fulfilled ideals of participatory development while outsourcing empowerment labor to those in need.[20] Such forms of work inscribed new forms of gendered vulnerability, risk, and precarity. The most extreme manifestation of risk was in the case of Bhanwari Devi, a grassroots state development worker who was gang-raped for attempting to stop a child marriage from taking place in rural North India.[21] The way her legal case was dismissed by the Indian courts also exemplified feminist critiques around the limits of progressive legalism and gender-sensitive state developmentalism.

It is in this story of neoliberal development that the gendered assumptions and consequences of voluntarism come into sharp relief (see, for example, K. Jenkins 2009). Yet Aradhana Sharma (2008) shows how the logic of voluntarism was consistent with gendered and class-based assumptions of welfare—insofar as women's labor was understood via the ideal of the upper-class and upper-caste housewife—and the neoliberal emphasis on pulling oneself up by the bootstraps. Sharma's ethnography is an important reminder of the convergence of distinct, even opposed governmental rationalities—welfarist and neoliberal, privatized and redistributive—in one and the same program. She asks what it means "to be co-opted by an entity that cannot be clearly demarcated or to seal oneself off from governmental processes that permeate the entire social formation" (A. Sharma 2008, 196).

If these kinds of feminist entanglements enabled the Indian state to be welfarist while neoliberal, then they also provided legitimacy to Hindu nationalist statecraft (Nilsen 2020). In Modi's first term in government, women's development schemes proliferated as a populist strategy that melded Hindu nationalism with neoliberal economic approaches.[22] The Beti Bachao (Save and Educate Daughters) campaign sought to empower *and* protect women but was called out as being "steeped in the same patriarchy that it claims to be fighting" (K. Krishnan 2020, 80). Similarly, the Swacch Bharat (Clean India) campaign—which linked toilets to women's empowerment—relied on gendered stereotypes, cultural ideas of protection, and even shaming strategies for enforcement.[23] The new popularity around building toilets to "save" women bolstered reasons to further confine them to their homes, in a context in which women experienced even a trip to the toilet as freedom from confinement (see K. Krishnan 2020; and chapter 5 of this book).

That some in the media described Swacch Bharat as India's "biggest women's movement" renewed feminist fears of co-optation and diminished the imaginative scope for resistance (K. Krishnan 2020, 84). The terrain I have mapped reveals, however, an intimate entanglement—a folding—of co-optation and resistance given the rise and legitimacy of neoliberal governmentality through its borrowing from and articulation of a range of transnational and local ideologies and idioms, both hegemonic and counter-hegemonic. The following discussions on NGO-ized and popular feminisms in India show just how much co-optation and resistance appear as two sides of the same coin, insofar as neoliberal dynamics are increasingly inescapable and hegemonic, even for our organizing against and resistance to it.

The NGO-ization Paradigm

Thanks to NGO-ization, young women are moving into an international field without going through the grass roots.
Queer feminist activist and consultant, Delhi, 2009

Who really represents the grass roots? Why does a group of twelve women who meet weekly represent the grass roots? ... To talk about grass roots, we would have to agree that only women's wings of political parties like the CPM [Communist Party of India (Marxist)] have that sort of reach.
Director of Mumbai-based women's rights organization, Delhi, 2009

One of the earliest motivations for this book was to appreciate the NGO as a site of the political, against its ready association with depoliticization.[24] My intention was not to uncritically celebrate laments about the NGO-ization of the IWM but to enquire into its meaning and effects, besides taking seriously the structures of feelings that mobilized feminist narratives of loss and melancholia. As the contrasting words of two feminists—of the same generation and involved in gender and sexual rights–based activism and NGOs—in the epigraph to this section suggest, NGO-ization was employed in discussions on Indian feminism not merely as a descriptive term—to refer to an increase in the number of NGOs working on women and gender—but a highly affective one. Sadia Hodžić (2014) refers to this affective structure as "the NGOization paradigm," which obscures as much as it reveals, especially through pitting NGOs against social movements. Or, as staff at an NGO in Bangalore remarked, NGO-ization "accentuates the polarization between the NGO sector and social movements."

The most abiding anxieties around NGOs and NGO-ization grew out of Indian feminists' attachments to the organizing and ideological principle of autonomy. Many of the autonomous groups of the 1970s and 1980s transformed into externally funded and professionalized NGOs given the expansion of work; "the need [to NGO-ize] came from within voluntary women's groups that we can't continue," explained one feminist academic I interviewed in Kolkata, who was also part of these groups. It was, moreover, these funded NGOs, and not informal collectives and campaigns, that were seen as taking important decisions on behalf of the entire IWM. While early law reforms were a product of the IWM, later ones—such as changes to the Domestic Violence Act—became, in Nivedita Menon's words, "the baby of an NGO and not representative of the grassroots." In my 2008 interview with her Menon observed (like many I initially interviewed for this project) how the politics of funding transformed the IWM entirely. While the first national-level autonomous women's conferences in the country were attended by women's groups who identified as neither funded nor attached to political parties, by the time of the Seventh National Conference of Autonomous Women's Groups, which took place in 2006 in Kolkata, it was almost entirely attended by NGOs (and thus only excluded left-wing political parties; Menon 2009, 109).[25]

These domestic shifts were fundamentally transnational in nature, making NGO-ization coterminous with processes of transnationalism and neoliberalism.[26] Liberalization made it far easier to obtain foreign funds to do activist and development work, just as the state receded from welfare provision and reconfigured its development goals. Global lenders like the World Bank and the International Monetary Fund deemed NGOs more efficient, accountable, and less corrupt than national governments. They were championed because of their assumed departure from the state; yet they were state-like and a site of governmentality (Bernal and Grewal 2014c). And just as structural adjustment and neoliberalism were the conditions for the possibility of NGO work, NGOs facilitated the neoliberalization of these states.[27]

In including NGOs alongside and on equal footing with governments, the UN brought unprecedented global visibility to NGOs as a new feminist form (Bernal and Grewal 2014b; see also Armstrong 2013; Devika 2016; Mukhopadhyay 2016; and Thayer 2010). The 1995 UN conference in Beijing signaled not only a change of the scale on which local struggles were operating—in giving feminist struggles from the South a global platform—but also a change in local institutional and organizational forms. Recognition was afforded, however, not just to any NGO but to those formalized and professionalized ones that were best able to receive the development aid that was on offer. While it was instrumental in constituting a transnational feminist counterpublic, especially through globalizing certain issues like violence against women and lesbian rights (Thayer 2010), the Beijing conference represented more worrying trends in excluding those struggles and activists who could not scale up their interventions and speak to the agendas set and resources offered by bilateral donors and international NGOs.[28] For those who were competitive in a "social movement market" (Thayer 2010, 166), the internal life of organized activism began to look very different as it moved from social movement or protest-oriented work toward service delivery, technocratic solutions, and hierarchical and managerial organizational cultures—or, in short, an "anti-politics machine" (Ferguson 1990). For many, these shifting scales of activism took activists literally and imaginatively away from those on whose behalf they spoke: "the growing cadre of well-trained full-time NGO feminists from the South had strategic visions that often aligned more closely with those of their Northern counterparts than with those of working-class women in their own countries" (Thayer 2010, 47).

In liberalized India, the transnationalization and professionalization of feminist activism exacerbated internal differences among women and among feminists. A new class of paid activists—"nine-to-five" feminists—contributed to the traditionally metropolitan, middle-class professional composition of the IWM (historical differences that were effectively masked by the NGO-ization paradigm),[29] but at a time when most Indian women were becoming poorer under the impact of neoliberal restructuring and globalization. Dave (2012) shows how efforts to overcome this paradox were negotiated on the terrain of sexuality, precisely at the time when the transnational proved an important scale for legitimizing local lesbian struggles. In recognizing lesbian rights as human rights, the Beijing conference countered domestic hostilities and homophobia and afforded "the lesbian" recognition as a rights-bearing subject. Yet these transnational challenges failed to push local feminisms in more intersectional directions, prompting Indian feminists to regurgitate long-standing formulations of lesbianism as elite, bourgeois, and irrelevant to shore up their indigenous credentials and to fortify a hierarchy of violence (Dave 2012, 123; see also Bacchetta 2002; Banerjea et al. 2019; and Menon 2007b). In fact, it was "possible for a number of feminists to evade the newer languages and challenges of sexuality movements—such as the gay and lesbian movement or struggles over sex work—precisely by seeing them as off-shoots of globalization" (John 2009, 48).

Indeed, when it came to the politics of sexuality, the implications of the concomitant processes of NGO-ization and transnationalism were more ambiguous than co-optation fears allowed. The genesis and rise of "counter-heteronormative" movements in biopolitical interventions around HIV/AIDS showed how state-centric governmentality and biopower could "spill over into forms of radicalization it could not have predicted nor desired"

(Menon and Nigam 2007, 130). As activists and academics I interviewed back in 2008–9 observed, "the queer movement was a product of but not contained by the NGO context" and, equally, "sex work has become an issue because of funding" (especially, as many agreed, that the IWM "did not talk about sexual rights").

Sex workers' struggles in the period of liberalization were, in fact, described as an instance of the transformation of governmental technologies into social movement work rather than the co-optation and collapse of the latter into the former.[30] As some of the earliest at-risk population groups, sex workers became visible to state biopolitical agendas and ends, but also as worthy of legal protection and rights (Ghose 2012; Lakkimsetti 2020; Mokkil 2019; Swati Ghosh 2017; and Vijayakumar 2021). While lesbians were not, as previously noted, a subject of HIV/AIDS risk and control, the 1990s created a space in which embryonic forms of queer feminist activism could consolidate themselves as more permanent fixtures in a changing terrain of sexual politics. Thus, by the time of the controversy around *Fire*, there was an emergent activist community to counter the right-wing attack on what was considered India's first lesbian film and also to challenge the mainstream feminist reticence toward homosexuality (see Menon 2012).

None of this is to suggest that global discourses of sexual identities and rights—which traveled to liberalized India via transnational funds and local NGOs—freed sexual subalterns, as accounts of globalization's liberatory potentials would have us believe.[31] Globalization constituted and limited an emergent field of political possibility around sexuality, which differently impacted marginalized groups and individuals. Not only were some sexual minorities afforded greater recognition than others in the entangled governmentalities around public health concerns and legal rights, but HIV/AIDS prevention programs also produced the very subjects of biopolitical intervention that they sought to regulate, manage, and empower (Boyce 2007, 2014; Katyal 2016). Many activists working in both community-based organizations and NGOs remarked how HIV/AIDS funding—the "HIV/AIDS industry" (khanna 2009)—had created a field of the proliferation of same-sex identity categories and competition among groups; "HIV money has divided the community," one transgender activist told me of the particularly intense site that was the city of Bangalore (see especially Vijayakumar 2021). The NGOs working in the HIV/AIDS sector were seen to be especially prone to using the labor of subaltern groups in extractive ways. But this was also true of women's NGOs, which relied on women's social reproduction to manage risk and provide legitimacy and care—dynamics that powerfully entrenched the gender, class, and caste dynamics of Indian society (see Govinda 2009; and Sangtin Writers and Nagar 2006). The NGO director from Mumbai whose words open this section powerfully noted, also as a way of bridging the gap between NGOs and movements, that "NGOs [are] a product of a social movement whose foot soldiers have always been poor women."

While critiques of NGOs hone our gaze toward important truths, as borne out in this book, they also take our attention away from other truths, and especially their more productive capacities and ambivalent effects. The strong affects that underlie the NGO-ization paradigm do not afford space to the feelings and desires of those subjects the paradigm incites or explain how NGOs attract and keep within their fold distinct types of individuals and groups. These include sex workers, lesbians, transgender persons, rural women, adolescent girls, and feminists. A common theme among the NGO workers I spoke to was one of encountering feminism on entering an organization; as one, located in Bangalore, explained, "I didn't really have access to this—I call this—the other world. I knew I didn't want to do certain things and had questions about certain things but to actually know that there are people who have thought about these things, there is literature available, there is a critique of these things.... It's also about class, accessibility. I didn't come from a family background which you would call well-read so you would know there's a world beyond; it had to be stumbled upon" (quoted in S. Roy 2011, 596).

The entanglement of feminism and neoliberalism in the NGO form makes it an especially significant site of *feminist* self-making in neoliberal times, and for asking, how NGOs might produce subjects who "could become feminist" (Grewal, quoted in S. Roy 2017b, 259), and whether such subjects are exhausted by the conditions that make them possible.[32]

Millennial Feminisms

If you want to "protect" anything, protect our fearless freedom, our bekhauf azaadi.
Kavita Krishnan, *Fearless Freedom*, 2020

Feminist entanglements in transnational and neoliberal flows of ideas and capital were perhaps most manifest in the new modes and technologies of public protest that marked the new millennium. The paradoxical combination of India's economic liberalism, which made women and sexual minorities newly visible on streets and in cyberspace, and political illiberalism, or the increased right-wing backlash against gendered assertions and sexual freedoms, shaped new geographies of protest. The postliberalization conjuncture made visible the (increasingly digital) forms of protest that young, urban, middle-class, English-speaking Indians engaged in, but also those that were marginal and intersectional and took as their object of critique Indian feminism itself.

Of course, the new millennium was not the first time that Indian feminism was subject to internal critique. The 1990s saw substantial challenges to its normative subject, making clear that *woman* was not a universal, stable, or homogeneous category but was, in fact, an exclusionary one. When confronted with the rising numbers of women in the Hindu nationalist movement—which even co-opted feminist slogans for its hateful and violent ends—Indian feminists were caught off guard (Bacchetta 2004; Sarkar and Butalia 1995). They had not only collapsed internal distinctions in crafting a universal Indian womanhood but had also failed to politicize the Hindu middle class, in favor of speaking on behalf of a poor majority.

The conjoint rise of Hindu nationalism and neoliberalism politicized the "new" middle classes in new ways; they spawned entire movements around good governance and urban regeneration, and against corruption (Anjaria and Anjaria 2013; P. Chatterjee 2004; Harris 2004). Women's issues were not absent from this trend but not reducible to it either and, beginning in the early 2000s, we see two developments: first, spontaneous and large-scale middle-class-led urban protests around gender-based violence against women of similar social backgrounds;[33] and second, more avowedly feminist responses against the backlash to women's increased visibility in public, including an Indian iteration of the global SlutWalk marches that took victim blaming to task, and the first local cyberfeminist campaign against right-wing "moral policing."[34] These were important harbingers of a new wave of urban feminist activism, which broke from the established political repertoires, technologies, subjects, and affects of the IWM. Critical events like the 2012 antirape protests in Delhi radicalized a generation of middle-class millennials, even as they added to generational worries around co-optation and loss.

Violence against women was at the heart of new feminisms, as it had been for older ones, but in dramatically different ways.[35] Unlike previous generations, for whom the state and law were the primary sources of redress, younger and newly politicized feminists rejected the protectionist logics of the state, which was less concerned with women's safety than their honor. The 2012 antirape protests were as much about the rising tide of public violence against women as they were about exploding the myth of paternal protectionism and the gendered forms of curtailment, even confinement, that it entailed. What women needed was not protection—which they invariably experienced as a form of violence—but equality of access to the public and unqualified and unconditional freedom for all. Feminist and radical leftist leader Kavita Krishnan's words in the epigraph to this section became a rallying cry after Jyoti Singh Pandey's murder. City-based campaigns and projects—which preceded the Delhi rape but gained visibility after it—encouraged women to "take back the night," to "break the cage" of discriminating women's hostels, and to engage in banal acts like sleeping in public parks or "loitering" in the streets, which were transgressive in gender and class terms (see S. Roy 2016a). Even as the urban dominated public optics, similar dynamics were discernible in rural India. Members of the North Indian Gulabi Gang gained mainstream attention for bypassing state and law to take into their own hands the endemic problem of (caste-sanctioned) violence against women and deliver justice to rural victims.

The immediate aftermath of the Delhi protests thus saw the emergence of new kinds of activist interventions.[36] Feminist and queer activists in Kolkata—who we will encounter in subsequent chapters—were part of this transforming landscape. As one explained to me in a 2016 interview, "We are creating spaces for protest outside rallies and marches.... We are challenging the people around us, challenging their gaze, and celebrating our variant identities." This activist was part of Take Back the Night Kolkata, which started with mostly cisgender middle-class women students in 2013 and developed into a more explicitly queer and transgender space through collaborations with working-class Dalit transgender feminists.

Such new kinds of coalitional politics expanded conventional leftist student organizing while foregrounding the class and caste dimensions of LGBTQ politics (which went unnoticed in NGO-ized spaces; Dutta 2019). They brought participants from diverse socioeconomic backgrounds—and people of all genders—onto common platforms around gender-based violence and rising right-wing nationalism.[37]

A new feminist repertoire of visible public protest was playful, sexy, and even fun. Popular initiatives like the Kiss of Love campaign, which deployed the idea of public kissing to counter the Hindu Right's violent governance of intimacies, expanded the parameters of engaging with sexuality.[38] They also invited leftist and feminist skepticism—for not being "revolutionary enough," for being frivolous and lacking "the seriousness of issues of labour/class" (B. Bose 2017, 281). In the hierarchy of oppression within which the IWM had historically operated, pleasure and desire, like

Figure 1.1 Take Back the Night Kolkata image. Reproduced with the kind permission of Take Back the Night Kolkata.

sexuality, could only amount to a distraction from more serious—structural and not subjective—concerns, with the added implication that these were elite issues of no relevance to the masses ("poor women are not sexual," as one queer interviewee summarized of the IWM). Initiatives like the SlutWalk marches and the Pink Chaddi campaign, while marking a turn toward play and sexual positivity, were declared "feminism lite" (Kapur 2012). As I heard more than once (and not only from older feminists), these initiatives had no engagement with class.[39] Of course, queers and sex workers were some of the first to face the sexual negativity of the IWM. Many queer activists, including those of SFE, agreed that the mainstream IWM was comfortable with discussions of sexuality if they pertained to sexual injury and women's victimization alone. "There is scope for the women's movement to learn from the queer movement that there isn't only victimology but celebration," a queer feminist I met in Delhi once said.

New ways of doing queer feminist politics—and being queer, feminist, or both—emerged in, were made possible by, and also reflected the logics and normativities of a neoliberal and digital India (Dasgupta and Dasgupta 2018a).[40] That the internet constituted a key site for feminist and queer counterconduct is another instance of the productive capacities of neoliberal governmentality, with unpredictable effects. On the one hand, observers note the extent to which the legal victory around Section 377, for instance, was helped by domestic and "transnational internet activism in the form of blogs, Facebook posts and the viral circulation of images from protest rallies" (Nagar 2018, 98). On the other hand, they warn that the digital was no utopian space (Dasgupta and Dasgupta 2018b).[41]

All major new feminist campaigns—from #WhyLoiter, #HappytoBleed, and #WeWillGoOut to larger initiatives like Blank Noise and movements such as Pinjra Tod (Break the Cage)—were instances of hashtag feminism, reaching somewhat of a crescendo in 2017 with the surfacing of the #MeToo movement. By this time, the early confluence of online and offline cultures of resisting sexual violence had been taken over by the digital. Initial concerns around exclusivity and (limited) reach in the face of India's digital divide seemed less pressing in the face of how seamlessly digital and mobile technologies entered the lives of young Indians, and not only the privileged ones.[42] India's #MeToo campaign, in particular, began with a new generation of vocal anticaste activists who made questions of caste privilege core to new technologies of resisting sexual harassment.[43] Their voices effected a radical expansion of the discourse of sexual violence by questioning Brahmanic feminism and by expanding intersectional feminist positions to decolonial ones (for ending India's occupation of Kashmir, for instance). Critiques of Savarna or upper-caste feminist practice traveled as "contemporary hashtag publics" (Gajjala 2018, 9) on Facebook, Instagram, and Twitter and strengthened forms of solidarity with marginalized communities elsewhere. Of course, Dalit feminist critique of Savarna feminist practice was established since the Mandal-Masjid years (see Guru 1995; and Rege 1998), but it took issues of caste-based discrimination and sexual harassment in higher education to catapult these to global visibility (thanks in part to the internet).[44]

Let me end this section by noting some of the critiques and countercritiques of digitally driven and youth-led millennial feminisms, which were plagued, from their earliest emergence, with accusations of being elite, exclusive, individualized, and neoliberal. Accusations of "neoliberal feminism" drew on the slippage between the highly individualized nature of some campaigns—through their reliance on individual participation and an ideological impetus to transform the self—with neoliberal ideas of atomized, individualized responses to social problems (H. Gupta 2016; Mani 2014). While they were entangled in neoliberal conditions of possibility, Indian activists' efforts did not, however, resonate with or produce uniformly neoliberal effects. The authors of the book *Why Loiter?* (Phadke, Khan, and Ranade 2011) and participants in the movement it nurtured were, for instance, careful to distinguish their vision of feminist freedom and fun from a neoliberal one rooted in consumptive and privatized sources of pleasure.[45] And even the most skeptical observers of #MeToo had to admit that it went beyond an individualized *me* and mobilized an ever-widening *too* (Clark-Parsons 2019).[46] But in the very specific regional context of Kolkata and West Bengal—with a poor history of politicizing the self—the transformations to the individual self that digital activism signaled needed no defending at all.

A Smaller Story

Hashtag movements seem to signal recognizable transformations of subjectivity.... Such impalpable transformations, in the realms of interiority, are sometimes the most lasting.
Kavita Panjabi, "Hokkolorob: A Hashtag Movement," 2015

In the prehistory of #MeToo in India, #Hokkolorob was a significant regional marker. A Kolkata-based student movement around sexual harassment in higher education, it was a first of many sorts: at the time it went viral in 2014, it was the largest hashtag movement, besides having a robust offline presence; it was emblematic of a new wave of leftist student politics that was consciously independent of the traditional Left; and free of single-issue fetishization, it produced novel on-the-ground alliances and solidarities. Even as the movement received tired critiques because of class and location (Samaddar 2014), it invited far more celebratory responses, of the kind expressed by Kavita Panjabi. That Panjabi chose to center, as this brief amorphous movement's greatest legacy, subjective changes—"in the realms of interiority"—tells us something of the historical conditions under which certain political strategies and their effects become desirable. What emerged at the transnational scale as neoliberal individualism was differently read—and felt—at the more intimate scale of the regional, where individualized modes of political engagement were historically granted little space.

The postcolonial and socialist legacies of the IWM meant a suspicion of more Western-styled personal politics as indulgent, individual, and depoliticizing; social change was imagined in strictly collective terms (M. Chaudhuri 2004; Kumar 1993, 195).[47] These dynamics shaped Kolkata's leftist feminist field—a field that Raka Ray (1999) found to be uncomfortable with attempts at politicizing the personal, which was read as "'bourgeois individualism,' as self-centeredness or selfishness" (Sarkar 1991, 217; on the self-effacing nature of Indian feminism, see also M. Chaudhuri 2004). Its concrete manifestations meant more political education than consciousness-raising when it came to working-class and poor women and the inability of middle-class women to share personal matters in feminist spaces. Even autonomous feminist groups were uncomfortable with "baring the soul" (Ray 1999, 82). Elsewhere in the country—in Bombay (now Mumbai), where such a leftist habitus was not as entrenched as in Kolkata—a more radical feminist politics centered the personal and even the sexual, laying the grounds for future campaigns around women's pleasures in risk and loitering.

Yet it was also millennial Kolkata that enabled a diversity that was not easily found elsewhere. As witnessed after the Delhi rape and at the time of #Hokkolorob, a range of individuals and activist groups—of oppositional ideologies and diverse socioeconomic circumstances—came together in unexpected alliances and solidarities. A leftist legacy of politicizing class developed into more intersectional and transnational struggles around class, caste, gender, and sexuality. And in their "hashtagged" politics that spread like wildfire, activists seemed to appreciate the significance of change in quotidian ways. What would it mean to turn to such "smaller" stories of globalized regional lifeworlds as a way of appreciating the entanglements in which Indian feminism currently resides?

For Navaneetha Mokkil (2019, 38), the "regional public" is an "unruly formation" whose sexual subjects and politics cannot be derived from the kinds of liberal vocabularies—of "rights, identity and recognition"—that permeate global and metropolitan imaginaries. She asks what forms of resistance and struggle—and agency—go unacknowledged when we look through one lens alone. Indeed, what do we miss in our affective drive to name contemporary political interventions and imaginaries as co-opted and apolitical, per inherited frameworks of post- and neoliberal feminism? In the Global South, where neoliberalism has a layered history, folded into other hegemonic projects that it does not easily or fully replace, pronouncements of a neoliberal feminism appear, at best, rushed, or, at worst, derivative of Western conceptualizations. As an intricate tangle of conditions, relationships, and possibilities that resist the kind of apartness assumed in "co-optation," the gender and sexual politics of the new millennium offers multiple readings, in telling us something about the instabilities of the neoliberal moment but also of the historic impurities of feminism and its subjects in this part of the world. The rest of the book explores some smaller stories of entanglements and exclusions, manifest in subjects whose actions, imaginations, and affects were transformed by a governmental impulse to which they could nevertheless not be reduced.

2
Queer Activism as Governmentality
Regulating Lesbians, Making Queer

There is no story to be told about how one moves from feminist to queer to trans. The reason there is no story to be told is that none of these stories are the past; these stories are continuing to happen in simultaneous and overlapping ways as we tell them. They happen, in part, through the complex ways they are taken up by each of these movements and theoretical practices.
Judith Butler, *Undoing Gender*, 2004

Lesbian feminism can bring feminism back to life.
Sara Ahmed, *Living a Feminist Life*, 2017

Oh, Sappho, they are so second wave!
Uma, queer activist, Kolkata, 2016

In the summer of 2016, I found myself in the Queer Café, the first such establishment in Kolkata. I had been invited there by Uma, whom I had recently met through feminist and queer activists in the city. Uma was a revelation to me—she was young, openly lesbian, and "living together" with her girlfriend. The Queer Café seemed to confirm what my first few meetings with Uma had suggested—that much had changed in Kolkata's queer scene. Or had it? While the café afforded space for queer sociality and community building, it still operated in the safety of the private and not in the public, implying the limits of a city that some were calling queer friendly. The café was in a solidly middle-class neighborhood that reflected the attributes of old, moneyed, respectable Kolkata as well as new patterns of urban consumption and purchasing power; homemade "continental" dishes along with Nespresso coffee were on sale. While the sale proceeds went to charitable purposes, the space was fairly elite. Notwithstanding some non-elite transgender persons, the bulk of those present reflected the particular demographic that the café's hosts belonged to: young, college-going, middle-class, and comfortable in both Bengali and English.

The café's clientele comprised not just self-identified queer individuals but also those who were part of an activist lifeworld around matters of gender and sex in the city.[1] These were the people who would, if nothing else, turn up to the annual Pride march and actively engage social media on queer issues. Barring one young woman who arrived late, there were no participants from Sappho for Equality (SFE), the only organization for lesbian and bisexual women and transgender persons in eastern India, which I had been researching for nearly a decade. The institutionalized activism of SFE in the region had played a crucial role in materializing this queer lifeworld.

In this chapter, I tell the story of SFE—and its roots in a support group called Sappho—which stretches over two decades from the beginning of the new millennium, a period in which the very possibility of queer Indian life changed dramatically. In the short life of this one organization we see how queer livability and political organizing in its name were actively enabled by, and came to embody, the configurations, convergences, and co-opting potentials of neoliberal India. A privately run, commercially viable queer café captured the paradoxical implications of these conjoint processes well—epitomizing, on the one hand, the materialization of the gay modern outside the West and, on the other, the commodification and depoliticization that accompanied what has varyingly been called, in the West, "gay normalization" or "queer liberalism" (Eng 2010; Eng, Halberstam, and Muñoz 2005; Love 2007).[2] For critical commentators observing the kind of mainstream visibility that queers and queerness achieved in a strikingly short period of time, such progress amounted to little more than the exhaustion of any radical promise that queerness might have held. The grounds for such pessimism were easily available in how queer success—in legal terms, for instance—appeared less and not more intersectionally driven, even more striking in a country like India, where queerness was so obviously inflected by class, caste, religion, and region. In a moment of hypervisibility and public recognition, what was progress for at least some Indian gays and lesbians turned out to be, for the vast majority, loss.

These dynamics of progress and loss—of success and co-optation—were fundamentally at stake in Sappho's trajectory and ones that such a self-reflexive set of activists were far from oblivious to. As they grew, from being a small support group for the few to a fully funded and highly regarded nongovernmental organization (NGO) for the care of many, they remained

committed to the radical potential of queerness by resisting seamless incorporation into neoliberal, elite, and exclusionary networks of power and privilege. The entry into neoliberal governmentality, primarily through the circuits of transnational funding and LGBTQ identity politics, did not amount, in other words, to any straightforward or uncontested process of neoliberal co-optation. Even as the organization's fortunes and ways of functioning transformed through the related processes of "NGO-ization," professionalization, and transnationalism, multiple genealogies of the political did not simply disappear; much changed and much endured.[3]

What endured most was a recent past of lesbian and feminist affect and politics, with clear regional and cultural inflections. Even as they changed the subject of Indian feminism, queer feminist activists took recourse to the established political repertoires and cultures on which early lesbian groups had also relied for legitimacy and effect (Biswas 2007; S. Chatterjee 2018). One thing we know of the queer feminist past, to whose scholarship my discussion is indebted, is that activism normalizes and marginalizes just as it creates the conditions for new forms of resistance and problematization (Dave 2012). These contradictions lie at the heart of the story of queer feminist activism as it unfolded in millennial Kolkata and presented local activists with real challenges around queer visibility and normalization. Activism constituted new norms and normativities on newer sites and created its own ghosts and space invaders.[4]

A key spectral figure is the *graamer meye,* the subaltern lesbian of rural Bengal, who haunted what metropolitan queer feminists could do and be in a new millennium. The story I tell here is as much her story as it is of those who spoke on her behalf, in a sharp reiteration of long-standing relations between *bhadralok* (middle-class, respectable) activists and subaltern subjects. Toward the end of this chapter, I show how a changed world of collective queer belonging, exemplified by the Queer Café, comprised a set of queer frictions among lesbian and transgender activists seeking to speak on behalf of the subaltern. While transgender feminism, in particular, might seem like the culmination of my story—what might have brought feminism "back to life" (Ahmed 2017, 214)—no such mode of recovery or redemption is on offer. Queer and transgender feminisms were the source of enduring and new governmentalities, haunted by ghosts of a feminist past at the dawn of a new queer future. Hauntings of this kind disrupt linear accounts and their progressivist logics, revealing the histories of Indian feminism (nonqueer, queer, and transgender) as not distinct or successive but as "simultaneous and overlapping" (Butler 2004, 4).

Beginnings

When Sappho began as an emotional support group for same-sex-desiring women in Kolkata on June 20, 1999, the lesbian was only just emerging as a political subject on the Indian landscape, on the back of the controversy around the film *Fire*. Unlike Delhi and Mumbai, Kolkata had not experienced the right-wing vandalism of local cinemas screening the film. Instead, supportive slogans—for freedom of expression and against right-wing censorship (but not for same-sex love)—prevailed. A leftist political culture also explained why Kolkata was not yet touched by any public consciousness-raising around nonnormative sexual identities and existence, which were lived in denial, secrecy, and invisibility. While other cities had witnessed the birth of informal networks and meetings of lesbians—under the umbrella of the single woman, or *akeli aurat*—Kolkata lesbians (*shomo kaami*, in the vernacular) did not even live this kind of "hidden life" (C. Shah 2005; see also Bacchetta 2002; and Bhaskaran 2004).

Akanksha and Malobika, young middle-class professional Bengali women, took this moment—brought about by *Fire*—and made the unprecedented step of giving an interview to a leading regional newspaper, an act of self-revelation that carried significant cost. In April 1999 the interview ran with the title "Chhaichapa Fire" (Fire beneath the ashes), gesturing to what was yet to be uncovered or silenced—even suppressed. Over three hundred women wrote to the mailbox number provided as part of the interview (negotiated as a condition for this media revelation). In an important reminder of the early origins of lesbian activism in gay male spaces, the mailbox belonged to the Counsel Club, one of the earliest support groups for middle-class gay men (Dhall 2020). The letters testified to the existence of other queer women and thus the idea of a support group for queer women, distinct from that for gay men, was born.[5] Within three months Sappho materialized in a small flat rented by Akanksha and Malobika; along with two other lesbian couples, they made up the six founding members. Akanksha and Malobika (2007, 363) later reflected on this moment of inception: "Two to four, four to six, six lesbians in the heart of the city of Calcutta exchanging laughter and tears—who had thought such a day would come in our lives? When we would be able to speak our minds freely without fear or shame, share jokes with people of a similar mindset? … The basic urge to meet our social needs led us to getting in touch with another couple in the same city."[6]

Members who had been part of Sappho from the start narrated similar desires for self-recognition and community—from how they could not even bear to see their own reflections in the mirror to recognizing themselves and eliciting recognition from others. Violence, especially at the hands of family and kin, pervaded their stories, and Sappho proved a literal lifeline: "If Sappho wasn't there, where would I have gone?" one member said, recalling horrific acts of abuse at the hands of her own parents. Like her, many of the lesbian women who first reached out to Sappho did so less for support or company than for survival, or "the fight to survive" (*beche thakaar loraai*). The initial letters that Akanksha and Malobika received even contained a suicide note, exemplifying the precarity of lesbian life. Their own lives were hardly free of risk, so much so that Akanksha and Malobika chose pseudonyms when coming out to the mainstream press.[7] The desire for public visibility and self and social recognition had to be balanced with the imperative for safety.

While gay male activist and support spaces had afforded initial and critical forms of support and solidarity, they had their own limits. In an interview with Sayan Bhattacharya published online, Malobika draws on her experience at the Counsel Club to mark some broader dissonances between lesbian women and gay men's experiences: "How does a homosexual man relate to a homosexual woman? Is their nonnormative sexuality enough to bridge the material differences of gender? And to this, when you add money matters, how do their power dynamics play out?" (Bhattacharya 2014).

The "material differences of gender" seemed to matter most when it came to lesbian experiences of violence, and it was violence that made the turn toward the women's movement critical. Sappho turned to local women's groups for help with domestic violence, for directing abandoned lesbian women to shelter homes, and even for setting up its own help line. Sappho's early history confirms the circuits of dependency that Naisargi Dave (2012) found in Delhi: how lesbian groups, without their own material resources and organizational infrastructure, had to rely on mainstream women's groups in ways that also necessitated certain ideological positions, such as the need to speak in the language of culture and nation that had served to marginalize lesbians in the first place. Sappho's activists also turned to highly regional and locally available tropes of vulnerability and empowerment, which constituted entangled leftist and feminist fields. Akanksha and Malobika insisted, for instance, on lesbian women's economic independence as a route to their emancipation, especially from the family. In my earliest conversations with them, they described SFE as an organization that did not provide any income-generating options to women, emphasizing instead their financial independence, the need to "stand on your own two feet" (*nijer paaye daaratei hobe*).

For their part, local feminist groups—under the banner of Maitree (Friendship)—formally included Sappho in 2000, but in conditional ways. As Akanksha (2009, 3) wrote in the SFE newsletter *Swakanthey*, "Not-understanding and trivialization of sexuality issues had always been the main challenge within the mainstream women's movement in West Bengal.... Sexuality per se was a taboo since inception of autonomous women's movement in this state. As the main leaders and activists came from a leftist background, sexuality was regarded as [a] bourgeois or private matter of individual choice." In early 2006 the newsletter's editorial page declared a turning point in these queer-feminist alliances: "This year, from 9th to 11th September, the 7th National Autonomous Women's Conference is being hosted in Salt Lake Stadium, Kolkata. We are part of it as a co-organizer. The issue of sexually marginalized women will be openly discussed for the first time" (Subhagata Ghosh 2016, 11).[8]

Given how previous conferences—and especially one at Tirupati in 1994—had been the site of open acrimony toward the issue of lesbianism, this one marked several important firsts (Biswas 2007; see also S. Chatterjee 2018; Dave 2012; and Menon 2012). In richly documenting the conference, SFE member Ranjita Biswas shows queer and nonqueer feminist convergences and tensions on issues of marriage, family, and violence, besides an early emergence of feminist contestations over transgender presence. While female-to-male transgender persons were part of the conference, a decision had been taken to not include men or male-to-female transgender individuals: "the conference was a platform for all who identified themselves as women and suffered similar kind of oppression as women," Biswas tells us, while noting the reessentializing of the sex/gender binary through this move in ways that the transgender question disrupted: "The category of anatomical sex as defining woman, no longer stands immutable and this was well demonstrated through the debates that emerged around the participation of transsexual and transgender people in the just concluded conference. Such questions remained unexplored throughout the four days of the conference in all sessions" (Biswas 2007, 2).[9]

Sappho's fortunes changed substantially with the creation of SFE some years later. Registered as an NGO on October 30, 2003, SFE embodied several related desires: the need to lobby the wider population in the struggle for decriminalization and destigmatization, and to move beyond providing support alone to demanding recognition and rights *as human beings* and not just as sexual minorities or as women. The oft-used slogan "Prothome ami manush, tarpor ami meyemanush, shob sheshe ami shomokaami meyemanush" (I am first a human, and then a woman, and only last am I a lesbian woman) captured activist reorientations from safety and emotional support toward a Bengali humanism and, eventually, human rights.

In Akanksha and Malobika's (2007, 367) words, "We started to visualize our issues from the human rights perspective.... While registering as a trust / public body, we took on the new name Sappho for Equality indicating our mission to work on a broader frame with marginalized women, starting with marginalization on sexual preference. Anyone who supports our cause can join this, irrespective of gender and sexual orientation."

The formation and rise of SFE had a lot to do with its ability to access international funds. Given state hostility, SFE had no choice but to NGO-ize. This was hardly a risk-free process given that NGO-ization also required ratification and recognition from the state, as Malobika explained: "We knew that we would not receive any state funding.... Right at the outset, we were very clear that when we would apply for registration, we would underline in bold that we were an LBT (lesbian, bisexual, and transmen) collective. There was no question of cloaking facts, even if it meant a tough time at work.... When we applied for funding, we did not have an idea about how to write proposals but soon picked the ropes. Mama Cash (an organization that provides funding support to activist groups working for the rights of women, girls, and transgendered people) granted us an amount in 2005 but it took us four years to get FCRA! Those years were so tough" (Bhattacharya 2014).[10]

The early history of SFE is an important reminder of the conditions under which activists take decisions to transform their activism—out of necessity, if anything. Transnational funds and human rights discourses—especially around violence against women—brought in obvious opportunities and resources; but it also provided key forms of institutionalism and continuity, denied to queer activists and not by the state alone.[11] As one SFE member put it, in my first meetings with the organization in 2008, "organizational expansion is the expansion of activism."

From the additive language of SFE's slogan—"I am first a human, and then a woman, and only last am I a lesbian woman"—activists turned to a more explicitly transnational and intersectional set of claims around "lesbian rights are human rights." Apoorva Ghosh (2015) shows how human rights approaches to queer politics are more likely to get funded by international donors than those that are advocacy based; such strategies enable LGBTQ organizations to be both queer and respectable, or "respectably queer."[12] These and other dangers of NGO-ization were not ones that SFE activists were unaware of. When I first met SFE members, the air was thick with criticisms of NGO-ized and professionalized activism, with members resisting calling their own organization an NGO and preferring as descriptor the terms *activist platform*, *organization*, or anything other than *NGO* ("not a NGO NGO," as one member described SFE). In contrast to NGOs, they said, SFE had grown organically, out of the needs of a community, and was motivated by their collective passion. As Malobika put it to me once, "[We] want this to stay a passion, not become a profession. This is very important ... we are not paying anyone to do the movement. It is *my* movement; *I* will do it. We want it to progress in this way ... with meaning, qualitatively."

Indeed, when I first encountered SFE in 2008, it resembled far more the autonomous women's groups of the 1970s and 1980s than some of the highly professionalized and polished sexuality rights NGOs in other major Indian metropolises. Members were employed in full-time work or study elsewhere, and meetings were scheduled in the evenings, reliant on individual invest- ment and participation or voluntary support. The organization took ex- ternal funds for individual projects only, turning to individual donations in crunch times. It employed one or two members to staff the office in a part-time capacity. The office consisted of a modest two-room residential house, and meetings involved sitting in a circle on the floor, with communally procured snacks being passed around as *adda* (informal conversation) ensued.

In our early discussions that took place in this space, members regurgi- tated well-worn divisions between autonomous and unfunded politics, on the one hand, and funded, professionalized, and NGO-ized politics, on the other, accusing both the Indian women's movement (IWM) and gay groups of "selling out" to external, donor-driven agendas and priorities. Declaring that the "market of sexuality is good these days," they insisted that they were not interested in expansion and that "the organization should not feed us." Notwithstanding their critiques of autonomous Indian feminists as being homophobic and co-opted, SFE members reproduced the very political logics and affects that these feminists had normalized, now remobilized to ward off the dangers of professionalization and NGO-ization. Theirs was a strong instance of the generational passage of Indian feminism, of how activism could turn and even "feel backward" while moving forward toward previously unimaginable queer futures.[13]

And move forward the organization did. It built a robust public advocacy program that included a biannual queer film festival; a three-day residential workshop for members; a national queer conference; and the regular publication of its bilingual mouthpiece, sold at one of Kolkata's most prominent cultural events, the international Boi Mela (Book Fair). The organization provided "self-empowerment" for its own members through a range of workshops, study circles, and the provision of peer support and mental health counseling. It also aimed at sensitizing distinct publics, from medical practitioners in state-run medical colleges to the local police to other NGOs (including Janam). A host of experts ("resource persons" and "trainers"), pedagogic models (in "counseling," "training," and "sensitization"), and activities (academic seminars, workshops) emerged to present community needs in the language of human rights, the law and citizenship, biomedical discourses, and even elite academic jargon.

Although the membership comprised primarily metropolitan, middle-class cisgender women, SFE was not a socially homogeneous group. A first generation of members consisted of college professors, lawyers, and those employed by the state. Subsequent generations moved beyond the public sector in ways that embodied changes consequent to neoliberal restructuring in the region, to work in call center and business process outsourcing services and industries. One younger member, a transman, Joy, explained generational shifts within the organization in employment terms: "If we look at Malobika-di or our parents' time, either you had to become a doctor, engineer, lawyer, or go for a government job. Now there are so many private companies and courses, like MBA, BBA, BCA.... How many opt for a government job, and how many manage to get one?"

Besides these generational shifts, there were also differences that marked even those queers—lesbian, bisexual, and transgender persons—who could inhabit the categories of the metropolitan and the middle class with some ease. Many came from families that lacked material wealth and were not English-speaking, an important marker of privilege in old and new neoliberal India alike. One member told me how not all SFE members were from the elite—*borolok* (rich folk) and "high flyers" were her descriptors—and that many were from the lower middle class (though with greater consumption potentials than previous generations).[14] And yet, SFE's organizational space was one in which *bhadralok* ways of making self, life, and politics endured such that queer community- and self-making was shaped by class distinctions and cultural markers that would not be easily legible to those outside the region.

Sappho and SFE: *Lesbian* and *Queer*

Throughout the organization's transforming fortunes, the need for a safe space persisted and materialized in the support group, membership to which was determined by sexual identification. This was a space that was not open to "noncommunity members" but only to self-identified lesbian and bisexual women and transgender people.[15] As Malobika explained, "Sappho still continues to be the informal space for interactions while Sappho for Equality (SFE) is the forum for activism. Anybody, irrespective of gender or orientation, can become its member. All the members of Sappho are members of SFE but not vice versa. So, this means that Sappho members who do not want to be open about their sexuality can still come to SFE and meet other people or even take part in activism because there is a cloak that SFE is open to all" (Bhattacharya 2014).

In instituting this division, SFE embodied two critical strands of the queer movement in India—one that linked sexuality to identity and one that attempted to unsettle this assumption. The support group embodied an identitarian and essentialist logic, while activist platforms like SFE and the Delhi-based People for the Rights of Indian Sexual Minorities (PRISM) enabled a collective ownership of sexuality, beyond being a minority issue (see khanna 2005; and Menon 2007a). The existence of a platform that included queer and nonqueer people also blurred the boundaries of who belonged and who was the appropriate subject of a queer politics (Menon 2007a, 2007b). As one member explained to me of SFE's politics, "many come [to SFE] who do not belong, sexually, to this group and are mistaken as being gay or lesbian. So, a conscious blurring of identities [between queer and nonqueer] takes place and is promoted." In a sharp illustration of the fluid and shifting nature of desire, members who originally joined SFE later attended the meetings of Sappho, which took place in the same physical space.

The move from a politics of identity to a politics of standpoint, as the organization put it, also resonated with critiques of single-issue liberal LGBTQ politics. These critiques had been in global circulation since at least the 1990s (Butler 1993; Warner 1993) and were enthusiastically taken up by Indian activist-scholars in the early 2000s. In a foundational volume, Arvind Narrain and Gautam Bhan wrote how queer was both "a deeply personal identity and a defiant political perspective" (Narrain and Bhan 2005, 4). Queer was meant to include and validate a range of nonnormative sexual identities (gay, lesbian, bisexual, transgender, *hijra*, *kothi*, etc.) that were specific to the postcolonial context and not sufficiently captured by the abbreviation LGBTQ. At the same time, queer acted as a critical lens on heteronormativity, forcing Indian feminists to take seriously the compulsory nature of heterosexuality (see Menon 2007a).

Sappho for Equality was a concrete manifestation of these queer possibilities, in adopting a nonessentialist position on gender and sexuality and moving beyond single-issue struggles to a broader platform. As Malobika said to me, early on, "it is very important to have alliances with nonqueers because otherwise how will you sensitize the mother or father who is forcing a gay son, daughter into marriage? Ultimately, we don't want to create an island and live by ourselves—this is not our objective." But the radicalness of SFE's logic was most manifest in the subsequent generations of queers who entered the organization, and especially those who were incited by the call to go beyond sexual identity. One member, Srimati, preferred *queer* over *lesbian* as a way of signaling that she was not heterosexual but not "LBT" either (she also refused to identify in religious and caste terms). For Joy, *queer* signaled what was against the norm in the widest possible sense. So, a single mother raising a child on her own was queer, even if not lesbian (reminiscent of a protolesbian politics that emerged around the category of *single woman* in urban India in the 1980s and 1990s; Bacchetta 2002).[16]

As *queer* emerged, at multiple scales, to mark a turn toward a more expansive, intersectional, and critical sexual politics—and to trouble identity categories around gender and sexuality—*lesbian* was also recast in specific ways, which evoked the anxieties of past forms of activism. Dave (2012) shows how, in the political expansion of early lesbian activism, the support group became the locus for meeting the needs of those Indian lesbian women who were construed as apolitical, in need of safety and support alone, and not political consciousness-raising. The separation between Sappho and SFE powerfully recalled these previous stakes in crafting authentic political subjectivity by keeping apart two imagined constituents of same-sex-desiring women. This is how Joy summed up the difference between Sappho's Sunday meetings and SFE's Thursday meetings to me: "A person might come from Durgapur to attend this one meeting. After traveling for such a long time, they may not want to attend a seminar on homonationalism. For that person, the more important issue is how much harassment they had to face from their mother or their friends. This is the difference between ... [the] Sunday and Thursday meeting."[17]

For many SFE members, the support group was vital for purposes of outreach, especially beyond the limits of the urban. It had to exist for the *graamer meye* who had never seen another lesbian like herself. What if she came to the organization from a faraway village and found noncommunity members present—even biological men? It would alienate her only further. Feminist scholar and SFE member Niharika Banerjea quotes Neena, a fellow member, expressing similar sentiments:

> Suppose a girl who comes to know about Sappho for the first time or comes to Sappho for the first time, think of her world!! A girl from an interior village or suburb, she does not get to see two girls roaming around! She does not know about *this life*! Maybe, she heard about Sappho and came here. Think of her fears and palpitations! So many thoughts are there embedded in her mind! That she is something different, that she is guilty, that she is giving pain to her parents, she just does not know what to do with life! So much of societal pressure! When these girls come here, what do you do? You just want to give her some warmth! Like a person freezing in cold! … Just as a person freezing in cold gets back the warmth within, when comes under a wrap! It is the same here. After a point of time, girls start feeling warm, stand up and face life in a different way. (Banerjea 2014, 8, emphasis added)

For SFE members like Neena, queer progress relied on a literal and symbolic journey from the rural, a space not conducive to same-sex livability, to the urban, the site of queer liberation and life itself. These kinds of metrocentric imaginaries, which were widely in circulation, posited specific kinds of relationships within a community of same-sex-desiring women, with the empowered metropolitan queer being posited as savior of—providing "warmth" to—the vulnerable and victimized rural lesbian.[18]

From the start, and in ways that intensified with NGO-ization and expansion, SFE had clear aspirations and anxieties around the reach of its activism. "Is our activism city-centric? Does it have no sway in rural areas?" SFE asked in *Swakanthey*, and it went on to illustrate in a January 2012 editorial how it did have such sway: "On 4th December, on the occasion of [the] anti-violence fortnight for women, we headed out with our leaflets to local trains running toward villages, where we directly talked to the daily passengers who come to the city to earn and go back every day. Our purpose, through these passengers, sending our messages … that we, your urban friends, are by you! Perhaps as a result of it, a village girl from close to the Sunderbans stands at our door, with her same-sex lover" (Subhagata Ghosh 2016, 33).

I was present for some internal meetings planning this campaign in late 2011 and was struck by how much it was done in the name of women's rights (*meyeder adhikar*), violence against women, and reaching the grass roots.[19] This rhetoric confirmed how international funds and donor-speak had extended activist (out)reach, while the constructs of the rural and the grass roots as the originating sites of need, risk, and vulnerability were handy in attracting such funds. If a "transnational politics of virtue"—centered around the virtuosity of the grass roots—was at play here, so were more local political affects around subaltern locations and subjects (Mindry 2001, 1189). In other words, NGO-ization recalibrated an existing terrain of affect and governmentality, marked by unequal historical power relations among different categories of women.

Take, for instance, the issue of lesbian suicide, one that had constituted crucial grounds for queer feminist mobilizing since the mid-1980s in India.[20] Through employing a familiar feminist lens around violence against women, queer feminists tried to call attention to the urgency of lesbian vulnerability in very literal ways. In the early days of Sappho, Akanksha and Malobika (2007, 366) asked, "Many lesbians have been forced to commit suicide in our country. How can lesbianism then not be a *life and death* issue?" Rural lesbian suicides epitomized women's marginal social status at the intersections of sexuality and violence, on the one hand, and poverty and underdevelopment, on the other, in ways that also assuaged the anxieties of the IWM that lesbianism was not a strictly metropolitan or middle-class issue (Dave 2012). Unlike in those early days when Akanksha and Malobika had to beseech mainstream feminists to care about the loss of lesbian life, their institutionalized status and greater resources meant a more interventionist stance on the issue, and one that would also extend the scope, scale, reach, and value of metrocentric queer activism.

Sappho for Equality's January 2012 newsletter documented a critical event:

> On 20th February 2011, at Nandigram, Swapna and Sucheta could only guzzle poison to die together in a paddy field.... And in the city of Kolkata all that was left for LBT rights activists was countless sleepless hours ... eternal days and nights ... endless months and years.... The two girls belonging to very underprivileged families from two neighboring villages ... proved by dying like Swapna and Sucheta ... that they have not died. Neither has our movement died. Rather our overwhelming empathy for them stirred our courage and will to be stronger. (Subhagata Ghosh 2016, 33)

Swapna and Sucheta belonged to poor, Scheduled Caste families and lived in a region of the state that had become infamous as a site of popular resistance

Figure 2.1 *Ebang Bewarish* (... *And the Unclaimed*), film screenshot.

to forced industrialization and dispossession. Not only did core SFE members decide to go to Nandigram to find out what had transpired, but they also produced a documentary film on the deaths. On arriving, they found a six-page suicide note left by Swapna, and the bodies of both women "still rotting along with many other unclaimed corpses in the morgue" (Subhagata Ghosh 2016, 31). The film, whose English title is ... *And the Unclaimed*, featured activists' conversations with the young women's parents, local police, and other villagers, interspersed with stories of abuse and the discrimination suffered by SFE's own activists. It was screened at queer film festivals, on local university campuses, and even at one of the villages in which Janam operated as part of SFE's collaboration with this community-based grassroots NGO.

Critical readings of the film accused it of a classic Spivakean error: of ventriloquizing on behalf of the subaltern only to further silence her, while fortifying the subjectivity and agency of those who cast themselves as her savior (Bhattacharya 2020; S. Chatterjee 2018). In other words, the film erased the *graamer meye*, who left little trace outside the desires of the urban activist even when she attempted to speak in death (as had the protagonist of Gayatri Chakravorty Spivak's original 1988 essay, "Can the Subaltern Speak?"). Solidarities and sympathies among queer women also ended by underplaying class and caste inequalities, besides the historical specificity of the region (Bhattacharya 2020). Bhattacharya (2020, 158) tells us that villagers turned hostile, forcing a stalling of the film shoot—which is evident in the documentary itself—and served to enhance, for SFE's activists, "the horror of the community's refusal to acknowledge Swapna-Sucheta's love."

Shraddha Chatterjee (2018, 86), who also reads the film critically, reports how some SFE members later regretted their entry into a space alien to them to place its inhabitants under investigation. This was a criticism that I heard from other queer quarters as well. But the ease with which urban individuals and groups could enter—and exit—rural areas is unsurprising and not unique to such types of activism or to this NGO. It speaks, in fact, to long histories of urban-educated Indian activists, whether Gandhian or Maoist, "returning" to the village for social justice and development work (S. Roy 2012c; Shah 2015).[21] The regional specificity of such metrocentric mobility matters. *Bhadralok* Bengali identity was historically constituted through specific imaginings of rural Bengal, as a site of the primitive and premodern, full of purity, innocence, and passivity, but also revolutionary promise that could be unleashed with external (urban) intervention. Documenting anti-industrialization struggles in West Bengal, of which Nandigram was a significant site, Sarasij Majumder (2018, 22, 26) provides rich accounts of how urban activists (re)produced "romanticized rurality . . . through images of peasants and nature" and how these informed the subjectivities, interests, and agendas of a range of actors, including "urban activists, leftists and postdevelopmentalists."

In the introduction to this book, I noted how postcolonial Indian feminism established its authenticity and relevance by speaking on behalf of poor, rural "others." While these representational economies had a direct bearing on how poverty came to be prioritized over the politics of sexuality, they endured in the affects, cultures, and modes of governance of queer feminisms before and after NGO-ization. Thus, while transnational funds might have necessitated the expanding scales of activism, a compulsion to reach or even save the *graamer meye* at the grass roots exceeded the demands of neoliberal governmentality, showing important continuities in governmentalities across time and specific to place. Whether in the name of lesbian rights, human rights, or development, such governmentalities were also experienced in similarly objectifying ways, from villagers who refused the investigation of two local deaths to those (that we shall encounter later in this book) who resisted outsider attempts to rescue young women from love and marriage. For now, I return from the rural to the urban—and the virtual—to show how the expansion of queer spaces and politics offered queers of this community unequal inclusion to participate in the promise of "this life."

Queer Spaces, Space Invaders

On a research trip in 2016 (having last met with SFE members in 2013), I was told that the support group had ceased to exist. Apart from that, there were other observable changes at SFE: its premises had shifted to a bigger space in the same neighborhood, or *paara*; salaried staff had increased to a number I had never seen before (six, though not all in full-time employment); and *trans* was a buzzword, with projects being developed around this new category. It was on this trip that I also visited the Queer Café. The changes in SFE—alongside the emergence of newer and younger activists of all genders and sexualities in the city—had me asking the same question: Had everything changed when it came to queer life and politics in Kolkata?

It seemed, from SFE members, that there was no longer the need for a support group, as there were now other spaces—both real and, especially, virtual—available to provide the kind of emotional support that it had offered. Even in prior conversations, in the period after Section 377 of the Indian Penal Code was first struck down by the Indian courts, there were mentions of increased queer visibility and the emergence of a "gay scene"— and even a queer market—in a city that was quickly transforming. Younger lesbian women found the city habitable (if not hospitable), in contrast to the fear and insecurity experienced by older lesbians. More than one SFE member pointed to an increase in "urban metropolitan queer spaces," as one young activist put it.[22] As even Akanksha and Malobika observed, "You can see lesbian women meeting freely in CCD [Café Coffee Day]."[23]

Since I had last met with them in 2013, a younger generation of SFE queers had graduated from being students to workers, and many now had access to increased privacy, even to actual rooms of their own.[24] Access to new urban spaces of consumption (coffee shops, multiplexes, and shopping malls) and a rental economy were, of course, contingent on class and locational privilege. When I asked about the fate of the *graamer meye*, SFE members claimed that she could come to the organization at any time since it now had a "drop-in center" on its premises; there would always be staff available to her.[25] Yet anxieties about reaching those located outside the metropolitan area had not disappeared: "We still brainstorm over the fact that we have made a world of our own and the [lack of the] Sunday meeting doesn't affect us as much, but what will happen to those who still don't have any access, what will happen to them? We still think about it," explained Joy. His own needs had changed, however: "I have a space to myself where I can bring some friends and hang out. If I can have conversation with them, why do I need Sappho?"

If villages were sites of lesbian impossibility, then the city was one of queer thriving, an assumption that the convergence of urbanism and neoliberalism only served to entrench (while erasing the contradictions, even cruelty, of the city; see Benedicto 2014). The transformations to the Indian city that came with liberalization—as sites of private consumption par excellence—were productive of urban gay cultures, global gay elites, and even queer activism, prompting both scholarly and activist critiques (see S. P. Shah 2015). Kolkata was hardly visible—to domestic or global audiences—as a gay city, or even one of radical queer politics, unlike some other Indian cities.[26] It offered only temporary and transient queer spaces, but it still attracted "a large number of queer people from suburban and small towns scattered around West Bengal as a sort of utopic place which provides the temporary fulfilment of queer desires" (Boyce and Dasgupta 2017, 217).

Queer women did not have unconditional access to public city spaces.[27] Jacquelyn Strey (2017, 247) quotes a Delhi-based queer feminist activist as saying, "Space is power, right? We don't have a lot of it.... Public space is problematic when it comes to women. You find less and less queer females moving around in public spaces." My respondent Uma also explained the lack of sociability for lesbian women in Kolkata in terms of the gendered organization of public space: "As girls, we do not have obvious cruising spots—I am yet to come across one—where we just meet and socialize or hook up." Members of SFE had previously been able to occupy some spaces in the city but were forcibly removed by hostile publics. Consequently, many younger queer women fell back on private or home spaces, in ways that an earlier generation of queer women had been compelled to (Bacchetta 2002).

What *had* changed in generational terms—and even during my interaction with SFE—was the digital dimension of queer lives, which had also created new possibilities for subcultural formation and belonging alongside political activism. Back in 2010, Srimati, who was then in her mid-thirties (and thus of the generation that came after Akanksha and Malobika), told me in a slightly affronted manner about how younger queer women were coming to SFE knowing their sexual orientation and of the existence of groups like SFE through the internet.[28] In contrast, when she had arrived at SFE in 2005 (two years after its registration as an NGO), through personal networks and with little knowledge of its work or politics, she did not even identify as queer. This expansion in knowledge—of the interior self and a potential queer counterpublic to belong to—was directly attributable to increased access to digital technologies in the lives of queer individuals who were just a few years younger and who joined queer communities later. Unlike Srimati, who belonged to the first generation of middle-class Indians to experience the advent of the internet with liberalization, younger, queerer women had unparalleled digital access, especially through their smartphones, fueled by inexpensive data packages.

The digital had several uses—not least for creating, like the support group, an alternative queer lifeworld where individuals could access crucial forms of community and care and have a virtual queer presence. Emphasizing the significance of when he, a transman, chose "male" on his Facebook profile, Joy remarked, "my comments and posts are also a sort of coming out of the [digital] closet" (see Gairola 2018). The digital also transformed the contours of queer activism, with activist protest labor and interventions taking place on Facebook pages and, later, WhatsApp groups. Members of SFE spoke of using Facebook to make connections with queer groups elsewhere in India and even across the globe. Evoking the student movement #Hokkolorob, which had attracted over twenty thousand people, an SFE member and college student claimed that, for students in nonmetropolitan areas who could not always travel to the metropole to join protest actions, "Facebook was the only space to show dissent."

The proliferation of online spaces also meant a reduced need for the support group. The increased use of digital technologies affected, in other words, physical spaces for in-person meeting, support, and intimacy: "What is the motivation to come [to a support group] if I can find like-minded people on Facebook?" Srimati asked rhetorically. Digital intimacies in the form of virtual spaces for dating and "hooking up" were, however, still in short supply for queer women. Even as Joy told me how dating and social networking websites had exponentially increased in just a few short years, "there is no dating space for lesbians," he qualified.[29]

Sappho for Equality had enthusiastically embraced Facebook as an extension of its activism, managing a group that invited its members (then numbering around five thousand) to post, discuss, challenge, and organize. It advertised its various ongoing outreach events besides sharing information on protest actions in the city. The public that the group constituted engaged in spirited discussion (which varied in terms of volume and intensity) on issues pertaining to queer lives and politics, sharing in the global circulation of queer media stories and politics. A queer friend from Kolkata referred to the group as *aantel*, a term that signifies a particular kind of middle-class Bengali intellectual distinction and one that was not observable in other Kolkata-based digital platforms with more mixed content (see Dasgupta 2017).[30]

Discussions in the group, shared with seriousness of intent and purpose, were interrupted by a post (or two) soliciting love, intimacy, or just "friendship with lesbians." These posts conjured another public that seemed, or was made to seem, out of place in this newly constituted virtual world of queer activism. They were not about pressing political concerns or sexy academic concepts, but invariably voiced the kind of longing, desperation, and isolation that the support group had been created in response to. Here is one representative post, which has been translated from Bengali (most of the posts on the page were in English): "I'm single. I have not found someone—and maybe I never will—to love me. I am very depressed. I am very simple ... if there is someone who is genuinely interested then contact me. I need *bhalobasha* [love]." The group's response to such posts was always the same: "Sappho for Equality is an activist forum and not a dating site." During one particularly painful exchange between the administrator of the Facebook group and another person who wrote, also in Bengali, that they had no other avenues available to meet *shomokaami* (lesbian) women, I reached out, via "private message," to the administrator. I said that I felt bad for these individuals who clearly had no virtual, let alone actual, queer community to be part of. She empathized with such individual predicaments, telling me how SFE often received dating requests and that there had been much internal discussion on the issue. The upshot was, "If dating is formally allowed, then members might feel alienated." There were also concerns about maintaining the safety of most of their female users, given the pervasive problem of cisgender straight men trying to penetrate and ambush the space.

In my conversations with individual members, many reiterated this need for safety; "we can't take the risk," I heard more than once with respect to the problem of "false profiles" online. Even if the possibilities of illicit pleasure might have brought them to SFE, it seemed that the prism of violence—as opposed to pleasure—had come to strongly resonate with these (mostly younger) members. Indeed, the blurring of boundaries between politics and pleasure gave rise to specific anxieties "in real life"—expressed, for instance, in SFE's assertion that "we are not a sex club." And yet the

Thursday meetings were saturated with desire and pleasure. One such meeting I attended included a new member who sat in one corner of the room. Opposite her and right next to me sat a young woman who munched *moori* (puffed rice), only half listening to the ongoing discussion as she played with her phone. For the greater part of the meeting, the two exchanged glances, smiles, and eventually gestures indicating the need for phone numbers. No doubt these silent expressions of desire were fully expressed at the close of the meeting, when participants lingered on and caught up with their queer families, friends, and actual and potential lovers.[31]

Increased online requests for lovers and friends prompted SFE on April 23, 2016, to publish some new guidelines on the use of its Facebook page, which stated,

> We do not appreciate people using this group as a dating space. Sappho for Equality is primarily an activist forum. We are here to reach out to queer community and definitely go beyond that to nonqueer community at large. However, we understand the need for dating space, especially for lesbian, bisexual, queer women and transmen. In such a scenario, we might not delete certain posts that publicly declare need for romantic/intimate friendships. But please remember, that SFE is not responsible for any unwanted situation that may arise, when someone shares their personal contacts, photographs or any other details. Time to time, we will regulate such posts, comments as we find necessary.

In response to the revamped rules, someone wrote on the page, "Was waiting for a post from you … else any random person will put up 'seeking friendship' post because they are not bother[ed] about Sappho's activity [in] the first place." The phrase "seeking friendship" is a nonidiomatic, vernacular use of English, commonly used by Indians not fluent in the language and evoked here precisely to mark (or mock) this lack of fluency.[32] Sappho for Equality was sensitive to how language structured queer livability and was unique in publishing a bilingual newsletter. By regulating Bengali posts "seeking love" and English ones "seeking friendship," however, its Facebook group normalized unequal access to both—queer sociality and political competence—as mediated by linguistic proficiency as indicator of class and caste privilege. In contrast to seekers of love and friendship, those seeking queer citizenship and rights expressed not just English proficiency but a degree of familiarity with an expert discourse and terminology not available to all and not reducible to economic class either. They expressed the uniquely Bengali capacity to be *aantel*, of which the familiarity and use of academic jargon was a key marker. Such regimes of normalization emerged in the name of SFE's political aspirations and in representing and responding to queers, whether online or offline, as rights bearing and not as desiring subjects. Indicating further how SFE's digital presence was geared toward neoliberal governmentalities, Joy was clear that dating was not, in fact, a service that SFE provided.[33]

The digital thus regurgitated divisions rooted early in the organization's life (and in the early life of urban Indian lesbian organizing; Dave 2012)—that is, between the properly political and the merely affective. The regulation of queer affect and conduct in the name of constituting a particular (political) public was, if anything, more evident in the digital milieu. In threatening to delete an online post—and even deleting members whose posts remained on the page, literally under erasure—SFE policed, more directly and more knowingly than queer feminist formations of previous eras, the contours of this new public that it had constituted. It also made the bearers of feelings of love and longing—marked by linguistic, locational, and political failure—seem out of place as space invaders.

We have, in this discussion, encountered an important marker in the history of queer feminist activism: the cessation of the support group. This moment of loss and closure marked other beginnings and possibilities: the availability of spaces for queer sociality and support (at least in an urban imaginary) and, relatedly, the expansion of activism onto other sites and scales, such as the digital and the transnational. The changed conditions that made activism possible—globalization, new digital technologies, and the urban neoliberal economy—also created new regimes of normalization and regulation in which older forms of inclusion, exclusion, and loss endured. Sappho for Equality strove to fulfill on social media its political aspirations, which the outpouring of affective excess—"the problem of feeling bad"—seemed to disrupt and upset (Love 2007, 158). Arguably, it was the support group that was meant to contain and direct such bad feelings, but with its disappearance, one was left asking where such feelings would now be held and stored. For years I had struggled to understand why such a radical and self-reflexive organization needed to hold on to a safe space, one that evoked an archaic model of activism and reductive ideas of sexual identity. But with its loss, I shared in the sadness that one member expressed when she said to me, "Nobody talks about their feelings. How will they? The Sunday meetings were meant for that, and they don't happen anymore."

Whose Life Is It Anyway? Regulating Lesbian Life and Making Queer Conduct

If it's legally allowed, we'll get married. If not, we'll have one big splash wedding. Whose life is it anyway?

Priyadarshini Sen, "Waxing Sapphic Gently," 2013

Like most NGOs, SFE undertook what it called outward empowerment, or training and sensitizing third parties (like the state and other NGOs) on gender and sexuality. What it called inward empowerment or self-empowerment, or raising the consciousness of and educating its own members, was even more important to its ethos and practice. The group's activism developed into a generative site of imparting knowledge (discipline) and normalizing (disciplining), which additionally showed how these queers lived with others, both lesbian and transgender, in the city.

Recall that in my first encounters with SFE members, in 2008, they engaged the issue and politics of NGO-ization and the wider challenges of the neoliberal moment. Fast-forward to only a few years later (2010–13), after the Delhi High Court decriminalized homosexuality, and "the terrain of struggle changed," as one SFE member put it. A clear sign of change was the increased visibility of queer issues and individuals in the mainstream media. Sappho for Equality had always been wary of the risk of exposure that came with visibility; homophobic hate crime had increased after the 2009 verdict, its founding members claimed. The media, they also maintained, was not interested in sensitizing but rather, in sensationalizing homosexuality.[34] A cover story by the Indian magazine *Outlook India*, which featured urban women loving and living together (one of whose words open this section), seemed to exemplify what SFE activists were especially wary of: a fetishization of individual choice and lifestyle, especially those that mapped easily onto class, caste, and metropolitan privileges, inadvertently scripting and normalizing an ideal queer life.[35]

The *Outlook* story indicated other worrying trends that Sayan Bhattacharya, a member of the Kolkata queer community, called in a critical article "the queer market," one that "co-opts emotions, histories, peoples, movements and struggles" (2013). It was not surprising that Bhattacharya used an advertisement for the youth fashion and accessory brand Fastrack as an example of market co-optation.[36] The advertisement featured a woman coming out of a closed pink closet with the tagline, "Out of the closet. Fastrack. Move on." Reflecting on it, Joy said to me, "The term *move on* can mean many different things. One meaning could be that you buy something new, use it, then get rid of it and then buy the next one." Both Bhattacharya and Joy made sense of these new market visibilities and their co-opting potentials as an instance of growing homonationalism in the Indian context.

During my fieldwork in 2013, terms like *lifestyle politics, gayborhood, queer market*, and *homonationalism* popped up regularly to signal the easy assimilation of queerness into the normative institutions of marriage, family, market, and nation. Alongside critiques of what could be understood as homonormativity in the broadest sense, activist desires to craft specific kinds of (nonnormative) lesbian desire, conduct, and life intensified in this moment of unprecedented mainstream queer visibility. While such efforts exposed the possibility of co-optation by state and market, they foreclosed others, such as taking seriously the irreducibly complex and messy nature of local lesbian desire. In attempting instead to discipline lesbians away from their normative attachments to capitalist futures, queer governmentality generated its own kind of friction, with the added consequence of alienating queer feminist activists from local lesbians.[37] The question at the heart of this conflict—"Whose life is it anyway?"—was, in effect, one of shaping, even regulating "who can and cannot embody the queer ideal" (Ahmed 2014a, 151).

It was then that I heard of Velvet, another lesbian support group in the city. Members of SFE described Velvet as being invested in *adda* and dating, or in a queer lifestyle alone. It turned out that toward the end of 2012, a very public conflict had ensued between SFE and Velvet's founders, Alka and Sonali, a well-known lesbian couple in the city (who were also featured in the *Outlook* story). Sutanuka Bhattacharya, an SFE member, wrote a long Facebook post on encountering their personal photo album celebrating the North Indian Hindu festival Karwa Chauth, during which wives fast for one day for the longevity of their husbands:

> I think it won't be irrelevant here to mention that the Karwa Chauth 2012 album came to me as a shock!! For me it is really disturbing to navigate through such an album where my fellow activists are showcasing the very heteronormative rituals which I am fighting against ... *the long history of the feminist movement* explains to us how patriarchy operates through such rituals. One may say that these are personal choices of the doers but *in today's world the space provided by Facebook and other social networking sites* are as much personal as political.... With that right I am asking Alka and Sonali who are a celebrated lesbian couple in Kolkata, my other community friends and my friends from the larger society, how do I understand these photographs, where, within young lesbian

couples the "wife" / "would be wife" or the "femme" touches the feet of the "husband" / "would-be-husband" / "butch" ... where only the "wife" / "would-be-wife" / "femme" fasts for the well-being / long life of their "husband" / "would-be-husband" / "butch"??? ...

Second, ... we have always worked closely with the women's movement and larger gender affinity groups, their support has been our strength. In this situation *can we blindly dismiss the criticisms raised by the women's movement against these rituals*?

Third, I believe exchanging gold rings and other expensive gifts as a celebration of one's couplehood is very personal. When it crosses this personal space, it is treated as exhibitionism leading to a class statement. We have friends who belong to adverse socio-economic background, how then to understand their life struggle with such a political notion! Can a norm be set where celebration of queer couplehood can only be done through economic affluence!! (Sutanuka Bhattacharya, quoted in Dasgupta 2014, 211–12, emphasis in the original)

In response to this post, Sonali sent a defamation notice to Sutanuka and to SFE for the use of their personal photographs, shared on Facebook, without their consent. On the public page for a Facebook group called About Breaking the Stone Walls, Sonali wrote in November 2012 of the bullying tactics of the homosexual as opposed to heterosexual community, adding: "nobody and I mean NOBODY has the rights to tell u how u should live, how u should love and how u want to spend ur life without harming another fellow human/nonhuman soul."

In the late 1990s, lesbian activists were also negotiating the question of how to live as queer Indian women (Bacchetta 2002; Dave 2012). Only ten years later, and with one major legal victory under their belt, the question assumed new meaning and urgency. In asking why a lesbian must desire what is patriarchal, heteronormative, consumerist, and classist, Sutanuka echoed long-standing concerns around queer lives becoming "homonormative lives" (Halberstam 2003; see also Ahmed 2014a; Butler 2002a; Duggan 2003; and Eng, Halberstam, and Muñoz 2005). She even offered an alternative art of living, rooted in different conceptions of life available in the critical traditions of the IWM. When Sonali, one of the women who were objects of her concern, retorted with "nobody ... has the rights to tell u how u should live" and asserted their rights to conjugality and consumption, she reiterated queer attachments to liberal logics of privatized neoliberal citizenship, engrained in the governmentalities of state, law, kinship, and market.

Like Sutanuka, scholar-activist Niharika also evoked queer feminist histories to remind Alka and Sonali what they risked, in forgetting past struggles:

> Unfortunately, irrespective of whether you want or not, Alka and Sonali are visible, and while they do portray a certain version of queerness, the question is: in the minds of the media and in public space that becomes representative of the entire "commumnity" [*sic*]. And hence, I request Alka and Sonali to be mindful of the implications of their visibility and what implications their cultural practices have on people who are unaware of the long history of queer-feminist struggle. You may say you are not political and driven by love, and I respect your love, but then your cultural practices do have deep consequences which involve more than you, thus many of us are concerned that some of your visible cultural practices are ending up reproducing those very norms that queer-feminists are struggling to change. I hope you will consider this. (Niharika, quoted in Dasgupta 2014, 213)

Memory work of this kind was selective, however; it forgot how seemingly personal matters, like marriage or wearing *sindoor* (which also came up in the context of this debate; see Bhattacharya 2013), were sites of internal contestation among Indian feminist and queer activists.[38] Marriage was, for instance, central to the emergence of lesbianism on the national mediascape (Bacchetta 2002), as well as to early lesbian community formation (Dave 2012).[39] And Indian feminism's stance on *sindoor* as a symbol of heteropatriarchy and therefore antifeminist had invited backlash by those ritually and socially barred from wearing it. A local transwoman and feminist activist responded to this conflict between SFE and Velvet by saying to me, "First, allow us to wear *sindoor* and then we can debate."

Excessive consumption, the public celebration of love, and an indulgence in "lifestyle politics" departed from the milieu that SFE had carefully crafted through its reliance on academic discourse and dispositions, in particular.[40] Right from the start, the organization invested resources in building a reference library of academic work on gender and sexuality and prioritized the hosting of regular study circles (and academic conferences); it also published a bilingual newsletter that featured writing by local and international scholars.[41] Referring to SFE as a place of discussion, study, and learning (*alochona* or *pawra shona*)—or, simply, a school—younger members rooted vital changes to the self in these disciplinary practices; as one SFE member put it, "When I joined Sappho, at such a young age, we used to call it our school. And all the elders would treat us like that." This intense traffic in ideas, which was not a dictate of transnational funding, rendered an academic disposition and the capacity to be *aantel* aspirational to many members. What they read in others as "homonormativity" could just as easily be read as lacking in respectability, education, and civility in a Bengali *bhadralok* culture, where economic status was not the only or even most significant marker of class and caste belonging.

Anxieties around class, location, and even academic or intellectual posturing haunted the debate around queer visibility in other ways, resurrecting the ghost of the *graamer meye* to reorient queer priorities. In May 2013, an enraged voice on SFE's Facebook group called out both warring sides for ignoring the real site and subjects of struggle, noting, "We hear brutal stories of torture, rape and abuse of lesbian couples in remote villages but what do we do about it? ... Debating over being a butch or femme or who touches whose feet won't bring any transformation, neither would the celebration of [the] Karva Chauth [ritual] change anything. Because our less fortunate brothers and sisters of the community don't understand terms like 'butch or femme' let alone complicated terms like 'heteronormativity' and 'heteropatriarchy.' I feel ashamed and enraged at what's happening here in Calcutta." Middle-class metropolitan queer activism had to function at appropriate scales—the nonmetropolitan, the village, the grass roots—and be oriented toward more worthy objects of rescue, through forms of grounded intervention and commitments to social change, which esoteric academic theorizing could seemingly not deliver. The question of which queers could most represent the poor (and "pure") sexual minority endured as a source of conflict when it came to a shifting terrain of sexual rights activism.

From Queer to Transgender: The Ghost of Indian Feminism

In this concluding discussion, I stay with moments of difference and conflict—and the bad feelings that fortified them—as they came to constitute the expanding life of local activism around gender and sexuality. These conflicts embodied many aspects of the story I have traced in this chapter; they spoke to governmental and developmental shifts (and the more general dependence of activism on neoliberal capital and forms of institutional stability via NGO-ization) but also reiterated and reproduced long-standing relations of subordination, exclusion, and invisibility as attached to diverse and unequal sexual minorities. If anything, a moment of queer (hyper)visibility and assimilation into power, through increased entanglements in the state, the market, and development, brought preexisting dynamics to the fore. Sharp feelings of disappointment and resentment turned toward familiar forms of critique. And the ghost of feminisms past haunted successive feminist claims to speak on behalf of subaltern others, across time and distinct spaces.

As noted in chapter 1, working-class and lower-caste sexual minorities were positioned, in both NGO and activist networks, in subordinate and marginalized positions even as it was their subjectivities and actual labor that sustained the legitimacy of these networks at both local and global scales. These relations both prefigured and came to inform the institutional emergence of transgenderism across state and nonstate regimes of recognition and governmentality, and afforded sexual subalterns new opportunities for rights, inclusion, and visibility. Yet the imperative to inhabit ever multiplying niche categories—almost in competition with one another—also reconfigured the existing landscape of LGBTQ organizing. New statist forms of recognition and redistribution were not only limited in terms of effect but also partial in how they were conceived; in the presumption that all gender-variant persons were assigned male at birth and desiring to be women, they failed to recognize female-to-male transpersons, for instance.

New transgender-led political formations also emerged in Kolkata.[42] One such organization, started in 2005, had close links to and collaborations with the Queer Café. But its profile was very different from these metropolitan, middle-class, and upper-caste queers. Most of its members were working-class and Dalit male-to-female transpersons, and the organization expressed its mandate intersectionally, working across gender, sexuality, class, and caste. Its work evolved into a somewhat familiar set of interventions: sensitization, counseling, and spreading awareness—around the problematic National Legal Services Authority bill and resultant law, in particular—but also lending support to those transgender persons involved in precarious and stigmatized forms of labor like sex work.[43] While this transgender organization garnered legitimacy for its embeddedness in the grass roots, from which it drew its members, it struggled to acquire material and symbolic ground in an inter/national market of LGBTQ activism without requisite forms of social privilege and capital. Its founder explained to me how transgender individuals had played a historic role in queer visibility but were themselves invisible: "We have been working in the NGO sector for a long time and we have encountered problems due to class, cultural difference, language. Due to these reasons the activism of our people went unnoticed.... It was clear that some people, who were from a particular background—the people who belong to a comparatively better class, they are economically sound, they know better English, they have good contacts—these NGOs are awarded a lot of fund[s]." Even as SFE had never been able to penetrate the grass roots, it was able to secure a share of this market with relative ease, owing to its position in urban and transnational circles.

Geographies of conflict and the affects that underwrote them shaped interactions between queer and transgender activists, positioned at the intersection of gender and sexual marginality, on the one hand, and class and caste, on the other. Some of the differences that transpired—around issues like marriage and (hyper)femininity—sounded like familiar sources of contestation between cisgender and transgender feminists and placed heteronormative and homosexual cisgender feminists in one camp and transwomen in another. In one instance, SFE's psychiatrist, a cisgender woman who provided support and counseling to LGBTQ persons and conducted city-based workshops on gender and sexuality, stood accused of denying a nonbinary transgender/*kothi* person—who was also non-elite and nonmetropolitan—access to hormones by refusing to issue her with a gender dysphoria certificate. Transwomen had long suspected cisgender women, even if queer and politically progressive, of being insufficiently aware of or unsympathetic to gender dysphoria, which they read as proof of their attachments to binary gender rooted in biological sex. That cisgender women had access to actual power that translated into material forms of gatekeeping transwomen's needs and aspirations was a great source of worry for them.

The fault line between cisgender and transgender women, however, went beyond issues of gender identification alone. It was experienced not only as forms of "femme-phobia" or transphobia but also as "classphobia," as one transgender activist put it. Transwomen activists accused middle-class activists (including those belonging to SFE) of class and caste bias rooted in deeply held prejudices against *hijras* and sex workers while questioning their legitimacy to speak on behalf of subaltern sexual subjects. As one transgender feminist activist said to me, "They [middle-class queer activists] keep looking for the grass roots and for the Dalit, and here we are, right in front of them!"[44]

But transgender activists were not the only ones accusing SFE of double standards. One summer day, at the Max Muller Bhavan in the heart of South Kolkata (where SFE hosted its annual film festival), I met some former Sappho members. They spoke of an early moment in the organization's history where there was "no money, no room, and [we] had so many ideas about what to do with money." In contrast, "today, we have funds, money and resources. So, what are we doing with it?" they asked rhetorically and concluded, "Money came, and everything changed." They were particularly despondent about the close of the support group, asking, "Who is this space for today?" and answering, in the same breath, "English speaking, well-connected, internet-savvy, from South Kolkata, middle-class and upper-middle-class [individuals]. That's not who we created Sappho for. Will Sappho go and stand next to the *graamer meye*?"

Here we come full circle in our backward and forward story of queer governmentality. Born out of resistance to homophobic exclusion and silencing—even at the hands of feminists—Sappho began its journey firmly attached to pervasive models and normative ideals of Indian feminism, around the political valence of autonomy and the dangers of co-optation. When I first met its members, they made robust critiques of the NGO-ization of the IWM, vowing that their movement would never become a "business" in the same vein. But once SFE was fully and successfully NGO-ized, they faced remarkably similar criticisms. Queer feminist activism was haunted by its failure to penetrate the grass roots, a powerful and enduring construct that historically worked to delegitimize the politics of sexuality vis-à-vis the politics of poverty in the postcolony.

As the risk of co-optation intensified with queer visibility in a neoliberal present, so did the desire to embody a politics of moral purism and cultural authenticity, in backward forms of activism. While queer feminists developed critical politics to homocapitalist and homonormative futures, they also instituted other kinds of norms and forms of discipline in which certain exclusions and inequalities—particularly those marked by class biases and social hierarchies—endured. And while the *graamer meye* embodied the metrocentric and classed limits of queer politics, she remained utterly reified and spectral in these conversations (and some actual interventions). Even as my writing in this chapter has drawn on calls to turn toward ghosts as a way of unsettling the incessant march of (queer) progress, the pull of the past can also be a pull toward the normative. "Feeling backward" can be a draw toward what is already known and established, as opposed to releasing the untapped and unrealized potentials of the past. For at least this group of queer and transgender feminists in millennial Kolkata, moving backward and forward served to obfuscate the historical specificity and complexity of the current conjuncture besides reproducing linear, generational narratives in which transgender feminism could only ever constitute progression over queer feminism, itself a dramatic break from and advance over a nonqueer feminism. Even if transgender feminism might have brought feminist ghosts to life, it was never freed of being haunted itself, as the words of one local transwoman made clear:

> Today I think of myself as trans, in order to get out of the male-female binary. So, I thought, I'll be part of this community, this different space that we inhabit. But once I entered this, it was the same. Instead of two boxes you have ten, and there are difficulties within these spaces as well. They will force me to enter one of these ten boxes, "Hey, what are you? Why is your hair long when you're wearing boys' clothes? Why are you wearing girls' clothes if you have a beard?" So, *this is part of the community as well*. And these divisions are important for funding; the more they divide the more power they have.

Newer and queer political possibilities were not outside the risk of normalization; they were the source of new governmentalities. As the story of queer Indian feminism—both cisgender and transgender—shows, the assimilation or co-optation of resistance by power was how the terms of power changed, how resistance was propelled into new directions, and how social change was made possible. It suggested that "what exists is far from filling all possible spaces," and thereby made "a truly unavoidable challenge of the question: What can be played?" (Foucault 1997b, 139–40). It is to this question that I turn in the technologies of queer and transgender self-making that follow.

3
Queer Self-Fashioning
In, out of, and beyond the Closet

To be gay is to be in a state of becoming ... the point is not to be homosexual but to keep working persistently at being gay ... to place oneself in a dimension where the sexual choices one makes are present and have their effects on the ensemble of our life. ... These sexual choices ought to be at the same time creators of ways of life. To be gay signifies that these choices diffuse themselves across the entire life; it is also a certain manner of refusing the modes of life offered; it is to make a sexual choice into the impetus for a change of existence.
Michel Foucault, quoted in David M. Halperin, *Saint Foucault*, 1997

Before I could ask anyone to share the truth about their lives with the world, I needed to do it first. I needed to come out as Dalit.
Yashica Dutt, *Coming Out as Dalit*, 2019

In 2015 an online lesbian advertisement went viral. It features two young Indian women awaiting the arrival of one set of parents to their beautifully decorated home, complete with sheer curtains, Indian rugs, and a MacBook computer resting on an antique wooden table. The couple are seen getting casually dressed and engaging in small, intimate chatter—switching between English, Hindi, and regional languages in the way urban Indians often do—while sharing a moment of doubt and anxiety over the impending visit. The short-haired partner asks, "Are you sure about this?" and the long-haired partner responds, at the video's climax, "I don't want to hide it anymore." They kiss and embrace before exiting the shot to go greet the parents. The advertisement was part of a series of three commercials on the predicaments of "modern Indian women" launched by the brand Myntra for its Anouk range of contemporary ethnic apparel.[1]

Figure 3.1 Anouk advertisement, screenshot.

The Anouk advertisement offers an unparalleled glimpse into queer intimacy, conjugality, and domesticity—queerness as a way of life—in liberalized and globalized India. It presents something improbable and even unimaginable for many urban middle-class queer women (and men), which is to live a life outside heteronormativity and unmarked by homophobia, and yet be recognizably and authentically Indian. The advertisement embodies the kind of queer visibility and assimilation that I began to mine in chapter 2, which was made possible by key convergences between global neoliberalism, urban modernity, and queer struggles for recognition even as the Indian state offered and withdrew sexual rights within a short period of time. *Suresh Kumar Koushal and Another v. NAZ Foundation and Others*, the judgment that reinstated Section 377 of the Indian Penal Code in 2013, alongside Narendra Modi's coming to power in 2014, renewed political energies to decriminalize homosexuality with the rallying activist campaign No Going Back. Seemingly propelled by a similar set of affective commitments, the Anouk advertisement suggests that once lesbianism is out of the closet, there is no hiding anymore; there is no going backward, only forward.

This temporal move—of coming out and never going back—is, however, a conditional one. Queerness is a way of life through (hetero)normative scripts of privacy, domesticity, parental approval, and conjugality. As the Anouk advertisement shows, access to queer freedom is tied to appropriate consumption patterns—the right taste, displays of distinction, and the right look, all of which are markers of the otherwise unmarked citizen of modern India, who is recognizably upper caste, staunchly Hindu, and solidly middle class. The question of intersectionality assumes prominence in these debates, with critical voices asking whether the "new" queer futures that a new India prefigures can only be envisioned in normative, neoliberal, and familial terms.

This chapter provides a glimpse into queerness as a way of life in millennial Kolkata, set against these wider tensions around classism and casteism, itself emblematic of a shifting horizon of possibility for queer living in the city (and the nation). I turn to accounts of embodied and lived queerness that younger members of Sappho for Equality (SFE) shared with me; members whose lives occupied a spatiotemporal register of being out of the closet.[2] While a first generation of queer women were caught between the desire for and fear of coming out, a subsequent generation had to negotiate the conditions under which to come out. Coming out did not mark the culmination of a journey, as the linear progression of queer political narratives of No Going Back implied. Some paid a much higher price than others for being out, while others could only be out by modifying their conduct or concealing aspects of themselves. Individuals engaged in strategic forms of revelation and concealment, beyond gender and sexuality, making it amply clear that Indian queers are not all the same.

As in chapter 2's account of queer entanglements in norms both old and new, we see here a similarly complex struggle with norms and normativities, including both a resistance to and reliance on—even attachment to—what might be considered normative. A critique of normativity and commitment toward antinormativity has constituted the heart of queer theorizing, prompting some to ask what even queer theory would be without an antinormative stance.[3] Attempts to "provincialize" queer theory's antinormative attachments show how these were, first, culturally specific (if not distinctly American) and, second, that queers could inhabit norms in capacious, contradictory, and even critical ways.[4] Against an assumed antagonism between kinship and queerness—rooted in queer theory's antifamilial posture—Brian Horton (2018), for instance, finds that young urban Indian queers do not reject natal kin networks so much as they inhabit them differently.[5] Ethnographies of this sort have revealed queerness in normative spaces, of family and kin, insisting that such spaces could be parsed for more "than domination or inevitable normativity" (Horton 2018, 1071).

If antinormativity was a clarion call of queer theory, then so was the recognition of intersectionality; the historical conjuncture of "queer liberalism" urgently expanded the need for more intersectional analyses and politics (Eng, Halberstam, and Muñoz 2005). While SFE exposed and politicized some intersections, it also presumed that these inequalities existed at a remove, in nonmetropolitan locales populated by poor lesbians; it thus left hierarchies within its organizational site unquestioned and even obscured their workings and implications (see chapter 2). Such logics and practices of *not* denying intersectional complexities but recognizing them in a limited way resonate with trends that Pawan Singh (2017, 722) finds in a post-*Koushal* India—what he calls "limited intersectionality." As we will see in this chapter, a limited intersectionality enabled some SFE members to fashion themselves as radical queer activists with relative ease, drawing on existing class and caste privileges, while others sought from SFE precisely those kinds of cultural resources and social capital that would otherwise elude them. Queer governmentality was a site of creative self-making in distinctly *bhadralok* (respectable, middle-class) ways; it produced a queerness that resonated with highly local currents of self-making and being made—currents that would be different elsewhere.[6]

The opening epigraphs of this chapter contain two classically contrasting paradigms when it comes to the politics of coming out. Michel Foucault held firm to his commitment that sexuality is not some inner or hidden truth that movements around it need to discover to free; rather, such forms of mobilization are about making new forms of relationships, new kinds of intimacies, and new ways of being and becoming.[7] In contrast, the words of journalist and writer Yashica Dutt evoke the more commonplace mode in which LGBTQ identity politics have proceeded by presuming an inner truth of the self that needs to come out for the purposes of community building, politicization, and social change. Dutt (2019) speaks of herself as coming out not as queer but as Dalit, and she is not even the first to employ the "epistemology of the closet" (Sedgwick 1990) to the experiences of a small percentage of Indian Dalits who are able to pass as caste Hindus. Technologies of concealment, denial, erasure, and passing are not, in other words, exclusive to the experiences of Indian queers; they are also strategic tools available to those who sit at the intersection of several marginalized identities. They also bear testament to what the narratives of this chapter show: that visibility is less about revealing an inner self than about navigating norms that afford one life and livability, recognition and inclusion. Queer self-fashioning assumes a creative and critical relationship to the norm—to governmentality—that asks not "how to become radically ungovernable" but "how not to be governed like that, by that, in the name of those principles, with such and such an objective in mind and by means of such procedures, not like that, not for that, not by them" (Foucault 1997b, 28).

Leaving Home or Staying Put: New Queer Domesticities

Indian lesbian lives were read as constituting a dramatic break with family, with coming out amounting to leaving the natal home, an option available to few unmarried Indian women, whether queer or not.[8] For one generation of lesbian women in and around Kolkata, the familial home was a primary site of repression and violence, with their queer feminist politics developing in resistance and opposition to, and even in exile from, the family.[9] Yet, SFE was adamant that the heteronormative family had to be confronted, even transformed, and *not* left behind. Insisting that they did not subscribe to or encourage the idea of running away from home, SFE founders Akanksha and Malobika regularly asked members, "How will you sensitize the mother or the father who is oppressing a gay family member?" This was also part of their consciousness-raising efforts: "Workshops create the knowledge base, provide the strength to face the world as well as family members. How will I speak to my father who is trying to force me to get married? Where will I get the knowledge to do this? To face reality with inner strength? More than knowledge, it is self-confidence." Against the imperative to leave home in order to gain social and sexual freedom, SFE seemed to advocate for "staying put," but not in ways that required the strategic silencing of one's sexuality or inhabiting it in secret ways (P. Singh 2017, 732).

As a measure of queer progress, Akanksha and Malobika pointed to the greater numbers of parents who availed themselves of SFE's help line—asking for counsel on how to raise homosexual children—and even instances of parents visiting the organization with their children. This signals an important shift—of middle-class Indian parents being increasingly aware and accepting of queerness in both public and private contexts (see P. Singh 2017).[10] Unlike Indian queers who were "closeted at home" (Horton 2018, 1071), SFE activists were out to their parents, in ways that signaled their learning at SFE, with members telling me how the organization had provided tools to deal with parents and not alienate them. Even as individuals spoke of tensions with family (especially around the compulsory nature of marriage), and living on one's own or with romantic partners and friends was a key aspiration for this collective, some also spoke affectionately of parents and siblings.[11] And, much to my surprise, two of the queer women I met and grew to know were living in family homes with their unmarried same-sex partners. They seemed, in fact, to be more emphatically out of the closet in private, to immediate family members, than they were in public, which was marked by a more staggered and strategic coming out.

In the case of Sushmita, an SFE member in her late twenties, leaving the familial home was undertaken suddenly, informing her parents only the day before she moved out. In a conversation in 2016 she told me, "My parents said, 'So you are leaving?' and I said, 'Yes, I will stay with her [girlfriend], since she stays alone.'" If Sushmita's ability to leave—especially at a time when relations with her parents were strained—might seem surprising, then it is altogether more surprising that this act of leaving was accompanied by an equally dramatic act of return, with her girlfriend in tow. The decision to move in with her parents was a practical one, prompted by sudden financial constraints. There was only one, seemingly natural, option available to them as a couple: "I decided to stay with her at home. Now we are four members in the family."

This turn of events took me by surprise. When I had previously met Sushmita in 2011, she was barely speaking to her parents, for all the predictable reasons. There was pressure to get married, and she was unable to even utter the word *lesbian* to them. Homosexuality was not even the most divisive issue but rather the fact that "I am not a girl who is like a girl [*meyer moton meye*]." Her parents knew her then partner but did not like or accept them. Comparing her current girlfriend to her previous one, who presented in ambiguous gender terms, Sushmita explained, "My mother likes chatting and gossip, but [her previous partner] lacked these [qualities]. Mohini [her subsequent partner] has these things in her. She enjoys gossip. My mother could not believe she could cook so well, even though she has short hair!" Sushmita ended this tale with what she called "the climax": "Now when we [she and her girlfriend] fight, my mother comes and tells me that relationships are built on sacrifices. 'If both of you have decided to stay together then why are you fighting?'" Sushmita stressed that her parents were fully aware of the romantic nature of her relationship with Mohini (the extended family knew they were "very good friends"). The family was fine with their relationship, as "we are girls and good girls [*bhalo meye*]." "A girl who is like a girl?" I asked. "Exactly," she replied; "a girl who is like a boy is a huge problem."

Acceptance of same-sex sexuality and intimacy was predicated, it seems, on gender conformity, on having socially recognizable gendered and, especially, feminine aesthetics and conduct—which were, in turn, conflated with sexual orientation. Shortfalls in one domain—signified by short hair or the loss of femininity—were compensated for in others, such as the ability to cook and take pleasure in gossip. These were also markers of a specifically Bengali *bhadralok* femininity that materialized in both hard work (cooking) and idle leisure (gossip).[12] Like the proverbial *bhalo chhele* (good boy) or the most suitable suitor of the *bhadralok* Bengali imagination, Mohini was a *bhalo meye* who embodied a mundane kind of respectable femininity that was not merely tolerated but enthusiastically included into the normative folds of the ordinary middle-class household.[13]

For people like Sushmita, being out to family was a nonnegotiable part of their political coming of age; coming to SFE and coming out to parents were simultaneous processes. But being publicly visible and making claims on a public that remained resolutely heteronormative and patriarchal was done more cautiously. Even as they were empowered by a wage packet to leave parental homes for their own, queer women had to pass as friends or even as sisters to access public spaces in the city, and housing proved particularly tricky. As SFE member Durba said, noting the irony of the moral policing of heterosexuality in India, "Two girls staying together is not a problem. In fact, they [the landlord] asked us not to get any guys, to which we happily agreed." Sushmita, however, implied that in an India that was queer aware, not all queer women and couples could pass in ways they might have previously. She and her partner were able to find a rental in the city only because they both wore their hair short: "Because they thought we are sisters, as the two of us look so similar that nobody ever got suspicious. But if one of us had longer hair, then that would've created some problem.... And the more important thing is that she is not that masculine. If she were more masculine, then we'd face to a lot of problems while hunting for a house." Both in public and in private, gender conformity—or what Dave (2012, 64) calls the "tight predictable alignment of sex, gender and sexuality"—seemed to be the crux around which nonnormative sexuality could be managed.

Sushmita was not the only one who was living this new queer domesticity in Kolkata. Uma was also "living in" with her girlfriend, Noopur, in her parental home. Uma came from a more privileged family than Sushmita. She and her partner resided in an apartment owned by her parents, and from that apartment they pursued their studies, social life, and activism. As with Sushmita, financial stability was a key driver for Uma to stay with natal kin: "[The] benefits are that we don't have to spend 30K a month on living expenses. The house is comfortable enough, it's in an accessible area, close to both of our colleges." In the case of both queer couples, then, the family was a unit of economic security, especially in the face of a lack of secure employment and the rise of insecure housing markets in liberalized India. The family enabled young people like Sushmita and Uma (and their partners) to move in and out of jobs, study for longer, and take for granted that they would live independently of kin once they were financially able to do so.

Uma voiced several of the complexities of affective family life, including its propensity toward exploitation. These were challenges, she insisted, that were not particular to queers alone but faced in all families, though concealed by an idealization of the normative family form as a locus of emotional support. Uma put it scathingly when she said, "Because she [Noopur] is close to us, she gets treated like family, and in this house, family isn't always treated very well." There were fights, often ugly ones, over domestic and interpersonal issues, and especially money. The economic security that the family provided was also precarious: "My father expects us to pay ten thousand a month for expenses, which isn't always possible, so we try to pay as much as we can. We would like to live alone soon, but in a sustainable manner. And generally, not every day goes badly at all. I still fight with my parents—nothing relationship specific."

Her father was not homophobic, she explained further: "I have told Baba that she's my partner, that I love her. Their problem doesn't seem to be about the lesbian thing at all, since maybe people don't suspect or register.... I think they are more preoccupied with social standards and acceptability." In fact, her father had greater reservations with the presence of men in his daughter's life than with women. Men, or the specter of heteronormative relations outside marriage, threatened the family's claims toward social respectability in ways that a lesbianism that was out in private but ambiguous in public did not. Outside the surveilling gaze of the community, the private afforded unanticipated forms of intimacy, care, and even pleasure and play. Uma's mother "bonded" with her partner over certain conventional feminine pursuits like makeup, dressing up, and cooking. Noopur did her mother's makeup, and "Baba makes fun of them both when they dress up."

Sushmita's and Uma's stories of queer domesticity reveal similar complexities as they provide a glimpse into how middle-class queer women were living intimate and domestic lives in Kolkata outside the bounds and expectations of heteronormativity but within the normative structures and spaces of family and kin and—unusually, especially for unmarried middle-class women—in their parents' homes. The positing of queerness in oppositional terms from the normativities of the family, home, and kinship elides the richness of these narratives of "staying put" and creating new kinds of queer intimacies, families, and feelings, in and through (rather than outside or in rejection of) the Indian family. Ultimately, though, queer acceptance relied on performing gender in strict and unambiguous ways, which entailed, in turn, specific costs for those who called into question binary gender.

No Going Back: Transmasculinity and
Queer Homelessness

Even after going through the process of SRS *[sex reassignment surgery], I don't understand how it is to feel like a man, and I don't want to either.*
Joy, SFE member, Kolkata, 2016

Not all who left home could return. Some could do so only in the dead of the night, when no one in the neighborhood could see them enter or leave. Joy had once told me this when speaking of the experiences of transmen who face not just exclusion but exile from their own families, who refuse to acknowledge their existence and cut off all ties with them.[14] The forward march to a queer future in which the transgender subject could return to who they were always meant to be, to being at home in one's "true" self, was defined by a specific kind of "no going back." Joy's words also remind us of the insufficiency of locating transgender and transsexual identities in an embodied home given that many, like him, experienced not a homecoming but homelessness in gender ambiguity (see Halberstam 1998).

I met Joy in 2011, at the same time that I met Sushmita and other younger members of SFE. Fast-forward to 2016, when much had changed in their individual biographies, as it had with the conditions for queer livability in urban India. Joy had started his transition in this period: "I didn't like hearing my voice before, but now I like it, so I speak more," he offered as an explanation of how he had grown in confidence and appeared chattier than before. As *transgender* emerged as a bureaucratic, governmental, and metropolitan activist category, making available new avenues for visibility, SFE began to work more systematically on transgender issues, especially for how they impacted a marginalized and hidden population of transmen.[15] Joy became involved in the organization's campaigning around this issue, even as transmen were underrepresented at SFE: "At Sappho, self-identified transmen are few in number.... Finding people in and around Kolkata who are going through a transition is a difficult task because of the lack of visibility." Following the National Legal Services Authority (NALSA) judgment (the Supreme Court of India decision that afforded transgender persons third gender status), he liaised with other transmen on issues of rights, recognition, and resources while beginning his own transition, changing jobs, moving out of his parents' home, and renting his own place. A lot had happened in a short period of time, he said to me more than once.

Even though they were of similar socioeconomic backgrounds and were all part of the city's queer feminist subculture, "coming out" for Joy was very different than it was for cisgender lesbian women. The conditions that made public and private cisgender lives livable—gender normativity—were those that made transgender lives, which most directly and visibly challenged the gender binary, unlivable.[16] Joy suggested that coming out was of a different order altogether for transmen, involving everything from a change of name, place of residence, and a new relationship to family and kin that could only take place in the shadows of the night. There was either no going back at all or only a return as a shadowy or spectral presence. "The situation of the transmen is so different that nobody wants to come out," he stressed.[17]

Joy was out and undergoing a process of self-fashioning that was considered the most literal embodiment of technologies of the self. Among feminists, and even queer cisgender feminists at SFE, there was a tendency to see such technologies of self-transformation as contributing to normalization, or as having a stabilizing effect on otherwise fluid gender identification and practices, in the service of heteronormativity.[18] An example of an early queer feminist rumination on the desire for surgical transition can be found in these reflections on the National Conference of the Autonomous Women's Movement in Kolkata, by Ranjita Biswas (2007):

> While the urge to move out of sex essentialism is welcome, one feels uncomfortable with the proposal to disavow one's body, its materiality, its pains, pleasures which are no doubt tied intimately to its specificity as sexed, male or female. Moreover, if sex was so redundant, why do some of our friends present there at that very moment, go to such lengths to add or remove specific parts of their body in order to achieve a more complete sense of being. And obviously such reconstructive surgery was not cosmetic but very significant for them, sometimes for survival even. What then becomes pertinent is perhaps not a total abandon of the body, but the need to rethink our notion of the body and sex as only biological and anatomical defined and determined by the specifics of chromosomes, hormones, gonads or genitals.

Knowing well of such responses that accused transsexuality of essentialism, Joy voiced his own deep ambivalence toward an embodied project of becoming a man. In fact, he sharply rejected narratives of transgenderism and transsexuality as entailing a process of gender stabilization, or reinscribing a normative gender order: "I wanted to become a man, but I am not a man and so, I also have these questions in my head: What am I, then? Although people tend to say that transgender people follow a binary, now being a transman, I realize how different I am from that thought." In our conversations, he insisted that the choice to change one's gender was not in aid of any simple desire to be the other gender, or even to access a hidden truth:

> For me, it's not that I like wearing short hair, jeans, and T-shirt, and hence I think myself as a male—I can't say that these are the reasons for which I identify as a transman. My understanding goes deeper than that. I have gone through counseling for days, attended workshops, have had conversations for days before deciding. So, when they [other transmen] say that "I think of myself as a male from my heart and soul" ... I can't say that to myself because I don't know what it feels like, to think of myself as male from my heart and soul.

Joy spent a lot of time explaining how transitioning into being biologically male did not entail inhabiting the conventions, behaviors, and aesthetics of a hegemonic masculinity. He spoke of himself as embodying a different kind of masculinity than the patriarchal masculinity on offer: "The picture that people, in general, have of a transman is that of a patriarchal masculinity. For me, a transman can exist outside of that realm.... I want to show that there exists a diversity [of maleness] and that we can talk about equality as well, which is not a face of patriarchy." He rooted some of the distance he felt from other transmen in their partaking of culturally distinct patterns of patriarchal privilege, like son preference, or how some were motivated in their choices and conduct by the belief that one had to become a man in order to legitimately love a woman.[19] As Malobika once told me, "If somebody really feels that in a relationship, they want to maintain a macho masculine attire and be in love with feminine girls, there is no problem. No problem. Everyone can practice their free choice, but we always say that you should be aware of what you are doing."

Indeed, much of the critical sentiments that Joy expressed were ones that circulated within SFE (and Indian feminist communities more broadly), to which he directly attributed his critical consciousness. Even as Joy found a fledgling community of transmen, his primary attachment was to a queer lesbian community in whose feminist consciousness-raising he rooted his departure from more conventional (trans)masculinity: "If I hadn't come to Sappho, I would've thought the same—[that] in order to become a boy I have to become certain things." Explaining further the continuing attachment to a community of primarily cisgender queer women, he said, "It is a very safe space; I can hang out with people, which I can't do with other trans brothers.... I seriously don't have anything else to talk about with them apart from the SRS-related conversations. I don't know what else to talk to them about."[20]

Even as an ethics of the self lay in a set of unfolding practices of becoming rather than being, such a project of self-transformation mired the individual into layers of governmentality that were outside one's control. These included subjecting oneself to regulatory—medical, psychiatric, and (newly) legal—norms, even as transmasculine communities were insufficiently represented in the NALSA judgment. Joy noted the many challenges he and other transmen encountered with doctors, for instance, given their inability to think beyond the gender binary: "They don't have any clue about gender-sexuality because they think that since she is wearing pants and shirt, has cut her hair short and likes a girl, she must be a boy—they can't think beyond this.... Doctors will say, 'You don't have a penis, then how do you have sex with your girlfriend?' They are so insensitive."

The reduction of transgender or gender-variant persons' identifications and desires in biologically deterministic and highly prejudicial ways made Joy even more aware of their constructed nature while exposing the fiction that is the natural body: "Had I not gone through this transition, I wouldn't have understood how many types of body there can be. Which hormone will react in which manner, in whose body, can't be figured out by any doctor, no matter how big that doctor is." Doctors, he said, were "simply experimenting with our bodies." Likewise, meeting the new terms of state recognition felt overwhelming, especially as the state authorized external agents for the purposes of verifying and approving transgender identity. So much so that Joy had even considered the possibility of refusing to engage the state in this manner: "I thought of changing medically whatever there is to change but keeping my name and gender unchanged in the documents. I have tried to think in many ways." And yet, being outside state governmentality—being *undocumented*—was also not an option.[21] Joy was able to rent an apartment in the city only because of personal networks: "It wouldn't have been possible [otherwise] because, while signing the contract, I had to fill in my current name and gender, which was different then. It was only possible because this person knew me."

To legally change his gender, Joy believed that he needed to show proof of "at least one top surgery."[22] The many layers of red tape that he was embroiled in powerfully revealed the limits of legal categories when it came to representing the interests of gender-variant individuals but especially those in a state of flux or fluidity—or, in transition. When it came to spaces outside the state—especially the *paara* (neighborhood) with the prying and potentially stigmatizing eyes of others—Joy faced a constant fear of failing to pass as a man. And even as his colleagues at work witnessed firsthand the embodied changes he was undergoing, they insisted on using the female pronoun as if to undermine and erase such efforts. But the greatest cost of undertaking such an intensely embodied project of self-transformation came from closest kin.

On the surface, Joy's life exemplified all the conditions that made a queer life livable, such as financial independence and the ability to live alone, even in a home of one's own—all of which were key aspirations of queer women (like Sushmita and Uma). And yet, there were costs that did not seem so evident in the lives of his friends: "They have their own spaces, but they are in contact with their families. They don't share the same kind of relationship as I do with my parents. They have girlfriends, sometimes they stay with them, sometimes they go home. Their situation at home is not like mine."

The "situation" stretched from the time he was a child, and he described it as a cultivated silence around his ambiguous gender presentation. "There was never any physical violence at home, but this silence," Joy said, recalling how his mother would simply leave a neat pile of washed and ironed men's shirts in his room. Things only came to a head because Joy had forced the silence to speak, confronting his parents with his decision to undergo SRS. They rejected his decision through both denial and dismissal (about his mother he said, "She still thinks I'm doing this playfully"), even as his decision materialized in the form of medicines displayed openly and, eventually, a change in voice. Even so, there was always a mother—and food on the table—waiting for him, no matter how late he arrived home from work. They ate in silence every night, an act he found more and more unbearable, and one he endured for over a year. But these could still be described as the ties that bind—the silent mother, the table of food, the light in the middle of the night—or the elaborate support system that is heterosexuality (Ahmed 2014a). This support system did not unravel for the queer cisgender women who came out to their families and who could still rely on them to provide a financial safety net and even give relationship advice, however unsolicited. But what happened when support was entirely withdrawn?

Once Joy moved out of his parents' home to a rental, the ties were severed. His mother phoned him very occasionally and even assumed that he had left Kolkata. There was some speculation that the family would leave the *paara* so they would not have to "face anyone." While Joy's life embodied the markers of linear queer progress—coming out, changing one's name, undergoing SRS, leaving home, and arriving at the home of one's true self—these were undone by the normative attachment to what was left behind, to even something as ordinary as a silent mother waiting with food on a table.

Multiple, intersectional histories determined what queers left behind, where they arrived at, and to where they could and could not return.

"If I Want to Use the Term *Gender-Queer-Heteronormative*, Then I Have to Do It in Cotton": Queer Aesthetics and the Caste Closet

I return to the experience of Sushmita, a space invader but in no obvious sense. In chapter 2, I identified those lesbians—and not queers—as space invaders whose beliefs, aesthetics, and conduct were read as being incommensurate with the political ideologies upheld by a majority of SFE's members. It so happened that such lesbians were also ones who bore the markers of certain class, linguistic, and locational conduct that placed them outside the metropolitan, liberal, *bhadralok* setting that SFE inhabited. But individual activists were also space invaders in less obvious ways, showing how intersections, inequalities, and exclusions within this organizational site were left unmarked—through, for instance, subsuming caste under class in ways that were typical of political elites in the region.

Sushmita joined SFE (and Sappho, the support group) at the same time as several twentysomething, middle-class, self-identified queer women. They were recognizably middle-class, with upper-caste names, and had inclusion into the new economy, through work in call centers, business process outsourcing companies, nongovernmental organizations (NGOs), and higher education. They celebrated hard and protested even harder when the Indian state decriminalized, recriminalized and, eventually, repealed the antisodomy law, risking full disclosure to family and friends via the media. Sushmita was a regular presence at SFE's meetings and major events. She seemed to instantly belong to the activist milieu and queer subculture that the organization represented. Yet, surprisingly, her conversations with me articulated moments of feeling like she did not belong and struggled to do so. These struggles to fit in centered, on the face of it, on dress and fashion, on how her own aesthetic jarred with the recognizable conventions of Kolkata's activist NGO world. With her friends, Sushmita undertook specific forms of aesthetic labor to fashion herself in socially rebellious, gender-nonconforming, and queer ways but also to achieve belonging in class terms and to fulfill class-infused aspirations. They rearranged their (literal) closets in ways that said something not only about gender and sexual difference but about class (and, as we shall see, caste) and offered us stories far beyond what we know of "gay men's closets" (Brown 2000, 23).

Sushmita spent some time telling me how her look had changed over the course of her time at SFE. This was somewhat to be expected. Many queer women described SFE as a place where they attempted a wide range of sartorial styles, aesthetics, and performances of the self—the kind of "lesbian aesthetics" found in queer subcultures more generally (Eves 2004). Hair was cut shorter, piercings increased, and clothing styles changed as these young people increased their online and offline visibility and enacted public ways of being millennial, Indian, and queer (a "pierced and tattooed gang" was how an older SFE member described this group). Uma, for instance, said of both herself and her partner, "Cutting hair gives us a sense of control in a society that is constantly dictating what we do with our bodies." Sushmita shaved hers off, and caused great distress to her parents, for whom the most divisive issue was that she was not a *meyer moton meye* (a girl who is like a girl).[23]

Forms of experimenting with and changing the self were not exclusive to Sushmita but also included her peers: "Everyone has been through a huge *makeover*," she said. In explaining their collective self-transformation, she told me, "I have a photograph clicked at Sappho, in 2010, when Sappho had its birthday. I was wearing a yellow *churidar* [a tightly fitted trouser worn underneath a tunic] with lots of bangles, lip liner, kohl ... since then my way of dressing has changed with each party." She contrasted her dressing with the circle of people in and around SFE who wore "cotton sarees, necklaces made out of safety pins, wearing all things queer." Apparently, most of the partygoers were speaking to these people and not to her given how "tacky" and "garish" she claimed to have looked. Her own friends were similarly styled, she explained: "Madhavi used to wear tight tops, tight jeans, bad shoes, plucked eyebrows.... She had nice, angular eyebrows, but they were plucked really thin." She described another—more "butch"[24]—friend thus: "I had seen Piya wearing a synthetic shirt, a thin gold chain with a pendant, and her hair—now she has spiked hair—but earlier it was curly at the bottom. She is totally unrecognizable now." Madhavi now sported an "ethnic" look with kohl-lined eyes (like Sushmita herself), while Piya was still butch but differently so. Women like her and her friends began to be mistaken as students of the Jadavpur University (JU) in Kolkata, an institution that was as politically radical and culturally subversive as it was respectable and elite (and at which none of them had studied). Sushmita explained how female students at JU were recognizable through certain trademarks: "[They] wear bindi, kohl, *jhumkas* [earrings], sleeveless kurta, *churidar* and if you have short hair, then it is a given that you are doing weed." The fact that she and her friends could pass as JU students suggested that they had won social acceptability; they were able to "craft one's look *as if* one belonged" (Kaur and Sundar 2016, 9, emphasis in the original).[25]

The self-fashioning that Sushmita spoke of echoed the "matte aesthetic" that Sahar Romani (2015, 73) found among NGO workers in Kolkata, which she describes as an "aesthetic of hand-woven textiles and indigenous prints on contemporary designs." The slum girls, who were the beneficiaries of these NGO interventions, differentiated this aesthetic, to which they aspired, from their own shiny kind of "flashy and sparkly clothing, of synthetic textiles and shiny accessories." At the heart of a matte aesthetic was simplicity "that serves to conceal any wealth.... But at the same time, this simplicity is of a particular aesthetic, which, I suggest, reveals wealth, class and, most importantly, respectability" (Romani 2015, 73). In strikingly similar ways, Sushmita described her makeover at SFE as going from a synthetic to a matte aesthetic, key to which was the consumption of ethnic wear in cotton. Feminist activists in India, from their autonomous to NGO-ized days, always favored ethnic clothing, exemplified in the fashion of Fabindia, the urban retail chain store that specializes in hand-loomed clothing.[26] Among urban consumers of a certain class and cultural milieu, Fabindia became a shorthand for denoting choice in values, and not merely dress and style, by virtue of its commitment to promoting indigenous textiles.[27] But the label, like pure cotton more generally, was out of bounds for most Indians, and even increasingly for the ordinary middle classes given the regular inflation in its prices.

With the rise of "the pink rupee," Fabindia produced respectable consumers, both straight and gay.[28] A majority of the cisgender queer women at SFE dressed in ethnic wear, and they were an ideal market—even the target group—for newer brands like Anouk: "We know NGO offices and home spaces with similar décor. We know gender and sexuality rights activists, working professionals, friends who dress like these characters [in the Anouk advertisement], women who dress only in cotton and ethnic fabric, who only wear silver and burnt clay, who cut their hair a particular way, who only wear certain shades of clothes and nail polish, in other words, women whose sense of aesthetics is Anouk-approved" (Bhattacharya 2015). Queer women of a certain class background, professional bent, and political leaning stepped out of one closet into another, which told specific tales of queer difference, distinction, and belonging.

Instead of these brands, Sushmita preferred buying her kurtas from the more affordable Khadi Bhandar outlets,[29] teaming them up with jeans purchased from mainstream department stores like Big Bazaar, Shoppers Stop, or Westside that offered a wide range of apparel at varying prices. But it had to be cotton, she explained with a slight grin: "If I want to use the term *gender-queer-heteronormative*, then I have to do it in cotton." Aesthetic labor, facilitated by the correct consumption practices, was thus undertaken for political belonging, to fit in with a crowd of gender and sexuality rights activists and NGO professionals whose political ideologies and beliefs were legible simply by virtue of their taste in clothes or, simply, their dress, or *saaj*. The work on dress, taste, femininity, and look were all technologies of (class) aspiration, self-improvement, and of passing as something else. Such labor enabled one to look and feel unique while also blending in. As Sushmita put it, "Everybody wants to feel exceptional; why should I be excluded?"[30]

Sushmita's desire to fit in with the class, cultural, and political aesthetic presented by SFE's members might not come as a surprise once we know a little more about her family. Her father was from the Scheduled Castes (SCs) : "The place where my father and his family used to live, that village was full of people belonging to the SC category.... That's why my grand-mother is so proud of her sons for being government employees [today]." Her father changed their name when she was born. Her own awareness of caste came much later: "It was only when I was in standard 11 or 12 [that] my mother got me a certificate [for affirmative action purposes]; that was the time when I realized that I am a SC." I asked Sushmita how she had felt at the time, to which she responded: "Nothing. It didn't matter. I was cool about it. My reaction was, I will get some facilities? Oh, good, that's good news."

Sushmita's story resonates with that of queer activist Sumit Baudh (2007), who writes compellingly of being doubly marginalized as Dalit and gay. Like Sushmita, his parents gave him a different name, which allowed him to pass as caste Hindu.[31] He thus remained, for most of his life, doubly closeted, first coming out as Dalit and later as gay. Dutt (2019), who also grew up hiding her Dalit identity, underscores the double-edged nature of such passing, which can generate comfort in concealment, but with the constant fear of being caught (see also Ahmed 2014a). Unlike Baudh and Dutt, Sushmita's coming *to*—and not *out* as—SC was not imbued with immense importance in her life story. She rooted the lack of caste-based discrimination she had faced in individual achievement and personality ("I can communicate, I am confident, I am not a shy person") but was in no hurry to disclose her caste identity either ("I have a different name"). Caste did not seem to matter to her, but it mattered enough to keep concealed, which might have brought, as the closet did for some queers, its own comfort and security, away from public scrutiny and the risk of stigma. Sushmita noted, for instance, the tendency of those belonging to the General Category to look upon those from the SC category with condescension: "They might pass comments on me, condescend me, so I don't tell them."[32]

One could also discern a degree of unbelonging in caste Hindu society when Sushmita spoke of her parents and SFE. To explain how her parents thought of and disapproved of SFE members, she used the descriptors *rich, modern, high-class, educated,* and *intellectual.* While her mother spoke no English, her father was educated and could "write very well in English." But even as his "class" had shifted from his original SC background, "my father doesn't belong to this class because he has seen poverty, and since my father had always belonged to the SC community, he can't relate to this class at all."[33] In her constant reference to what was "intellectual," "knowledgeable," and "academic" in describing her father's disdain for "this class," Sushmita revealed how being *bhadralok* was much more than having economic wealth and financial security.[34] It denoted a way of life, from deportment and dress to intellect and know-how—so much so that even those SCs who could pass, whether through fictitious names, the acquisition of class capital, or by rearranging their consumptive practices (and closets), were still treated and treated themselves as space invaders. In the absence of strong regional assertions around caste and the growing belligerence of a Savarna Hindu nation, coming out as lesbian might have appeared safer and less queer than it was to come out as Dalit.[35]

Limited intersectionality means that while being openly queer, individuals are still in the closet—hiding some parts of the self while performing the labor of being middle-class, upper-caste global, aspirational Indians. Such technologies of the self underscore at least two things: first, the extent to which respectability mediates social recognition and belonging, even in spaces that are antinormative; and second, that being included in these spaces does not occur along a singular axis of gender or sexuality, with a disproportionate burden being placed on those marginalized, intersectional subjects to perform the labor of inclusion and belonging, even if such labor is simply sartorial. Sushmita's aesthetic labor was double-edged: to produce a visibly rebellious queerness that was against all norms, but also to adhere to (class- and caste-based) norms, to secure the invisible comfort of normative belonging. These were the practices of coming out and staying in, not (only) in a world structured by heteronormativity, but in a uniquely Bengali *bhadralok* one, as I stress in the next section.

Coming Out, Staying In: The Queer Communist

There are ways of staying in, even when one gets out.
Sara Ahmed, *Queer Phenomenology*, 2006

Sushmita's interactions with SFE lessened over time, for various practical reasons. But it also had to do with how she experienced change in the organization. She told me that it had become far too "academic" and "hard-core" and catered to the needs of those with an academic or theoretical interest in sexuality: "Nobody speaks in the mundane language anymore, everybody started using words like *hegemony*."

Let me now turn to one of the youngest members, who epitomized the kind of disposition that Sushmita described. While technologies of the queer self involved somatic practices, from sex change to everyday aesthetic labor, they also included the philosophical labor of thinking differently (Foucault 1985; see also Dave 2012). This labor entailed a firm rejection of what was considered normative while also expanding queer politics in more explicitly intersectional directions. An individual project of self-making drew, moreover, on a deeply embedded left-wing political stance and sensibility and revealed some of the wider shifts to leftist hegemony in Kolkata. It showed, in fact, remarkable continuities between "old" and "new" leftist political cultures, so much so that growing up in a communist family provided seamless entry and inclusion into queer subcultures and activist circles (notwithstanding the "old" Left's reticence toward gender and sexuality, and the antipathy of young SFE activists toward all political parties, including communist parties). Unlike the queer and transgender stories told so far, the master narrative of coming out plays little role in this final one, showing a different history of arrival into a "true" queer self, mediated by a leftist normativity that rendered coming out more like staying in.

A young, self-identified queer feminist, Durba joined SFE when she turned eighteen (the minimum age of membership), even as she had been ready to join for a while, having read SFE's newsletter *Swakanthey* while still in high school.[36] Her reasons for joining embodied key logics underlying the expansionist agenda of the organization, from the support group to the activist platform. While a first generation of queer women joined Sappho to secure a safe space, free from violence and discrimination, subsequent ones were in search of people "like us," for companionship and love. Durba seemed to represent a third generation of queer women, who consciously distanced themselves from any personal or identity-based reasons for joining a queer feminist organization.[37] Instead she desired to be part of a movement attached to a framework for LGBTQ rights. In her long interview with me she said,

> When the Delhi High Court released its verdict, I read the news, I felt good that I was aware of a Section named 377, because none of my friends knew of [it]. It wasn't even that I was very sure of my identity, but somehow I was reading these articles very mindfully—what the Delhi High Court was saying, why it was saying certain things, is it only applicable to Delhi, or to the rest of India?—and so on. But the fact that there is a movement behind it, for which so many people are fighting, they are fighting for their rights.... I wanted to contribute to this. I didn't come to Sappho to find a friend, or a partner, or love or support.

No longer a support group for LGBTQ individuals but an activist platform that anyone could be part of, SFE was, in Durba's description, involved "in solidarity building and not dwelling in identity politics." Of the few support group meetings she had attended, just before they dissolved, she said, "I liked them. We would watch films, gossip, or somebody would share their personal stories. Maybe I couldn't share my stories, initially—I would have a problem to talk about myself at the drop of a hat—but that didn't mean I couldn't connect with anyone. I started making connections through those meetings—my personal connections. I didn't expect much from the meetings as my main priority wasn't to make friends, not in that way." Her primary motivation was political: "My orientation was just a practice for me. It was not associated with my identity.... The reason behind coming to Sappho was somewhat political to me. And finding friends there, a support system, was a bonus."

Unlike most queer women I met at SFE whose politicization began there, Durba spoke of a longer history of "being political" that started at home. Her uncle was a party man, which meant far more than just being a member or supporter of a communist party; it signaled an affective tie that partly explained the social reproduction of leftist hegemony in the region—how its ideology infused families and entire *paaras* and informed successive generations of communist supporters and activists.[38] In gesturing toward this familiar inheritance of Bengali communism, Durba told me, "I was raised in a very polemic environment. Instead of saying that I grew up in a biased space, I would say that I grew up in a very argumentative space. So, I knew why there was a land movement happening at Nandigram, what it's about.... I mean, I was aware of these issues."

As I noted in chapter 2, activists at SFE were also invested in wider, nonqueer political issues and struggles, even as a way of marking their difference from other lesbian groups in the city. Yet Durba's speech contained a more recognizable imprint of the Bengali Left than theirs did. Take, for instance, her resistance to marriage. While other queer women at SFE resisted the institution of marriage, a key way of channeling their sexuality toward heteronormativity, Durba emphasized a Marxist rationale focused on property ownership and rights in relation to the state: "By getting married I am handing over the power to the state. And is it for companionship, for property lineage? For what? What have you gained from marriage? I will think about getting married if someone answers these questions."

Durba came of political age in college, having befriended "left-inclined independent students" through on-campus student movements. But these activists had left her disappointed, with their constant relegation of sexuality to what was "merely cultural" (Butler 1998) and therefore of no value to the masses; as she explained, "We have epitomized food, clothes, and shelter so much that we will not let any question of gender and sexuality in." Even so, Durba maintained that she had gained much from her association with student politics, moving beyond gender and sexuality to understand their intersections with class and caste. She offered, as an example of a "huge change" in her thinking, a shift in her position on caste-based affirmative action: "I used to think that reservation policies should be class based. Why should it be caste-based?"

In subsuming caste under class, Durba reiterated a dominant Bengali communist tendency of ignoring caste while fueling casteism. In being open to newer and more intersectional concerns around gender, class, *and* caste, independent strands of leftist organizing in the city represented dents in leftist hegemony. Evoking directly the legacy of the antirape protests in Delhi, Durba said, "When I walk in [a] Pride [march], my slogan says, 'VHP se azadi, khap se azadi, baap se azadi' [Freedom from the VHP, freedom from the *khap*, freedom from the father/patriarch]."[39] Forms of solidarity around right-wing Hindu nationalism were, in fact, instrumental in countering leftist skepticism of sexuality politics in Kolkata. Independent left-wing student organizers showed how central sexuality was to the imagination of the Hindu *rashtra* (nation) and to Hindutva's violent materialization.[40] While noting the growing phenomenon of the right-wing Hindu gay in neoliberal India, Durba underscored the incommensurability of queerness with right-wing politics: "Believing in right-wing politics and then going into a same-sex relationship is very paradoxical, isn't it?"

Sappho for Equality had greatly expanded her existing political knowledge and consciousness: "Previously I used to see the world in black and white, but now I can see six different colors. The dimensions of the lenses have increased." She emphasized its critical and creative labor of knowing differently: "Sappho is trying to reach the root of [our] thought, and to ask, Why do you believe in this? Is it because you were taught this?" To question our most normalized beliefs was, she explained, the organization's goal. A normative practice of thinking differently was thus common to both her communist upbringing and to SFE; it had made her "too political," such that she had nothing in common with her peers: "Firstly, people from my generation, of my age, people that I interact with are dumb.... There are friends who practice same-sex love but who do not have this [queer] identity. To them the concept of fighting for these rights, the need to fight for these rights, ... is an alien concept." Asked if this was related to their class position, she replied, "They have less exposure. Wealth buys you exposure in a way. Education gives you exposure; they don't have this."

Durba did not come from a wealthy family, but she had the right "exposure" and access to forms of cultural, social, and symbolic capital. In embodying a kind of *bhadralok* sensibility that was rooted not in wealth but in intellectual, philosophical, and respectable dispositions, she was the JU girl that Sushmita desired and that Sushmita's father derided. Durba's arrival at politicized queer selfhood, at SFE, via studying humanities in college and being part of left-wing circles, was a way of staying in—in a deeply familiar and intimate world. These shared spaces, of the family and the party, of the Old Left and the New Left, of the nonqueer and queer Left, functioned as a caste kinship.[41] As the subaltern studies scholar Sudipta Kaviraj (2014, 380) claimed of his upbringing in Kolkata, "I was a communist by caste—that is, born into a communist family, and therefore expected by communists and others alike to act in a perfectly casteist fashion—to have the same occupation as my fathers, and the same opinions." It is striking that the edition of *Swakanthey* that Durba first read, in which she located an initial pull toward SFE's queer politics, was about the double suicide of two rural women: "the representation of Sucheta's charred body left an impression on me ... they [had] committed suicide for their choices." The charred body of the subaltern constituted an enduring ground for the politicization of generations of upper-caste *bhadralok* activists, whether leftist, queer-inclined, or both.

If there were latent hierarchies with respect to class and caste in Durba's explanations, then there were also attachments to gender norms that could translate into forms of transgender skepticism. Durba claimed that in a post-NALSA conjuncture, SFE attracted greater numbers of transmen over lesbian women; those who were "manly men" and interested in "girly girls." The latter were not interested in becoming members of SFE, as they believed that they were in a "normal" heterosexual relationship, "so [the 'girly girl'] doesn't need to be with people who are lesbians." Her views echoed wider feminist anxieties around transmasculinity, expressed by cisgender queer and nonqueer feminists in India who assumed that transmen were driven to transition because they believed they had to become men to legitimately love women. Such explanations—which presented transsexuality as derivative of and the answer to lesbian desire and in service, ultimately, of heteronormativity—were in circulation at SFE, even echoed in Joy's critique of transmasculinity. Durba admitted to being transphobic in the past: "I had a MTF [male-to-female transperson] phobia...various experiences in the streets had triggered that phobia. I have overcome these after Sappho, and my friendship with Joy has prompted me to understand gender even more closely." She herself had been subject to the regulatory potential of gender: "I used to love dressing up, wearing kohl. It used to baffle me a lot: Am I not a lesbian enough? For me being a lesbian meant that the person must think of themselves as a man.... Now, I can't think of myself as masculine or feminine. I am comfortable in both, and that, too, because of Sappho." If SFE was a site of transgender skepticism and cisgender normativity, then it was also one in which these were undone, perhaps less through the cultivated art of thinking differently than through friendship, community, and embodied practices of the self.

Durba's queer selfhood epitomized the antinormative and intersectional values that SFE valued. Yet the ability to reject certain norms relied on specific and often material configurations, like class and cultural distinction, the invisible privilege of being from an upper caste, gender passing, and—especially in a Kolkata context—being from a Communist Party family. Antinormativity relied, in other words, on a limited intersectionality.

Antinormativity and Intersectionality

The queer Indian lives and subjectivities at stake in this book entail a complex play with norms and normativities. They offer support to those analytics that have sought to question queer attachments to antinormativity and to provincialize antinormative critiques from outside the Global North. In any case, it is not individual relations to social norms but the social life and reproduction of norms that queer self-fashioning lays bare—from "staying put" to "leaving home," "coming out" of the closet while reshaping one's closet, and "staying in" while being out. Who could afford the mobility to transgress norms or remain stuck in them—to come out and to not go back—was a deeply intersectional question in millennial Kolkata.

Even within a queer community of relative homogeneity and privilege in terms of class and caste, language, and location, all queers were not the same; indeed, what some rallied against emerged as the locus of aspiration, desire, and the crux of inclusion and belonging for others. Such contestations emerged from (unmarked) social differences and normative attachments—in the materialization of queer activism as a caste kinship, for instance—and ultimately made for a limited and not robust intersectionality. A limited intersectionality offered paradoxical queer possibilities, in and against norms. Queer activists in Kolkata not only aligned with social norms for highly practical purposes but also desired the invisible comforts of the normative—social stability, respectability, and "the feeling of kinship" (Eng 2010). Gender conformity enabled criminalized same-sex-desiring women to live and love at their parental home, while gender nonconformity, though newly recognized by the state, led to family severance. Queer play and aesthetics were a powerful individualized strategy of upward social mobility and, even, of caste concealment: of achieving upper-caste invisibility while being visibly queer. And even a properly intersectional and antinormative individual queer life remained attached to and was partly enabled by the unmarked ordinariness of social, cultural, and familial capital, or the enveloping invisible comfort of upper-caste *bhadralok* privilege. That queerness at these various scales—in public and at home—entailed conformity, complicity, and contingency raises questions for a queer feminist politics that assumes antinormativity as its primary sensibility and stance while also struggling with the kind of intersectional challenges that developed as Indian queer visibility grew.

Sappho for Equality's way of negotiating both—its intersectional and antinormative commitments—was true to the leftist political tradition in which it was embedded, even if it displayed little organizational or individual support for the organized Left in West Bengal. The organization turned to the rural, subaltern queer as embodying the utopic potential of the queerness it desired, while rendering such subjects as spectral figures with shadowy subjectivities who cannot be co-opted. It is to these possibilities that I turn in chapter 4, in a feminist governmentality that leads us to the wayward figure of the subaltern as one who constitutes and exceeds the contours of metropolitan queer feminist imaginations.

4
Feminist Governmentality
Entangled Histories
and Empowered Women

Concepts do not enter an empty unmarked conceptual space. They have to affect the operation of established practices and their implicit conceptual structures.
Sudipta Kaviraj, *Filth and the Public Sphere*, 1997

Shaadi karne ki azadi / na karne ki azadi. (Freedom to marry / Freedom not to marry.)
Feminist slogan in urban protests, quoted in Mallarika Sinha Roy, "Inside/Out," 2020

I began this book by suggesting that the recourse to neoliberalism as an analytic for explaining the emergence, the actual doing, and the co-optation of feminist and sexuality politics is, however vital, a partial one. Its explanatory potential could end up flattening the multiple spatiotemporalities at work in the neoliberal present. In India, millennial neoliberal feminisms were deeply entangled in political formations and feelings that emerged in a radically different preliberalized era, even if only a few years earlier. Queer feminist activists turned both backward (to past autonomous feminisms) and forward (to expanding ones around human and women's rights and development) in their legitimacy-seeking claims and interventions. These distinct governmentalities converged around the powerful construct of the subaltern and offered metropolitan activists access to sites and subjects they knew not and on whose behalf they nevertheless spoke.

In the organization I call Janam, I encountered a quintessentially millennial development initiative centered on the financial inclusion of women whose class, caste, and location marked them as subaltern. Its microfinance institution (MFI) embodied key global dynamics in attaching the promise of poverty alleviation, through financialization, to human and women's rights. Janam's everyday work echoed with multiple genealogies of educating and empowering women and girls, however. Besides transnational and corporate development, these included colonial governance and postcolonial state-led developmentalism and nationally and regionally specific understandings of women's vulnerability. The density of intimate governance that these lineages produced, especially around the governance of "child marriage" as a specific site of women's victimization, were manifest in a number of strategies adopted by Janam: in the unquestioned value of women's education and economic independence (in its injunction to subaltern women to "stand on one's own two feet"); the pedagogical tools of conscientization and collectivization; its mobilization against violence and for women's rights; and the spatial and affective arrangement of the women's self-help group that acted as the locus of preexisting and newer emancipatory pedagogies.

Like queer activism, a neoliberal developmentalist feminism did not erase what came before it. It did not enter an "empty unmarked conceptual space," in Sudipta Kaviraj's words (1997, 92), and it built on existing political literacies and affective ties and structures, especially those of the local Left.[1] A market-oriented and rights-based NGO that was fully embedded in feminist networks in the region, Janam was a good example of how layered governmentalities shaped neoliberal development but also of shifting claims and agendas on a terrain of organizing around women's rights and development.

Toward the end of this chapter, we will see how the feminist government of child marriage proved highly contentious, with subaltern women rejecting offers of rights, rescue, and rehabilitation. Such women were wayward, even unruly, subjects whose agency was not directed to feminist or secular ends, and constituting them as such was not something that could be done without struggle. Subaltern counterconduct revealed the instability of governing rationalities, the relations of power they produced, *and* a tenuous relationship between governmentality and self-making. Queer feminist governmentalities in Janam and Sappho for Equality (SFE) were many things at once: backward and forward looking, global and highly local, and co-opted and autonomous, in ways that opened distinct possibilities for (re)making the self.

Introducing Janam: Credit plus Rights

Janam belonged (like SFE) to Maitree, the face of the regional women's movement. At the time of my fieldwork, several of Maitree's member organizations, and certainly the more visible ones, were involved in addressing violence against women, especially domestic violence. They provided services like the provision of legal aid, victim support and counseling, and legal mediation.[2] Domestic violence emerged as a core issue of women's mobilizing in the 1990s, a period in which microlending also gained traction as a distinct development strategy.[3] Janam started as a community-based NGO in 1990, acquiring registered status a few years later. From the start it saw itself as undertaking rights-based claims and struggles even as it only later took on a more explicit rights-based approach to development (much like the belated turn toward human rights of SFE). Unlike some of the other organizations in Maitree, which emerged to address violence against women, Janam represented a different trend, which was the gradual expansion of existing organizational priorities—around economic empowerment and poverty alleviation—toward antiviolence activism. Both trends represented what Poulami Roychowdhury (2016, 796) has described as the hegemonic status that women's rights against violence gained in West Bengal.

Janam's conjoint commitments to microlending and women's rights were representative of still other trends, especially the pro-rights rationalities underpinning market-oriented neoliberal development strategies. Women (not gender; see Grewal 2005) emerged as a key site for the merging of human rights with development.[4] As development became conceptually yoked to human rights, in the right to development itself, rights emerged compatible with neoliberal imperatives, with access to credit and inclusion into the market being brandished as a human right (Karim 2011; Ananya Roy 2010). Framed as a right—"credit is a human right," the slogan went—access to credit was positioned as key to an ethical capitalism, with the third world woman embodying such "millennial ethics" (Ananya Roy 2010, 33).[5]

These shifts in neoliberal development rationality and practice—through human rights and specific articulations of women's rights—informed Janam's self-identification as engaged in a rights-based approach to MFIs.[6] Senior staff explained to me what this meant: going beyond credit, linking credit with rights, or acting as a "credit-plus program." Janam's staff emphasized women's rights to establish the unique if not exceptional nature of what they aspired to achieve in an increasingly competitive, crowded, and highly lucrative business of giving loans to poor women in the Global South. Echoing what some have called an empowerment approach to microfinance, the founder of the organization described microcredit as a Trojan horse that could be used for entering a community to gain acceptance to do women's rights work (see Kabeer 1994; Keating, Rasmussen, and Rishi 2010; and N. Sengupta 2013).

Women's inclusion in the market was a significant first step toward their empowerment, given how manifest women's exclusion from economic life was in rural West Bengal, but it was not enough, he claimed. There was a need to go beyond credit, as access to money alone could not instigate massive and lasting change in rural women's lives. In concrete terms this meant that Janam took up various income-generation activities and, in what indeed appeared to be an original move, it belatedly engaged in rights projects to protect rural women from patriarchal violence. By all accounts, MFIs that began with the intention of using credit to promote social change were increasingly marginalized from an intensely financialized and commercialized sector. They also rarely took up issues beyond their financial activities.[7]

Janam's trajectory showed the reverse and provided weight to its founder's claims of beginning with but going beyond credit. Staff admitted, however, that the pursuit of women's rights had taken a back seat given the more pressing demands of ensuring the viability and efficiency of the MFI. This tension mirrored a deeper contradiction—between "doing well" (financially) and "doing good" (socially)—or the need to be sustainable and efficient while attending to the needs of the poor (Kar 2018, 32). In one of the first meetings with women borrowers that I observed, in 2008, Janam's director, Dia, emphasized how important it was for the MFI to be professionally organized and not appear to make allowances for women simply because it was a woman's bank. At this time efforts were also in place to reorient organizational energies from doing financially well to doing social good, of which Janam's more direct investment in antiviolence activism (through new sources of funding), rights rhetoric, and feminist networking at Maitree were possibly all a part.

The first of its interventions into violence, which I call Leading Light, was initiated to address the growing cases of domestic violence in the rural areas in which the MFI operated. Emblematic of the kinds of services that were ubiquitous to antiviolence activism in Kolkata, the group's fifteen-odd members—all drawn from self-help groups, or *dols*—dealt with cases of rape, forced abortion, dowry, and domestic violence by providing legal advice, obtaining lawyers, and following up cases with the local police and courts. By the time Janam initiated a new campaign, to address an increase in early or child marriage, led by members it named the Vigil Group (VG), the use of community women as peer educators to combat gender-based vulnerability and violence was well in place. Both groups engaged in wider outreach activities, such as theatrical performances and awareness-raising events in villages and in Kolkata.

A common critique of MFIs was that they disarticulated conscientiza-tion from collectivization. Janam anticipated this critique, and countered it through the historically specific and spatial construct of the *dol*. "Why do rural women come to Janam?" the founder asked rhetorically and answered this question with "I go for *dol*, not money." Janam's staff echoed its founder in insisting that the *dol*'s primary objective was social: to raise conscious-ness, collectivize, and create leadership on the ground. Ultimately it was these noneconomic affects and intangible goods that drew, they claimed, rural women to Janam. It was not the tangible, or money. The *dol* lay at the heart of the realization of distinct and potentially incommensurate agendas: of providing and going beyond credit; of fulfilling both social and market-based goals; of tangible and intangible empowerment; and of rooting indi-vidual empowerment and even neoliberal entrepreneurialism in collective processes of social change. With the expansion of Janam's rights-based imag-ination, it became an ideal site from which to produce empowered feminist subjects who returned to it, armed with pedagogies of consciousness-raising and collectivization, as well as a new sense of self.

Women's collectives, a key locus of the Indian state's attempts to develop women and ensure their political participation at the grass roots, consti-tuted a readily available site upon which to experiment with new techniques of feminist governance.[8] It was through the *dol* that statist governmental-ity attempted to incorporate rural women into its visions and strategies of collective empowerment, rural development, and local governance. In communist West Bengal, *mahila samitis* (women's collectives) were meant to assist the panchayat councils in local governance but also to awaken and empower women (Munshi 2005; Tenhunen 2009). Over the course of the 1990s, *mahila samitis* were incited by both state and national governments toward neoliberal economic measures, especially through the adoption of microcredit strategies to help the poor to help themselves, which were chan-neled through NGOs. In the light of the commercialization of MFIs, NGOs like Janam reterritorialized the *dol* as a locus of collective empowerment. Optimistic assessments of NGO-led MFIs evoked the *dol* to show that even in the face of limited economic impact their group and peer dynamics had positive effects: they enabled solidarity and sociality among women; collec-tivized them around common issues and goods; and promoted their social capital, networks, and mobility while also increasing their decision-making power in the household and even resistance to violence in the family (Sanyal 2014). More critical and damning accounts of MFIs attributed, in contrast, to these very group dynamics the proclivity to reproduce rather than disrupt power and hierarchy, not least given the unspoken but widely recognized imperative of the *dol* to act as a collateral to ensure timely loan repayment.[9] While the *dol* embodied the convergence of multiple impulses—of credit plus rights, for instance—it did not erase their tensions.

I will end this section reflecting on one final tension that flowed from the dual goals of providing credit and upholding women's rights. Unlike MFIS that simply used women as instruments to avail microloans on behalf of the family, Janam prioritized the individual woman over the family. Janam's way of putting this rhetoric to work was in the guarantor principles of its microcredit program. Dia, its staunchly left-wing and feminist director, told me that they decided to do away with the idea of a male guarantor or cosignatory so that a woman could provide a guarantee for herself. The significance of this move should not be underestimated given how most MFIS required women to have a male guarantor to obtain an individual loan (Kar 2018). Janam's female clientele argued that rural women, the majority of whom were housewives, had no resources to secure themselves. Even some staff resisted the removal of the guarantor on similar grounds. Midranking staff led varied socioeconomic lives, with some young women assuming the role of the sole breadwinner in their natal families; they did not come from left-wing or "party" lineages, like Dia, or with women's studies training, as some of SFE's staff had. Many were armed with graduate degrees in social work and circulated within the governmental and nongovernmental development sector. It was at Janam that they often encountered consciousness-raising, feminist, and rights rhetoric for the first time and exposed tensions between, as Dia put it, "women's feminist and nonfeminist interests."[10]

Consciousness, conduct, desire, and mindsets were the stuff of Janam's everyday feminist labor. Whether it privileged doing well (credit) or doing good (rights), the intention of this feminist governmentality was the production of a particular kind of subject directed toward specific ends. Both microcredit and rights were subject-producing forces that evoked convergent and contradictory governing logics and even relied on similar disciplinary techniques that were not reducible to neoliberalism alone.

From the Office to the Field: "Rurbanization"

My visits to Janam followed a predictable pattern: I would arrive at the office, located on the southern fringes of Kolkata, at its opening hour and then head out with agents on its rights programs to the neighboring villages in which the *dols* were located. Janam described at least three available routes of transportation—the "bus-cum-auto route," the "auto route," and the "puddle route"—indicative of the proximity of some of the villages to the office as against the more interior ones. Generally my travels involved all three modes of transportation: by bus, by auto-rickshaw, and on foot, past if not through puddles. Let me set the scene before turning to some of the interventions and events that took place between these settings and the NGO's office.

The population and pollution density of Kolkata, even thicker with continuous construction work, gave way as we stepped off the bus into a packed auto-rickshaw that drove through a main road flanked by open fields and ponds. This scenic ride would eventually end at a "stop" with small shops and tea stalls, from where we would turn off the tarmac road onto a dirt track flanked by clusters of houses made from mud or concrete. As we walked along this final route to the borrower's home in which the loan meeting was taking place, women would be seen bathing or washing clothes in small ponds or sweeping the courtyards of houses as they settled into the rhythms of the afternoon. In this short journey from the urban office to the rural household the setting was richly reminiscent of the pastoral image of rural Bengal as Sonar Bangla (Golden Bengal).

This apparent divergence in cityscapes and rural landscapes belied many obvious truths, not least that rural areas were hardly remote (or especially idyllic), even when spatially removed from urban ones. There was also a more manifest urbanization of the rural, or what Kenneth Bo Nielsen (2018) has called "rurbanism," including the area in which Janam had operated since the 1990s, the South 24 Parganas.[11]

Though the district was largely rural, with 84 percent of the population living in rural areas, the rate of urbanization was high, and this was true of where Janam worked given its proximity to the southern part of the city of Kolkata. Signs of "rurbanization" were everywhere, from incessant highway construction to real estate ventures announcing plans for "smart housing." Increased rural migration to urban areas, greater rural and urban connectivity, and the diversification of rural livelihoods, especially from agriculture as the primary source of income generation, were all contributing factors.

The lives of the individuals I encountered at Janam—and especially the rural women integrated into its everyday functioning as beneficiaries, workers, or both—were set against these wider shifts. They were primarily housewives, dependent on male breadwinners. As women of middle- to lower-middle-class *bhadralok* (respectable) backgrounds, they did not work in the fields or engage in salaried work outside the home as a way of

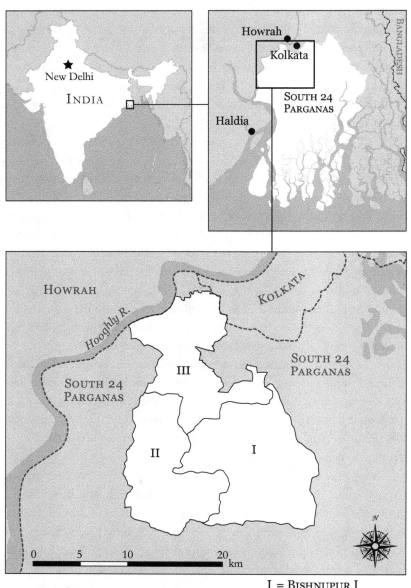

Map 4.1 Map of the peri-urban South 24 Paraganas. Drawn by Geoff Wallace.

producing and maintaining the respectability of their families. They conformed to hegemonic ideas of class, caste, and domesticity that served to restrict women to the household, and regulated their mobility in the rural public (even if strict female seclusion was no longer in practice; see Nielsen 2014, and my discussion in chapter 5). While the majority did not engage in paid labor outside the home, they undertook home-based work that, while poorly paid and temporary, enabled the women to supplement precarious household incomes. They mentioned jobs like tailoring, making umbrellas, offering beauty treatments, and "tuition," all done from home. Some were involved in a booming rural outsourcing industry, undertaking embroidery of *zari* saris, or rolling bidis (see Chattaraj 2015). Given that work in a declining agricultural sector could no longer furnish a livelihood and that there were not enough nonagricultural jobs available (and rural unemployment was on the rise), the households to which women belonged were hardly financially stable. At the same time, the cost of living was comparatively higher in these southern fringes of the city. Rising costs constituted the primary reason for women's turn toward MFIs, whether state- or NGO-run; they came to Janam, in other words, for money and often to meet immediate consumption needs.[12]

The rurban was also a site in which new opportunities and aspirations—especially for middle-class status and futurity—were being crafted. Many of these were expressed through previously unavailable urban consumptive potentials and practices, with some of the women telling me that all rural households now had certain basic consumer goods, such as scooters, refrigerators, cell phones, and televisions. Not all households I encountered had these items, and I glimpsed varying degrees of affluence and scarcity in the villages I visited. *Pakka* houses, built of cement with plastered walls and even window grilles, featured alongside brick houses with no plaster and *kaccha* (mud) houses with thatched roofs. I rarely had access to the interiors of villagers' homes, as *dol* meetings would take place in outdoor areas such as narrow concrete front porches or courtyards, which ranged from those with concrete or tiled floors to others where members in attendance simply sat on mud floors next to an open hearth. Contrast such a setting with one in which a meeting took place inside a home with a four-seat dining table and curtains. The presence of a motorcycle by the door was another marker of financial stability, while a small car would denote affluence.

Signs of an emerging urban and middle-class lifestyle were thus on display, however unevenly, in these peri-urban and rural settings. One no longer had to venture into the city to satiate urbanized tastes—for saris, cosmetics,

Figure 4.1 Janam workers. Photo by the author.

or cheap smartphones—given their easy accessibility within rural areas. The women of the VG embodied many of these metropolitan and modern sensibilities, which symbolized their upwardly mobile class status and their "empowered" and "NGO-ized" sensibility. As opposed to the traditional *tant* (cotton), they wore synthetic saris, and increasingly, tunics with trousers (*salwar kameez* suits) and even jeans. One young member of the group told me how change had come to her *graam* (village) in the form of women wearing jeans and riding cycles. One of its older members attributed, in turn, the large numbers of elopements that were taking place to the high usage of cell phones among adolescent girls, through which they "did love" (*prem korche*). Indeed, the smartphone embodied specific and highly gendered anxieties in the "rurban" (see Tenhunen 2018).[13]

As this discussion will unfold, we will hear women in these locales voice anxieties that contain within them the specter of still greater social transgressions, such as the possibility of illicit relationships and love affairs across religious divides. In the religiously heterogeneous rural communities in which Janam operated, these fears, together with anti-Muslim sentiments, were commonly expressed. Located in the same district, there were villages of (lower- to middle-caste) Hindus living in close proximity to Christians and Muslims, and neighborhoods—and self-help groups—were often divided in terms of religious makeup.[14] In a clear instance of the limits of taking a more intersectional approach to development, one NGO staff member admitted to me the "big challenge" that talking across religion had proved to be. She reported the circulation of common stereotypes about Muslims, such as "they marry a lot," "they make lots of babies," "they are very dirty," and "they don't work a lot," adding, "among ten [*dol*] members, if we have three Muslim women, these words hurt them a lot. A sense of hurt is born within the group." While gender training was "saturated," there was no training for how staff members like herself could negotiate such communal sentiments.[15] This was not an oversight on the part of the NGO; senior staff tended to reiterate the Left Front's deliberate silence on caste and religion in West Bengal. One male staff member, in fact, told me that the introduction of religion or caste would serve to divide women as a group. At work here was not simply the kind of limited intersectionality that we saw in SFE but a more anti-intersectional stance in the spirit of a leftist humanism.

Gender Training and Consciousness-Raising

Let us move back from the lush paddy fields of South 24 Parganas to Janam's dusty office and to some of the gender training sessions and workshops that I observed and found myself drawn into through small group discussions and even self-defense. Gender training is an important site for tracing the entanglement of older and newer disciplinary technologies on the terrain of millennial feminist development. A common criticism of gender training (and not in Indian feminist circles alone) pertains to depoliticization—of making development beneficiaries gender aware but hardly feminist (Batliwala 2007; Gilbertson 2021). Instead I found Janam's attempts to make rural women aware of their oppression (*nirjatan*) as continuous with local left-inflected feminist idioms and practices of consciousness-raising, even as they overlapped and merged with, but never collapsed into, global vocabularies of women's empowerment.

Consciousness-raising was common to the otherwise ideologically opposed autonomous and affiliated strands of the regional women's movement given their common assumptions around women's "ideological backwardness"

(R. Ray 1999, 76). They owed this formulation to the organized Left, which spearheaded self and social transformation as part of its decentralizing effects in rural West Bengal and with a far greater reach and impact than urban women's groups. Sedimenting into the rural everyday, the language of *jagaron* (awakening), *sachetana* (consciousness), and *pratibad* (protest), the goal of such left-wing consciousness-raising, was less about politicizing the personal than restoring to the poor their status as rights-bearing citizens.[16] Kolkata-based autonomous feminist groups attempted to wed class consciousness with more explicitly feminist awareness-raising techniques, but with limited impact (see R. Ray 1999).

Janam's peer education model for intervening into patriarchal violence embodied mixed legacies; it was often specific to an individual trainer's own background, ideological leanings, and experience. The practice of some, as we shall see in this section, was reminiscent of the rhetoric of the established Left, while others were responsive to new trends in the development industry that focused on challenging social norms and changing the self.[17] However distinct, these approaches shared assumptions of transforming the "unchanged" by "acquiring knowledge as defined by the changed" (Gilbertson 2021). Trained—"changed"—subaltern women were tasked with the responsibility of educating and empowering their peers and constituted key nodes of millennial feminist development on the ground.

Here I stay with Janam's MFI, which was less a designated site of rights education but one that was conducive to the crafting of new, especially rights-based subjectivities. The session I reflect on was rich in its borrowing from an array of universalizing (leftist, feminist, humanist) discourses, and yet the entangled logics at play were also, ultimately, in aid of neoliberal market-based logics. As a significant site upon which credit and rights converged, Janam's MFI represented less a decentering of entrenched neoliberal rationality than the amenability of existing arts and techniques of government toward specific ends.

"Today we have all come together for a reason; we are here to realize our own rights," explained Ila, a project coordinator at Janam, while further clarifying that the aim of the session was much bigger than simply discussing the rules and regulations of the MFI. The thirty-odd trainees present were primarily married women—housewives—and *dol* members. In a long monologue over a long morning, Ila charted a woman's life course (she was joined in this training by another midlevel staff member). If a woman was even allowed the luxury of birth, this moment was marred with disappointment and despair ("she is a burden") amid pervasive son preference, she said. These affects extended from early childhood to adolescence and youth, and they marked consecutive deprivations in a young woman's life that was directed toward marriage and motherhood alone. The denial of personal freedoms and educational opportunities was a key indicator of the societal difference between boys and girls. Her colleague asked the women seated in front of her, "Can we come home at eleven or twelve at night? We can't, even if we wished to. This is how society differentiates between men and women." In a statement deeply iterative of millennial metropolitan feminist activism around women's mobility, Ila declared, "A girl is as much a part of the society as boys; she has the same rights of going out."

Gender inequality was most manifest in women's lack of power, or shakti,[18] and men's monopoly over it, which Ila explained through familiar tropes like men's control over women's earnings and mobility, and, especially, men's violence against women: "[Men] repress her by not letting her go outside, or expressing her opinions, by not letting her spend money, and hitting her after [they get] drunk," said Ila. Even as alcohol-induced domestic violence—"wife-beating"—was mentioned more than once, Ila qualified that "it is just an excuse to hit; one can hit with or without being drunk." The problem, she explained, was not only about gender differences but that women were denied human rights (*manushik adhikar*).

For these women staff members, power attached closely with money— men's control over it and women's lack of access to it. The patriarchal organization of domestic relations centered on money: from husbands who drank away their money and hit wives, to parents who chose to save money by not educating their daughters (over their sons), to daughters who could, in turn, be educated or trained to earn money on behalf of parents, money was the crux around which women's marginalization and agential possibilities hinged. Pervasive social ills like dowry were also explained, less through recourse to custom or tradition than to a logic of commodification. The daughter, Ila explained, "is an object; one needs a lot of money in order to get her married, so one should get her married as soon as possible by paying dowry." Ultimately, "the main reason for all of these [discriminations] is women's lack of economic independence," the solution to which was also economic: "If I can earn money somehow, contribute some money to the household, then I will have some right to speak." Money, she said more than once, is "huge power."

Ila's words established a close, almost casual connection between women's access to money and their ability to take decisions and exercise rights, expressed through the vernacular idiom of having the capacity (*khomota*) to stand on one's own two feet. While commonly used across India, the expression "to stand on one's own two feet"—used to signal individual autonomy, security, and mobility—was an especially enduring aspirational idea in communist and postcommunist West Bengal (see Romani 2014). It embodied activist attachments to the need for and importance of economic independence as a direct conduit to personal autonomy and empowerment. Even newer (and queerer) political imaginations remained entangled in such leftist logics of what individual empowerment looked like and how it could be achieved.

Knowing all too well that she was addressing not women workers but rural housewives, Ila raised the issue of women's unpaid domestic labor: "Just think about it. If you had to keep *kaajer lok* ["a person who works," the Bengali term to replace *chakor*, or servants; see Ray and Qayum 2009, 4] to get [house]work done, then how much would you have to pay? Your husband is not paying you anything [and] yet you are doing everything, isn't it [so]?" She asked the women present to list all the chores that occupied them from morning until night and asserted, "These are work." Capitalist precarity was implicit in the following chain of effects she evoked: "What if suddenly a person who is earning a wage in our family, let's assume, at the factory, or a jute mill, becomes unemployed overnight? In that case, we will have to cut down on our costs. If both son and daughter are studying, then the daughter's education is stopped. That was an extra expense, we took care of it as long as we had the money, but now that we don't have money, we can only continue the son's education. So, from the very beginning I am distributing an unequal amount of power to boys and girls."

Janam's staff thus resurrected the "magic wand of economic independence" (R. Ray 1999, 74) that pervaded leftist feminist thought of a preliberalization era—but, of course, with an important caveat.[19] The magic wand was now credit (or debt). Consider here a longish quote from Ila in which economic independence—standing on one's own two feet—was resignified in distinctly neoliberal terms:

Suppose somebody gives me fish to eat every day, then it will become my habit, I will never think that I have to earn and work hard. For instance, you look after your son now, but you will not look after him forever. After a certain age he will have to become empowered so that he can earn for himself. So Janam's main aim was to see that *graamer meyera* [village girls] come together and take their empowerment to a point where they are able to do something on their own. They will need help till a certain point of time, till they are able to stand on their own two feet, but after that, if we don't come away, then it will transform into a habit. If I keep giving fish to somebody, then it will become their habit to consume fish; but providing them with fish is not our aim; our aim is to see how they can fish for themselves. So, our aim is to see how we can empower rural women and through that they can, without outside help, make their own organization, run their own business, improve their skills. Janam started working with this aim.

Ila's words were evocative of the popular proverb and clichéd development slogan "Give a man a fish and he will eat for a day. Teach a man to fish and he will eat for a lifetime." It was also emblematic of neoliberal reasoning—in emphasizing the merits of moving away from dependency to self-sufficiency via the acquisition of intangible skills, as opposed to tangible goods such as charity, welfare, or waged labor. In his book *Give a Man a Fish*, James Ferguson notes that the popular development aid slogan "encapsulates a certain development ethos, economically expressing a core belief that the object of development work is *transformation*, not charity, and that recipients of aid should get productive skills and the opportunity to work, not handouts and dependency" (Ferguson 2015; emphasis added).[20] Rural Bengali women needed not actual fish but a fishing lesson, or a new set of skills and dispositions to wean them off dependency and direct them toward self-reliance. A loan from Janam facilitated this and more; staff emphasized how women's loan taking increased their decision-making capacity. Ultimately, to stand on your own two feet, with the crucial but limited investment of an external agent like Janam, conjured a vision of individual success rooted in hard work and enterprise, strikingly compared to rearing a child who "after a certain age [will] have to become more empowered so that he can earn for himself." The analogy between development and child-rearing was one that the rural women present would have been especially receptive to given their discursive construal, in a range of governmental and disciplinary frameworks, as good mothers responsible not just for the future of the family but of the nation-state.[21]

Core to development intervention is transformation, writes Ferguson, and it was indeed individual transformation that was at the heart of Janam's imagination of what a feminist solution ought to consist of. A large part of Ila's explanation of women's specific vulnerability drew, for instance, on their lack of self-confidence or internalized sense of inadequacy cultivated since childhood. Ila evoked an example from the field when she told a victim of domestic violence: "When they hit you, why don't you hit them back?" These kinds of individualized and subjective solutions were commonly on offer in NGO-driven antiviolence work.[22]

The training provided a glimpse into how mainstream neoliberal development-speak articulated with older and newer rationalities and pedagogies of modernization to craft particular subjectivities for poor women and futures for the rural poor. As with Janam's rhetoric more generally, project coordinators rarely mentioned capitalism, class, or the state. Consciousness-raising was not intended to generate rights-based claims toward the state but was directed inward, toward individual agency and responsibility. Even as market-based solutions were offered in the light of the failures of the state, women's empowerment relied for its actualization on resources (education and employment) that only the state could provide. These contradictions were manifest in Janam's rights program on early marriage, to which I now turn.

Genealogies of the Girl-Child and Child Marriage in India

Child or early marriage was a new entry to Janam's litany of rights work, broadly centered on violence against women, and was prompted, staff explained, by high rates of such marriages and elopements in their areas of intervention. Janam's new emphasis on the rights of adolescent girls was concretized by project funding from an international nonprofit, emblematic of the rise of global interest in the adolescent girl and her potential to champion a "girl effect." Local NGOs like Janam were especially well placed to access transnational development funds given their penetration, via MFIs, into the grass roots and their intimacy with at-risk groups and individuals. While antiviolence work entailed the provision of concrete services like counseling and legal aid, the intervention into early marriage centered on intangibles alone—awareness, sensitization, and changing social norms—in ways that were commensurate with the development sector's valorization of intangibles as objects and ends in themselves (see Jakimow 2013). Janam's child marriage program relied, like its rights-based activism more generally, on trained and changed members from the community who were tasked with facilitating interactive sessions with *dols* on child marriage.

Before I turn to the richness of these sessions, let me return to the subject positions of "at-risk" and "can-do" girls that drove rights-based and even market-driven claims to empower the adolescent girl of the Global South (see chapter 1). Janam was a good instance of the entanglement of these neoliberal and corporate feminisms in older assumptions, around how the girl-child was constituted as an object of rescue and rehabilitation and how child marriage was imagined as a governmental and legal problem to be addressed and solved in independent India. We know that the question of reforming or "modernizing" women emerged central to a thick terrain of competing colonial and nationalist governmentalities, as well as to a prehistory of rights (see Sarkar 2001). Child marriage constituted a major site of contest between colonials, reformers, and conservatives in the late nineteenth century in ways that made clear that the status of the girl-child was more about managing conservative and liberal anxieties around female sexuality than recognizing women as rights-bearing subjects. As the history of Bengal alone shows, campaigns to improve the status of women by increasing the age of consent in and outside marriage, allowing widow remarriage, and expanding education (for at least upper-caste Hindu women) were far more about preserving, on the one hand, colonial power and paternalism and securing, on the other hand, decolonial and nationalist futures.

Unlike the social reformers of the nineteenth century, for whom the governance of marriage was part of the regulation of women's chastity and sexuality, women's organizations of the early twentieth century turned to concerns of women's health and education. It was their prolonged campaigns, as well as socioeconomic factors such as increased urbanization and expanded opportunities for women's education, that led to a steady increase in the mean age of marriage, from fifteen to eighteen for girls and eighteen to twenty-one for boys.[23] Statist frameworks, however, reduced consent to a biological category that limited the breadth of imaginative emancipatory possibilities for women of all ages.

The more recent shift in terminology—from *child marriage* to *early marriage*—is traceable to the rise of the adolescent girl as the latest figure of risk, resilience, and enterprise in global development. In Nike's Girl Effect campaign, for instance, child marriage was identified as a key risk, a "cultural" or "traditional" practice that conjured a set of related risks, such as pregnancy, ill health, and lack of education and employment for girls and subsequent generations. The delay in marriage assumed, in turn, a transformatory chain of positive effects: for the United Nations, empowered girls will "stay in school, marry later, delay childbearing, have healthier children, and earn better incomes that will benefit themselves, their families, communities and nations" (quoted in Koffman and Gill 2013, 95). Education, in particular, was key to the Girl Effect, to unleashing the hidden potential of young girls for their own empowerment, that of the wider communities to which they belonged, and, needless to say, for the expanding frontiers of corporate capital.[24]

While local NGOs were at one with the Girl Effect resolve around education, they did not always regard child marriage as a problem of culture or tradition. The Delhi-based feminist organization Nirantar argued that the culturalist framing of early marriage rendered invisible its structural determinants, like poverty, poor access to education for women, and the specter of gender-based violence (Agnes 2013; Bhog 2017). In the Indian context, Flavia Agnes (2013) also points to the law's failure to curb early marriage; in fact, the law strengthened familial and wider societal control over young women's sexuality. She tells us that around one-third of rape cases filed in India are by parents who, together with the police and community leaders, use the legal provision around child marriage to control young women's choice and consent in intimate relations, especially when it exceeds the bounds of community or family-sanctioned consent. The girl is falsely represented as a minor and the boy slapped with a case of abduction or rape. Many feminists thus feared that the raising of the age of consent would only serve to further criminalize "contentious" forms of love, intimacy, and marriage (Chowdhry 2007).[25] The conversion of women's choice into force—consent into coercion—became routine to the Hindu Right's efforts to violently curb interreligious intimacies and unions (of which vigilante campaigns against "love jihad" were exemplary).[26]

It was this terrain that Janam entered with a clear injunction to prevent child marriage through the education and empowerment of adolescent girls. In a brief document, a concept note prepared for donors, Janam stressed that it was "natural for young girls to fall in love and to have relationships/friendships. The immediate family, the community, and the school authorities (including teachers) need to understand and respect this instead of clamping down heavily on the mobility and sexuality of the girls and thereby blocking their path to growth and development." Instead, family and communities exercised "severe control over sexuality of young girls" and left them "with no other alternative but to elope with the partners of their choice." Janam understood, then, the specific entanglement of elopement and marriage well, or how young women were, ironically, forced to elope because of the pressure to marry. The intimacy between elopement (as an expression of women's choice and agency) and marriage (the site of women's governance and subservience to social norms) made it difficult to discern a woman's choice ("elopement") from her lack of choice ("marriage").

Unlike statist discourses that ended up prioritizing family and community choice over the rights of individual women, Janam foregrounded their sexual rights. As the concept note put it, "Janam believes that in order to curb the rising phenomena of child marriage it is necessary to ensure and promote the sexual rights of girls, challenge the control over their sexualities and mobility and provide an ambience for the girls where they are free to exercise their choice and have access to all opportunities for growth." It further stressed the importance of creating an environment in which women had choices—where marriage, whether entered voluntarily or through coercion, would not be the only option for adolescent girls. Janam remained resolute, as it did in its MFI, that "woman must trump the family" (as Dia put it to me when discussing Janam's guarantor policy). To achieve such goals, the concept note proposed "a change in the mindset of the stakeholders and to create community consensus against early marriage of girl-children." How were mindsets changed? What strategies and techniques were employed, and how successful were they?[27]

In the Field: Schooling Girls, Delaying Marriage

Janam founded the VG, with selected *dol* women, with the aim of stopping child marriages from taking place. It was meant to undertake "preventive" work through advocacy, consciousness-raising, and work with state agencies.[28] While we shall meet the individual women who made up this group in chapter 5, let me state what is most relevant about their personal biographies—namely, that a majority of these young women who were keeping a "vigil" (*nojor*) on their compatriots had themselves married before the legal age of eighteen. In speaking about her marriage at a young age, one of the workers, Purnima, evoked the complexities Janam identified: "The environment at home was very strict, and my parents were trying to arrange my marriage elsewhere. Therefore I decided to elope and get married. But I didn't want to get married. I was a good student, I could have studied further, but there was too much pressure at home."[29]

These women had an especially strong hold on the uniqueness of what adolescent girls in their community went through given their own experiences. In the training sessions that I observed, it was this highly individualized experience that the trainer—feminist, academic, and middle-class—mined. These trainings revolved around a primary question ("Who am I?") as a way of building theory from experience. ("Am I only a mother?,"

"What do I see myself as?," and "How do others see me?" were questions around which exercises were typically organized.)[30] Issues (like child marriage) and the language of rights and legal training came later. The training also emphasized how self and experience were key resources in the field for building empathy and gaining trust. In explicitly fusing self and social transformation, the trainer described the VG women to me as being "agents of change for [themselves] and for others."

In the sessions I observed, though, the workers described the consequences of early marriage in highly formulaic ways. "We can tell them [dol members] that girls who get married at eighteen face a lot of trouble which they're unaware of," explained one of the trainees, in anticipation of what she would say in the field. Even when the trainer pushed a member to define the nature of "trouble," the responses were predictable: having a baby at a young age harms women, state and law do not allow child marriage, women have rights, and so on. The transformatory capacity of education was at the front of their rhetoric, with the workers regurgitating, in training and later in the field, well-worn clichés like "A girl can get an education and stand on her own two feet."

Finally came the field visits. Two staff members accompanied the members of the VG to dol meetings, who together facilitated interactive sessions on the problem of child marriage and the need to build awareness around it. Organized at lunchtime, just after a loan officer had wrapped up her business, these sessions followed a standard pattern: NGO staff and workers introduced the discussion on child marriage to dol members seated on the floor in that part of the house in which the loan meeting was taking place—typically a courtyard or porch.[31] Through the use of flash cards, the speakers raised questions about the oppression (nirjatan) of early marriage, inviting their audience of mostly married women to ask questions and share their experiences. The visually coded flash cards (prepared by Janam's staff) contrasted the life courses of two adolescent girls, one who had married early, and another who had completed her schooling. The former's life course was marred by marriage and dowry, early and multiple pregnancies, ill health (of self and children), and violence within the family. It was described as being one of sadness (dukho). The second figure evoked an entirely different affective landscape: the adolescent girl was primarily one who attended school and was shown to be engaged in a range of tasks—like winning prizes, doing homework, being computer savvy, and even driving a van—with the support of her parents (no other kin were presented). Here's a taste of the commentary that accompanied the contrasting images, delivered by one of the project coordinators:

If we follow the picture of that girl who was married off young, had a child when she was barely eighteen, what will happen to her? Does it paint a happy picture? It is not what we call happy. She has already had so many children at such a young age, and she is pregnant with another one. [*The coordinator turns to the alternative image.*] If you look at this picture closely, you will see that she has the entire world in her grasp. I have power [*khomota*] because I have got education, or I have learned some work or the other. I can do many things. The entire world is there for me. She is a very confident girl.

The reasoning was clear: by not getting married and instead being in school, a young girl was guaranteed not just an alternative, empowered future but also hope, happiness, success, and joy. Alongside the standard presumed benefits of schooling, such as the health and well-being of mother and child (and, implicitly, health of the community and nation), there were newer affective and aspirational ones on offer that also gestured toward middle-class futurity. Janam's staff repeatedly stated that education was a conduit to a range of jobs—not just the usual sewing but making jams and pickles, working as a plumber or electrician, and so on.[32]

The divergent flash cards constituted not only a parable on happy and healthy gendered adolescence—and its opposite—but also on what "good" responsible mothering ought to look like. While mothers were presumed and spoken of in one life course as treating the girl-child as a "burden," they were associated with "support" and being a "guide" to their daughter in the other (all these words were said in English, which is indicative of how NGO-speak folded into local everyday talk). In one image a young mother was shown to be helping her daughter with what looked like homework, conjuring up a distinctly bourgeois lifeworld in which mothers were free of productive and reproductive labor and were literate, if not school-educated, and could guide their school-going children. The "mother-teacher" was always a classed and not just gendered subject; it interpellated middle-class women as good mothers in ways that were meant to be emulated by, even if not directed to, the working classes (Khoja-Moolji 2018, 72). Indeed, the special status that NGO personnel afforded to the mother-teacher, the child, and childhood accrued from their own class status. While not elite, staff members were resolutely middle class and metropolitan and conformed to ideas of childhood as a special chapter in one's life or, in neoliberal logic, "a time free from and prior to marriage and child-bearing—to be spent instead in education" (Koffman and Gill 2013, 88).[33] Given, moreover, the legendary valorization of women's maternal roles in West Bengal, not least by the Left Front, it was natural for Janam's staff to address rural women in their roles as mothers, responsible for the health, happiness, and futures of their daughters (see R. Ray 1999). There was no mention of husbands, sons, or fathers in these discussions.

Dol women's responses to these interventions veered between disinterest and rejection; they seemed far more concerned with their loans. Even as they did not necessarily disagree with the notion that child marriage was bad for women, they tried to complicate the narrative presented by repeatedly raising the problem of elopement. They stated, not without a touch of irony, that they were not marrying off their daughters; they were themselves running away and getting married! What could they do? "I will educate my daughter till class six or seven; after that she will work at home," some asserted, even defiantly defending the use of their young daughters' labor.[34] Women also shifted responsibility back onto state and government, stating simply that education was not being provided. I once asked a younger VG member, herself enrolled in a local college, what kind of schooling facilities existed in that village. Very few, she explained, and most families could not afford the associated costs, such as the purchase of books and bags and the escalating price of private tuition.[35]

In these early days VG members did not share their own experiences of early marriage and motherhood, so there was little possibility of solidarity building, key presumptions of empowering MFIs. In telling rural women which aspects of their actions and beliefs were wrong—in using words like *bhul* (mistake), *beyani* (illegal), and *oporadh* (sin)—they produced themselves as apart from the women in front of them. Given their newfound proximity to power and upward mobility through Janam, VG women established relations of difference and hierarchy—not sameness and equality—between themselves and their peers.[36] They presented themselves as educated and empowered, and their peers as ordinary village women. *Dol* women, in turn, identified NGO staff and even VG members, drawn from the *dols*, as being from town and not *graam*, and insisted that their own domestic matters were of the village, not the town (*eita town-er byaepar na, graam-er*). By 2016, however, the VG had consciously moved away from this structure of intervention. It was now organized in a far more intimate manner, involving one or two workers for each *dol*, thus constituting a support group for rural women. Group members told me how they would consciously try to draw attention away from financial deliberations and direct it instead toward casual conversation around daily routines. They would ask community women to speak "from the heart," choosing to sit back and listen in a decidedly more noninterventionist fashion than had originally been envisioned for them. They also shared more freely their own lives and experiences. While this approach was more along the lines of Janam's own commitments of going beyond credit, it still focused on transformation: on rearranging women's desires, affects, and consciousness. As one staff member put it, "Stopping a child marriage is not our focus; we work on changing mindsets."

Coercion, Care, and Other Incommensurables

I turn now to an event that occurred while I was in the field that vividly displayed the limits of feminist governmentalities, composed of translocal logics, practices, and technologies of power. At the heart of this assemblage was an unresolved tension between the incommensurate agendas of providing credit and going beyond credit. In its offer of a credit-plus-rights program, Janam staff sought to produce, as did global rhetoric around ethical capitalism, commensurability between its strictly economic function and its commitments to ethical and emancipatory ideals. But none of this mitigated a central fact: that Janam was not only in the business of "doing good" but also in that of "doing well," and while these twin dynamics were irresolvable in most ordinary MFIs (Kar 2018), their fault lines were experienced in more intense ways in explicitly rights-based and feminist-inspired ones.

One day in November 2011, I entered Janam's office at its usual opening hour to find an unusual level of excitement among the members of the VG. They told me that a *baccha meye* (an adolescent girl) was being married off in one of the villages, and that the marriage was taking place against her will. Janam was going to stop the marriage from taking place, and its members, together with the project coordinator Ila, the loan officer, and even the director Dia, were gearing up to go to the village in question (a panchayat member had also been summoned). Before I knew it, we all piled into several auto-rickshaws and set off, in convoy, with the NGO *didis* (sisters) ahead of us. As we entered the *graam* the excitement of VG members turned to unease, and they worried about what their own kin in that village would make of their presence. Concerns around risk and repercussions began to permeate their conversation.[37]

Janam's staff summoned members of the local *dol*, as well as the underage girl. On being asked about her situation, the girl declared, quite defiantly for someone who looked about fourteen (she said she was seventeen), that she loved the boy and wanted to marry him out of her own volition. She went so far as to say that she would kill herself if she was not allowed to do so. The entire situation turned hostile, with a crowd of about thirty-odd women declaring Janam members to be homewreckers and moneylenders and demanding that they leave. Amid angry screams and shouts that verged on a riot, Dia stood up and gave a dramatic speech about how Janam's primary focus was women's rights and not the giving and taking of money; it was not a local moneylender [*mahajon*], she said. And if this was not clear, then Janam would no longer work in the area and no loan officer would go there. After an explosion of opposition from *dol* women, Dia softened her stance and said she would take care of the girl herself, besides offering her paid work at Janam. The crowd took a while to quiet down, with some agreeing with what Dia had said but insisting that the young girl's situation had to be considered too — namely, that she was poor and had no "guardians." On my way back to the office with Dia and Ila, the two remarked on how good the intervention had been. Nonetheless, the marriage went ahead in the weeks that followed.

Shortly after this incident, evidence emerged to suggest that the adolescent girl was being sexually abused in her home at the hands of male relatives. Her vulnerability was only accentuated by the fact that she had no parents and was under the care of an aged grandmother. Members of the VG responded to this revelation with silence while Ila said that there was nothing that could be done: publicizing this information would render the girl unmarriageable. While fear of sexual violence was one of the drivers of early marriage in poor families in India, Ila's response underscored just how normative marriage was. Sexual violence was merely one of the factors that rendered complex the set of motivations that might have constituted consent to early marriage in this instance. The lack of resourceful guardians and abject poverty were other considerations that the rural women present on the day of the intervention repeatedly drew attention to, insisting that the young girl's *poristhiti* (situation) needed to be understood.[38]

Rather than considering the wider social determinants of consent, as it did on paper, Janam's staff sought to dismiss the girl's expression of consent and even interpret it as evidence of coercion—that she was being forced into marriage against her will. They stated, matter-of-factly, that the question of the girl's *icche* (wishes) was irrelevant, since she was a minor and child marriage was illegal. Outside the legal categories of the girl-child and child marriage, NGO staff reduced the adolescent girl to a *bacha* (child), as juxtaposed to elders. Dia, for instance, repeatedly addressed the crowd of women gathered on the day as elders—*borora*—a term laden with connotations of age, experience, wisdom, and responsibility, while reducing the girl to an innocent, asexual, unknowing, immature, and irresponsible ("rash") child. Someone in the crowd said, "The girl wants to get married, so why are you stopping her?" Dia responded, "So if your child wants to jump into fire, would you let them?" She continued by saying, "We cannot let our girls jump into the fire of marriage when we know what it is about, and they do not know." The child would simply be in the household, at the mercy of her husband. This logic of false consciousness was equally at play when the young woman rejected Janam's offer of work in its office, declaring that she did not want a stitching job.[39]

Dia, in particular, adopted a punitive and paternal disposition toward the young woman and the wider community of rural women present, emphasizing concern and care, on the one hand, and mobilizing threats and punishment, on the other. She told the women more than once that Janam could have involved the police but was choosing not to because of the NGO's long-standing relationship with the village through the loan program. In deploying this tactic she presented Janam as considerate yet reaffirmed, in the same breath, a relation of power between the organization and its beneficiaries in which one could operate with a degree of proximity to state power not available to the other. While NGOs like Janam had no law enforcement authority or capacity, they did work closely with state agencies. On the day of the incident, Janam seemed more state-like than ever, given that the literal embodiment of the state—the local panchayat member—was entirely ineffectual. He not only arrived late on the scene (only because Janam had asked him to) but he apparently suggested that the marriage go ahead as planned. His reaction spoke volumes to the lack of law enforcement and how women's organizations and NGOs employed "extra-legal contextual solutions" (S. Basu 2015, 187) to fill this "vacuum of institutional power" (Roychowdhury 2015, 799).

Perhaps most strikingly, Dia threatened to suspend the *loan-er-subedha*, or the benefit of getting a loan. She employed the debt relation that Janam's MFI had instituted—a fundamentally unequal one between the creditor and the debtor—as leverage to achieve the gendered social change that she desired in the world. Money—and not any ethical claim toward rights or empowerment—was evoked to compel subaltern women to change their conduct (even if their mindsets remained unchanged). This instrumental usage of indebtedness also, ironically, brought a feminist NGO into proximity with the vilified position of the moneylender and, unsurprisingly, elicited accusations from beneficiaries along these lines. South Asian MFIs were, in fact, haunted by the figure of the moneylender, given their use of coercive loan repayment strategies and increased turn toward making a profit.[40]

That MFIs articulated both care and coercion—or a system of rewards and punishment—was one chief manifestation of their attempts to reconcile incommensurate agendas of credit and empowerment.[41] Janam's mobilization of coercive rhetoric was not—at least in this instance—in the service of its MFI but served to fulfill its emancipatory feminist aspirations, especially when faced with subaltern subjects who did not appear to comply with what was presumed to be in their best interest. As unruly subalterns who articulated nonfeminist desires and antisecular fears—and placed a feminist NGO as continuous with the state and even with the culturally maligned position of the moneylender—the responses of the wider community of village women brought feminist governmentality to its limits. And even when executing Janam's ethical and emancipatory agenda, the VG operated with a different set of assumptions, which undermined relations of power between children and adults and between NGO workers and their objects of rescue and emancipation.

Limits and Compromise

In the days that followed, I asked VG members about their reaction to what had transpired. All agreed that Janam had done the right thing by attempting to stop the marriage from taking place, though they saw the fact of the girl's consent as a snag. If she had withheld her consent, they said, it would have been easier to stop the marriage from going ahead (barring the small detail of a dowry that had already been given). Even if the intervention had failed, it would still have the positive effect of instilling fear in the larger community such that families would think twice before getting their underage daughters married. Some seemed frustrated that the girl had changed her story, from claiming that she was being forced to marry to saying that she was freely consenting to do so. She must have been tutored by family members to say so, they speculated, or she was a *badmaish* (deviant) who had changed her story of her own volition. Or maybe she had had another romance on the side and was being married off to prevent her from eloping. Runu had apparently met the girl the evening after Janam's involvement and asked her how she could afford a cell phone if she "cannot eat" (*kethe paaey na*). These kinds of rumors and subjective assessments served to confirm, for VG members, the girl's status as a *baaje meye* (bad girl), used to signal any young women who exercised sexual agency. This status was also confirmed in the girl's choice to get married over accepting low-paid and intermittent employment at Janam.

Members' mobilizing of stigmatizing tropes of dishonesty and moral deficiencies—*baaje meye* and *badmaish*—were familiar vernacular idioms used to frame the disobedience of subalterns, especially when it involved someone from a more vulnerable social position. Rather than associate the girl with innocence, passivity, asexuality, and false consciousness, as in Janam's usual rhetoric, VG members presented the adolescent girl as treacherous (lying about not being forced to get married), potentially manipulative (changing her story), sexual (having a romance on the side), and ungrateful (refusing the offer of rehabilitation and rescue). They transformed her from a passive object in the hands of metropolitan middle-class development professionals and bestowed upon her an agency that they did not approve of.

Given Janam's obligation to empower rural women constituted as lacking agency, it was obvious why it would be invested, like metropolitan queer feminists, in images and narratives of victimhood. While the VG members—themselves subaltern women (in being mostly from lower-caste and lower-income families)—also mobilized such stereotypes, they seemed less moved by the affective force of victimology. Young girls, they seemed to say in response to Janam, lie, run away, and have sexual relations with men they are not married to. Even as they did not approve of such behavior, their ascription of agency to the adolescent girl allowed the writing of another kind of narrative, at the center of which was a subject, however wayward and disobedient.

If the girl was no innocent victim in the eyes of VG members, then Janam was no noble savior for the larger community of rural women. Early field interactions that involved the NGO lecturing *dol* women on the ills of child marriage were also sites of dissent and resistance. Mothers refused the moral imperative to send their daughters to school and even insisted on early marriage to control their daughters' sexuality. Their accusations of Janam being a homewrecker, a popular term of abuse hurled at feminist organizations doing this kind of intimate governance, were not surprising. But it might not be sufficient to read rural women's response as non- or antifeminist in the face of Janam's feminist campaign against what it considered patriarchal and antiwomen. On the contrary, rural women asked for intervention and empowerment in the name of women and their rights, but not in the ways it was being offered. For instance, on the day of the incident with the adolescent girl, they asked Janam staff why they did not break the local distilleries in which alcohol was being made in the village. In asking such questions, they placed millennial and neoliberal feminist interventions in a long-standing tradition of rural Indian women's activism around alcohol abuse.[42]

Women's responses at the scene of Janam's "successful" intervention into early marriage revealed the limits of feminist governmentality in other ways, especially in its reliance on the *dol* for achieving incommensurate agendas and ends. In constituting the locus of Janam's aspirations to provide but also go beyond credit, the *dol* was the principal guarantor of the feminist potentials of its MFI; in the founder's words, rural women came to Janam for the *dol*, not for money. On the day of the event, Dia similarly insisted that the *dol* was not just for the giving and taking of money. It was the *dol*'s obligation to take responsibility for an underage, vulnerable girl who had no guardians: "Eta ki doler kaaj na? Doler ki kaaj khaali taka poisha?" (Isn't this the work of the *dol*? Or is it simply taking and giving money?) In invoking the *dol* in this capacity—as the potential guardian of the prospective bride—Dia displayed her concerted efforts to put Janam's feminist commitments to work: to constitute out of the *dol* a female or even feminist public whose members would take responsibility for each other's well-being and stand in solidarity with one another.

Rural women refused to partake in such attempts to build a more expansive and ethical *we*. They refused to take *daito* (responsibility) for the girl, challenging Janam by asking, "What will happen if she runs away tomorrow—with a Muslim boy?" This was not the *kaaj* of the *dol*, they firmly asserted, reducing the *dol* to its economic function alone—one that was moreover sustained through technologies that were not conducive to egalitarian and collective projects. They asked angrily about the "informer" who they presumed briefed Janam about the marriage. In the field interactions that I witnessed, NGO staff encouraged *dol* members to report cases of early marriage on the basis that "we are each an agent of change." All these newly constituted subject positions, from the loan officer to the peer educators to the peer group itself, were thus deeply enmeshed in technologies of surveillance and discipline, exercised in the name of responsibility, collectivization, and care and not just of credit. We know that an implicit function of MFI-based SHGs was to discipline their members through forms of surveillance, and while such disciplinary power was primed for loan-repayment purposes, it also came in handy in the enforcement of women's rights. *Dol* members' responses showed, in turn, the incommensurability of using technologies of discipline, coercion, and surveillance for building a feminist collective out of a group of rural women.

The expansive and ethical *we* that Dia tried to constitute included not just subalterns but also middle-class metropolitan feminist agents of development like herself. Much like the commonality that metropolitan queer activists strived to establish between themselves and subaltern lesbians, Dia mobilized gender to build bridges to women whose social position was vastly different from her own.[43] Her *we* was rooted in a shared and culturally resonant maternal common sense, one that would intuitively know the "fire" of marriage and the "evils" of husband and household. It was not without purchase given that many of the women standing around me on the day loudly agreed with her. But they also undermined her efforts. When Dia, in one instance, compared the adolescent girl to her own daughter, a woman next to me responded sardonically, "As if your [Dia's] daughter is the same as mine."

Throughout this chapter I have shown a lack of intersectionality at work in Janam's feminist governance, with one staff member presenting the grass roots as a "safe" repository for gender and sexuality education but not for mobilizing around caste or religion. Yet in the religiously heterogeneous spaces in which Janam's MFI operated, where communal sentiments surfaced easily, women's aspirations and fears for their daughters were shaped in fundamentally intersectional ways. When they asked what would happen if a daughter ran away with a Muslim boy, they spoke as a group of not just women but Hindu women, whose fears around their daughters' sexuality were haunted by historically "sticky" stereotypes of Muslim masculinity (Ahmed 2014a). The young Muslim man played a key role in the violent imagination of Hindu nationalism, "cast simultaneously as lustful seducer and a dangerous jihadi" (K. Krishnan 2020, 58; see also Sarkar 2018). By disregarding the complexity of subaltern women's anxieties—in favor of an enforced commonality and solidarity—feminist interventions not only failed to fulfill their mandate around women's rights but also ended up normalizing internal fault lines in a time of Hindutva-fueled "love jihad."

The responses of the *dol* and the VG, while not necessarily sensitive or progressive, brought into relief the historically embedded and subjected nature of individuals and their life choices. They underscored specific contradictions on the ground, which local, even feminist NGOs could not easily reconcile, including the possibility of early marriage and elopement as routes to standing on one's own two feet, and the violence of early marriage with the safety net that it seemingly provided against sexual violence. Rather than ignorance or false consciousness, rural women's defense of early marriage was of the nature of compromise, "of conscious knowledge and understanding of what is being gained and given up" (Li 1999, 298). Just as the liberatory potential of education and employment were, at best, ambivalent, some compromises (like elopement and early marriage) were also necessary.[44]

Feminist Failure

Part of the VG's campaign around child marriage was the staging of a play on this issue for a string of advocacy-related events. Members of the group told me that the play originally ended with the line that a girl's wishes ought to be respected in matters of marriage. Given that young women were eloping and getting married at alarming rates, Janam staff thought it was best to remove it. The young VG member who told me about this was furious. The line should have been kept, she insisted, and it should have been the VG's decision to do so and not Janam's. This same woman wholeheartedly supported Janam's concerted efforts to stop child marriages, even against the wishes of individual women.

I end this chapter by foregrounding the messy life of feminist governmentality embodied in a range of social actors, historic forces, forms of power, and technologies of rule intended to conduct, through changed mindsets, the conduct of poor women of the Global South. This governmentality was not straightforwardly neoliberal, nonstatist (or state-like), or feminist. These were certainly the qualifiers of Janam's ideological imperatives, even as its everyday development work accommodated other ideologies. Located in the legacies of Indian feminism, the developmentalist and neoliberal state, the local Left, and global efforts around an ethical financialization were a variety of governmental techniques intended to empower individual and groups of women. These included microfinance as a mode of individual self-reliance and collective solidarity; subjectification through the ascribing of liberal legal rights; protection through the pastoral power of the family and community; and the mobilization of threat and coercion via the sovereign power of law and state. Janam's belated emphasis on women's rights established its presence on a shifting local feminist field, where the hegemony of the Left loosened but also endured in translocal activist pedagogies and everyday practices across feminist and queer feminist organizing.

At the intersection of older and newer governmentalities and tools sat a fragile project of (in)commensurability. That providing credit and using credit to emancipate were fundamentally incommensurate possibilities was more than ethnographically evident in the everyday enactment of feminist government in forms of care and control, paternalism and punishment, and discipline and empowerment. In Janam's governance of early marriage we see the increased propensity of feminist governmentalities—whether rights based or development oriented—to employ punitive logics to save women and secure their rights, not least given the institutional vacuum created by the state. Subaltern groups *contested* the more explicitly punitive stances taken by NGOs in their name—even when couched in a benevolent paternalism—but they also *consented* to feminist governmentality for multiple reasons: access to credit and other income-generation opportunities, employment, and—indeed, as chapter 5 will attest—for female friendship and community, for *dol*. Ultimately, however, consent shaped a relationship of dependency (not reciprocity) that NGO staff could use as leverage for projects of rescue and salvation.

The achievement of commensurability was impossible; it was also haunted by the needs and desires of the subaltern women in whose name credit plus rights was brandished. This book has already shown how such subjects assumed a strong but spectral presence in postcolonial queer feminist imaginaries. As with metropolitan middle-class queer activists, the spectral subaltern was key to the aspirations of development professionals who saw themselves as ethical and feminist. Recast as the face of the global microfinance movement, "the Millennial Woman" (Ananya Roy 2010) not only produced for local NGOs the desired commensurability between fundamentally incommensurate ends but also afforded moral authority, purpose, and legitimacy, besides greater material reach, in highly local—and not only transnational—ways.

As significant players in Kolkata's feminist field, both Janam and SFE were sites of feminist success but were also vulnerable to failure. While SFE was perceived as failing to penetrate the grass roots to stand in solidarity with the *graamer meye*, this failure, I argued in chapter 2, exemplified queer activism's tethering to a normative feminist past that haunted queer feminist possibilities in a neoliberal present—to ghosts who were never brought to life. The subaltern women who spoke on behalf of themselves in this chapter constituted the material and not merely imaginative possibilities and limits of millennial development; in refusing the offer of rescue and rehabilitation, they even propelled feminist governmentalities to failure. In far exceeding the imaginative scope of postcolonial queer feminisms, they failed feminism and embodied the rewards of feminist failure.[45] In chapter 5 we see the full rewards of such failing, in the subaltern reconstituted as an agent of development and a millennial feminist in her own right.

5
Subaltern Self-Government
Precarious Transformations

I was caged for life, in this life there will be no escape for me.... I was snatched away from my own people ... and was given a life sentence.... I would shed tears in secret but since I had to spend my life with these people, I eventually became a tamed bird.

Rashsundari Debi, quoted in Tanika Sarkar, "A Book of Her Own, a Life of Her Own," 1993

For so many days we were used to living in a closed box, spending our days inside it, but today we are out, and we are seeing a new world on this earth.

Supriya, Janam Vigil Group, Kolkata, 2013

She, too, refused to be governed.

Saidiya Hartman, *Wayward Lives, Beautiful Experiments*, 2019

From the ninetieth to the twenty-first centuries, the cage appears as a poignant metaphor for women to describe their experiences of public and private spaces in India. For an upper-caste Hindu Bengali woman of the nineteenth century, Rashsundari Debi, the household into which she was married at the age of fourteen was her cage. Her life entailed endless cooking and domestic service, from which she was released only with prior permission and under strict supervision, "like a prisoner out on parole" (Sarkar 1993, 47). At a time when education was out of reach for Indian women, Rashsundari secretly taught herself to read and write and emerged as author of the first full-length autobiography in the Bengali language. Fast-forward to the period just after the 2012 gang rape and murder of Jyoti Singh Pandey in Delhi, when women across the country sang songs, shouted slogans, held up placards, and asserted, against the wisdom of governments and families alike, that women should not be caged for their safety.[1] To "break the cage" became a rallying cry of urban feminist protest in millennial India.

The women that form the crux of this chapter—conscientized and politicized development workers in the nongovernmental organization (NGO) that I have named Janam—readily employed the metaphor of the cage or prison to describe their lives. These were mostly middle-class and lower-caste women who were married off young and whose lives had, not unlike the life of an upper-caste Brahman woman of the nineteenth century, been entirely absorbed by the demands of the *sansaar* (household). They questioned the purpose of their schooling given their days of endless unpaid domestic labor. If they undertook any paid labor at all, it was at home. This was the principal way in which women of their communities supplemented familial incomes, even as they were further folded into relations of dependency and invisibility within the household. Involvement in a local feminist NGO was their first encounter with the world of paid public work.

For Supriya, one of the women whose words begin this chapter, Janam had opened a door in a dual sense: it facilitated her literal movement, a "coming out" from the confines of the private to the public, while undoing the seeming ignorance that came with confinement, to see the same world anew.[2] Rural women employed well-worn spatial and visual metaphors to convey the depth and scale of personal transformation that Janam had enabled. Even these felt inadequate at times. As Supriya once said to me, "I don't know how to put this into words, but I used to be someone, and now I am someone else."

What Supriya struggled to convey was not simply a story of personal or self-transformation but one of self-creation, of how feminist development had provided the tools, techniques, and vocabulary to create oneself anew. The movement from being imprisoned to being free, from darkness to light, and from someone else to someone new were all suggestive of the same dynamic: of transformation in a queer feminist mode. Women like Supriya stepped out of the threshold of the home into the public with the highly intentional aim of challenging and transforming women's selves and souls—their "mindsets"—in line with widely circulating and increasingly normative ideas around gender equality, women's rights, and their empowerment. As opposed to its intended beneficiaries, it was the mindsets of these agents of development that were most changed, with their raised consciousness impacting spaces, relationships, aspirations, and intimacies that were not ordinarily imagined as sites of intervention and change. As Supriya put it, in an emblematic way, "Naam chhara shob bodle gaechhe" (Everything about me, except my name, has changed).

In presenting practices of self-work, self-transformation, and self-creation, I delve into the heart of the productive capacity of governmentality, or the self's ability to govern itself in novel, creative, and resistant ways. Like young urban queers, these rural women developed complex ways of relating to social norms. Their projects of self- and world-making were far more in the spirit of refusal and defiance, embodying the kind of wayward will that Saidiya Hartman (2019) describes.[3] Refusal was not, however, some site of purity; the space to critique, resist, and even refuse some norms also enabled subjection to others. Such messy entanglements revealed the contradictory effects of projects of self-making and asked what their implications might be in historical and regional contexts in which feminist and leftist struggles did not center the politics of the self.

The art of existence that feminist government enabled meant that these women workers returned to a lifeworld whose conditions of possibility had been both made *and* compromised by NGO-ization and neoliberal development. From my first encounter with this group of women, belonging to Janam's Vigil Group (VG), I wondered what it was that sustained their interest and investment in precarious and poorly paid development work. I returned to this question repeatedly as my relationship with them deepened and they openly and bitterly complained about pay at Janam. That I end on a cruelly optimistic note—in showing how new capacities and affective attachments were continuously frustrated by the very impulse from which they were born— shows how neoliberalism offers dreamworlds that do not materialize (see Kaur 2020). It also shows how some neoliberal variants of feminism become especially productive in this historical conjuncture and how their productivity draws on the intimacy of government and self-government. But that this chapter ends with negativity and "stuckness" (Berlant 2011) should not be read as undermining the deep and enduring attachments and positive affects that it otherwise uncovers. On the contrary, the projects of self- and world-making that this book foregrounds, queer and feminist, show the depth and complexity of our attachment to what is "nearly utopian" (Muñoz 2009).

Ghare and Baire in Liberalized India

In her book *Fearless Freedom*, Kavita Krishnan (2020, 12) provides staggering evidence to show how—across class, caste, and the rural/urban divide— Indian women live in cagelike conditions, under "almost-total surveillance." Krishnan is categorical that such confinement in the home is less about women's safety than a denial of their autonomy and personhood. Even as education and employment constituted the only plausible reasons for women to leave their prisonlike home, they could hardly do so unsupervised or without seeking permission from someone in the household. Education, in fact, "contributes only marginally to freedom of movement" (K. Krishnan 2020, 11–12), in contrast to the hopes of Rashsundari Debi that education would be the key to women's emancipation from dependency and domesticity. On the contrary, India presents a paradoxical situation in which the more women enter the world (*baire*) through education, the more they are folded back into the household (*ghare*).[4]

Since Rashsundari's time, when education was denied to women, India has witnessed a remarkable increase in women's access to and entry into education—especially higher education. Women of varying classes, castes, and religions have been able to claim the space of higher education in unprecedented ways, such that it has constituted "an exceptional bubble of relative gender parity" (John 2020, 146). It is all the more paradoxical, then, that India has one of the lowest female workforce participations in the world, which has dropped even as education levels have increased.[5] Unlike the reverse pattern in much of the world, Indian women's increased educational qualifications have resulted in an opting out of rather than into the labor market, for a range of reasons, including reduced employment opportunities for women in the postliberalization era, but also normative— and aspirational—ideals of domesticity and respectability. Unique to our context is the association of women's wage labor with the stigma of being from a lower caste or indigenous; Adivasi and Dalit women are those who labor out of necessity (John 2013). One of the major markers of upward social mobility in India is, then, to withdraw women from paid labor and farmwork into domesticity or housewifery. Megan Moodie (2015) calls this move "domestic respectability," or the acquisition of forms of status and capital through the ability to be nonworking women or housewives. She notes, "Domesticity in this sense is not a cage from which one must seek release, but a space of security and freedom from worry" (Moodie 2015, 91).[6] Ideals of domesticity and maternal self-sacrifice have found deeper, more resilient roots in West Bengal, where they have fueled political and not just social change. What Raka Ray and Seemin Qayum (2009, 122–26) call a "*bhadralok* patriarchy"—in which men earn and women run the household as a measure of being respectable (*bhadralok*)—means that women only earn if men fail to fulfill their patriarchal obligations. The women servants that

Ray and Qayum interviewed in Kolkata aspired to marriage and domesticity not as enslavement but as freedom.[7]

While female workforce participation in West Bengal is even lower than in comparable Indian states, women's participation in home-based cottage industries, key to the informal economy, is on the rise. Like social reproduction work, such highly feminized forms of labor tend to elude official governmental records and are prone to more general forms of societal nonrecognition. "This work was mostly coded as leisure time activity in which they engaged to earn some extra income to support the household and the husband," writes Sarasij Majumder (2021, 337) of small landowning middle-caste households in peri-urban West Bengal. The women of Janam's VG were of the middle to lower castes, with some identifying as Scheduled Caste.[8] If agricultural labor was not an option for them, then forms of home-based labor that nearly all of the women were involved in (sewing, crafting jewelry, or making umbrellas) were considered appropriate and not at odds with household chores or class and caste status. Husbands, on whom they were financially dependent, did *kaaj* (work) ranging from electrical to construction to business. Those women who came from more financially secure families took loans from Janam to support households—for instance, in the payment of ever-increasing tuition fees for children. Others took loans to afford more vital forms of support, like the purchase of auto-rickshaws for husbands. At one end were those women who claimed to be doing *shauk-er kaaj*, or working at the NGO for pleasure, while at the other end were those who told me that they worked for need, given the hard times the household had fallen upon due to an unemployed husband or a fallout with in-laws; their households had "only enough to eat."[9]

While four of the group were unmarried—though two married in the course of my knowing them—others had married young and had small children. Recall from chapter 4's discussion on early marriage that a majority had married early, certainly before turning eighteen, and some had chosen their own partners, even eloping to do so. All were literate and spoke Bengali (and little to no English). Otherwise, they formed a varied bunch of mostly young women, ranging from eighteen to their early thirties (with one middle-aged member), even as their status as wives and mothers would place them outside the category of youth and youth cultures in India. I heard different versions of how they were recruited to Janam, but the completion of some secondary schooling seemed to have been a determining factor. The compulsions of domestic respectability weighed heavily on this group of women as they entered the world of work: "Stepping outside the home, returning with money, and doing a *baaje kaaj* [bad deed]" was how Madhuri described her family's initial response to her working at Janam. Several of the women echoed these thoughts, with one vowing that even if paid work ended, she would persist. Such rhetorical strategies were also part of women's efforts to be respectable while undertaking not just (poorly) paid work outside of the home but activities like marching through the streets of Kolkata, a city that few had accessed on their own.[10]

It was testament to the closeness of this group of women that they represented their views in almost one collective voice, and I struggled to gather individual perspectives, which were only made possible in subsequent years through the mediation of technology (like, chats over WhatsApp).[11] Their self-making was, to this extent, a shared project, not least because the collective that Janam had willed into existence provided the possibility and pleasure of caring for one another as an intrinsic part of the care of the self.

Aesthetics: Styling the Self

In late 2018, I received a photo via WhatsApp from Mousumi in response to my asking how they all were doing. It was a photograph of the entire group, and they wore tunics with slacks or leggings. They all wore sunglasses. Over my years of interaction with this group of women, I learned to take talk about dress and style seriously as a site of actively working on and re-orienting the self. I had anticipated such talk when it came to urban queer activists, given the extent to which queerness is manifest in transgressions of gendered codes of dress and deportment (see chapter 3). For these rural women, who were also young but not considered youthful, technologies of styling the self were about fulfilling gender and class aspirations, for producing themselves as modern, middle-class, aspirational subjects. Styling was an embodied and deeply pleasurable labor of the self.

Married rural women engaged in meaningful sartorial choices as a way of indicating their changed—that is, NGO-ized—affects and dispositions, to produce themselves as urban and modern consumptive subjects, and to play and subvert the very idea of the mature respectability that their bodies were meant to embody and signify. In a theme that will recur throughout this discussion, these choices were articulated as changes to gendered con-sciousness that, while acquired at Janam, were not reducible to the NGO's interventions alone.[12] They spoke of wider transformations in the "rurban" (Nielsen 2018) with globalization, liberalization, and modernization, but also of regional histories and anxieties around changes to women's status, partly articulated through contestations over dress.

We know that the fashioning of the *bhadramahila* (respectable woman) in colonial Bengal was scarcely about clothing but instead about changing ideas of the nation at a moment of high nationalism. Respectable attire for middle-class, upper-caste women became, from then on, synonymous with the reformist sari, blouse, and petticoat. Well into the postindependence period, it informed the organized Left's disciplinary ideas on dress and "decency." For instance, in the 1990s West Bengal was rocked by several public scandals around a dress code for college students and women teachers of government-aided higher education institutions. The sari emerged in these debates as the only appropriately modest attire for working women to wear in public, with even the North Indian *salwar kameez* (tunics with trousers) being deemed unacceptable or less modest. The *salwar kameez* was subsequently deemed respectable for Bengali women in the public sphere, but newer items of clothing joined the list of "indecent" attire, including *churdiars* (tightly, as opposed to loosely, fitting pants), leggings, capri pants, and basically anything that women found physically comfortable to wear. Schoolteachers in Kolkata faced harassment, even violence, for not following the unwritten dress code of the sari, while there were media reports of schoolgirls being traumatized for wearing leggings at the district level. Neither the Left nor feminists were "able to contest the hegemony of the image of the *bhadralok* which had its roots in upper caste and Victorian moralities" (Choudhury Lahiri and Bandyopadhyay 2012, 20; see also Datta 2009).[13]

It is against such local constructions of gender and class that rural women's sartorial journeys—from saris to slacks—must be located and their subversive value mined. When I first met members of the VG, only the unmarried younger women of the group wore *salwar kameez*; the rest all wore saris, draped in a modern fashion, like Janam's middle-class *didis* (elder sisters). But as the demands for mobility grew, the sari quickly felt cumbersome. The first claim, then, for its relegation in favor of the *salwar kameez* was made on the basis of practicality and comfort. When I interviewed Dona, she gave me an example of how she would reason with her father-in-law about her preferred style of dress, affirming rather than negotiating what she wanted and needed: "Baba, I have to travel a lot and it is not comfortable to do that in these clothes ... it is problematic for me. I will wear them on days that I feel confident to run around in them, and on other days I will not."

If wearing a sari limited the body's capacities to labor in public, it was also restrictive in private, where the bulk of a woman's labor-intensive work was undertaken. A common story that the women shared with me was around their desire to wear a loose-fitting nightgown—a "nightie"—in their conjugal homes. Most in-laws (and some husbands) refused to allow newly married women this small luxury, arguing that it was inappropriate for brides to dress in such an immodest or sexualized fashion.[14] Women argued that it was inhuman to be in a sari all day, cooking in a hot kitchen. When not openly confrontational, they developed creative ways to evade such discipline, as another interviewee, Purnima, explained to me:

> I have taught my sister to wear her sari to lower the *kuchi* [pleats]. One day when she has gone to light the evening lamp, she intentionally tripped over her lowered *kuchi*. Hearing her scream, her mother-in-law came running and asked what has happened. Then she said, "I don't know how to wear a sari, but yet he [her husband] will force me to wear it and now I think my leg's broken!" Then she [her mother-in-law] said, "You wait, the moment my son returns I will tell him to buy two nighties for you!" Now she wears [a] nightie at home.

Purnima told me this story in her classically amusing style, embellishing the characters involved and making everyday gendered struggles all about creativity, agency, and play.[15] There was obvious pleasure and playfulness in these narratives of styling and performing the self (and of growing, concomitantly, in confidence and defiance). A playful performativity was similarly at stake in a *natok* (theater play) scripted and staged by Janam, which I happened to observe, as part of a series of events raising awareness around gender-based violence. Despite peals of laughter from other group members and protests from Janam's *didis*, Supriya stripped herself of all feminine and marital markers and reinvented herself as a male character for the play, wearing a T-shirt and a pair of men's jeans smuggled in by one of the women from her unsuspecting husband. This playfulness continued beyond the staging of the play and into individual homes, where wardrobes began to include a pair of jeans, much to the bewilderment of husbands. Dona's husband asked why she had not told him before purchasing jeans, to which she answered, "Your words wouldn't have mattered anyway." What mattered was women's expressions of desire, choice, individuality, and autonomy and their ability to imagine what could be possible through something as everyday as fashion.[16]

Still more transgressive were experiments with traditional markers of Hindu marriage. All the married women of the group wore the mandatory *sindoor* (vermillion) in their hair and a combination of white and red conch shell bangles called *shankha pawla*. These markers of the married self were absent only in the unmarried or widowed. Removing them not only raised questions about one's wifely devotion but even placed one's husband's actual well-being at risk, as they "aimed toward protecting the longevity and well-being of their husbands" (Lamb 2000, 224). In the aesthetics of the Indian women's movement, these markers of Hindu heteropatriarchy had little place and were challenged in urban feminist and queer feminist circles. Rural women, too, acquired—through their raised feminist consciousness—a criticality toward such symbolism; they asked why husbands did not display any markers of marriage.

The newest married member of the group, Dona, had none of the trappings of a new bride, wearing only one of the designated bangles as opposed to three, a smidgen of *sindoor* on her forehead, and *salwar kameez* as opposed to a sari. This kind of body work had been undertaken consciously, so when Dona's husband asked, snidely, "Is this what Janam has been teaching you?" she aggressively asserted, "Yes, a hundred times, yes." Eventually Dona overheard her father-in-law tell one of her nieces, "Bouma [daughter-in-law] wears things that I see actors in TV serials wearing, like *sindoor teep*; she looks quite lovely."

The *sindoor teep*—a small rather than a wide mark of vermilion on the scalp—was popularized among women following Hindi television serials that centered on the family life of the rich and the valorization of domesticity. In adopting this new, "barely there" *sindoor* style, rural women produced themselves as continuous with middle-class, metropolitan, modern—and not only feminist or NGO-ized—femininities. While the workers' new *saaj* (style) might have distinguished them from their rural peers—in terms of signaling mobility, modernity, and even empowerment—it did not mimic the NGO *saaj* on offer. Unlike the pure cotton that draped the "matte aesthetic" of NGO staff (Romani 2015), rural women opted for machine-produced synthetic saris that were cheaper and popularized in the Hindi television serials.[17] They also embraced aesthetic excess—gold jewelry, blingy sunglasses, shiny smartphones—reminiscent of the "shiny aesthetic" that queer activists felt they needed to shed to properly belong to radical queer activist circles in the city (Romani 2015; see also chapter 4). Rural women development workers were not so straightforwardly seeking belonging in middle-class spheres; their aesthetic labor was more in the nature of fashioning a distinct self. As one of the workers, Radha, put it, "The biggest thing is that I am a human being. I have something called choice, taste, and distaste ... why should I follow others?"

Affect: *Adda*, *Ghora*, and *Bondhura*

Young urban Indian women made a woman's rights to seek pleasure and have fun, especially in the public, central to a new repertoire of feminist resistance; it was also a way of demarcating themselves from "joyless" feminisms of the past.[18] These debates appear so removed from the everyday lives of rural women that the rural girl doesn't even make it to the typology of pleasure-seeking behavior ascribed to distinct categories of women—like rich girls and Muslim girls—in the pathbreaking book, *Why Loiter?*, which inspired many movements (Phadke, Khan, and Ranade 2011). Globally and historically resonant discourses—from international development to local feminisms—have endlessly produced her as joyless, submissive, and devoid of pleasure and desire. Tropes of exploitation, marginalization, and victimization have, in fact, proved handy for projects of "saving" subaltern women at scales both global and local.[19] From her interpellation as an "at-risk" girl in global development to her association—at the hands of local, metropolitan, and even queer feminists—with both lack and authenticity, the rural girl, it seems, just cannot have fun.

Women face such degrees of restriction and lack of sociality in rural India that even the opportunity to defecate in public is perceived as a welcome release from domestic confinement. In complicating the Bharatiya Janata Party's attempts to "empower" women through the provision of indoor toilets, Krishnan quotes a young daughter-in-law in Haryana as saying, "The reason that [I and my sisters-in-law] go outside [to defecate] is that we get to wander a bit.... You know, we live cooped up inside." Others explained how they, in fact, preferred outdoor toilets to indoor ones because they served as "our only excuse to get some fresh air, take a walk together and speak to friends without someone overhearing us! We make the most of it, dragging out the outings as long as possible" (K. Krishnan 2020, 91).

In rural Bengal, the idealization of domesticity—key to *bhadralok* patriarchy—entails that rural women's daily interactions occur in highly specific, circumscribed ways, involving mostly kin or, at most, neighbors (see Sanyal 2014). Men, on the other hand, have easy access to market areas and can be found hanging out at village tea stalls.[20] Gender itself was constructed, in the West Bengal village that Sarah Lamb (2000, 182) studied, "through people's movements within and beyond the home."

There was no "scope," as my interviewees would put it in English, for women like them to move beyond the confines of the household, suggesting not only a lack of opportunity and access but also the unavailability of spaces for sociality, leisure, friendship, and fun. Married—and especially newly married—women faced the greatest restrictions on their mobility, at the hand of in-laws. But it was no different for younger, unmarried women to move beyond preordained spaces, involving school, home, and tuition classes—so much so that some felt compelled to elope at a young age to escape the structure of suspicion and control that accompanied their every move. Drawing continuities between such surveillance before and after marriage, Mousumi remarked, "Before marriage it was [the] father's permission and, postmarriage, it's the husband's permission."

Women's access to the public sphere was conditional on their ability to cultivate and demonstrate the dispositions of being respectable. But was the restriction of mobility a worthy price to pay for being a good woman? As Dona asked, "What good is there in being *lokkhi* [compliant]? If one is *alokkhi* [disobedient], then she can roam around freely, but if she's *lokkhi* then she will never be able to get out of the home." Dona underscored the poor set of choices that Indian women were faced with between freedom and respectability, one that closely mapped onto the choice between freedom and safety that urban women came to reject after the gang rape and murder in Delhi in 2012.

From negotiating time outside the home for work, the workers began to extend work hours for fun and pleasure by using their purposeful time in the public to do other, unpurposeful things. At the close of almost four years of working at Janam, it had become quite common for them to "do *adda*" (catch up) for an hour or two after office hours, returning home at seven instead of at five p.m. It was these unpaid, unpurposeful, and highly public activities that ultimately came to constitute the basis of their abiding attachments to poorly paid development work. In anecdote after anecdote, VG women emphasized how *mawja* (fun) boiled down to the twin possibilities of catching up and going out—*adda* and *ghora*—with their friends (*bondhura*). Fun was informal and spontaneous, and in direct contravention of the norms that restricted women in the private sphere and masculinized public spaces of sociality and friendship. That work produced unproductive fun—the office itself was transformed into a space for *adda*, as I witnessed several times—also undermined neoliberal presumptions of the unlimited productive capacities of third world women (see Wilson 2015). Women's unproductive time was ultimately used in service of remaking the self; they contrasted a new self with an older one who never found the time to leave the household. Making this distinction, one of the VG members, Basanti, declared, "No, I will have to go out; going out is necessary."

Aside from the obvious echoes of such words ("I will have to go out") in a new feminist repertoire of resistance in contemporary India, Bengal had its own historic and exalted version of purposeless action, or *adda*. The quintessentially Bengali ritual of engaging in long, informal, and "useless" conversation was, however, a strictly homosocial and middle-class practice. If women partook in its pleasures at all, they would do so in their own separate sphere; Dipesh Chakrabarty (2000) writes of men and women's *adda* as replicating distinct male and female spheres of public culture in twentieth-century Bengal. He further notes the "noninstrumental pleasure" of *adda*, to which the demands of household and family acted as an impediment, and how, conversely, "every married woman looks on *adda* with poisoned eyes" (2000, 208). When rural women engaged in *adda*, they overturned the gendered and class-based segregation of public life upon which the terms of sociality, intimacy, homosocial friendship, bonding, and even the possibility of being *bhadralok* had long relied.

An old established cultural practice, *adda* was part of a new culture of fun and "hanging out" that the women created around their working life. Fun could be as simple and fleeting as coming to the office on a day that one was not required to go to the field and to opt for an outing instead—going off for a picnic and consuming a prepacked lunch elsewhere. On other occasions the women went to a *mela* (fair) that happened to be taking place in the area, and their memories of the day included eating street food (*phuchka*) and chatting (*golpo kora*). The pleasures of personal consumption, made possible by their meager earnings, were obvious in these accounts. While they may have included newer, more global, and status-defining consumer goods (smartphones), what was more striking were attachments to strong signifiers of the everyday, the ordinary, and the highly local, like *phuchka* and the *mela*. Fun was not organized; it was spontaneous, outside the routine, unpredictable, and even risky. Once, as we walked together to a *dol* meeting, the women hailed down an SUV, which we all piled into, and we were driven a short distance by a strange man: a small but telling incident of rural women's ability to court risk in public places.

These experiences illustrated a larger point about the self: that after several years of paid development work, family members would no longer question women's whereabouts; as Purnima explained, "Now when I come home late, nobody says a word." The women had one time consumed alcohol, and even this downright illicit act was later communicated to their husbands. "We don't keep anything secret," they said. Unlike other working-class women who tended "to enjoy" in secret (Gjøstein 2014, 150), there was no secrecy or shame involved. If anything, the burden of shame was shifted onto husbands who were made to feel inadequate in the face of the newly found pleasures of female friendship and sociality; as Dona stated, "We tell our husbands, 'Since you don't get the time from work, we will go out by ourselves!'"

Friendship is elusive for most women, given the maleness of public sociality and the fact that friendship itself is a "male social-relations category in India" (Gjøstein 2014, 150). Writing on Kolkata, Henrike Donner (2016) notes how self-chosen relationships among (urban) women, not belonging to the immediate family, tended to end with marriage. For rural women, development emerged as an unexpected site for developing a social network of friends outside kin relations and across castes and villages (Gjøstein 2014; Sanyal 2014; on the youthful urban poor, see Romani 2014). The VG women formed intense friendships with one another; the distance that they produced from *dol* women whom they considered "beneficiaries" of their labor contrasted with the closeness they developed with each other. Such intimacy—which continued after working hours, thanks to mobile technologies[21]—appeared to transcend social differences of caste and class; they were friendships "across difference."[22] Friendship also formed the basis of a solidarity politics, especially when it came to registering differences with their employer, Janam. The same Janam had provided a way of life—a *jibon*—whose defining feature was *bondhutto* (friendship), or friendship as a way of life.

Increasingly, women came to see the productive power of friendship in their empowerment work with other women. They evoked friendship as a considered strategy to curb the problem of elopement, echoing the views of middle-class and metropolitan Bengali mothers who stressed greater intimacy with their children for greater control (and not necessarily for more individual autonomy; Donner 2016). "I tell them to treat their children as friends so that they don't go tell their neighbors about their lovers but come home and tell their own parents about it," explained Supriya. She linked a lack of friendship with one's own children to parental failure: "We never learned how to build a friendship with our children and talk to them like a friend—in such a situation the girl *will* escape. I mean, my own child is not trusting me, and trusting somebody else. Why are they doing that? We are at fault. This is the main reason why they are escaping, eloping."

Having married at the age of fifteen, Supriya had two grown sons. One of them had recently fallen in love and was able to confide in Supriya with no fear of rebuke or retaliation. Alluding to the risks of teenage romance, like unwanted pregnancies, Supriya explained, "I say openly that if you, by chance, end up doing something wrong, then come and tell me. Tell me; as a friend, I will help you. You might ask me that, as a mother, how could I have said all this? I have. I have discussed this very frankly with my son." For Supriya, this growing trust and intimacy with her children and peace (*shanti*) in her *sansaar* was the best outcome of her *kaaj*.

Women's participation in paid work—a disciplinary domain imbued with new regulatory potentials—enabled the development of new skills, techniques, capacities, and affects in an entirely other domain of nonwork. It was in this domain that some of Janam's intended objectives and ends—to form bonds and friendships, to conscientize and collectivize, to challenge the self and grow in confidence—were more realizable than in the site designated as work, which was prone to the production of hierarchy, suspicion, competition, and control. Feminist work brought this group of respectable, mature rural women to fun, simple and frivolous, that did not compromise their ability to be good women, was not always couched as resistance, and might have had only transient or limited liberatory effects. Yet this embrace of joy mattered given the structural impossibility of female sociality, pleasure, and friendship, or for the rural girl to have a bit of fun.

Ethics: Care of the Self

Self-care: that can be an act of political warfare. In directing our care towards ourselves we are redirecting care away from its proper objects, we are not caring for those we are supposed to care for; we are not caring for the bodies deemed worth caring about. And that is why in queer, feminist and anti-racist work self-care is about the creation of community.
Sara Ahmed, "Selfcare as Warfare," 2014

Sara Ahmed's words—especially the redirection of care from others to the self—echoed in what VG members felt and said. They provided several illustrations of the "proper objects" of women's care, epitomized in the housewife who disproportionately cared for others over the self. "If I can keep others well, then I am well," was how Purnima explained this sociocultural expectation to me. Turning this norm on its head, she declared, "I can only look after others when I have looked after myself. If I don't eat and fall ill, then how will I look after my son, daughter-in-law, husband, home?"

Empowerment work acted—even as it might not have explicitly aimed—to foster "a kind of attentiveness toward the self" (Heyes 2007, 81; see also O'Grady 2004). It enabled not only a novel way of relating to the self but access to and a privileging of a previously unavailable individual self, as Monu's words attest: "In the past I never thought about myself, but now I see that, apart from my *ghar-sonsaar* [household], I am a person, and I will have to see to it as well." In such evocations of the "I" of a liberal humanism, we hear the echoes of Janam's gender-based training and consciousness-raising projects that were themselves a product of mixed and complex genealogies. Feminism was part of this lineage, but not one in which the imperative to politicize the personal had found a ready home. I evoke this history recalled earlier in this book to emphasize what the workers themselves insisted on— namely, the unprecedented ability to foreground the self, as an object of thought, care, and love, as powerfully captured in the words of Dona: "Unless *we* learn to love *ourselves*, none of this will work."[23]

Efforts to take care of the self made evident the everyday workings of power in the quotidian, where their gendered, disciplinary, and normalizing effects were especially opaque to recognition. Conversations around food, for instance, were sharp reminders of how power was exercised in the household not only through controlling women's access to food but through norms of docile femininity manifest in consumption practices. Hindu Bengali women were long expected to engage in ritual fasting, or to eat little, as a way of demonstrating their virtue, their selflessness, and their ability to care for others. "I used to eat the bare minimum," Mousumi once told me.[24] In my interviews, women voiced a newly acquired sense of individual entitlement, even a right (*adhikar*) to food. Dona expressed this entitlement rather matter-of-factly: "I mean, I will have to eat as well; why should I not?"

"Why should I not?" was a direct challenge to the patriarchal discipline that gendered unequal access to the production and consumption of food, in which women were meant to be indifferent to the food they themselves produced as a marker of womanly virtue. As she resisted such norms, Dona voiced new ones—"I will have to eat"—and, through it, shaped a desiring, consumptive, unashamed self.

If some of the queer activists in this book asked the subjects of their activism to know themselves *epistemologically*, development workers asked their peers to relate to the self *attentively*. While this attentive technology might have emanated from their training by Janam, the workers also expanded the remit of women's rights. Yes, women have rights to education and to a life free of violence, but they also have other rights, they explained. Rural women have the right to ask for and to receive care from others, and especially from the family members who are the primary beneficiaries of their care labor but on whom they can rarely make any claims for care: "The girl takes care of so many family members, and if she really falls ill one day, and if her husband looks after her, then what is wrong in that?" they asked.

Self-care required time—time that had to be stolen away from the mandatory care of others, from unending domestic chores that also left little by way of leisure time. Dona implored *dol* women to make time for themselves, while underscoring their lack of (nonproductive or leisure) time:

> I asked them, "You work in your household, but there is a different life outside of work. Do you need to think about yourself, or do something for yourself?" Everybody fell silent, and then they said, "Yes, [but] when will we get time for ourselves? Our whole life is spent on household work." Then I said, "I mean watching TV for five minutes, or listening to some songs—you could do that, right?" When I said this, one of the women said, "Didi, you are right. I want to watch TV, but I don't get time to do that either."

"Think about yourself, look after yourself, do something for yourself; why is this attention to the self so important?" I asked Dona. Rural women lacked space, privacy, and control over their leisure, even in their own homes; "I mean, they are not even allowed to watch TV!" she exclaimed. They could not envision the possibility of their own pleasure, whether in going out, eating something nice, or purchasing something small and personal. Instead, "their whole day is consumed by cooking meals. When I ask them what have they cooked, they give me a list, but when I ask them, 'Have you cooked anything of your choice?' then they wonder, 'My choice?' I mean, they can't even think about it!"

Dona's exasperation at rural women's inability to think of themselves would be readily shared by more class- and caste-privileged housewives in Kolkata. While these women (in Gooptu and Chakravarty 2013) bitterly complained of the neglect of their well-being and devaluation of their affective labor by the family, Dona implied that the rural women in her midst were unconscious of such dynamics. Her empowerment labor thus turned to the rearrangement of women's desires in this very specific respect, away from prioritizing the needs and interests of the family and instead toward caring for the self.[25] Knowing that care of the self had to be balanced with care of others and had to take place in a context of limited, even stolen time, Dona asked these rural women to carve out a mere "five minutes" for leisure—for watching TV or listening to the radio. She even provided a strategy by which the family could embrace and not reject women's expressions of autonomy and choice, however minimally expressed: "We tell them to make what they like eating and to feed [it] to the rest of the family. Then they [family members] will also pay heed to the women's choices." New technologies of the self enabled self-care to take place alongside—and not in contradiction to—the care of others. One's own access to and enjoyment of food did not compromise that of others in the household. On the contrary, one's own choices literally shaped the taste of others.

Consumption, it should be clear by now, informed these technologies of self-fashioning and self-care in key ways.[26] Returning to the sunglasses evoked earlier in this chapter, several of the VG women sported them in their WhatsApp profile pictures. The smartphone itself—which got bigger and shinier with each of my visits—was key to how the urban consumer was produced in peri-urban and rural settings. Fashion and consumption were not merely sites upon which the workers scripted new modern and middle-class futures for themselves but also sites that proved handy in their empowerment work with other women. They made women's ability to consume—or the lack of such ability—central to their thinking and mobilization of what "women's empowerment" meant and looked like on the ground.

One of the women, Monu, once told me that she worked on the "basic *adhikar*" that rural women were unaware of. She gave me examples of such rights, which included women's mobility (*cholaphera*) and buying and wearing clothes of one's own choice. She also reported from her field site: "You know what happened when the girl came all dressed up? Other women asked her, 'Have you started dating someone?' I have taught her to say yes to such remarks. So, she says, 'Yes, I date someone too. What is stopping me?'" What comes to view in this brief anecdote is a postfeminist repertoire in which individual women work on themselves—through forms of consumption, self-care, and aesthetic labor—to shape new subjective capacities and even to question the existing gender and sexual order. [27]

These dynamics are especially evident in Mousumi's narration of the strategies she employed to ensure that rural women were able to better receive care from others. Mousumi met a thirty-year-old mother of two whose husband was having an affair with another woman. When the woman wailed, "What should I do?" Mousumi advised the following: "We have plucked our eyebrows, pleated our saris; I have worn a [hair] clip that looks stylish. You should also try this.... The days when we are more dressed up, our husbands love us more."

Mousumi's story brings into view some of the more ethically ambivalent ways through which self-care operated—through a reliance on women's new consumptive potentials as well as the commodification of their bodies. Mousumi embodied and modeled a self-stylization that demonstrated dress, look, and consumer potential as indexing a new type of femininity, one that is sexualized, agential in working on the self, and possibly modern in abandoning traditional and modest demeanor and dress, all in the aid of the age-old goal of "keeping a man." Women's empowerment appears here as a "makeover paradigm" (Gill and Scharff 2011, 4) in which empowered women offer their own self-stylization to others, who appear ready for postfeminist subjectification (Dosekun 2020).[28]

We might worry of the effects of these postfeminist and neoliberal technologies of caring for the self: how they could enmesh women further in capitalist consumer circuits, normalize individual routes to empowerment, service heteropatriarchy, and even strengthen class divides among women. In her wonderful musings on Palestinian women's pleasurable public pursuits, mediated by their limited consumer capacities, Laleh Khalili (2016, 596) observes, "I can see how such pleasures are consumerist, although I do not know how to find a space outside of consumerism today if the consumption even of '15-cent nail polish' traps us in the circuits of exchange."[29] For lower-caste and lower-class women who were unevenly—and unfairly—included in an expanding consumer culture in a "new" India (through their wage-earning husbands, if anything), it is perhaps unsurprising that their ideas of pleasure and leisure and the ability to care for the self relied on small claims on consumption—for smartphones, street food, hair clips, and nighties. "Neoliberalism sweeps up too much when all forms of self-care become symptoms of neo-liberalism," writes Ahmed (2014c).

Politics: Intimate and Everyday

New technologies of the self—caring, attentive, and consumptive—provided an expanded repertoire of rural women's conduct and agency, especially within the household and in relation to immediate intimate others. The family is "one of the most vexed arenas for feminist activism," being among the most impervious to subvert and change "given its multiple sources of support and power (such as, religion, the law, and capitalism)" (Sunder Rajan, quoted in A. Sharma 2008, 173). Grassroots development workers were not able to intervene in power relations and decision-making in these arenas, in spite of the injunction to do so in state developmentalism.[30]

There was no similar obligation placed by Janam on its VG members. Yet their new sense of self, as agents of development and change, naturally seeped into the intimate structures and organizations of their own households. The VG workers not only advocated against the early marriage of their own children but also confronted what they saw as blatantly gendered and illegal social practices, like the giving and taking of dowry. In narrating, for instance, how she negotiated dowry in her affinal family, which entailed a common strategy of insisting that the amount being demanded as dowry was instead given to the bride as a financial investment in her name, Basanti remarked, "I use my own sense of just and unjust. I don't even spare my family."[31] Changing the self came to include changing one's family, just as women's commitments to changing their families emerged as an important marker of a changed self.

Women's earnings from paid work most obviously impacted the running of the household—through supporting school or tuition fees, for instance—besides fully funding their own personal expenses.[32] These women emphasized their financial independence—"we can take care of our own expenses"; "we are not dependent on anyone"—which linked to but also departed from the needs of the family and the household. But changes to personal and even family life were not reducible to monetary factors alone. Women took greater pride in rooting changed household dynamics in subjective changes in themselves, because of who they were and not merely because of what they did or how much they earned. The art of self-making accrued to women what money could not always guarantee: forms of acknowledgment, worthiness, respect, and respectability that they greatly lacked in private.

Women reported changes to the self that elicited new forms of recognition, including being subjected to sarcastic mockery and ridicule. Radha said that her family members would roll their eyes and say, "Look, she's started [arguing]." Laughing, she added, "They hardly expected that I would return from this job, as someone who protests (protibadhi)." Family members accused women of the arrogance of the educated, captured in the label of didimoni (a working woman, usually a teacher, one of the few genteel professions open to the bhadramahila; R. Ray 2000). Other common comments heard around the house included, "She has become too smart for her own good" and "God knows where she goes."

None of these aspersions could dampen the obvious joy and pleasure women took in performing these new identities of the feminist killjoy—

the *protibadhi* or the *didimoni*. Women seemed, in fact, to revel in these, especially in their newly entrusted skills to guide, shape, discipline, and govern the conduct of others. The household was a site for enacting such new epistemic and pedagogical skills—"we can present our thoughts with logic"; "now they ask for our opinion before doing something"; "now we understand what they are talking about"—with tangible results. "Previously," said Purnima, "they [family] didn't pay heed to our words. They wouldn't care about what we have to say. Now when the men of the family have a meeting, they call me and [then] I call the other three wives at home. They also need to listen to them."

Marital relations emerged as a key site of contestation and (re)configuration, reflective of wider expectations, aspirations, and ideas around love, conjugality, and intimacy in these peri-urban and rural areas. In a long tradition of women's participation in public political life in India, these development workers relied on the consent and support of their spouses: "We wouldn't have been in this position without their [husbands'] support," they all agreed (see Ciotti 2012; and Nielsen 2018). Two of the women had, in fact, left the VG owing to unsupportive husbands. Overwhelmingly, though, husbands did not seem to obstruct women's entry into the world of work, even as they might have struggled with the impact of a working wife. They appeared in women's narratives to be kind, reasonable, cooperative, and loving. Especially when it came to intimate struggles between mothers-in-law and daughters-in-law, husbands were reported as reining in their own mothers, supporting wives in domestic disputes, and affirming love and care as part of their rights and responsibilities toward them.[33]

Not all husbands were so forthcoming, however, and certainly not from the start. Supriya, for instance, was faced with constant questioning as to why she would arrive home late. She knew that implicit in this concern for her safety was a thinly veiled accusation that she might be abusing her freedom to work to do other (not respectable) things outside the home. Mousumi had to negotiate her husband's unwillingness to take on additional childcare responsibilities accruing from the new demands made on her time (mothers generally outsourced childcare to extended kin and in-laws).[34] Both women protested—Supriya through quiet but persistent negotiation and reasoning and Mousumi by threatening to leave her husband for her natal home. These narrations ended similarly, presenting pictures of transformed marital bliss, powerfully symbolized through the pleasures of food. Mousumi reported, "People say that when the husband returns home the wife is there to bring him water, but I ask my husband to make a good cup of tea. Sometimes I ask him to fry some *papad* [wafer bread], sometimes I buy some *chop* [a fried snack], and we eat it with *moori* [puffed rice] and *shingara* [samosa]." And Supriya explained, "On some days, I'm running late, then he makes the tea and calls me, saying, 'What is taking you so long? The tea will go cold.' I feel so happy inside!"

Couched in these narrations of intimate caring life were aspirations toward companionship, mutuality, and equality between husband and wife, or a warm companionate conjugality. In her rich reading of even richer love letters in 1990s Nepal, Laura Ahearn (2001) shows how changing ideas around romantic love, courtship, and conjugality stand in for wider social transitions, enabling individual men and women to produce themselves as particular kinds of people—modern, progressive, and developed. New literacy practices and social development programs facilitated such changes, of which consensual unions, elopements, and love letters were signifiers with contradictory gendered effects. In West Bengal, youthful choice in matters of love and marriage was evident in the rising numbers of elopements, enabled less by letters than by WhatsApp, and represented aspirations toward modernization but also anxieties around social and sexual transgression.[35]

Evoking the gender and sexuality training at Janam that they had all undergone (some of which was administered by Sappho for Equality [SFE]), Madhuri said, "In the past, we couldn't say anything.... I couldn't tell him when I wasn't in the mood and he was forcing me. Now, after these trainings, I tell him, 'It feels like you are raping me.'" Purnima asserted her own need for sexual pleasure, asserting with a laugh how she no longer even needed her husband since she had learned "the magic of two fingers." At other moments, the women mentioned intimate transgressions that questioned conjugal sacredness. Monu, for instance, had started to "chat" with a previously unknown man via her cell phone. Even as she couched this relationship in friendship, she expressed disbelief at how she had been raised to believe that "marriage meant being with one's husband alone." Women's reflections on consent, self-pleasure, and even illicit affairs could be located in, but were not reducible to, the wider governance of intimacies that NGOs like Janam and SFE undertook. Governmentalities directed at reforming marriage and motherhood facilitated talk of sex and not through the anticipatory logics of risk and violence alone.

Aspiration: "We Need a Future"

Let us return now to the notion of the caged home that women aspired to be free of. For Rashsundari, freedom served a specific set of class- and caste-based desires, including outsourcing domestic labor to servants (John 2013). The aspirations of rural women development workers of twenty-first-century West Bengal were modest. They desired a salary to continue doing what they loved, what they referred to as a *bhalo kaaj* (a good deed). Such new aspirations and capacities to aspire were rooted in and sustained by the unrealizable promises of NGO-ized feminism in a neoliberal age.[36]

Vigil Group women's aspirations for freedom had not been met through education. "Did I study to sit at home and stir a *khunti* [spatula]?" was a rhetorical question that conveyed considerable frustration at education's inability to deliver freedom from the confinement that came with early marriage, domesticity, and motherhood. Employment at Janam had the possibility to set things right—to put to productive use wasted years and unused capacities, and to make good of the failed or even false promises of not just schooling but of a new, shining India. We know that one of the hallmarks of neoliberal India was an expanding horizon of aspiration, especially (but not only) on behalf of the urban middle classes. Yet the structural and material conditions for the realization of these aspirations were never put in place; new aspirations and hopes were "weighed down by real structural impossibilities," write Jostein Jakobsen and Kenneth Bo Nielsen (2020, 151).

Janam's insistence that rural women stand on their own two feet felt like a recognition of the specificity of this context, where women's earning capacities could meet not only their own individual aspirations (for autonomy and agency) but also collective ones (for security and social mobility). The theme of economic hardship was ubiquitous in the narratives of the VG women—of unemployed or poorly employed husbands, of children who were fed only rooti, of households suddenly plunged into poverty. These were the concrete circumstances that obligated women to supplement men's earnings, not just to maintain precariously middle-class households from slipping back into poverty but also to meet the new kinds of consumptive desires that liberalization had produced and normalized. "What does even two thousand rupees amount to these days?" Radha once asked me as a way of rationalizing why it was not enough for one person alone to earn.

Unlike previous cohorts of volunteers at Janam, the members of the VG were paid a small stipend from the start, but this did not mean that the monetary and nonmonetary worth of their work was not a deep and constant source of tension (see S. Roy 2019). Their anxiety was also temporal, accruing not just from the paucity of the amount of stipend that they received but also around the promise of better pay, a promise that kept getting indefinitely deferred even as the demands of work and the remit of responsibility increased. What Janam defined as voluntary work included daily trips to the field and the office, writing up reports, performing plays, and participating in advocacy action. At one small-scale rally against a case of sexual violence in Kolkata, VG members worried about how they would return to their villages as the event carried on into the evening. Well-known city-based activists arrived and left by car, while the mobility of these women, whose presence swelled the ranks of any protest, remained dependent on their employer's will.

In our conversations, the women veered between expressions of their love for rights-based work and their bitterness at not being adequately paid or properly recognized for it. It seemed that wage labor eluded worth and value in the same way that domestic labor in the household did. There were, however, specific "economies of anticipation" (Cross 2014, 13) attached to paid work—a concrete sense of what investment in productive labor would return, in the form of greater purchasing power if not the kind of economic self-reliance that feminist development promised. Yet their efforts returned little, jeopardizing not just a precarious present but also possible futures. As one of the later members of the VG, Radha explained, "When my son is eighteen, he will know that I left him at home [when he was little] because I was working at Janam. He will ask, 'What was [the] point? What can you show for it?'" She evoked this imagined future conversation between herself, as a worker of neoliberal capital, and an adult, discipling son to underscore the "wasted" nature of her productive capacities (*bekar khete khete*). "We need a future," she put it candidly.

The present was lived in anticipation of a better but continuously deferred future. While women waited for a performance review with its promise of better and steadier pay, they were faced with an arbitrary mode of evaluation, through the introduction of an internal pay grade. Purnima, who received the lowest amount on offer, was a casualty of the new policy and told me, "I was very sad inside. The money is not the main thing. I was constantly thinking, Am I doing something wrong, and is that the reason why this is happening? I was feeling within myself that maybe I am not being able to do it right. Maybe I am not being able to change myself." Her sense of inadequacy—at being unable to change herself—showed the affective dimensions of this kind of precarious labor and how it translated into successful technologies of self-governance, discipline, and responsibility, on the one hand, and competition, individualism, and inequality, on the other. Supriya, who was paid the highest amount, directly challenged the inequality of the internal review by telling Janam staff, "If you want to pay, pay an equal amount or don't pay at all."

If the workers harbored fantasies of gendered and middle-class futurity, Janam was equally invested in its own fantasies and future. Staff members described the women who worked at the organization not as volunteers but as activists, even commending their choice to engage in activism "full-time." Funders, I was told by one project coordinator, wanted a "pure volunteer." This language, of "subaltern altruism" (A. Sharma 2008, 57), provided crucial moral legitimacy to NGOs that saw themselves as part of social movements; one staff member even surmised that if the volunteers were paid, then they would lose their fighting spirit.[37] The evocation of activist autonomy and altruism was also the clearest instance of Janam looking "backward," to secure local legitimacy through the norms of the Indian women's movement, and "forward," to align with the dictums of ethical financialization on a global scale. As we saw in chapter 4, subaltern women were key to the production of commensurability between credit and rights, where there was, in fact, none. These tensions also drove desires and justifications of voluntarism and reinforced the deeply gendered, class- and caste-based assumptions underpinning this kind of low-paid and precarious labor. Janam's staff were not elite but ordinary middle- and lower-middle-class upper-caste women for whom the idea of contributing to development voluntarily would also have little meaning. When I raised questions of pay with some of them, they provided a stock response: there was not enough external funding available to facilitate the kind of salaries that the volunteers expected for what was, ultimately, limited time and involvement at Janam. It was the volunteers' aspirations and anticipations that were, in other words, out of sync with the prevailing realities of the NGO sector.

When it came to interpersonal dynamics within the organization, the VG reported both seemingly insignificant incidents, such as *didis* taking credit for reports they produced, as well as serious instances of disciplining for poor performance and absenteeism. Most poignantly, VG women claimed that they were treated as *chakor*, the Bengali term for servant and deeply evocative of regionally distinctive class- and caste-based "cultures of servitude" (Ray and

Qayum 2009). Janam's director, Dia, once pointed out to me how midlevel staff came from modest backgrounds with limited social and cultural capital of their own. Their modes of disciplining volunteers were less ascribable, she argued, to a sense of hierarchy and entitlement than to feelings of insecurity and vulnerability relating to their own job and standing within the organization (she herself consciously challenged the reproduction of power and inequality within it). While such an explanation provided an important corrective to our tendency to view NGO staff as an undifferentiated and class-privileged whole, it did not explain why a sense of precarity among staff at this level was channeled into disciplinary behavior toward the most vulnerable of workers, themselves recipients of development.

Individual VG women understood these logics and their productive—and not only repressive—capacities well. They also behaved in distinctly class- and caste-based ways to the only other worker who was farther down the organizational hierarchy than they were—namely, the domestic worker who cleaned the office space. In treating her as socially unequal if not inferior—as a *chakor*—they were able to anticipate and manage some of the effects and expectations of being the precariat both within and beyond the organization. Ultimately, aspirations toward freedom and possible futures could only be secured, as Rashsundari's trajectory also made clear, through reconfiguring distinction in highly gendered and class- and caste-based ways.

Cruel Attachments

Was it all a waste? Many of my conversations with the VG women would certainly indicate so given the unfair exchange of women's labor in an empowerment market where they obtained little in return in both economic and noneconomic terms. Their own description of their productive capacities—time, labor, and affect—as "waste" confirms a wider recognition of neoliberal capitalist accumulation as relying on the disposability of women's labor and the dispensability of their attachments and aspirations.

Women workers struggled to abandon their attachments to forms of labor that were poorly paid, irregular, and even exacerbated their existing vulnerabilities. Faced with such limitations, the only option available to these women was to return to the normative folds of the household—to domesticity and dependence on men. Yet, many felt, in ways that echoed the linear temporalities of queer advance previously encountered, that there was no going back. As Supriya exclaimed, "Look at what they have done to us! We can't go back [to our households], but we can't continue like this, either."

Her words expressed a curious kind of impasse, of being stuck between newly available sets of aspirations, promises, and even "fantasies of the good life" (Berlant 2011, 3) that were structurally unrealizable *and* the inability to return to the only horizon of possibility formerly available—namely, conjugal domesticity.

Laurent Berlant (2011) describes attachments as being cruelly optimistic when they impede our thriving or flourishing, when they are not merely unrealizable but actively harmful, poisonous, and destructive. Her idea of cruel optimism goes some way to explain why poor and lower-caste women remained attached to a lifeworld despite its precarity and cruelty.[38] Moodie suggests, helped also by Berlant (2011), that young women whose lives were "defined by marriage as its horizon" experienced the same ambivalently, given how the conventional was a site of frustrated promises of "love, security, reproduction and futurity" (Moodie 2015, 136, 137). While for the rural women of this chapter marriage constituted the only available horizon of possibility, parallel horizons had opened up for them through waged labor in the business of doing good. New conditions produced a changed set of relationships to the conventional, thickening aspirations toward marriage, motherhood, and respectability, with desires for employment, earning and consumptive capacities, personal autonomy, mobility, and modernity. The conventional—especially the domestic household—was too slim to hold the density of these affective changes, expressed above all through a transformed mode of relating to the self.

At the heart of these rich accounts of self- and social transformation was the emergence of an aggressive resolve—a wayward will—to conduct one's self according to one's own norms. In place of ambivalence and acquiescence there was a resistance to dominant social norms—especially those that governed women's subjectivities, conduct, and mobility and restricted their agency to the private while offering little recognition or care. The work of the self on the self traversed these boundaries of the public and private to expand women's capacities and agencies—to enable them to literally "come out"—and generated forms of sustained critique, action, and new identifications. In the intimate folding of technologies of domination with technologies of the self—which we might call governmentality—lay the unexpected risks, pleasures, and possibilities of self-making within and against norms. This kind of governmentality, charged with the administration of life, also acted as a way of life that could yield a culture, an ethics, a new self, and intimacies that were not yet institutionalized—a way of life rooted, to recall one of my interviewees, in love and friendship.

Feminist governmentality produced forms of critique, self-reflexivity, problematization, and even resistance to an empowerment that these women knew to be nothing more than a waste. Some attempted to sever such cruel attachments in using their newly acquired skills in state feminism to seek other jobs, especially in government.[39] A few managed to do so and left Janam. For those, like Supriya, who stayed because they felt they had no choice, the lack of choice in *not* going back tells us something important about changing the self via one set of norms ("empowerment") against another (domestic respectability). Not going back held the queer promise of "a future world that resided in waywardness and the refusal to be governed" (Hartman 2019, xv).

Like the forms of queer governmentality encountered in earlier chapters in this book, individual and collective practices of the self disrupted some norms while enforcing, in their cruel attachments, the tenacity of others. We have witnessed the successful "hailing" of feminine subjects by older and newer technologies of making gender, sexuality, and class in idioms of self-care, individual autonomy, and even aesthetic makeover. We could assume, too hastily, that the care of the self that emerges from these narratives is nothing more than an instantiation of the governmentalities in which it is located—that is, neoliberal governmentalities that incited rural women to be thrifty, responsible, productive, and altruistic but also playful and desiring in specific (market-oriented, consumptive, profit-gaining, and respectable) ways. Neoliberal technologies of gender appear to dominate these projects of the self, recalling and even fulfilling fears around the co-optation of feminine and feminist subjects by neoliberalism. I hope this chapter shows that there is much to gain by parsing the ordinary outcomes of those lives and subjectivities shaped by long histories of care and development, of which neoliberal empowerment was only the latest iteration. The economies of anticipation at stake in the feminist development initiatives of the present need to be understood through the specificity and fullness of this history as well as the burden of the local.

As beneficiaries of entangled feminist governmentalities, rural women responded to age-old feminist injunctions to "stand on one's own two feet" in convergence with newer calls to be modern, developed, consumptive, and empowered. In taking up what was generally considered to be youthful activities—of fun, fashion, and friendship—these projects of self-making also responded to other currents transforming feminine subjectivities at present. I do not think it is a mere coincidence that, at a particular historical moment in which urban Indian women were incited to take fun seriously, rural women isolated fun as the affective force of feminist development. To take what *they* say seriously would entail greater scrutiny of how and why women, rural and urban, elite and subaltern, take up some technologies of the self, through their cruel attachments, in the face of the availability or absence of others. In a context where a feminist politics rarely foregrounded the politics (or the pleasures) of the individual self, older and younger women seem to be turning to the call to take care of themselves, which originates in dominant rationalities—of consumption, neoliberal modernity, and urbanism—that do not necessarily empower women. We can hear this as an iteration of the age-old problem of women's complicity in their own oppression, or we can listen to a call for the need and expansion of sites in which women can care for and develop new ways of relating to the self without entrenching their oppression.[40] For feminists in India and elsewhere, this might mean staying with the uncertainty and ambivalence offered in projects of self-making rather than accepting the closure of co-optation as a way of maintaining our own cruel attachments to proper feminist subjects and desirable feminist futures.

Conclusion
On Critique and Care

Letting go allows us to put the visionary genius of black feminism to work otherwise.

Jennifer C. Nash, *Black Feminism Reimagined*, 2019

Let me return to the politics of telling feminist stories on and from the Global South with which I began. I want to recap the stories I tell in this book while also drawing attention to other, unfolding stories of feminist self- and world-making. The preceding chapters have offered a partial and subjective—"motivated"—account of the feminist present (Hemmings 2011, 16). Even as this book has centered the "other" of feminist subject-agents in the Global North, it has excluded still others; the multiplicity and diversity of feminist politics and subjects complicates efforts to be exhaustive and representative. Clare Hemmings (2011) reminds us that exclusions and partiality are intrinsic to all accounts in ways that elude forms of "corrective labor" (Nash 2019, 49). Instead of striving to provide more inclusive and representative—better—stories, Hemmings urges us to write stories differently. I want to end by taking her invitation to tell stories differently—rather than tell different stories—and do so with nuance, complexity, and responsibility. This returns us to the question implicit at the start of this book: Who judges? Who judges which stories should be told and in what way, and how does the power to judge interpellate the feminist as critic, as located outside and not within an imagined *we* with which this book began?

In the inaugural essay of the British journal *Feminist Theory*, Sara Ahmed (2000, 97) asks, "What counts as feminist theory?" This, of course, begs another question: What is feminism (and what is theory)? The question conjures the ghostly image of someone who is doing the sorting, the classifying, the counting: "Upstairs in the dusty attics of our institutions, counting out theories, counting out feminisms . . . I can almost hear her voice, gleeful and joyous, as she throws out some works, names them as impostors, saying that they don't count, that they can't be counted. Am I that woman? Have I been her? Are you her? Have you made such judgements with the ease of the one who is counted, of the one who counts?" (Ahmed 2000, 97).

Many activists will recognize this figure as the feminist academic who, notwithstanding her politics and claims around solidarity, has the institutionalized authority and power to engage in the business of counting—and critique—and not just of knowledge production. Given long-standing anxieties around the divide between academia and activism, feminist theorizing might feel incommensurate with the will to change the world. Feminist critique has also been heard as causing friction within activist communities and foreclosing the possibility of a shared *we* that academics and activists might together inhabit.[1] This book tries to undo certain normative claims—about the feminist present and its horizon of political possibilities—but also engages in normative assumptions of its own, which will, no doubt, "be judged as judgmental" (Ahmed 2017, 2). In closing, then, I explore how the book interpellates me as a critic whose "bad feminist habit" is to undermine, rather than understand, activist affects and efforts (Ahmed 2014b). I follow the mediations of fellow feminist theorists in reflecting on what might it be for our critical practice to offer other possibilities through, for instance, the offer of critique as care in sustaining queer feminist selves and worlds. I take this deeply generative and ethical notion from Mayanthi Fernando's (2019) reflections on the life of scholar and teacher Saba Mahmood, whose critical practice was in service of care and hope—for others and for the world. Against the polarization of critique and care, Fernando looks to Mahmood and, through her, to Michel Foucault for critique as a way of both undoing and repairing. Critique pushes against the limits of what we know to be certain of the world—and of ourselves—and, simultaneously seeks to move beyond those limits to transform what exists. It is thus not only reparative but a fundamentally transformatory practice. "There is something in critique that is akin to virtue," wrote Foucault (1997b, 25).[2]

Stories within Stories

This book has told a specific story of the making of queer feminist government and subjects in a time and place of global neoliberalism. It has provided an account of some of the new (nonstate) arts and technologies of governance that emerged in India, postliberalization, as constituting the conditions for individuals to make themselves in a novel fashion. I thus tell two stories at once—of government and of self-government—and of their intimate entanglement that matters in ways that I stress in what follows.

But first a recap of the story of government against an environment of expanding global neoliberal capital, which informed nongovernmental (NGO) and activist sites of queer and nonqueer feminist interventions. The two organizations examined in this book, Sappho for Equality (SFE) and Janam, appeared less products of distinct, even antagonistic (queer and feminist) histories than part of a conjoint world of human rights and millennial development in which they traded in sexual and gender rights in the empowerment of selves and others and in the business of doing good. Funding pushes and pulls meant that they often spoke in one voice through the language of rights, empowerment, education, and entrepreneurship. They found themselves on common platforms—united by common city-based causes around gender-based violence—and in mutually beneficial collaborations. Sappho for Equality provided sexuality training to Janam's rural beneficiaries in ways that fulfilled funding obligations around outreach, with Janam being able to reposition itself around gender and sexual rights to attract new kinds of institutional support. Not all could equally participate in the new flows of state and transnational development funds that ran through the region, even as these shaped its feminist counterpublic and transformed the imaginative and material scope of a preceding leftist era. And even those who could participate did so in precarious and transient ways; circuits of entry into neoliberal global capital were ones of inscribing new forms of dependency and precarity. Queer activism—marked by "an abundance of marginality and insufficiency of stability" (Rubin 2011, 356)—was also compelled to enter these circuits, in ways that are not always captured by the term and feelings around "NGO-ization."

If these felt like very global stories, then they were also intensely local. Notwithstanding their newness, millennial forms of queer feminist organizing revealed sharp continuities between the past and the present. This book thus reiterates, alongside others, the significance of place and time in processing traveling or even placeless dynamics, like NGO-ization and neoliberalism, and highly contemporaneous configurations, like millennial development or neoliberal feminism. In making sense of contemporary interventions into the lives of the gendered and sexualized poor, I turned not only to transnational forces but also to long, resilient histories of managing and empowering subaltern groups in the Global South. Neoliberal governmentality built on but never erased these existing rationalities and practices, repurposing them to new, market-oriented logics and effects. If these dynamics were obvious in the case of Janam's everyday empowerment efforts, then they were implicit in SFE's intimate governance of queer lives, which drew on a leftist humanism and pedagogical technologies of guidance, schooling, and discipline. The Left informed the embodied orientations, aesthetics, and sensibilities of activists—from NGO *didimonis* (teachers) to *aantel* (intellectual) queer feminists—whose personal biographies were not traceable to the organized Left and to which they, and the organizations of which they were part, bore little to no allegiance. And yet their bodies—just their *saaj* (dress)—spoke of the multiple political traditions that had seeped from one governance project to another, "constructed as new or antithetical" (Salem 2019, 3).[3]

Millennial feminisms were shaped by the historical structures of knowing and feeling that shaped the contours of postcolonial politics, both leftist and feminist. In ghostly figures like the *graamer meye* (the subaltern lesbian of rural Bengal) we see that organizations like SFE and Janam were ridden with specifically metropolitan burdens and anxieties around what politics ought to look and feel like in the postcolony. The ghost of the *graamer meye* embodied some of the limits of metropolitan feminisms, but she also fortified, in her assumed passivity and reification, their own subjectivity and agency. Normative assumptions—around what feminist politics ought to look like and on whose behalf it ought to mobilize—thus shaped specific relations of power and inequality. Queer feminists were deeply attached to these normative logics, which had marginalized their own injuries, in setting up false hierarchies between merely cultural and more material concerns. And while both queer and nonqueer feminists attempted to resolve the tensions of middle-class metropolitan feminisms, they created their own exclusions in ghosts and space invaders.

Spectral figures and their capacities to haunt the postcolonial present have been hailed for their capacity to disrupt global temporalities and their hegemonic subjects, but my story of postcolonial haunting comes to a different conclusion. For millennial feminists, both queer and nonqueer, the burdens of the past—its unfinished business and afterlives—did not always propel the telling of different stories of Indian feminism, its subjects and objects. On the contrary, the normative weight of the past served to sustain relations of paternalism, exclusion, and othering, in ways that reproduced rather than challenged structural inequalities *within* non-Western metropolitan feminisms, especially along the lines of class, caste, and location.

Postcolonial hauntings produced "defensiveness" (Nash 2019) as a key feminist affect in the neoliberal present, even as this moment contained the possibility of encountering the ghosts of the past in a different way and of telling feminist stories differently.

Throughout this book we have encountered the *graamer meye* as both a spectral and embodied figure who inhabited a series of complex subjective positions. In the villages in which Janam worked, she was an oversexed adolescent, a child who lied, and a Hindu woman who voiced anti-Muslim rhetoric. A key object of feminist governance, she frustrated transnational efforts around rescue and rehabilitation, even bringing them to their limits and ends, and confounded metropolitan feminist desires for feminist subjects sutured to secular, leftist, queer values. The *graamer meye* directed the course of a metrocentric queer feminist activism, not letting it stray from appropriate objects and ends, especially in a time of unprecedented queer progress. We glimpsed her desires—for friendship and love—as invaders of online and offline queer worlds, leaving us to imagine what a story of queer feminisms in India would look like with the complex desires of the *graamer meye* at its center and in which metropolitan activists and their fantasies would figure as *other*.

On the flip side of government—that is, self-government—this book began to mine the stories of metropolitan Indian feminism's others (queer, transgender, subaltern) as feminist subjects in their own right who are worthy of recognition, complexity, and critique. In positing, moreover, an intimate relation between government and self-government, I showed how one constituted the conditions—the ground—for the emergence of the other in creative and critical forms of self-transformation. Even as activists and NGOs might have acted in a regulatory and disciplinary manner toward their objects, their practices also constituted the grounds for other kinds of possibilities to emerge. It is thus not surprising that in their explicit call to work on and change the self, feminist queer governmentalities nourished rich projects of self- and world-making in which Indian millennials from very different social backgrounds could experiment in new acts, tastes, relations, and subjectivities. Development and activist spaces proved far more productive for individuals to work on, care for, and transform themselves than to empower others.

Projects of individual self-making—and not just being made—enabled me to think of the diverse and messy subjectivities constituted in and through multiple governmentalities in the current neoliberal conjuncture. It also afforded me insight into the intimate labor—the costs and the pleasures—of crafting self and life under precarious neoliberal conditions that tend to squeeze out possibilities of caring for and nourishing the self. The diminishing possibility for the care of the self is reiterated in those analytics that tend to reduce subjects to the hegemonic conditions through which they are produced, as if these could so easily and exhaustively extract all agency. Neoliberalism's unique extractive potential should, if anything, propel greater scrutiny of how it incites individuals (women, queers) to relate to themselves in new ways. This rings especially true of locales in which cultures of emotion and selfhood are poorly developed, as I noted in this book's introduction.

If there is room for more complex reckonings of the becoming of neoliberal selves in the Global South, then this is especially true for subaltern subjects. When not silenced or static, they speak to either confirm the despairing effects of power or register resistance against it, the exemplar of feminist agency. We place, in other words, a disproportionate burden on subalterns to act as an antidote to neoliberal hegemony and its detrimental effects while rationalizing any positive affects as false consciousness. In the intimate lives of the rural women who constituted the core of this book, "empowerment" translated into both a heightened, and previously unavailable, individualism and new forms of intersubjectivity, conjugality, consumption, and care. Affects of joy and pleasure persisted *despite* the knowledge that the horizon of possibility opened by feminist developmentalism and rights discourses would not necessarily materialize. The disappointment of this world did not negate its many and varied pleasures—from the embrace of nonproductive, frivolous fun in public to changed forms of domesticated conjugality at home—and illustrated a simple truth that Sami Schalk (2018, 143) stresses: "Pleasure does not exist outside of oppression because none of us exist outside of these systems of power, but pleasure can nonetheless arise in the midst of oppression, in the face of it, in spite of it, or sometimes even because of it."

The entanglement of pleasure and power is merely one instance of how self-government was less a site of purity than one that exemplified the messiness of the everyday. I have been careful to show that self-government did not always nor necessarily amount to a disruption of dominant governmentalities. On the contrary, it is because self-government relied for its productivity on government that it did not constitute any resistant agency. It is also owing to this intimate entanglement of government and self-government—of making and being made—that neoliberal variants of feminism appeared especially productive in my ethnographic sites. Young women and queers relied on new cultures of consumption, intimacy, and enterprise for propelling an empowered self. Against an expanding urban economy and intensification of a middle-class consumerist common sense across an urban-rural divide, these were the concrete forms of neoliberal subject and self-making.

Feminist and queer selves also articulated aspirations to chart nonnormative futures, but not without normalizing effects. These contradictions were especially tangible in the case of queer activists, and even drove new forms of moral regulation and discipline in the name of queer livability. Individual queers performed an intricate dance with norms, in and out of multiple closets, which made only partially visible the complex intersections of class, caste, gender, and sexuality. These everyday negotiations with norms, normalizing practices, and antinormative aspirations took place, moreover, at a time when queer Indians were coming out of closets that literally bore the markers of globalized, metropolitan, and upper-caste privilege. Who chose to rearrange what was in their closet said as much as who chose to come out or remain in the closet and under what conditions. The closet thus tells a specific story of queer "success" in neoliberal India, of how queerness relied on the normalization and reinforcement of class and caste privilege even as it disrupted gender and sexual hierarchies. It offered activists more complexly intersectional struggles rather than clear lines of resistance. And while they looked toward the *graamer meye* for moral direction—as a way out of the co-opting potentials of the present—she, too, engaged in acts of coming out and crafting a new closet for an empowered, sexualized, even postfeminist self. Against the tendency to set apart elites and subalterns—and make one the repositories of the fantasies and fears of the other—this book has strived to show them both as subjects equally mired in but not exhausted by power.

Critique beyond Co-optation

I have been motivated, in no small measure, to tell these stories to expand the scope of existing accounts of the feminist present, to make room for the kinds of messy subjects and their contradictory desires, aspirations, and capacities that I discerned in liberalized India. But in telling different stories, this book does not provide cause for celebration. On the contrary, it has uncovered the need for a sharper set of reflections and critiques than is currently available—in arguments around co-optation, for instance.

Indeed, co-optation is a powerful mode of structuring knowledge and feelings around feminism's changing fortunes under neoliberalism. Co-optation articulates with a kind of defensiveness that Nash (2019) finds core to the affective universe of contemporary Black feminism, manifest in how intersectionality is defensively thought of as being appropriated by and in need of rescue from others, beyond Black women and Black feminists. Feminism's co-optation is similarly imagined as "misuse, wrongful circulation, and theft" (Nash 2019, 43) in ways that trap feminists into property logics and forms of defensive corrective labor, and it ultimately limits feminism's expansive or world-making capacities. This book turns from co-optation to entanglement, especially at a time in which contemporary feminist struggles find themselves in a peculiar position of being not excluded from power but able to access and exercise it. Entanglement offers a way of grappling head-on with the contradictions and tensions of the moment while reminding us that feminism's proximity to power is not newly experienced in the Global South. Feminism's co-optation is, in other words, better understood as an entanglement in historic and ongoing relations of power, in ways that complicate assumptions of purity and desires for solidarity.[4]

In the *graamer meye* we find some of the historical and regional entanglements in which millennial queer feminist activism found itself: how socioeconomic difference, linguistic and locational hierarchies shaped newer, queerer, and more global forms of millennial Indian feminism and its relation to others. Local activists' access and ability to remain in a competitive market of social movement activism relied, for instance, on highly local forms of capital, which were amenable to global upscaling. It relied on subaltern subjects as not just imagined objects of discipline and rescue that provided visibility and legitimacy but also as the actual deliverers of millennial development on the ground. These entanglements—that I have also thought of as a confluence of "older" and "newer" governmentalities—produced their own opportunities and tensions that activists were far from oblivious to. And yet, organizational modes of mitigating some forms of exclusions and inequalities—or even navigating the contradictions of the neoliberal conjuncture—had the paradoxical effect of naturalizing and depoliticizing others.

For instance, to assuage their class, caste, and metrocentric limits, both SFE and Janam (re)produced the grass roots as a space outside time and place—as reified Bengali rurality—with a "pure" feminist subject to speak on behalf of and to save. They turned backward to prior models of passion-driven autonomous Indian feminism to legitimize forms of moral regulation and even material inequality. Queer activisms that resisted being consumed by neoliberal and homonormative (homocapitalist) governmentalities were nevertheless spaces in which social hierarchies endured such that caste markers were lived in closeted ways. As a limit where "queerness failed or queerness couldn't reach" (Kang 2016), caste has perhaps the greatest potential to expose the frictions and foreclosures of more privileged modes of queer life-making in India today.

It is only by tracing these longer and more intersectional histories that we see how, in their efforts to ward off the co-opting dangers of the present, queer and nonqueer forms of feminist organizing could normalize and even reproduce certain biases and hierarchies. In a curious reversal of activist- and funder-speak on intersectionality, I found a limited kind of intersectionality at work in these spaces; organizational logics could only partially recognize and thereby obscured some of the complexities of Indian lives, both middle-class and subaltern, and the needs and desires these signaled. When confronted with a range of feelings—from queer women's desires for inclusion into market and marriage, to the depth of subaltern women's communal attachments—activists opted for moral regulation to convert bad queer subjects into good ones or denied subaltern women's expressions of politically ambiguous affects. Organizational strategies that fall short of doing the genuinely complex work of building solidarity across differences, even when they demonstrate commitments to intersectionality or diversity, have been attributed to global funder-driven obligations. But in this feminist field, single-issue, top-down vanguardist politics had other lineages that had struggled with difference; they had adopted a liberal humanism to eradicate rather than recognize and politicize difference.[5] Whether a product of left-wing humanism, or the tensions of the neoliberal conjuncture, or even attempts to negotiate these very tensions, fears around co-optation undercut alternative possibilities of naming difference, challenging exclusion, and thinking intersectionally.

Critical observations of this kind—of the reproduction of inequalities and hierarchies in spaces meant for their undoing; of inadequate or even anti-intersectional orientations; of denied difference and unspoken feminist frictions—confirm existing critiques of NGOs as co-opting and emptying feminist struggles of their radical potential. My story might well reiterate the analyses and feelings that I have been trying to move away from—namely, that some forms of feminism are "bad" and doomed to co-optation and failure. Such bad feminisms ensure, in turn, that there are good uncompromised feminist projects and subjects to preserve and protect—and defend—in the world.

Notwithstanding this book's attempts at a different critical orientation, I have little doubt that the activist and NGO communities who constitute its core will either not recognize themselves in my judgments or receive them as a form of injurious critique that can hurt and harm. It will also be easier to receive such critique as emanating from *outside* than from within these spaces, even as it is those subjects who unequally inhabited the activist *we* who pushed against the limits of activist and NGO governmentalities. That the "spectral figure of the critic" might end up being the most audible says something about the academic's participation in the politics of speaking for, but also how internal critique becomes externalized and attributed to an outsider (Nash 2019, 35).[6] And finally, at a time when civil society is not simply being squeezed out but fundamentally starved of resources and criminalized by authoritarian governments, it might prove impossible to hear of the contradictions inherent in these very spaces.[7]

My anticipation, in a paranoid vein, of the responses that my own writing might generate resonates with the defensiveness I have attributed to those I critique. Defensiveness might well be the preferred affect of the feminist academic who feels too much the weight of judgment for her own capacity to judge, to count, and to discount. She becomes the lonely woman of Ahmed's (2000) paranoid image and reiterates the logics of the good versus bad feminist. In considering how critique produces the bad feminist, Ahmed turns to Karen Barad, who says, "I am not interested in critique. In my opinion, critique is over-rated, over-emphasized, and over-utilized, to the detriment of feminism" (quoted in Ahmed 2014b). Barad's words imply, explains Ahmed, that the problem is feminist critique rather than *what* feminists critique, with the added implication that "to free feminism we need to let go of critique" (Ahmed 2014b).[8] Yet there might well be other things that we need to let go of, rather than critiquing (or caring about) feminist politics.

Instead of trying to defend and save intersectionality from its (non-Black feminist) critics, construed as violent and destructive, Nash advocates a "letting go" of defensive corrective labor while accepting that "letting go is a risky proposition.... To speak on behalf of black women is politically powerful, a seemingly virtuous form of agency. And yet ... it locks us into feelings of defensiveness" (2019, 130). Under neoliberalism, practices of speaking for and affects of defensiveness are intensified in how they create currency for those who can most demonstrate unmediated access to subaltern subjects in the expansive grass roots that is the Global South. "Letting go" of these might well expand, both imaginatively and materially, what feminism can do and be in neoliberalism.

Letting go

Sappho for Equality's own trajectory offers a powerful moment of "letting go," with activists embarking on new ways of relating to others and to the self, beyond defensiveness. In 2020, on the eve of the twentieth anniversary of Sappho, SFE's forerunner and support group, a statement issued on the SFE Facebook page included the following:

Our location in an urban middle-class setting has brought with it certain advantages and resources. We remain aware that such privileges often tend to create a divide with other geographical and social cultural settings that might not be equipped with the resources that we have been able to access. While we have taken this critique seriously keeping the lens of reflexivity focused on ourselves, we are also careful not to self-flagellate ourselves to the extent where we end up producing locational binaries between an "authentic non-urban" and an "inauthentic urban." After all, the urban, middle-class is not a homogenous reality, and numerous individuals, who despite being located in urban middle-class settings, are the target of different forms of violence within domestic and familial spaces. Therefore, we stand to work across this locational difference. We are reflective of the fact that there is a need to unpack and understand such labels that tend to reduce the complexity of lives lived at intersections of diverse marginalizations and privileges in different geographical scales.

These words offer a different orientation toward critique, where self-critique sits alongside or at least does not substitute for self-care. They resurrect the more expansive role of the critic as one who practices critique as a form of letting go, to care concomitantly for the self and the world. Indeed, millennial India offers many moments to let go—of what we think feminism must do or can be—and to begin anew.

Care: Feminist Life- and World-Making

It's a home, a daily routine of sending kids to school, cooking and taking turns for household tasks, it's a women's protest, it's shyness and anger, it's "I have never spoken in a public place," it's "I have always been a housewife, but I am here."
Sarover Zaidi and Samprati Pani, "If on a Winter's Night, Azadi . . . ," 2020

In Shaheen Bagh, the women's full-time job—carework—has taken the shape of a revolution.
Rajvi Desai, "In Shaheen Bagh, Muslim Women Redefine Carework as Resistance," 2020

Care has been an implicit thread running through this book. If the activists of SFE were in the business of offering others care and protection through human rights, then Janam's workers offered forms of support, information, and resources that have become core to women's social reproductive labor at the community level. Both sets of individuals were involved in the kinds of activities that sustain, if not transform, everyday relations and forms of social life, ones that have been thought of as life-making work under capitalism and disproportionately undertaken by poor, minority women (Jaffe 2020).

In the years after the data for this book were collected—and when its written form took final shape—questions of care gained renewed, even unprecedented urgency, amid successive kinds of national and global catastrophes. The end of 2019 and start of 2020 saw the eruption of protests against the government of Narendra Modi around the Citizenship Amendment Act (CAA), a law that was passed by the Indian Parliament on December 11, 2019, that made it possible for non-Muslim religious minorities from Afghanistan, Bangladesh, and Pakistan to obtain Indian citizenship. Alongside the equally controversial National Register of Citizens (NRC), oppositional forces considered this move as one of disenfranchising Indian Muslims of citizenship and fundamentally writing secularism out of the Constitution of India.[9] These steps were only the tipping point of an aggressive Hindu majoritarianism that showed no signs of slowing down since Modi came to power in 2014. During Modi's first term in power (2014–19), the lynching of vulnerable minorities—predominantly Muslims, but also Dalits—in the name of protecting the holy cow, and the hounding down, intimidation, and arrest of activists, journalists, and academics as "antinational" became commonplace.[10] The second term—which began with a resounding electoral victory in 2019—witnessed the rise of Hindu nationalist statecraft in the form of successive legislative measures geared toward the consolidation of the Hindu rashtra, including the abolition of Kashmir's statehood, the NRC initiative in Assam, and the Supreme Court of India's ruling in favor of the Hindu Right in the Ayodhya dispute (see Nilsen 2020).

The protests sparked by the CAA were the first nationwide challenge to the hegemony of the Bharatiya Janata Party (BJP) and brought Indian democracy—in ways only comparable to the Emergency of 1975–77—to "nothing short of a breaking point" (Nilsen 2020). In a matter of weeks they swept across the nation and gathered up people from all communities, classes, and castes, from towns, villages, and cities. Thousands of arrests and utterly blatant acts of state-sponsored violence—on, for instance, resisting students at Delhi's Jawaharlal Nehru University and Jamia Millia Islamia—did little to stop their expanding reach and intensity. Women were at the forefront of this uprising around what was ostensibly not a women's issue, with 333 women-led protests, including 165 sit-ins, being registered in a period of just a month and a half. The most famous of these was the sit-in at Shaheen Bagh, a working-class Muslim neighborhood in Delhi that emerged as the face of this revolution.

For one hundred days and nights, hundreds of Muslim women, some in their eighties, sat in a tent and braved an unusually bitter Delhi winter; they were undeterred by right-wing threats, police intimidation, and media slander in their demand that the government roll back the new laws. As the words of some observers that opened this section suggest, these women spoke on behalf of themselves and their families, as both Indian and Muslim. They spoke of domestic routines and of speaking out in public; of being housewives and protestors; of shyness and anger; and of doing carework as revolutionary work. Shaheen Bagh inspired similar women-led sit-ins across the nation, including a significant one in Kolkata's predominantly Muslim neighborhood of Park Circus. Anchita Ghatak (2020) observes how many of the hijab-wearing women who joined had "never before thought of themselves as active political agents" and how "the past few days have changed them in ways that they can't yet fathom." Through their criticism of the government and their care as the work of the revolution, they had changed. Would they be able to change the world, they wondered? (Ghatak 2020).[11] In making space for incommensurate categories, spaces, and affects—self and collective; private and public; shyness and anger; critique and care—to sit alongside each other, the women of Shaheen Bagh and Park Circus orient us again toward the messiness of fashioning new selves and worlds.

The individuals and groups of this book were not absent from these new resistant geographies. Alongside young students and queer, transgender, and sex worker groups in Kolkata, individual activists at SFE were deep in this wave of resistance, shaping its direction and the substance of its critiques in robust and creative ways. Queer activists ensured, on the one hand, that resistance to the mechanisms of unequal citizenship registered other kinds of vulnerabilities—of transpersons and sex workers to the conjoint might of the NRC and CAA[12]—and, on the other hand, that their own homegrown queer spaces materialized in more visibly intersectional ways than before. The annual Pride march in Kolkata, which coincided with the protests against the CAA and NRC, was, for instance, a powerful platform for publicly decrying the BJP government as fascist and showing the incommensurability

Figure C.1 "Affection as resistance." Photograph of Shaheen Bagh protests by Ishan Tankha, reproduced with his kind permission.

between its politics and queer politics. New kinds of commensurabilities also emerged upon this protest landscape that went beyond the convergence of queer politics with antifascist futures. Arundhati Roy (2020) observes how a love politics had arisen against a fascist politics of hate in India: "A battle of lovers against haters. It's an unequal battle because the love is on the street and vulnerable. The hate is on the street, too, but it is armed to the teeth and protected by all the machinery of the state."[13]

It took a global pandemic, which shut India and the world down, to end the mass uprising of Indians against the CAA and NRC. Even Shaheen Bagh, which escaped the orchestrated carnage against Muslims during US president Donald Trump's visit to Delhi, could not survive the new world order that literally descended overnight in the middle of March 2020.[14] A hastily declared lockdown in the wake of the spread of COVID-19 enabled the police to finally clear the area, leaving no visible trace of the uprising's existence.[15] In a farewell to Shaheen Bagh, Raghu Karnad (2020) writes: "In those hundred days, Indians have gone from radical gathering to radical distancing—from physically converging as a public and laying claim to their republic to waking up isolated in a world of private boxes insulated from touch. But the two are not opposite. A spirit of collective action and care, of protecting each other, drives both."[16]

activism is a form of care

The COVID-19 crisis was a crisis of care. It laid bare both how essential social reproductive labor is to any society and how little capitalism invests in those very institutions and resources—essential services—that support the furthering of life and not profit. Tithi Bhattacharya (in Jaffe 2020) distinguishes care work—which is deeply racialized and gendered—from the main impetus that drives capitalism, which is profit-making, the very opposite of life-making. While the pandemic forced capitalism to temporarily care about more than profit, it could not stop states from indulging in their carceral capacities and necropolitical fantasies.[17] Ignoring a humanitarian crisis of its own making, the Modi government used the pandemic to actively pursue its broader agenda of persecuting religious minorities and defending the Hindu *rashtra* (nation) against dissenters.[18] The national lockdown of 2020 created an environment perfectly conducive to arresting journalists, academics, activists, and human rights defenders—especially women—for their alleged role in the CAA and NRC protests. And on the ground, activists—like those of SFE—were resuming their resistance, on- and offline, in a brave new world of socially distanced but unceasing protest.

Throughout this lockdown, the workers of Janam—with whom I was intermittently in touch—maintained a web of solidarity and care with the communities in which they worked and with the women they knew best. Through regular phone calls they asked after children and schooling, health and safety, and the new rhythms of a new normal. When the vicious Cyclone Amphan ripped through the entire region of Bengal, which was already grappling with rising cases of the virus and plunging economic precarity, Janam workers were more than ready to resume their field obligations. There was much work to be done—in the face of submerged agricultural lands and destroyed homes—and they had little to offer on behalf of a fund-strapped NGO that was overwhelmed by relief efforts; but they offered what in a sense was always their essential commodity—care—to repair and hold, however minimally, the social world and human relations amid unending devastation, disease, and despair.[19] This form of care was too important for them to give up on, even as they knew well its limits and ambivalences.

Even as this book began and has ended with spectacular forms of collective resistance—the 2012 antirape protests and the 2020 movement against the CAA and NRC—it does not tell a story of revolution. It tells a story of what happens in periods of quietude, where individuals and groups engage in silent, sustained action; negotiate co-optation and friction; and manifest insignificant if not negligible social change but also great amounts of criticality, care, and even transformation in intimate, individualized ways.

Such stories would not easily find their way into tales of revolution, being more amenable, as we know, to accounts of feminist co-optation than to its unexpected revival. I do not intend to correct such a narrative by drawing any simple, causal connection between everyday forms of organized activism—"nonmovements"—and the sudden flash of a revolution, even as we know that revolutions do not come out of nowhere (Bayat 2009).

Whether or not a straight line can be traced from the daily, humdrum, behind-the-scenes activist affects and life-making labor to the spectacle of the social revolt might, ultimately, depend on what kinds of stories we wish to tell—and hear—about global feminisms in the new millennium. I, for one, wish to hear stories not of feminist capitulation or success (carried on the shoulders of good or bad, sufficient or failed feminist subjects) but of complexity, compromise, complicity, and even conflict—the stuff of every social revolution and everyday life. Alongside the frictions and failures, the rough edges that cannot be smoothed over or wished away, I wish to hear and feel the deep pleasures, the joy and fun, and the sense of imaginative and utopic possibility in the making of feminist subjects and worlds. And I want to sense such worlds in their making, not as completed projects for me to report on or, even less, for me to judge. Finally, in movement or nonmovement, I wish to be moved by allowing myself to feel many different things at once: surprise, exuberance, loss, disappointment, tension, hope. By letting go of a story of Indian feminism, in which middle-class queers, lower-caste workers, and working-class Muslims can all successfully embody and fulfill feminism's revolutionary potential, we might find a different starting point and tell stories differently.

I have told stories in this book that have both uplifted and frustrated me. They have left me with loose ends, in more material ways than I ever imagined, when catastrophe upon catastrophe rages through the sites that are at once my field and my home. As opposed to trying to resolve these tensions, I have held on to them in ways that allowed me to hear the diverse, incomplete, and fundamentally contradictory ways in which feminist subjects are made and are making themselves in times of upheaval and uncertainty. This is also where I believe our work as feminist academics and activists ought to begin: in assumptions of impurity, messiness, and entanglement rather than in purity, cleanliness, and freedom. Instead of engaging in the business of counting and clearing, I advocate for entanglement as our starting point—as "the space of work, rather than the space that must be cleaned up in order for judgments to occur" (Hemmings 2011, 226). To presume—and inhabit—a messy ground that cannot be cleaned up is not to defend against critique but to enable a letting go that would simultaneously make us more accountable to critique while not being paralyzed by it. It would enable academics and activists to produce and receive critique as care, to be open to scrutiny (as opposed to being armed with self-defense) and to make room for surprise, for uncertainty and risk, for failure and hope, and, ultimately, for new stories of the world in which we live and that we seek to change. Feminist world-making is a project that requires critique and care in equal measure.

good

NOTES

Preface

1   The 1990s were a decade of rising communal tensions that culminated in the demolition in 1992 of the four-hundred-year-old Babri Masjid in Ayodhya. The demolition was orchestrated by the Hindu Right–led Ramjanmabhoomi (Ram's birthplace) movement with the participation of members of the Hindu nationalist Bharatiya Janata Party. Large-scale communal riots followed the destruction of the mosque, particularly in Mumbai, under the stronghold of the local Hindu right-wing Shiv Sena. The period, and especially the events at Ayodhya, signaled a fundamental shift in the basic tenets and practices of Indian secularism.

Introduction

1   On the Delhi rape and the protests that ensued, see Baxi (2012a, 2012b); Dutta and Sircar (2013); Kapur (2013); Anupama Roy (2014); S. Roy (2014, 2016b); Roychowdhury (2013); and Shandilya (2015).

2   The largely urban-based postindependence IWM has a national profile and presence but cannot be thought—and does not claim—to represent all Indian women. Its history, internally contested nature, generational dynamics, and effects have produced a vast body of scholarship that this book engages with throughout, and most fully in chapter 1.

3   In this introduction and in chapter 1, I draw on interview data with feminist academics, activists, and NGO workers in Bangalore, Delhi, and Kolkata gathered in 2008–9. This constituted a pilot study that preceded the ethnography of SFE and Janam, whose members appear from chapter 2 onward.

4   Neither *feminist* nor *queer* are straightforward or stable terms in India; they are unpacked throughout this book. The long and complicated association of feminism with colonialism, Westernization, and elitism led early Indian activists, like others in the Global South, to reject the label altogether; for an overview

of this debate, see Chaudhuri (2004) and S. Roy (2012b). Younger women and queers are far more comfortable with self-identifying as feminist. Similarly, while the term *queer*—like *gay* and *lesbian*—is used with ease by certain individuals and (activist) communities, there have been concerns that nonmetropolitan, subaltern sexual minority groups cannot envision themselves or be understood as LGBTQ in the same way (see chapter 2).

5 My mobilization of governmentality draws principally from Foucault (Foucault 2008; Martin, Gutman, and Hutton 1988) and is helped by W. Brown (2015); Cruikshank (1999); Lemke (2001); Lorenzini (2018); Oksala (2013); and Rose (1999). On literature on South Asian governmentalities, see Agrawal (2005); P. Chatterjee (2004); A. Gupta (2012); Kalpagam (2019); Legg (2007, 2014); Legg and Heath (2018); Samaddar (2016); and A. Sharma (2008).

6 In thinking through the life of neoliberalism in the Global South, I have turned to Dosekun (2020); C. Freeman (2014, 2020); Gooptu (2013); Grewal (2005, 2017); Li (2007); Ong (2006); Peck (2013); Ananya Roy (2003); and A. Sharma (2008).

7 On NGO governmentality, see Bernal and Grewal (2014b); Grewal (2005); and Hodžić (2014).

8 "Shaping today's NGOs in India there lies a history of women's mobilisation that has flowed like a river through Indian modernity," writes Kalpana Ram (2008, 141). This is a history that can be discerned in contemporary NGO practice, such as the issues NGOs choose to prioritize, besides the highly embodied "readiness" that Ram finds in subaltern women to be trained or educated in a specific manner.

9 In a volume of essays I have edited with Alf Gunvald Nilsen, we use *subaltern* to move beyond the original deployment of the term in the field of subaltern studies to offer a more intersectional and relational account of subalternity (Nilsen and Roy 2015; see also Nilsen 2018).

10 Sangari (2007, 53) describes these changes to the IWM—in ways that echo some of the responses cited at the start of this introduction—as signaling a "shift away from mass-based political struggles, broader coalitions, and structural critique to neo-liberal modes of governance." For academic commentaries on issues of co-optation, generational shifts, and depoliticization of feminist politics within and beyond the context of the IWM, see Batliwala (2007); Cornwall, Gideon, and Wilson (2008); Madhok and Rai (2012); Menon (2004); Mukhopadhyay (2016); Sunder Rajan (2003); and Wilson (2008). For more critical engagements with the idea of co-optation, see Dean (2010); De Jong and Kimm (2017); and Eschle and Maiguashca (2018). For my own work reflecting on and summarizing these debates with respect to India and South Asia, see S. Roy (2009, 2012a, 2015).

11 The idea of "feeling backward" (see Love 2007) will recur through the book, most centrally in chapter 2.

12 Mokkil (2019) turns to "lesbian hauntings" to show how loss and mourning—of actual Indian lesbian lives—offer an alternative and more locally grounded

politics of sexuality than liberal sexual identity politics. For similar readings of lesbian ghosts and hauntings, which draw on the foundational work of Avery Gordon (1997), see Hemmings and Eliot (2019), as well as my discussion in chapter 2.

13 Dalit (literally, "crushed," "ground down," and/or "broken to pieces") is a political category coined and embraced by the formerly untouchable castes and now defined as a Scheduled Caste in the Constitution of India.

14 Lefebvre (2018) convincingly employs Foucault's arguments around the care of the self to show that human rights, generally considered tools to care for vulnerable others and not one's own self, are in fact about self-care and personal transformation. For similar observations with respect to aid workers, see Malkki (2015); on human rights and LGBTQ activists, see Chua (2018).

15 For how neoliberal and postfeminist logics are presumed to be the preserve of white and Western girls alone, and mimetic of similar effects when they travel to distinct locations in the Global South (like Nigeria), see Dosekun (2020). Dosekun's book is part of a broader effort to explore these logics in more transnational and grounded ways while offering rich accounts of cultures of consumption, gendered neoliberalism, and postfeminist self-making. See also Iqani and Simões de Araújo (2021).

16 Eschle and Maiguashca (2018) counter—both conceptually and empirically— the prevailing tendency to erase actual instances of resistance to neoliberalism's dominance (in the writings of Nancy Fraser and other contemporary feminists). Dean (2010) also provides concrete evidence as to how the analytics of co-optation and depoliticization erase from view political—including feminist—resurgence in the United Kingdom.

17 It is no wonder that Foucault turned, in his thinking on neoliberalism, from perceiving power as conducting the self to how the self conducted itself in a relatively autonomous fashion, and thus he afforded a rich account of the self's relation to and care for the self. Some have argued that this turn to ethics of the care of the self shows Foucault's sympathy with neoliberalism. On this debate, see Lorenzini (2018).

18 Foucault's reflections on the practices of the care of the self—especially their inventive and transformative possibilities in constituting "a modern form of ascesis" (Halperin 1997, 78)—have been read into feminist and queer politics, ethics, and selves, including in specific postcolonial locales; see, for instance, Dave (2012); C. Freeman (2014); Livermon (2020); Mahmood (2005); Najmabadi (2014); and Nuttall (2009). I have also benefited from commentaries on the care of the self by the following feminist philosophers: Heyes (2007, 2020); McLaren (2002, 2004); Mitcheson (2012); Oksala (2013); and Taylor and Vintges (2004).

19 *Governing*, rather than *fashioning* or *making*, grasps more fully, I believe, the nonvoluntarist sense of this model of individual agency, or how "the subject constitutes itself in an active fashion [though] these practices are nevertheless not something invented by the individual himself" (Foucault 1997a, 291).

On Foucault's technologies of the self as offering agency, but not of a voluntarist kind, see Lorenzini (2016); and Mitcheson (2012).

20 In showing the limits of Marxist feminist critiques of neoliberalism, Oksala (2013, 44) similarly argues that "we also need a politics of ourselves that acknowledges that it is through us, our subjectivity that neoliberal governmentality is able to function."

21 On this point, see Lefebvre (2018); and McLaren (2002, 2004). The self and the collective are not, in any case, so easily disentangled from each other; as Chandra and Majumder (2013, 7) note, "anthropological studies of these micro-practices cannot simply be read via narrow empiricist lenses as simply individuation or monolithically as subject-formation, but as emblems of wider social transformations ... micro-practices of the 'self' and 'self-making' are key sites to study the workings of theoretical abstractions such as power, capital, culture, and gender."

22 Gooptu (2016), who maps the neoliberal reshaping of individual subjectivity on a range of sites (from retail to religious and spiritual), locates this limitation in the more general lack of attention to the politics of the self and self-making in India—a limitation to which Indian feminists have contributed their fair share, as I show in chapter 1. Glover (2021, 2) observes the same of the Caribbean, where individual actions are evaluated not on their own terms but "through the prism of communal politics," with Black women primed to fulfill social expectations of self-sacrifice and solidarity.

23 As Glover (2021, 2) notes, self-making "do[es] not plainly generate or gesture toward programs or possibilities for political change."

24 See Rao's (2014) wonderful piece on how the "Woman and Homosexual Question" had "intertwined trajectories" in (post)colonial India; he shows how questions around gender and sexuality are both posed and disrupted by feminist, queer, and transgender politics. For historical detail on how caste, gender, and sexuality operated in mutually reinforcing and co-constitutive ways, see Mitra (2020).

25 I refer here to the state-commissioned report titled *Towards Equality*, published in 1971, that contributed (together with the Indian state of emergency in the 1970s) to a weakening of the IWM's nationalist aspirations. In generational accounts of the IWM, the 1950s and 1960s are characterized as a silent period that saw great feminist faith in the emancipatory potential of the state.

26 Especially in this "second wave," the IWM took two organizational forms: affiliated and autonomous women's groups. The former referred to women's wings of political (usually left-wing) parties, while the latter were structurally and ideologically autonomous from political parties. On these feminist formations and reflections on autonomy, see Gandhi and Shah (1991), Kumar (1993), and R. Ray (1999); for further evaluation, see M. Desai (2016) and S. Roy (2015).

27 This is not to suggest that subaltern women did not have political agency of their own or did not speak or act on their own behalf; this is evidenced by a long history of collective action, whether to do with gender-specific issues or

not (see Kumar 1993). In West Bengal alone there is robust mapping of the participation of rural, Adivasi, lower-caste, and working-class women in land and labor struggles; for a good overview, see Sinha Roy (2011).

28   Masjid refers to the demolition of the Babri Masjid in Ayodhya in 1992, which engulfed parts of the country in communal riots and significantly eroded the secular edifice of the republic. Mandal is short for the Mandal Commission recommendations, announced under the government of V. P. Singh, "for reservations of 27% for backward castes, apart from 22.5% for SC/STs [Scheduled Castes and Scheduled Tribes] in government service and public sector jobs" (Tharu and Niranjana 1994, 97). It sparked a major backlash from the upper castes, including dramatic acts of self-immolation by student protestors fearing unemployment. Upper-caste women protestors pitted themselves against lower-caste men, thereby making clear their caste-based allegiances and dependency on forms of Brahmanical patriarchy (Arya and Rathore 2020; Tharu and Niranjana 1994).

29   For a posing of this question in the context of this period, see Menon (2004). The beginnings of this question can, however, be traced to *Mohd. Ahmed Khan v. Shah Bano Begum*, the iconic pedagogical moment in the 1980s when the rights of an individual (female) minority subject came into sharp conflict with collective rights, and feminists found themselves on the side of conservative political forces. Shah Bano, a divorced Muslim woman, sought alimony from the Supreme Court of India, while her ex-husband argued that he was not obliged to pay her, per Muslim personal law. While the Supreme Court ruled in favor of Shah Bano, the Rajiv Gandhi–led Indian National Congress Party government passed what later became a law—the Defense of Muslim Women's Act of 1986, commonly known as the Shah Bano Act— which overturned the Supreme Court ruling and removed Muslim women from the right to maintenance. The rising BJP took this opportunity to call out the Congress Party's appeasement of religious minorities and shore up its own feminist credentials by supporting a uniform civil code for all women, regardless of their religion. In 2019, at the same time as Muslim men were being hounded and lynched by right-wing Hindu nationalists, the BJP government under Modi criminalized "instant triple talaq" divorces to show its deep commitment to the protection of Muslim women. On the *Shah Bano* case, see Sunder Rajan (2003).

30   Class analysis has been central to critical queer organizing and scholarship (though less ethnographically mined in the case of queer Indian women). For a good overview and extension of existing arguments, see Khubchandani (2020).

31   Chandra, Heierstad, and Nielsen (2016) argue against such exceptionalism, especially in how it made caste appear irrelevant to local politics, a position replicated in scholarly work.

32   The idea of Sonar Bangla was core to Bengali nationalism, "developed by a host of predominantly Calcutta-based Bengali nationalist writers since the 1880s" (Nielsen 2018, 42). The song "Amar Sonar Bangla," written by Rabindranath

Tagore at the time of the first partition of Bengal, became the national anthem of Bangladesh.

33 While there is a long history of valorizing the peasant in nationalist and left-wing rhetoric, the Left Front instrumentalized this figure to constitute a myth of peasant unity and bolster its claims toward rural progress (while masking its failings toward the urban poor). The "stickiness" (Ahmed 2014a) of this figure has endured in postcommunist politics, from the anti-industrial movements at Singur to development projects and even shaping the queer feminist politics that I uncover in this book (see chapter 2).

34 There is a vast literature on the Left's rural reformism, and I have benefited from analyses by A. Basu (1992); Nielsen (2018); Ananya Roy (2003); and Ruud (2003).

35 The solidly upper-caste, elite communist leadership of the state thought caste, in comparison to class, was of little relevance, exemplified in one leader's proclamation that there were only two castes in Bengal: the rich and the poor (Mukherjee 2019).

36 Note, however, the long history of lower-caste struggle, as documented by Bandyopadhyay (2011). See also Chandra, Heierstad, and Nielsen (2016).

37 While the Left Front's greatest achievement (besides land reform) was the maintenance of communal harmony (Tenhunen and Säävälä 2012), the 2006 report on the socioeconomic conditions of Indian Muslims by the Sachar Committee, headed by Justice Rajinder Sachar, revealed that Muslims in left-ruled Bengal were worse off on every count than their counterparts in most other states (Paul 2010).

38 The government, including the chief minister, Banerjee, has resorted to blaming victims while linking rapes to sexual permissiveness under globalization and urbanization. Boyce (2014, 1211) also shows the concrete implications of the Trinamool Congress for sexual rights organizing in the state given moves to cut funding for community-based NGOs for HIV/AIDS prevention and sexual rights work.

39 During the thirty-four-year reign of the CPM, the terrain of the local women's movement was dominated by its women's wing, the Paschim Banga Ganatantrik Mahila Samiti (PBGMS). With a membership of two million women in 1990, its reach was unparalleled, largely due to its "piggybacking on the strength" of the party (R. Ray 1999, 54). City-based autonomous women's organizations—some of which later became NGOs—were unable to compete with a mass-based organization of this sort (Datta 2009) and remained skeptical of its feminist claims. The peculiarity of the West Bengal political scene is, of course, that these oppositional forces were themselves embedded in the same leftist field (R. Ray 1999). This book, in turn, shows how even as the official dominance of the CPM and the PBGMS has waned, leftist ideologies, cultures, and affects hold firm and inform feminist and queer feminist NGOs, as it did the autonomous feminist activists of a previous generation. Even today, NGOs, political parties, and other civil society organizations come together on only

some rare issues and occasions (like during the Singur movement; see Nielsen 2018).

40 The Naxalbari *andolan*, which began as a peasant revolt but had a significant urban dimension, played a critical role in consolidating the dominance of the Left in West Bengal. It is also considered a predecessor to the new social movements that emerged after the Indian emergency had been lifted in 1977, by which time many of its activists ("Naxalites") had been killed or arrested.

41 Leftist suspicion of "foreign funds" were related to concerns around imperial domination and the erosion of national sovereignty (which explains the belated boom in NGOs in Kolkata, in comparison to other parts of the country). In discussing the All India Democratic Women's Association (AIDWA), Armstrong (2004, 41) reveals an alternative model of women's organizing that draws on a pool of members. She rightly argues against pitting funded and unfunded politics against each other, noting instead how "no politics, however populist, informal or momentary, can wholly evade the complex range of problems raised by the increasing privatization of activism. Neither fiscal purity nor simply defined autonomy fully circumvents the processes of globalization that folds organizations that fight for social change into the logic of capital." Even though AIDWA presents itself as independent of the two leading communist parties, it is generally perceived as their women's front: "[It] could not seriously challenge the male-dominated top leadership [of the mainstream communist parties]. Women's entry to the top decision-making bodies of the democratic communist movement is still a rarity" (Sinha Roy 2011, 29).

42 There is a rich body of feminist literature on sex worker struggles in liberalized India that also considers tensions around sex work within the IWM (Devika 2016; Kapur 2005; Kotiswaran 2011; Lakkimsetti 2020; Menon 2007a; Mokkil 2019; S. P. Shah 2012; Sukthankar 2012; and Vijayakumar 2021).

43 Depicting a love affair between two sisters-in-law in a traditional Hindu joint family, *Fire* was made by a Canadian Indian, Deepa Mehta. Labeling the film as alien to Indian culture and as insulting Hindu religion, right-wing political groups vandalized cinema halls screening the film and called for it to be banned.

44 Some of these later interviews with transgender feminist activists were conducted by a research assistant who identified as a queer woman and was involved in feminist and transgender organizing in the city.

45 I present as a cisgender woman, and heteronormative in ways that were never questioned by my queer interlocutors. In those early days, and as evident in SFE's discussions on sexual identity (see chapter 2), the use of self-descriptors like *queer* were merely emergent on this terrain. In subsequent years I have come to align more consciously with this category and the communities it hails, for the potentialities that bell hooks (2014) identifies when she defines queerness as not belonging, as being at odds with everything, and as signaling an alternative kind of thriving (even as such usage might constitute its own kind of "postured privilege"; Ballakrishnen 2021, 194).

1 "One would be hard-pressed," John (2009, 47–48) says of India, "to find any period when women's issues emerged autonomously or authentically 'in their own right,' so deeply mired have they been in the complex histories of colonialism and nationalism."

2 For Eva Giraud, it is not enough to acknowledge the entangled nature of the world and its problems; such a move, on its own, can even obscure the constitutive role of exclusions in social actions and who bears these burdens the most. Giraud advocates for a greater emphasis on an ethics of exclusion, parallel to the recognition of entanglement: "emphasizing and politicizing exclusion is not just a means of complicating narratives of entanglement but offers alternative trajectories for grounding ethical and political intervention" (2019, 4).

3 In considering such structures of feelings among Indian feminisms, I have been inspired by conversations on the idiom of loss and failure in feminist politics elsewhere (Adkins 2004; Hemmings 2011; Scott 2004; Wiegman 1999, 2000, 2002).

4 Section 377, which dates back to 1861, criminalized sexual acts against "the order of nature" and was used to target sexual minorities, homosexual couples, and gender variant persons and communities, especially of economically and socially marginalized communities. In 2009, in what was a major win for the queer movement in India, the Delhi High Court struck down Section 377 to decriminalize consensual and private sex between adults of the same sex. In 2014 the Supreme Court of India overturned this lower court judgment and upheld Section 377, thus effectively recriminalizing consensual gay sex. In 2018 the Supreme Court upheld the right to privacy as intrinsic to the right to life and liberty and included sexual orientation as an essential attribute of privacy. For a close reading of Section 377 set against the Indian state's wider regulation of sexuality, see Puri (2016).

5 In an introduction to a series of essays in the journal *Interventions*, Stephen Legg and I show the role of the Indian state in institutionalizing heteronormativity (in what we term heterosovereignty), of which its preservation of Section 377 was a clear instance; see Legg and Roy (2013).

6 The first efforts to decriminalize homosexuality came in 1994 from a Delhi-based unfunded human rights collective named AIDS Bhedbhav Virodhi Andolan, which found that the illegality of homosexuality hindered its HIV/AIDS prevention work. A petition filed in 2001 by Naz India, which was working on HIV/AIDS prevention, mainstreamed the cause of sexual citizenship. It was later joined by a broad-based campaign called Voices against Section 377, which expanded a legal petition into a social movement (Dave 2012; Lakkimsetti 2020; Narrain and Gupta 2011; Puri 2016). The predominance of groups in Delhi, funded or unfunded, had a marginalizing effect on groups elsewhere in the country, including SFE. On the internal tensions among Delhi-based activists themselves, see Dave (2012) and Puri (2016).

7 These engagements and outcomes with law mirrored the uneven effects of long-standing feminist struggles for gender justice and women's rights. The belief that the law could function as an instrument of social change made legal activism, especially around violence against women, core to the IWM's organizing from the 1970s onward. Feminists found, however, that even positive wins, as a consequence of their struggles, could have unintended and even negative effects. On these debates with respect to the law, which became constitutive of Indian feminism itself, see Agnes (2002); S. Basu (2015); Gangoli (2007); Jaising (2005); Kapur (2005); Kapur and Cossman (1996); Kotiswaran (2017); and Menon (2004).

8 For details of how various other Indian laws adversely affected queer Indian women, see Thangarajah and Arasu (2011).

9 Alliances, however, emerged between gay men and female sex workers mobilizing around Section 377 and the Immoral Traffic (Prevention) Act (ITPA)—the primary legal rubric for regulating sex work—to mitigate their conjoint vulnerability to HIV/AIDS (Sukthankar 2012, 321). Yet sex worker mobilizations did not garner the kind of public attention and support that the campaign against Section 377 did. Some argued that the afterlife of Section 377 served to further marginalize the concerns of sex workers and left them open to more intense forms of harassment and precarity (Aditya 2018). We know far less of *queer* feminist positions on sex work and related forms of sexual commerce. Sukthankar (2012) mentions queer feminist solidarities around the state's banning of bar dancing, which also saw the emergence of tensions between Marxist feminists who were against the ban and Dalit feminists in favor of it (see Arya and Rathore 2020). In Kolkata, tensions between cisgender middle-class queer feminist activists and transgender feminists, including sex workers, were refracted through class and caste divides (see Dutta 2019; and my discussion toward the end of chapter 2).

10 Chatterjee quotes activist Chayanika Shah as saying, "The women's movements were the first to articulate concern over the control over sexuality and the societal constructions of gender and are hence the closest link and support for the nascent 'queer' movements in the country" (2018, 153; see also chapter 2 of the present volume).

11 The emergence and trajectory of CALERI embodied an important history of how Indian feminists, both autonomous and affiliated, responded to lesbianism. Influential leftist women's groups like the All India Democratic Women's Association refused to march with CALERI on International Women's Day in 2000. Many autonomous feminists boycotted the march for alienating lesbian comrades, even as some of these groups preferred the sanitized politics around "single women" over lesbian or queer politics (see Bacchetta 2002; Chatterjee 2018; Dave 2012; and Menon 2007a).

12 Critiques around privacy were widely in circulation and taken on and responded to by activists, especially lawyer-activists belonging to Voices against Section 377 (see Narrain 2012). For criticisms of sexual rights based on privacy, and as part of a growing queer liberalism in North America, see Eng (2010).

13 The terms *hijra* and *kothi* describe gender-variant persons who were assigned male sex at birth and are invariably stigmatized on account of their feminized gender expression and same-sex desire. On *kothis*, see Boyce and khanna (2011); Cohen (2005); Dutta (2012b); and khanna (2009); for an intimate ethnography of the *hijra* community in India, see Reddy (2005).

14 Oishik Sircar (2012, 563) notes that the court's judgment made this logic clear—specifically, that "India needs to live up to the progressive developments in other parts of the (Western) world by decriminalising sodomy." See also Dasgupta and Dasgupta (2018a).

15 The constitutional category of Other Backward Classes emerged out of the work of the Mandal Commission to recognize and provide reservations to lower-caste groups—that is, groups who are neither upper caste nor Dalit and that are also called *bahujan*. For the complexities of treating transgenderism as akin to a marginalized caste, including how some trans activists and communities rejected the Other Backward Classes label, see Dutta (2014).

16 The NALSA judgment, as it came to be known, refers to the Supreme Court decision that recognized transgender persons as full citizens of India. It followed from a public interest litigation filed by NALSA on behalf of the *hijra* community. For some observers, transgender subjects found easy inclusion into Hindu nationalist India because "the collation of 'transgender' and hijra identities provides a particular 'Hindu-ised' historicisation of transgender existence" (Loh 2018, 47).

17 "The feminist response has the consequence, among other things, of denying the self-identification of male-to-female trans* persons (including many *hijras*) as women," writes Rao (2014, 10). For feminist takes on these contestations, see Dave (2011); Gangoli (2007); Kotiswaran (2017); and Sukthankar (2012).

18 Before the HIV/AIDS pandemic, sexual minorities in India were objects of state surveillance but not of welfare or development (Lakkimsetti 2020). Rao (2020b) shows when and why global development and finance began to take sexuality more seriously (even as it was always present, though implicit, as a development issue).

19 Scholars attribute a general decline in Indian women's labor force participation to neoliberal economic restructuring. As Chacko (2020, 208) explains, "In the period between 2005 and 2012, the female LFPR [labor force participation rate] declined dramatically to twenty-three percent." See also Armstrong (2013); J. Ghosh (2009); Gooptu (2009); John (2020); and S. Sen (2001). On West Bengal, see Ganguly-Scrase and Scrase (2009); and Nielsen and Waldrop (2014).

20 The rise and popularity of participatory approaches to development from the 1980s onward made it incumbent upon NGOs to show legitimacy by demonstrating involvement at the grassroots level (Cooke and Kothari 2001; Jakimow 2013; O'Reilly 2006).

21 Bhanwari Devi was employed as a *sathin* (female friend) on a government program to stop child marriage in rural Rajasthan. As "punishment" for her work in the community, she was gang-raped while her husband was severely beaten

in September 1992 (for an interview with her, see Madhok 2012; see also Madhok and Rai 2012). Even as justice eluded her, the legal case led to the landmark Supreme Court judgment, called the Vishakha Judgment, that laid down strict guidelines to protect women against sexual harassment in the workplace.

22 Chacko (2020, 210) observes, "this focus on women is partly the product of electoral imperatives. Women's participation in politics as voters has risen significantly since the 1980s, with a particularly rapid increase since the 1990s."

23 The protection of Hindu women, especially from predatory Muslim men, gained new impetus in the Modi government's first term in power. The campaign against "love jihad" became central to the everyday vigilantism exercised by right-wing groups to victimize Muslim men and erode the sexual agency of consenting adult women. On "love jihad," see C. Gupta (2009); for an overview of the gender and sexual politics of Hindu nationalism, see Baxi (2019).

24 For making sense of the NGO-ization of feminist politics within and beyond South Asia, see Alvarez (1998); De Alwis (2009); Kamat (2002); Karim (2011); Lang (1997); and Sangtin Writers and Nagar (2006). For an overview, see S. Roy (2015).

25 These national conferences started on the back of the activism that gathered around the rape of a fourteen-year-old Adivasi girl named Mathura while she was in police custody and the subsequent acquittal of the accused by the Supreme Court (a critical event in the struggle around women's rights and changes to the rape law). Manisha Desai notes how "activists in Bombay called a national conference on 'Perspectives for the Autonomous Women's Movement [AWM] in India.' Thirty-two groups from all over the country came to Bombay in what was to become a regular meeting of the AWM until 2006.... These conferences became important venues for debate and dialogue within the AWM" (M. Desai 2016, 98). They were a conflictual site for engaging not just issues around NGO-ization but also the politics of sexuality. The 2006 conference represented a significant shift given that SFE was part of its organizing committee, but not without a struggle; see chapter 2.

26 In contrast to the tendency to reduce the IWM's transnationalism to its globalization from the 1990s, John (2009) argues that the preglobalization years saw a more intense international traffic in feminist ideas. The same has been shown of lesbian activism in India; see Dave (2012, 110).

27 Note that the sites of state withdrawal were highly gendered ones—"of women's paid and unpaid labor and feminist struggles for resources and services"—and amenable to NGO-ization because of the similarity, and not the difference, between states and NGOs (Bernal and Grewal 2014b, 9).

28 For transnational feminist scholarship on gender and sexuality that best represents the limits and possibilities of these new globalized flows and funds, see Alvarez (2014); Chowdhury (2011); Chua (2018); De la Dehesa (2010); Hodžić (2016); and Thayer (2010).

29 The ideal and practice of autonomy was rooted, after all, in privilege—in, at least, having other (familial) sources of financial stability. These factors also served to consolidate the traditionally elite leadership of the IWM.

30 Toorjo Ghose makes these observations of the unique and powerful Durbar Mahila Samanwaya Committee, which evolved from an HIV prevention program to a sex workers movement and union in Kolkata, with notable international visibility (it was "completely isolated from the mainstream women's movement," one Kolkata-based activist remarked as a way of showing the conservative bent of the local women's movement). Ghose (2012, 302) argues, contra Partha Chatterjee, that "governmentality, seeking to manage political society claims, also provides opportunities for politicized members of political society to inject subaltern subjectivities into civil society." Dutta (2012b) and Menon (2010) equally turn to feminist and sexual minority struggles to complicate Chatterjee's dichotomous rendering of postcolonial Indian society into civil and political society (he associates political society with governmentality).

31 There is robust academic debate on the transnational travel of LGBTQ identity categories, sometimes called—after Altman's (1996) essay, which perceived this phenomenon critically—"global queering." These critiques were also popularized in Massad (2002), who termed Western LGBTQ organizations the "Gay International," as implanting Western-style gay identity onto postcolonial contexts. While such scholars have been right to call out the liberatory assumptions of Western (or Americanized) LGBTQ politics and queer theory, they have been met with counteraccusations of erasing local agency (see, for instance, Mourad 2016).

32 A growing body of ethnographic work shows the varied and deeply generative effects of NGOs, especially at the affective and subjective levels; see, for instance, Cody (2013); Hodžić (2016); Jakimow (2015); Leve (2014); Ram (2008); and Thayer (2010).

33 One such case was the murder of Jessica Lall, a model who was shot dead by Manu Sharma, the son of a politician, for refusing to serve him a drink at a private party. The trial court first acquitted Sharma but later convicted him, following an appeal backed by huge popular pressure. People thronged to Delhi's India Gate in what became a regular feature of middle-class protests in the city (Dutta and Sircar 2013).

34 I refer here to the well-known Pink Chaddi (or Pink Panty) Campaign, in which several Indian women were urged to send pink underwear to a right-wing vigilante group who had attacked women for sitting and drinking in a pub in Mangalore in 2009. The history of social media use for feminist activism can be traced back even farther, to 2003, when Blank Noise was formed as a response to sexual harassment in the street (see Mitra-Kahn 2012). Useful summaries of this period can be found in Gajjala (2018); Jha and Kurian (2018); and Sinha Roy (2020).

35 Even as I employ here a language of generational difference that mirrors academic discussions around "new" feminisms in India, this book will trouble the

idea of generation and its reliance on linear temporalities. I have also attempted to do so elsewhere (see S. Roy 2009, 2017c).

36 While Delhi has been hegemonic to the formation of queer feminist fields across India, the first years of the new millennium also shifted these scalar hierarchies. When protests traveled from Delhi to other regions—and across borders—they decentered an originary site, producing instead a protest assemblage (S. Roy 2016b). Students and activists I interviewed in Kolkata agreed that Delhi as the center of a protest landscape made little sense anymore.

37 Networks like Das Theke Das Hajar (from Ten to Ten Thousand)—which emerged out of Maitree (Friendship), a conglomerate of local women's groups and activists in Kolkata—included radical leftist queer and transgender activists and sex workers, as opposed to being solely focused on women's issues led by cisgender women. The network represented a new generation of left-wing activists who were more open to concerns of sexual rights.

38 Visibility was at the heart of these public protests. But visibility had its own tensions and limits, which Mokkil (2019, 34–35) summarizes from the perspective of Dalit feminists. Dalit women's bodies have historically been marked for their publicness, always available to a public gaze, in ways that new feminist politics around visibility did not always recognize or register. On the limits of visibility in popular feminisms in the United States, see Banet-Weiser (2018).

39 Established women's groups did not participate in SlutWalk marches, leading younger and queerer activists to ask, "Is our discomfort with SlutWalk about urban elitism or about our unease with a positive (rather radical) articulation of sexuality?" (Borah and Nandi 2012, 4).

40 On the use of digital technologies by the neoliberal state to "protect" women from violence, including the use of safety apps launched by the Delhi police, see Datta, Ahmed, and Tripathi (2018); and Gajjala (2018).

41 Even as queer feminist politics and lesbian experiences have merited little attention in these conversations on queer digital spaces, my observations confirm the role played by the digital in legitimizing some—respectable—queer bodies to the exclusion of others.

42 Indian journalist and writer Snigdha Poonam (2018, 34) reports how non-elite millennial Indians in nonmetropolitan locales lived their lives and their "truest" selves on the internet: "it was only on social media that Indians of a particular age were willing to present a complete picture of themselves: personal, political, professional."

43 A crowdsourced list of sexual predators in the academy went viral at the end of 2017. Its anonymous nature—it was simply a list of names—gave rise to disquiet around the politics of naming and shaming. Some Indian feminists penned a statement asking for caution and a return to "due process," prompting a backlash not along generational lines alone but also around caste divides within Indian feminism. For summaries and analyses, see Gajjala (2018); John (2020); Kannabiran (2018); Lukose (2018); Menon (2019); and S. Roy (2017c).

44 Digital activism around the death of Indian PhD scholar Rohith Vemula, as evidence of systemic discrimination against Dalits in higher education, was one catalytic moment (Arya and Rathore 2020).

45 Lieder (2018) also notes that participants of loitering movements had a more ambiguous class position than had been generally assumed. This is true for Kolkata-based initiatives like Take Back the Night Kolkata.

46 For many commentators in the Global North, #MeToo was another instance of the atomization inherent to "hashtag feminism" in prioritizing "the individual and her resilience and survival" over "collective political demands for systematic change" (Rottenberg 2019, 45; see also Phipps 2020). Across the Global North and South, such complaints were also generationally articulated, with younger activists described as vigilantes, social media centered, or "fingertip activists"; for a summary, see Gajjala (2018).

47 Poonam (2018, 7) notes the uniqueness of a banal question—Who are you?—in a society like India where caste, class, and religion already determine the answer. Millennial Indians, she argues, are the first to be confronted with the full weight of this question.

2. Queer Activism as Governmentality

1 Throughout this chapter, I use the self-descriptors used by my interviewees (whose names are all pseudonyms), such as *transman*, *transwoman*, *transperson*, and, especially, *queer*, as not only referencing a broad set of gender identities and sexual orientations (including lesbian, bisexual, and transgender persons) but also as performing important political and activist labor.

2 Arguments that engaged these debates extended their critical insights to the entanglement of queerness in Hindu nationalism, neoliberalism, and globalization in India. Nishant Shahani (in Rallin 2019, 365) draws on Jasbir Puar's homonationalism to show how Indian queers went from the "life and death politics" of HIV/AIDS to being productive of India's neoliberalizing and globalizing aspirations. See also, in the same roundtable forum (Rallin 2019), the contribution by Oishik Sircar and Dipika Jain, as well as their earlier curated volume on the neoliberal normalization of queerness (Sircar and Jain 2017b). More broadly, on homocapitalism, see Rao (2015, 2020b).

3 I have been inspired by the idea of enduring forms of politics and subjectivities in Kenny's (2019) historical sociology of retail workers' labor politics in South Africa.

4 This chapter is in critical conversation with writings on the liberatory possibilities of feminism's ghosts, or that which is erased, repressed, or buried in dominant histories (see Hemmings and Eliot 2019; and Mokkil 2019). The lesbian is a spectral figure par excellence, one who has long haunted the boundaries of mainstream feminism and the stories it tells about itself (Hesford 2005). The concept of "space invaders" comes from Puwar's (2004) book of the same title.

5 Letter writing has played a constitutive role in lesbian self- and community building since the 1990s, comprising an "archive of feelings" (Cvetkovich 2003;

see also Dave 2012). On how a broader genre of lesbian writing keeps alive what would otherwise be lost, see Sukthankar (1999); but see also Arondekar's (2010) critique of the compulsion to recover, in relation to sexuality and the colonial archive.

6 Before the materialization of this space, Malobika and Akanksha had even reached out to lesbian groups in Delhi and Bombay, "just to know if there were any lesbian couples in Calcutta at all" (Akanksha and Malobika 2007, 363). It is also worth recalling Sukthankar's (1999, xvi) powerful words: "every lesbian who claws her way into self-awareness in a society that insists upon heterosexuality, has surely experienced the horror of that complete alienation from herself, the perilous feeling of being the only one."

7 Akanksha and Malobika were pseudonyms used by the women, by which they were known at SFE and in the broader queer community (though their real names were widely known too). On similar forms of collective coming out in feminist queer counterpublics in Lebanon, including the use of pseudonyms or first names alone, or "anonymous authorship," see Mourad (2016, 207), who argues that such rituals enable "degrees of publicness rather than a public/private binary" (2016, 208).

8 Ghosh's editorials from *Swakanthey* (the title means "In her own voice"), spanning the period 2004–16, are compiled in a volume that was published by SFE (Subhagata Ghosh 2016).

9 Biswas (2007, 2) also expresses ambivalence toward transmen and those who opt for surgical transitions: "If sex was so redundant, why do some of our friends present there at that very moment, go to such lengths to add or remove specific parts of their body in order to achieve a more complete sense of being?" I return to tensions among queer and trans feminists later in this chapter, and to queer feminist ambivalences toward transsexuality in chapter 3.

10 The abbreviation FCRA refers to the Foreign Contribution Regulation Act of 1976, which gave NGOs legal permission to obtain foreign funds or aid from outside India.

11 In the context of Myanmar, Chua (2018) uncovers the deeply enabling aspects of human rights discourses as a way of facilitating the self-transformation of local and otherwise marginalized lesbian activists. For more critical perspectives on human rights discourse, for taking a neoliberal approach to gender and sexuality and even attaching homosexuality to economic growth and development, see Shahani (in Rallin 2019) and Rao (2020b).

12 Regarding Kolkata, Dutta (2012a, 123) shows how the convergence between humanity (*manushotto*) and human rights (*manobadhikar*) served to discipline unruly working-class queer subjects into "being respectable, dignified and responsible citizens."

13 Love (2007, 147) cautions against queer temporalities that repress "the stubborn negativity of the past" in a rush to move forward, to queer success and positivity, increasingly expressed in (homo)normative terms. Her caution is widely registered by several queer theorists for whom queerness disrupts linear progression, including the idea of a future grounded in "institutions of family,

heterosexuality, and reproduction" (Halberstam 2005, 1). Love (2007, 7) is clear that she is not rejecting the idea of the future itself (as Edelman [2004], for instance, does), but is interested in "celebrations of perversion, in defiant refusals to grow up, in explorations of haunting and memory, and in stubborn attachments to lost objects." My discussion in this chapter shows that the turn to the past can also prove constraining for radical politics, as arguments that draw on Brown's (2003a, 2003b) "left melancholia" have established. On "backward" temporalities in affective politics around caste and sexuality in India, see Mokkil (2019); Ramberg (2016); and Rao (2020b). For a nuanced take on queer pasts and futurity, see Muñoz (2009).

14 On the distinct category and lived experience of the *nimno madhyabitta*, or lower middle class, in West Bengal, see Donner (2008); Ganguly-Scrase (2003); and S. Roy (2012c).

15 The category of transgender people included transmen but not transwomen, though the early life of the organization included at least one self-identified transwoman.

16 There was also some skepticism among Indian queer activist-scholars as to whether queer traveled well to "our" context and spoke to its multiple complexities. See, for instance, Kang (2016); and some SFE activists in S. Chatterjee (2018).

17 As will emerge in this chapter, "homonationalism" was widely discussed by SFE members, prompted by Dasgupta and Banerjea's (2013) piece in *Swakanthey*. They extended Puar's original thesis on homonationalism to stress that "in India it is important to ask whose queer body is being recognized by which forms of the Indian state, and if strategies for enhancing life are our primary political goal, then we need to ask: whose life? What constitutes good life? And, whose life is rendered bad/unlivable?" (Dasgupta and Banerjea 2013, 1). Puar, too, reminds us "to note the divergences and differences that create multiple kinds of homonationalisms" (2013, 32; see also Puar 2007).

18 For instance, an editorial in *Swakanthey* once stated, "In rural areas, where there have not reached the touch of anything western, women who have willingly exited life send us their cryptic messages through their suicides" (Subhagata Ghosh 2016, 34). For critiques of metrocentric assumptions in Indian queer politics, as attaching queerness to developed, modernized, and globalized metropolitan centers against premodern, underdeveloped, or "backward" nonmetropolitan locales, see Boyce and Dasgupta (2017); Dutta (2012b); Gopinath (2005); S. P. Shah (2015); and P. Singh (2017). For writings on nonelite and nonmetropolitan "women loving women," see M. Sharma (2006). For critiques of "queer metronormativity" outside India, see Halberstam (2005).

19 I made consistent research trips to Kolkata from the start of this project in 2008 until the beginning of 2013. After my children were born, I struggled to travel every year, but managed two robust rounds of interviews in 2016 and 2019.

20 Bacchetta (2002, 958) tells us how lesbianism first entered the national mediascape in relation to lesbian suicides and marriage: "Lesbian suicide appeared

first, in 1979, when partners Jyotsna and Jayashree, after forced marriages to men, jumped in front of a train together." For rich readings on the visibility and politicization of the issue of lesbian suicides, see Bhattacharya (2020); S. Chatterjee (2018); and Mokkil (2019).

21 Svati P. Shah further shows how the Bharatiya Janata Party (BJP) deployed metrocentric arguments that pitted authentic rural "Bharat" to elite and urban "India" to paint homosexuality as an elite issue and argue against its decriminalization. Shah also notes that "the BJP, more than a decade later, frames its criticism of gay rights in relation to class, and the urban frame, identifying itself and 'real' Indian culture with 'Bharat' and, in a strange twist, claiming that English speaking, urban queers now belong to 'India'" (2015, 647).

22 Queer activity was increasingly observable in smaller cities, too, like Chandannagar in West Bengal, which had been hosting its own Pride march since 2012.

23 Café Coffee Day, a coffee shop franchise that was a ubiquitous marker of India's neoliberalization, first opened in 1996. My interviews with younger activists regularly took place at one of its outlets, as it was more affordable than the competitor, Barista. Local coffee chains first appeared in urban India in the mid-1990s (McGuire 2011) but did not gain popularity until a decade later in places like Kolkata. On how Kolkata's modern café culture is a site for performing class, cultural distinction, and upward social mobility for youth from different sections of the middle class, see R. D. Chaudhuri (2019).

24 Queer women were able to rent homes of their own, a clear marker of generational advance and that of increased earning and consumptive potentials in liberalized India. As one SFE member put it, "You can now buy your freedom." I detail these shifts and their implications in chapter 3.

25 SFE's staff now included not only community women but those with an academic background in women's studies or work experience in the NGO sector, part of a new class of professionalized women's rights and sexual rights activists (and development professionals; see chapter 4).

26 In explaining his "elision of Bombay and Delhi for Bangalore," Khubchandani (2020, 20–21) describes Delhi and Mumbai as well-known centers of queer activism associated with long-standing local support groups or the legal fight to decriminalize homosexuality. Even as it hosts established organizations for sex worker and LGBTQ rights, Bangalore, popularly known as India's Silicon Valley, does not enjoy global queer visibility. Kolkata is even less associated with queer lifeworlds and energies, whether political or social, precisely because of its lack of urban and economic development as compared to these other global Indian cities (notwithstanding its unique political culture). Lesbians in the city are still more invisible. When I first started research on this project, a cousin who had lived her entire life there asked, with incredulity, "There are lesbians in Kolkata?"

27 Writing on space and sexuality in the postapartheid South African city, Zethu Matebeni (2011, 121) suggests that lesbians have a different relationship with space than gay men, noting that "while the latter dominate space (such as clubs,

bars and cafés etc), lesbians rarely have territorial aspirations. They attach more importance to social and interpersonal networks and relationships."

28   Another SFE member observed a similar trend, noting that "young women are coming [to the organization] for orientation, not politics." These words sharply evoke the sentiments of a previous generation of Indian feminists who felt that young women entered the Indian women's movement for a job and not for politics (see the introduction and chapter 1 of this book).

29   In one of the few accounts of the digital intimacies engaged in by middle-class women, S. Krishnan (2018, 156) mentions her respondent, a young user of the Pink Sofa gay and lesbian dating site, as turning to the space for a lot more than dating, and "indeed it was more a place for her to make friends with other queer women and build something of a community."

30   Being *aantel*, or intellectual, was deeply fetishized by Left Front leaders, themselves patrons and even producers of arts, literature, and high culture who prided themselves on intellectualism, cultural refinement, and educated tastes. Subsequent leader Mamata Banerjee's populism was partly rooted in her lack of such cultured and genteel dispositions and was seen as shaping a political culture of crass spectacle (Nielsen 2016).

31   I also heard of more structured attempts to direct, if not discipline, queer desire. A residential workshop that took place at a location outside Kolkata was one such site. Even as SFE members acknowledged that this was inevitably the first opportunity for several young queers to stay overnight with their partners, there were rules to ensure that the workshop was not used for romancing. The organization defended these rules on the basis that coupledom should not take precedence over friendship and community building. In discussing these tensions, one SFE member put it thus: "Sappho does not fully repress the play mode, but it does police [it]." For a critical counter to the divide between queer activism and pleasure in gay nightlife, see Khubchandani (2020).

32   Dasgupta (2017) shows the hegemony of English on the Indian queer internet (as on the internet more generally; see Benedicto 2014), with gay users being marginalized for posting in the vernacular, notwithstanding an increased online presence of people from small towns with varying proficiencies in English.

33   Similarly, when I asked Durba, who features more prominently in chapter 3, whether anyone at SFE discussed sex toys, she responded, "Sappho is a platform for emotional support and rights-based politics. So, I don't think people here would ask for a sex toy." The organization had, however, conducted workshops on polyamory and monoamory, she said. This kind of language—of services and workshops—was quite different from that used by SFE members interviewed in 2008–9, including Srimati, who said that Sappho was the only place in the city where she could think about sexuality, desire, and the body, in contrast to women's groups that only engaged these issues in relation to violence (see S. Roy 2014).

34   Sappho for Equality even stayed away from the annual Pride events as a way of maintaining the politics of making visible "the issue and not the individual."

The organization found the space of the actual Pride march to be dominated by gay men and transwomen, and also worried about its growing corporatization and the dominance of celebrities.

35 On the complexities of scripting a queer life, Ahmed (2014a, 151) writes, "For already in describing what may be queer, I am also defining grounds of an ideality, in which to have an ideal queer life, or even to be legitimately queer, people must act in some ways rather than others. We need to ask: How does defining a queer ideal rely on the existence of others who fail the ideal?"

36 The advertisement, as well as the article by Bhattacharya (2013) on the politics of queer visibility, were discussed at SFE meetings.

37 Such dynamics are, of course, recognizable from histories of "political lesbianism"—or the idea that being a lesbian was more a political belief, or even practice, than a sexual identity—in US feminisms in the 1970s and 1980s. Rubin (2011, chap. 4) mentions several problems with the idea and how it manifested in tensions around sadomasochism, including how it made it difficult for politicized lesbian women to accept lesbians who were not feminist; how it led to feminist lesbians identifying more with the women's movement than with the lesbian community; and how it prevented the recognition of lesbian desire and ultimately impeded the development of lesbian politics and consciousness. Andrea Long Chu (in Chu and Berg 2018) finds this kind of political lesbianism as being essentially about governing desire—premised in one's capacity to change one's desires—in ways that are highly amenable to the forms of moralizing that I discern in this feminist queer community. On moralizing and the divides it created between "politically advanced" lesbian women and "politically flawed" gay men in North American HIV/AIDS activism, see Gould (2009, 345).

38 *Sindoor*, or vermillion, placed in the parting of the hair is a key marker of a married Hindu woman's fidelity to her husband. In offering a genealogy of *sindoor* in Indian film and feminism, Das (2020, 1034) reminds us how the film *Fire* plays with the cultural practice and "effectively destabilises the heteronormative marriage ideals and creates a strategic disengagement with the ritualistic value of sindoor." See also Dasgupta and Banerjea's (2013) discussion of this celebration of Karwa Chauth by local lesbians, where Banerjea cautions against adopting an uncritical secular queer position.

39 In the late 1980s, the marriage of two policewomen, Leela and Urmila, constituted a critical event in this history. This is, of course, not to say that marriage—and homonormative aspirations around domesticity, consumption, and family—were not contentious among Indian queer activists, especially in the aftermath of the decriminalization of homosexuality, when it was obvious that same-sex marriage would be the next struggle goal. Activists in SFE had long anticipated and resisted the materialization of a privatized queer liberation, which made available, in the words of one member, "an easy access to a kind of liberal agency."

40 It is worth noting that the Bengali communists were also deeply uncomfortable with forms of excessive consumption—with their male leaders preferring

simplicity and modesty in dress, for instance. I explore the politics of sartorial styles, especially of left-leaning Indian feminists, both queer and nonqueer, in chapter 3.

41 Sappho for Equality had a substantial network of queer academics, within India and from the diaspora, who were key to the circulation of scholarly books and activist ideas. These kinds of transnational exchanges and links have been common to histories of queer activism in India; see Dave (2012).

42 A marker of a more explicit "trans" turn in SFE was available in *Swakanthey*, where the editor noted a change in terminology from "lesbian, bisexual and transgender women" to "persons assigned gender female at birth" as a way of correcting previous patterns of excluding transgender identities (Subhagata Ghosh 2016). For the reflections of some members on transgender issues, and especially transmasculinity, after the National Legal Services Authority verdict of 2014, see Biswas, Beethi, and Ghosh (2019).

43 Sex worker organizations—with the exception of the Durbar Mahila Samanwaya Committee—ignored transgender sex workers, they argued.

44 They also claimed that the only transwomen who were welcomed into elite activist/NGO circles were those who had *poisha* (money), were *shikhkhito* (educated), and had "class" (said in English), pointing to divides *within* the transgender community. Their critiques have wider resonance when we consider how some transgender persons have found easy inclusion in Hindu nationalist neoliberal India. The transgender activist Laxmi Narayan Tripathi, founder of the first *hijra akhara* (*hijra* Hindu collective), is evoked in these critical readings as an instance of the convergence of Hindutva, neoliberalism, and nonnormative sex and gender (Dasgupta and Dasgupta 2018b). On transnormativities that have emerged within transgenderism, beyond the Indian context, see Pearce, Steinberg, and Moon (2019).

3. Queer Self-Fashioning

1 The production house behind the Anouk advertisement was quoted in the mainstream media as saying, "We tried to avoid the stereotypes associated with gay people. There was no one woman looking more masculine or feminine in the film. We tried to give it a candid feel like it is any other couple being apprehensive about meeting the parents" (Hebbar 2015). Critical readings of the advertisement can be found in Bhattacharya (2015); P. Singh (2017); Sircar (2017); and Strey (2017).

2 Rahul Rao considers the postdecriminalization period as marking a specific temporality, of what happens after liberal rights are achieved—or, in Jasbir Puar's words, "what happens when 'we' get 'what we want'" (Puar, quoted in Rao 2020b, 2). The intimate projects of queer self-making at stake in this chapter unfold against the gaining of some measure of success, but also embody some of the temporal and affective complexities that Rao (2020a, 2) lays out, in spaces where "people had not got what they wanted, or had only just got what they wanted, or had felt implicated in the fact of others not having what they wanted."

3 Offering a robust overview of queer theory's foundational attachment to antinormativity, Wiegman and Wilson (2015, 2) show how it served, in fact, to flatten norms, which were "more dynamic and more politically engaging than queer critique has usually allowed." Beyond the specificities of this debate on queerness and antinormativity, my discussion in this chapter has also been helped by broader takes on queer (and nonqueer) relationships and investments in social norms; see, especially, Ahmed (2006, 2014a).

4 "Normativity as a relative ideal might not be accessible for many people in most parts of the world," writes Yau Ching of contemporary East Asian societies (quoted in Henry 2020, 24). Ethnographies on queer Asia align with queer-of-color critiques that "have sought to expand the purview of queer studies beyond the privileged vantage point of white, middle-class, gay men. Through transnational and diasporic approaches, queer-of-color critiques have exposed the subordinated status but insurgent agency of racial minorities who inhabit the contradictory cracks of liberal societies in North American [sic] and Western Europe" (Henry 2020, 13). For similar critiques and interventions that also take seriously the (in)commensurabilities between queer and area studies, see Arondekar and Patel (2016); and, in the same volume, Macharia (2016).

5 Queer theorists like Bersani (1995) and Edelman (2004) have famously posited queerness as being antithetical to community, the family, and the social, exemplified in Edelman's rejection of reproductive futurism in the figure of the child. For critiques of antirelationality, which center queer feminist and queer people of color positions (like Gopinath 2005), see Muñoz (2009). For efforts to render queer politics more commensurate with reproductive logics and futures, see Sperring and Stardust (2020).

6 Joshi (2012) argues that respectability is more salient than ever in queer politics in the Global North (and globally); even as the gap between heterosexuals and queers might have narrowed, there is a widening gap between "respectable" and "not respectable" queers. On how LGBTQ organizations can function as respectable middle-class spaces, contra a more queerly intersectional politics, see Ward (2008).

7 The closet and attendant rubrics of coming out, visibility, and pride were also subject to critique, for essentializing homosexual identity and for universalizing Anglo-European queer experiences. The master narrative of the closet and coming out could end up marginalizing other tropes and categories through which queer existence and experience is made sense of, especially in the Global South; see, for instance, Gopinath (2005); khanna (2005); Mourad (2016); and Najmabadi (2014).

8 As opposed to coming out, Dave (2012, 24) finds leaving home to be "a more salient rubric" for queer Indian women. The imperative to leave home extends beyond queer women and includes poor rural development workers, who experienced the home as confining, even cagelike (see chapter 5).

9 Gopinath (2005) usefully summarizes how the home is a key site of contestation in both postcolonial feminist scholarship and queer theory. Foundational

to feminist theorizing in South Asia was the nationalist configuration of the home as the site of the emergence of a new bourgeois domesticity and a new patriarchy (see P. Chatterjee 1989). In queer studies, in turn, the home is "a primary site of gender and sexual oppression for queer and female subjects," and thus to be "left behind, to be escaped in order to emerge into another, more liberatory space" (Gopinath 2005, 14). The queer South Asian diasporic texts that Gopinath considers imaginatively transform the idea of home beyond these (post)colonial and queer analytics.

10 These shifts have been noted elsewhere, where "the visible participation of some parents in support of their 'out' children at recent pride festivals and other public events marks a highly controversial dimension of a queer politics that, in South Korea as elsewhere, remains as much family-oriented as individually based" (Henry 2020, 2). Eng (2010) observes, in an early instance of queer liberalism in the United States, how queers moved from coming out via a severing of ties with family and kin to reinhabiting familial structures in public and visible ways. This shift is also reflected in the desire for state recognition of same-sex marriage.

11 Horton (2018, 1065) shows how renouncing marriage was also a way of coming out for the urban queer Indian women he interviewed who, in their refusal to marry, confronted the heteronormativity that women "expected and [were] conditioned to want."

12 There is a vast literature on *bhadralok* femininity, especially on the nineteenth-century figure of the *bhadramahila*. See Borthwick (1984); Sarkar (2001); and, for a postliberalization take, Donner (2008).

13 While Sushmita spoke of the *bhalo meye* in terms of gender and sexuality alone, class and caste were also constitutive of this figure. The *bhalo meye*—or *chhele*—of the Bengal marriage market would have to be middle-class, upper-caste, and Hindu besides being gender-conforming. She is also reminiscent of the lesbian couple in the Anouk ad, which P. Singh (2017, 729) describes as configuring lesbians as "homely," after Geeta Patel's critical appraisal of this term (2004).

14 Najmabadi (2008, 31) reminds us of the trauma of "family severance" among transgender and transsexual persons in Iran, especially for female-to-male (FTM) transpersons:

> Severance from family often means not only emotional hardship and homelessness for prospective transsexuals, but also a loss of education and job opportunities. While transsexuals tend to find each other and form alternative kin worlds of their own, they often face enormous problems in the immediate period of being thrown out into a hostile world. MTF trans persons are much more likely to face this predicament than are FTMs. Correspondingly, family reconciliation is often easier for FTMs than for MTFs. Several close relatives of (pre-/non-/post-op) FTMs explicitly said their acceptance of their daughter/sister becoming a son/brother would have been unimaginable if it had been the other way around.

15 The NALSA judgment contained only one reference to FTM transpeople, thereby erasing a minority within an already marginalized community (Loh 2018; Semmalar 2014).

16 In other contexts, however, this would play out differently. I thank one of the reviewers of the manuscript for this book for drawing my attention to the documentary film *Manjuben Truckdriver* (2003), in which it is transmasculinity that makes queerness livable in rural India.

17 Coming out was also very different for transwomen, and especially those belonging to subaltern communities of historical disadvantage, like *hijras*. "Becoming a hijra does not leave much room for selective coming outs, or for romanticism around the paradoxical safety of the closet," writes U. Sen (2018, 89), speaking, in contrast, of her own coming out as a middle-class cisgender lesbian woman in Kolkata.

18 On feminist suspicion of transsexuality as normative and normalizing, see Heyes (2007); Butler (2004); and Halberstam (1998). Iran presents a very different story of the relationship between transsexuality, transgenderism, and homosexuality, as richly told by Najmabadi (2008), who shows how state discourses and forms of religio-legal regulation of transsexuality were "productive of paradoxical, and certainly unintended, effects that at times benefit homosexuals.... As one pre-op FTM (female-to-male transsexual) succinctly put it: 'Once I was diagnosed as TS (trans-sexual), I started having sex with my girlfriend without feeling guilty'" (Najmabadi 2008, 25; see also Najmabadi 2014).

19 Ashwini Sukthankar, an Indian LGBTQ activist, attributes an initial wariness toward transsexual rights claims as aggravating the belief among lesbians that for two women to make a life together in India, "one must metamorphose into a man in order for the relationship to be acceptable or recognizable to society" (2007, 91). This belief was not absent from the understanding of some queer feminist activists at SFE, as we see in this chapter. Queer feminist positions on transsexuality were also not static, as the critical self-reflections of some SFE activists show (Biswas, Beethi, and Ghosh 2019).

20 Commenting on the early visibility of transsexuality in the United States, including "border wars" between lesbians and FTM transsexuals, Halberstam (1998, 293–94) shows that distinctions between FTMs and lesbians can be blurry (even as lesbians might have subsumed transgenderism in their own history and politics): "Many FTMs do come out as lesbians before they come out as transsexuals (many, it must also be said, do not).... Once they have transitioned, many transsexual men want to maintain their ties to their queer lesbian communities."

21 These highly limited choices—of being mired in the rubrics of state recognition or not being afforded any recognition at all—intensified when the Indian state introduced, conjointly, the National Register of Citizens and the Citizenship Amendment Act in 2019. I turn to these and the unprecedented forms of mass protest that they ignited in this book's conclusion, but let me note here

how these proposed new laws risked further exiling transgender individuals and communities from the nation-state.

22 "Top surgery" refers to SRS that alters or removes a person's breasts. The NALSA judgment did not specify surgical intervention as a requirement for formal recognition and registration purposes, but this remained unclear and open to local interpretation and enforcement. The eventual law made surgical intervention a prerequisite for revising gender identity and further eroded the individual right to self-identify. Hinchy (2019) traces statist logics on transgenderism to nineteenth-century debates, which similarly turned to medical expertise when wrestling with diverse forms of gender identity and expression in India.

23 The cutting of feminine hair went beyond norms policing gender and sexuality, however. Upper-caste Hindu widows had to shave their heads as a marker of shedding their femininity and sexuality, while Dalit women were forcibly shaved to shame them for alleged caste-based transgressions. For a deeper exploration of the symbolism around hair, see Lamb's (2000) ethnography on gender and aging in a Bengali village.

24 *Butch* and *femme* were terms used by this group of queers.

25 The evocation of JU is an important reminder of the extent to which, especially in Kolkata, class distinction mediated belonging to specific subcultures and countercultures.

26 Fabindia is considered synonymous with the revival and preservation of hand-loomed clothing in India. It has branches in most major cities, selling men's, women's and children's wear, furnishings, jewelry, and organic food; see R. Singh (2011).

27 My thanks to Srimati Basu for reminding me of Nilima Bose, in Amitav Ghosh's novel *The Hungry Tide*, who marries into Bengali communism and subsequently runs a nonprofit in the Sunderbans for women's development. The novel describes her strikingly as "small in height and her wispy hair, which she wore in a knot at the back of her head, was still more dark than grey. It was her practice to dress in saris woven and crafted in the workshops of the Badabon Trust, garments almost always of cotton, with spidery borders executed in batik." Her dress embodied her "selfless devotion" to working for the betterment of the people of the region (2005, 21).

28 One important argument for decriminalization was rooted in queer contributions to overall economic growth in India (see Nishant Shahani, in Rallin 2019; and, for transnational dimensions of the same phenomenon, see Rao 2020b). Joshi (2012) shows how the emergence of gay markets and respectable gay consumers was key to the production of a respectable queer politics.

29 The Khadi Bhandar state-run outlets sell khadi, the homespun fabric that, under Mahatma Gandhi, became a symbol of India's self-sufficiency in colonial times.

30 Kaur and Sundar (2016, 9) note that, in postliberalized India, "the art of self-makeover does not affect a real shift to another identity, it does create caste or

class ambiguity that is at least provisionally less exclusionary in nature." The work of appearances, they suggest, is twofold: "'standing out' in order to draw attention to oneself, and for 'blending in' with dominant groups."

31 Speaking of Baudh's essay, Menon (2009, 99) writes, "In an intensely caste-defined society such as India, such 'passing' is rare, as one's caste identity is almost the first thing made evident by any Hindu name." Bandyopadhyay (2014) notes that, in West Bengal, upwardly mobile lower-caste families did at times hide their caste identity (of which surnames are not always an exact indicator).

32 A landmark case by the state of California against an information technology company for caste-based discrimination not only exploded the truth around caste in Silicon Valley but also showed the extent to which caste atrocity was speakable only under the condition of strict anonymity. Writing the story for the *New York Times*, Dutt (2020) spoke to Dalit workers, one of whom she quoted as saying, "If they knew I was Dalit, it could ruin my career" (the complainant behind the lawsuit was unnamed). For similar forms of concealment and passing in premier Indian institutions of higher education, see Subramanian (2015, 2019); and on how discrimination against Dalits endures in the name of meritocracy in Kolkata, see Bandyopadhyay (2014).

33 In a common use of the term, Sushmita employs *class* to signal caste-based hierarchies; see Roberts (2016).

34 While the *bhadralok* includes many castes, it is dominated by the three upper castes of Brahman, Kayastha, and Baidya; "but they claimed their superiority on the basis of culture and education, not caste" (Bandyopadhyay 2014, 34).

35 Caste became a prominent concern in Indian queer activist circles, with an emergent body of public writing on being a "Dalit queer" (Jyoti 2017). Kolkata's queer community was not shielded from the internal politics of caste. Casteist slogans were allegedly raised at an event after the *Koushal* judgment, prompting some tense discussion in social media forums, including SFE's Facebook group.

36 Younger members first encountered SFE at the annual Boi Mela (Book Fair), where they later sold the organization's newsletter. As one member, Sutanuka, recounts in *Swakanthey*, "I joined Sappho for Equality in November 2005 and in the last Kolkata Book Fair (Jan–Feb, 2006) many of you must have seen me with some others, distributing Swakanthey in the fair.... The 2006 Kolkata Book Fair found me moving around excitedly not as a book lover but as a news hawker trying to voice the anguish of some of my friends who have been labeled by our society as sexually marginalized women and denied their right to live" (Sutanuka 2007, 8).

37 These generational divides did not always hold. There were older queer women who had joined SFE for explicitly political over personal reasons, and there were younger members who, like Durba, were involved in left-wing student activism. Overwhelmingly, though, and across generations, members did not come from the kind of communist backgrounds that were otherwise commonplace to activist trajectories in the region.

38 On how the idiom of family shaped the internal patriarchal culture of communist parties, making it hard for activists to recognize sexism and sexual violence within, see Da Costa (2010); and S. Roy (2012c). On the social life of Bengali communism, see Kar and Bradbury (2020); and Ruud (2003).

39 The Vishwa Hindu Parishad (VHP) is a right-wing Hindu nationalist organization. *Khap* references *khap panchayats* (caste-based village councils) that acquired international notoriety for their violent policing of intercaste marriages in North India.

40 Dutta (2019, 7) quotes one left-wing activist: "I've heard many left groups decrying, 'no thought to food-clothes-shelter, but excessive attention to sexuality!' But think once, brother, what if you were told that you cannot kiss your wife? If you kiss her cops will haul you to jail? Brother, the BJP [Bharatiya Janata Party] is coming to power.... It is this BJP that, along with some Hindu and Muslim fundamentalist groups, had opposed the Delhi High Court judgment." The same activist adopted a classically paternalistic stance toward transwomen, however. In mapping emergent and shifting activist assemblages comprising independent student activists and non-funded LGBTQ groups, Dutta (2019) reveals multiple possibilities and limits around solidarity, unavailable in spaces of party politics and in funded LGBTQ formations.

41 Subramanian (2015) describes premier engineering institutions in India as producing an intimacy between Tamil Brahmin male students and their professors that is rooted in assumed, and not even actual, Brahman status as a caste kinship.

4. Feminist Governmentality

Parts of this chapter previously appeared in Srila Roy (2019), "Precarity, Aspiration and Neoliberal Development: Women Empowerment Workers in West Bengal," *Contributions to Indian Sociology* 53 (3): 392–421; and Srila Roy (2017a), "Enacting/Disrupting the Will to Empower: Feminist Governance of 'Child Marriage' in Eastern India," *Signs: Journal of Women in Culture and Society* 42 (4): 867–91.

1 As Cody (2013, 12) notes of literary activism in southern India, we can hear in it "the echoes of socialist politics in a decidedly neoliberal age."

2 Changes to the Protection of Women from Domestic Violence Act of 2005 recognized NGOs as "official 'service providers' with wide discretionary powers over legal aid and case registration" (Roychowdhury 2015, 800). Women's groups, whether autonomous or NGO-ized, have long provided such extralegal interventions when it comes to marital breakdown and domestic violence (S. Basu 2015; Grover 2011).

3 The Indian state promoted microcredit as an alternative to rural banks adversely affected by banking reforms in the period of liberalization (Nirantar Trust 2015).

4   Critical approaches to rights discourses point to their easy co-optation by the state or market, their universalizing and homogenizing tendencies, and their abstraction from particular social contexts such that they only served rhetorical functions (Kapur 2005; Madhok 2012; with respect to development, see also Cornwall and Molyneux 2006).

5   The initial noncommercial approach to MFIS soon gave way to an increased commercialization of this sector led by private companies. On corporate microfinance, see Radhakrishnan (2018).

6   The use of the descriptor *rights-based* is appealing for development actors, for whom it provides not just international legitimacy but also "moral authority and purpose" (Cornwall and Molyneux 2006, 1179).

7   As Wilson (2015, 11) writes, "Significantly, issues of gender relations within the household and domestic violence were generally not considered to fall within the purview of these groups, whose stated objective was women's empowerment, even when these issues were raised by the women members of the groups."

8   The self-help groups typically comprise anywhere between ten and twenty people, usually women, who take part in rotational savings and credit programs. Since the 1990s, "the expansion of SHG programmes throughout India has perhaps done more than any other programme to produce sites conducive to development" (Jakimow 2013, 29). Regional governments addressed social problems, such as child malnutrition and rural credit, through SHGs (Menon 2009; Tharu and Niranjana 1994). On SHGs in West Bengal, see Sanyal (2014); Sen and Majumder (2015); and Tenhunen (2009). For an account of the origins of SHGs in low-caste women's protests against alcohol abuse and their subsequent co-optation by government-led microcredit schemes in rural Andhra Pradesh, see Still (2017).

9   These accounts uncovered the SHG not as a site of empowerment but of new techniques of surveillance, shaming, and the reproduction rather than disruption of patriarchal power and privilege; see Karim (2011).

10 This book does not tell their story, but there is a story to tell, especially as NGOs constitute a huge source of employment for women of a range of backgrounds. I have elsewhere explored the experiences of middle-ranking NGO staff in Bangalore and Kolkata, and especially how NGOs politicized a particular generation—and class—of professional women; see S. Roy (2011).

11 On changes to the political economy of rural West Bengal and on rural subjectivities, see Chattaraj (2010, 2015); A. Majumder (2018); S. Majumder (2018); Nielsen (2018); and D. Roy (2014).

12 The use of microfinance loans for consumption purposes is a widespread tendency.

13 Gender and sexuality were at the heart of more anxious accounts of the impact of rapid industrialization and urbanization and featured in high-level political contests in West Bengal. Both the Left Front and social movements resisting its plans for industrial expansion evoked cultural associations between women and

romanticized rurality to argue their opposing positions (Nielsen 2018; see also Chattaraj 2010).

14 I met one Christian woman volunteer for Janam; none of the volunteers I met were Muslim, and there were no programs and projects that specifically targeted Muslim women or girls (who were present at meetings and trainings).

15 It is interesting to note that a report on SHGs conducted by the Delhi-based Nirantar Trust indicated how gender, and especially violence against women, was not a safe issue to discuss in the context of microcredit SHGs (Sharma and Parthasarathy 2007).

16 Unlike feminist traditions of sharing experience, leftist consciousness-raising was premised on the cadres knowing the answer. I thank Raka Ray for this nuance.

17 Gilbertson (2021) tells us that the "social norms approach" became popular in the development industry in the new millennium, especially around gender and violence; social norms were identified as a barrier to the successful implementation of development programs. While Freirean and gender and development frameworks saw empowerment as a process of collective consciousness-raising, these ideas proved amenable to resignification in peer education strategies focused on changing social norms and even individual mindsets under neoliberal development.

18 On shakti or feminine power as an idiom of women's agency in development-speak, see Berry (2003); and Cody (2013).

19 R. Ray (1999, 48), writes how, during the long communist reign in West Bengal, "literacy [was] an issue that enjoy[ed] unquestioned legitimacy within this political culture."

20 Ferguson (2015) proposes cash transfers as a foundation for a new leftist political imaginary centered on distribution; for a critique of this position, see Nilsen (2020).

21 The rural women received such broad humanist-leftist explanations of their social condition(ing) with appropriate affective responses—loud approval or quiet nodding. They even interjected Ila's speech with their own anecdotes on domestic violence, dowry, and feticide.

22 S. Basu (2015, 201) reports very similar trends in her ethnography of antiviolence counseling and activism in Kolkata. In the face of limited state capacity, she writes that women's organizations "can at best proffer less patriarchally coded solutions."

23 Tambe (2019, 153) reads the trajectory of raising the age of marriage as marking several moves: "from protecting girls from unwanted sex, to seeing girls' potential fertility as a population threat, to then seeing girls as targets of investment." For historic and contemporary takes on child/early marriage, see S. Basu (2015); Sunder Rajan (2003); Sarkar (2001); and S. Sen (2000).

24 For the best critical appraisal of this campaign, see Moeller (2018).

25 With the raising of the age of consent as part of the 2013 Criminal Law (Amendment) Act (the principal state response to Jyoti Singh Pandey's gang rape and murder in 2012), India established itself as having the highest age of consent. This has put the Indian women's movement into the curious position of "arguing against, rather than for, raising the age of consent" and given, moreover, the use of child marriage prevention laws to police the consensual choices of young people, of "raising the age of consent would, in fact, curtail, rather than extend, young women's freedoms" (Tambe 2019, 146–47).

26 On how the Hindu Right's spectacular governance of intimacies included the girl-child of the Beti Bachao (Save and Educate Daughters) campaign, see Baxi (2019).

27 Janam also engaged SFE for sexuality training purposes. The workshop delivered by SFE was remembered by one NGO employee as offering a "scientific" view on women's sexual health, from periods to pregnancy. She seemed less persuaded by the group's treatment of same-sex desire, arguing, in a familiar mode, that talk of women's sexuality alienated poor rural women who could not even think about sex (let alone lesbianism) because they had "no *bhaat* [rice] in their tummies."

28 This included the district's child protection officer, part of the bureaucratic machinery of the Integrated Child Protection Scheme that was launched by the government of India in 2009. The officer ensured the implementation of the governance around child protection and development at the district level.

29 In contrast, another member, Supriya, had been married at age fifteen and had a *shukher jibon* (life of happiness). She felt that revealing this positive personal experience might set a bad example for other women in the community (even as she agreed with me that women who get married after the legal age of eighteen may or may not have a *shukher jibon*).

30 This trainer's pedagogical model was one of collective consciousness-raising, filled with good humor and wise feminist lessons. She asked the women to collectively reflect on hard truths emerging not just from what they had experienced in the field but also vis-à-vis their interactions with one another.

31 On the differences between rural and urban microfinance meetings and how these "were both absorbed into and disrupted the domestic everyday," see Kar (2018, 113).

32 As one of the staff involved in the early marriage project explained to me, their discussions with the community would begin with comments such as "Why is she [a daughter] not going to school?," "Admit her to a different school," or "Put her in a crafts program" as a way of emphasizing schooling and its links to training and employment.

33 On longer histories of childhood and child-rearing in colonial Bengal, see P. K. Bose (1995); on respectable women teachers in colonial Bengal who were meant to model modern bourgeois feminine behavior to their students—as future good wives and mothers—and how teaching itself was a "set of learned

gendered behaviors," see P. Sengupta (2005, 49); on parenting and education in liberalized Kolkata, see Donner (2008).

34 Rural households were fast transforming with the availability of greater home-based income-generating possibilities, some of which, like rolling bidis and embroidering *zari* saris, necessitated the use of the labor of younger members of the household (Chattaraj 2015).

35 Writing critically about the link between schooling, security, and empower-ment in rural West Bengal, Da Costa (2010) shows the ambivalent benefits of schooling for women (and men) given structural insecurities born out of rural dispossession, gendered asymmetries of the Left's redistributive policies, esca-lating unemployment, and violence against women. Some rural communities even described education to Da Costa as the cause for and not the solution to poverty; see also Sen and Sengupta (2012).

36 Such relationships serve as a powerful reminder of how development, especially of the participatory variety, produces new hierarchies among communities of women (A. Sharma 2008; Jakimow 2018; Pigg 1992).

37 In one feedback session back at the office after a regular field trip, a worker reported being threatened by villagers who had apparently said that if the *mahila samiti* came to their area, they would make them strip and flee the village. Dia presented such risk as an expected part of feminist labor, of doing *mahila samitir kaaj*.

38 As S. Krishnan (2020, 9) observes of consent in relation to young Indian women's participation in public sex, "While a great deal of attention is rou-tinely focused on the circumstances in which young women can say 'no' to sex, choosing to say 'yes' is far from uncomplicated."

39 On how victims of trafficking are presented as suffering from false consciousness when they refuse to be rescued and rehabilitated, see Soderlund (2005). In unpack-ing how feminist governance manages such wayward subjects, I have turned more than once to the rich accounts and critiques of antitrafficking practice in Agustin (2007); Bernstein (2010); Cheng (2010); and O'Connell Davidson (2005).

40 The founder—father, even—of microfinance, Nobel Prize laureate Muham-mad Yunus, was referred to by local people as Moneylender Yunus (Kar 2018); Karim 2011. The accusation that MFIs were moneylenders was also one of the few acts of resistance available to subaltern women to disrupt humanitar-ian claims toward poor women's care, rights, and freedom. Jakimow (2018) describes how accusations of being a moneylender—of profiting from the indebtedness of others—adversely affected development workers in Indonesia who saw themselves as doing good.

41 "This power dynamic subjects the poor to mandates of the NGO that are often in conflict with local norms, and it sometimes creates new opportunities of violence against the very people (poor women) the NGOs seek to empower," writes Karim (2001, 93). Sanyal (2014, 145) reports on her fieldwork in West Bengal, where SHG members forcibly removed a "child bride" from her wed-ding and "smashed her shell bangles." It is widely recognized that MFIs turn to force and violence to recover loans.

42 Self-help groups have been known to both co-opt women's antiliquor ag-
itations and unexpectedly address alcoholism across socially marginalized
communities (Still 2017; Mosse 2019). See also Radha Kumar's history of the
Indian women's movement that includes the important anti-arrack movement
as constituting one important stream of women's mass mobilization (Kumar
1993).

43 On queer feminist efforts, see chapter 2. Feminist critiques of state developmentalism have repeatedly warned of the dangers of presuming that women
exist in natural solidarity with one another based on their shared gendered interests and identities, thus erasing internal hierarchies and contests (see Sharma
2008).

44 Janam made strategic compromises too. In locating its income-generating
program in its own premises to facilitate women's mobility outside the home,
Janam knew it was prioritizing rights over credit. For *dol* women, travel to and
from the office was, however, complicated; many could not afford the travel
costs, while the risk of sexual violence served as a deterrent.

45 Instead of a liberal feminism that is invested in projects of saving others to
fortify its own legitimacy and agency, Halberstam (2011, 128) advocates, as part
of a wider project of recognizing the ambiguous promises of queer failure, for
"a feminism that fails to save others or replicate itself, a feminism that finds
purpose in its own failure."

5. Subaltern Self-Government

1 K. Krishnan (2020, 177), a radical leftist leader who gained prominence during
the 2012 antirape protests, also turns to Rashsundari's life as a "caged bird" to
underscore Indian women's lack of autonomy in the current conjuncture. For
an overview of urban Indian women's mobilizations to "break the cage," see S.
Roy (2016a).

2 Younger SFE members similarly spoke of the organization as opening several
doors for them, with one claiming that the space offered "knowledge about
so many issues, not just LGBT." Recall, however, that they did not uniformly
experience the heteropatriarchal home as a cage, as is generally assumed of
queer women.

3 Moodie (2015), like Mahmood (2005), writes of women's acquiescence to social
conditions and to norms as a way of countering the (Western) imperative to
equate agency with resistance, even as she stresses how norms are inhabited
with deep ambivalence. In contrast, I wish to make room for the open refusal of
norms, and the imagining of others, as central to the kinds of "wayward" if not
explicitly resistant forms of self- and world-making I encountered. To channel
Hartman's ideas further, we could say that development transforms "the imagination of what you might want and who you might be" (Hartman 2019, 24)

4 This section's title evokes Rabindranath Tagore's 1916 novel *Ghare Baire*, or *The
Home and the World* (later adapted into a film of the same name by Satyajit Ray).

The novel exemplifies tensions around "the woman's question" in the high tide of the anticolonial struggle, in the transgressions of its female protagonist Bimala from the domestic (*ghare*) to the public male world of politics (*baire*). Reading Bimala's exit from the *zenana*, or women's quarters—a site of intense contestation among Indian nationalists—as a literal coming out, Rao (2014, 5), writes, "The Woman Question was, in this astonishingly literal sense, always already queer."

5   At a moment of high economic growth, John (2020, 147) notes how only 15 percent of women have any kind of paid work, while the rest of the female population—apart from a small percentage of upper-caste and class-privileged women in urban India—were basically dependent on male breadwinners, tied to households and the family, through their provision of "some form or other of unpaid family labour."

6   In her ethnography of South Indian Dalits, Still (2017) observes how such trends are not just persisting but growing in a postliberalization moment; Dalit women are being educated for marriage rather than employment, as a way of improving the social standing of their community. Still also shows how the neoliberal view of the "developed" or "empowered" woman—promoted through microfinance institutions and self-help groups—comes into conflict with cultural expectations of domestic respectability. Across castes and communities, Indian women must balance the economic needs of the household with the symbolic imperative to produce class- and caste-based distinction by conducting entrepreneurial activity, under the guise of being a dutiful housewife, for instance (see D. Sen 2017).

7   On working-class mothers' aspirations for a better life through "happy domesticity," see Sen and Sengupta (2012, 74); on the ideology of domesticity and the significance among poor women for "nonworking housewife roles," see S. Sen (2001); and on the extension and modernization of the housewife's role in neoliberal West Bengal, see Gooptu and Chakravarty (2013).

8   By *lower castes* I mean those who fall below the three upper castes in Bengal (the Brahmans, Baidyas, and Kayasthas) but who are not classified as of the Scheduled Castes. On the caste hierarchy in rural West Bengal, see Nielsen (2018); and S. Majumder (2018). S. Majumder's (2021) observations of the caste and gender discourses surrounding women's informal home-based work in small landowning middle-caste households are especially relevant to this peri-urban terrain.

9   The Bengali word *kaaj* can signify different things in different contexts, including paid work, a vocation, or even a morally good or bad deed.

10   Workers invariably spoke of their workplace as an "office," thus implying a space that produced respectability for women like themselves (see Khoja-Moolji 2018, 105), and they also dressed as urban office-working women (see S. Majumder 2021). These were just some of the ways in which they ensured that their entry into a world of paid work did not disrupt their gendered and classed social standing in the communities to which they belonged.

11   On the conscious use of a collective rather than individual voice as a way of undermining academic—and NGO-ized—expectations around representa-

tion and expertise, see Sangtin Writers and Nagar (2006, 151), who claim that "our collective voice allowed us not only to explore how we could produce new forms of knowledge but also to gain a space and legitimacy for our critique and reflections."

12 As Mosse (2019, 222) remarks about the inadvertent social impact of developmental policies in Madhya Pradesh, "the project could not claim to have *produced* these and other social and lifestyle changes, but it did provide a context in which social aspirations could be expressed, whether these concerned gender relations, or a feeling for modernity or freedom" (emphasis in the original).

13 Left-wing and autonomous women's groups found themselves to be uneasy bedfellows with the Hindu Right on issues of women's dress and fashion when it came to India hosting beauty pageants as a direct result of liberalization. Both sides cohered in their objection to such new forms of commodifying women's bodies (Oza 2006).

14 The intimate struggle over this piece of clothing reminds me of Abu-Lughod's (1990) marvelous observations on generational conflicts around lingerie in Bedouin communities.

15 Digital technologies played a significant part in these crafty plans. Some of the workers advised women to use their smartphones to record their mother-in-law's disapproval as "evidence" of what was transpiring in the absence of husbands. One reported a story of success: "She made her husband listen to that recording, after which her husband said, 'Wear nighties, you don't have to wear sari anymore.' Now she wears nighties."

16 Lukose (2009, 68) refers to jeans as a "key commodity" underlying the refashioning of the body as "urban and consumerist."

17 Janam staff wore mostly cotton saris. The sari is still very much the gold standard of the working *bhadramahila*.

18 On the subversive potential of fun, including feminist fun in South Asia, see Kirmani (2020); and Phadke (2020). Both essays are part of a special section, "*Mazaa*: Rethinking Fun, Pleasure and Play in South Asia," in *South Asia: Journal of South Asian Studies* 43 (2); the section editors, Anjaria and Anjaria (2020, 233), seek to establish "why *mazaa* matters, how it offers a methodology and mode of analysis, and what new features of everyday life in South Asia might be brought to light if we put *mazaa* back in the story."

19 Kirmani (2020, 4), for instance, notes how ideas of Muslim women's victimization permeate Pakistan, and how a focus on joy and pleasure "disturbs this very narrow, simplistic, Orientalist image, which objectifies women as passive victims of violent and backward cultures and of men."

20 There are rich ethnographic portraits of young Indian men idling, loitering, or indulging in "timepass," while "good" Indian women are meant to direct their time purposively toward productive or reproductive activity alone (Jeffrey 2010; Lukose 2009).

21 Supriya once told me how some of her VG friends would send her "greetings" via WhatsApp at all times of the night and day, wishing her good night or good

morning. Her husband ultimately asked why she was getting so many messages, and from whom. His playful response—"Baba, what a friendship!"—suggests new marital shifts, which are significant in light of the more general spousal disapproval of wives' friendships beyond the family.

22 For McLaren (2002, 199–200), friendships "across difference" can challenge and even disrupt social norms; these include female friendships that fall outside the parameters of "patriarchal normativity" and, following Michel Foucault, friendships between men that escape the limits set by heteronormativity. On "dissident friendships," see Chowdhury and Philipose (2016).

23 Dona's words beautifully encapsulate the significance of caring for the self as constituting the principal affect and effect of development and human rights work. In making this argument, Lefebvre (2017, 6) warns that "Foucault is not saying that care of the self is by nature individualistic or egoistic, as if it must take place at the expense of other people or by ignoring them. He claims, rather, that in ancient morality the care of the self is a self-sufficient moral end." On how self-love in the Black feminist tradition is a prerequisite for other kinds of affects and relations and stands at the heart of a womanist project (for someone like Audre Lorde, for instance), see Nash (2011).

24 Nineteenth-century feminine ideals included "professed indifference to food, to habitual neglect of eating," relegating women like Rashsundari Debi "to a lifetime of non-eating in the middle of endless feeding" (Sarkar 1993, 53).

25 Spivak (2012) identifies the goal of humanities teaching to be the rearrangement of desire, or the possibility of developing intuitions, affects, and dispositions that enable critical thinking beyond the logic of capital.

26 On consumption in rural contexts and as central to upwardly mobile rural families, see Chattaraj (2010, 2015); Moodie (2015); Mosse (2019); and Ramamurthy (2004). In thinking through the complexities of new globalized cultures of consumption and their ambivalent gendered implications in India and in the Global South more generally, I have also learned from Donner (2008); Dosekun (2020); Fernandes (2006); Ganguly-Scrase and Scrase (2009); Gilbertson (2017); Grewal (2005); Iqani (2016); Lukose (2009); and Nuttall (2009).

27 The easy evocation of individual choice and consumption as sites of women's freedom indicated that the consumptive and aesthetic practices these women were engaged in were also widely in circulation in these locales.

28 Even as I use Mousumi's case to foreground these complexities, it should not take away from the many occasions in which these women counseled other women to stand up to errant or abusive husbands and in-laws.

29 A key criticism of neoliberal feminism in India, and one often laid at the grounds of millennial feminist campaigns around women's mobility, is its interpellation of women as good consumers of neoliberal capitalism; for instance, Gupta (2016, 155) writes, "What I call 'neoliberal feminism' [has] been produced—and deeply shaped by—contemporary forms of marketization that link rights to consumption with feminist freedom." In contrast, Phadke

(2020, 10) argues that the pleasure in reclaiming public spaces belongs not to "the docile bodies of neo-liberal consumers but the rebellious bodies of women who refuse to stay within limits defined by a patriarchal culture." For counter-critiques of millennial feminisms as neoliberal ones, see Lieder (2018).

30　In making these observations on Mahila Samakhya, A. Sharma (2008, 176) suggests that "empowerment in one context does not easily translate into another—that a change in women's self-image and public image through consciousness-raising activities may not influence their power and status across various social contexts. Mahila Samakhya women often spoke about gender equality and yet were not always able to implement these ideas in their own households."

31　What is significant in these accounts is that, in raising the issue of dowry, women disrupted marriage negotiations between uniting families, often putting the alliance at risk.

32　The women's thoughts on their own earnings, and insistence on spending them according to their own wishes, reminds me of these words by the Sangtin Writers and Nagar (2006, 101): "When I first received money after joining work, I thought, in whose hands should I place my earning? My husband's, my mother-in-law's, or my father-in-law's? For two days, I struggled with this dilemma. After much reflection, I decided that it is my earning; I will keep it in my hands, and only I will spend it. Whatever things I am asked to buy, I will get them all. Even if all the money is spent on these requests, it will be spent only by my hands." Sharad Chari (in Pratt 2008, 226) notes the importance of hands in this passage as reflective of an "embodied feminist consciousness."

33　Mothers-in-law are typically the only women able to exercise a degree of power in the joint family, and "wives, particularly young wives, are lowest in the household's power hierarchy" (Sanyal 2014, 44). They appeared, in these women's accounts, as deeply resistant to changing power relations within the household (even as they enabled women's paid work through the critical provision of childcare).

34　Mousumi speculated that part of the male reticence to take on more caring responsibilities had to do with several surveilling gazes, from extended kin to neighbors. Her husband's presence at the village water tap, for instance, prompted others to ask, "Is your wife not home?"

35　Ahearn's (2001) observations of the coexistence of consent and coercion in narratives of elopement are sharply reminiscent of chapter 4's discussion of elopement and early marriage. On the increased role of WhatsApp in shaping intimacies in the rural quotidian, see Tenhunen (2018).

36　On the neoliberal shaping of specific sets of aspirations in India, see Cross (2014); Gooptu (2013); Jeffrey (2010); Kaur and Sundar (2016); Lukose (2009); S. Majumder (2018); Mankekar (2013); and Moodie (2015). Jakobsen and Nielsen (2020, 148) note how existing scholarship has neglected the rural and "has generally fixated on the country's urban middle classes."

37 "Altruistic social work imagines a middle- or upper-caste and class housewife as its paradigmatic subject," writes A. Sharma (2008, 57), while showing how such assumptions reproduced gender, class, and caste norms in state-development projects like Mahila Samakhya.

38 Writing on India's special economic zones, Cross (2014, 151) finds that male workers consent to—even as they contest—exploitative labor "in order to pursue material desires and projects of self-fashioning." It is the pursuit of these projects that keep individuals attached to "structural conditions that mitigate against the collective realization of dreams" (Cross 2014, 136). While Cross sees special economic zones as "arenas of imagination, hope, aspiration and desire in which people construct and assemble possible future worlds for themselves and others from existing ideas and images" (2014, 4), Jakobsen and Nielsen (2020, 146) suggest, in contrast, that aspiration as "social praxis may ground hegemonic processes of neoliberalisation in lived experience."

39 This shows the intimacy between states and NGOs, which "may make it possible for some women to move from being gender advocates within NGOs to filling more influential official positions of authority or at least to find more stable employment within the state" (Bernal and Grewal 2014a, 306).

40 Foucauldian-inspired feminists have long been alive to the normalizing and nonnormalizing potentials of one and the same technologies of the self. See, for instance, Heyes's sharp observations (2007) on how specific practices of the self—dieting, for instance—might operate as both a strategic practice of freedom and a technology of domination.

Conclusion

1 My discussion on feminist critique is informed by Nash's (2019, 34) provocations on how criticism, in the context of what she calls the "intersectionality wars," is constructed as destructive, even violent practice, with the critic "imagined as inflicting harm."

2 On Foucault's ethos of critique, see Butler (2002b); Lemke (2011); and Mahmood (2005).

3 Salem (2019, 1) mobilizes Avery Gordon's idea of haunting to show continuities across political projects, thereby "problematizing the notion of a linear teleological or providential trajectory consisting of distinct eras."

4 I am reminded of Pumla Dineo Gqola's (2021, 47) remarks on the limits of Western feminist-led international solidarity efforts: "The argument for internationalist feminisms and solidarity networks demands honest reflection, not romanticisation of feminist intent. Even for feminist women, sisterhood may be possible, but it is not automatic. It is chosen and earned in processes that are as reflective as they are committed. This is not a paradox."

5 Hemmings (2018, 105) describes the deep humanism of the anarchist Emma Goldman as a different, nonintersectional mode of recognizing oppressions

"whose goal is ... the *eradication of difference* as the starting point of a new communitarianism" (emphasis in the original).

6 Millennial Indian feminism is marked by frictions and tensions between majority and minority feminist voices, which precisely foreground these questions of critique and representation. They also mark other shifts, with Dalit feminists reestablishing their right to speak on their own behalf, as opposed to being spoken for. Williamson's (2019) response to critiques of intersectionality by Nash (2019) reminds us of the history of African American feminists who pledged to speak in defense of themselves: "No one will speak for us but ourselves." Williamson uses this historical evidence to show how defensiveness can also work as a critical posture.

7 In India, the Modi-led BJP government attempted to systematically marginalize NGOs by canceling their registration or revoking their ability to access foreign funds; see Alam (2016).

8 Ahmed (2014b) counters this claim by arguing that "surely what critique does depends on *where*—and *where not*—critique is directed. I doubt very much that critiquing whiteness is something students have learnt to spit out. In fact, much of what needs critiquing still seems to go unnoticed in our academic worlds" (emphasis in the original).

9 The CAA offers expedited citizenship for persecuted religious groups from Afghanistan, Bangladesh, and Pakistan who can prove that they have been living in India since before December 31, 2014. Yet it only extends this right to Buddhists, Christians, Hindus, Jains, Parsis, and Sikhs and thereby excludes Muslims. The CAA must be seen in conjunction with the NRC, under which the right to Indian citizenship is linked to whether individuals can prove that they were born in India between January 1950 and June 1987 or that they are children of bona fide Indian citizens. While the CAA affords entry to non-Muslim religious minorities, the NRC intends to flush out "infiltrators," as the home minister, Amit Shah, declared in what was widely considered a euphemism for Muslims.

10 There were more than a hundred such attacks between May 2015 and December 2018, leaving a total of forty-four people dead. Thirty-six of these victims were Muslim (Human Rights Watch 2019).

11 Self-transformation becomes the condition for utopic possibilities—of what could be rather than of what is—and suggests how "individual change, while not sufficient enough on its own for macro-level change, is nonetheless a necessary part of changing oppressive cultures" (Schalk 2018, 143; see also Muñoz 2009; and Nash 2011).

12 Transgender activists and groups were visible in all protest actions because of their specific vulnerability to the combination of the CAA and NRC. Leaving aside that many transgender individuals have names different from the ones on their birth certificates and might have even been abandoned by their families, many had, in fact, changed their name and gender after the 2014 National Legal Services Authority judgment, the Indian Supreme Court decision that recognized transgender persons as full citizens of India (Desai 2019).

13 There were many intersectional moments in the high tide of the protests against the CAA and NRC; for instance, at Shaheen Bagh, three elderly Muslim women alongside Radhika Vemula (the mother of Rohit Vemula, whose death sparked widespread outrage over caste discrimination in Indian universities) hoisted the Indian flag and sang the national anthem (see Rao 2020a).

14 With the incitement of BJP leaders, local vigilante groups tried to forcibly remove protestors, and especially Muslims. The ensuing "clashes," as the media called them, turned into large-scale violence against Muslims, who were the majority of those killed and whose homes and properties were vandalized. Of the fifty-three people killed from February 23 to February 26, 2020, thirty-eight were Muslim. During the national lockdown that followed, the Delhi police arrested hundreds for their alleged involvement in this violence; these were, again, mostly Muslims, including victims themselves. It is widely accepted that those arrested were being punished by the state for protesting the CAA and NRC (Lalwani 2020).

15 In Kolkata, protestors left behind objects like their clothes, shoes, or name tags at the protest site; they protested "from home," one media story reported, embracing the new terminology that accompanied the pandemic (Lahiri 2020).

16 Anti-CAA activists were found in forms of COVID-19 relief work across the country, including Delhi-based groups like Karwan-e-mohabbat and, in Kolkata, Dhorshok Tumi-i (Bakshi 2020).

17 In the United States, the police murder of George Floyd stirred massive protests not only across the country but elsewhere in a world conjointly facing a global pandemic. These mass demonstrations against racial discrimination and the carceral state were far larger than previous ones, with a greater transnational reach and impact. In India, for instance, the online collective, FeministsIndia, used the Black Lives Matter movement to highlight the Indian state's violence against Dalits and Muslims.

18 The humanitarian crisis was generated by a hastily announced lockdown that afforded no time for some of the poorest in India's workforce, who lost livelihoods overnight. The face of the 2020 pandemic became migrant workers who were left with no choice but to embark on a journey of many thousands of miles, on foot, from the city to their hometowns and villages. Citizen groups and journalists estimated massive deaths owing to starvation and financial distress, as well as exhaustion and accidents during migration; as the Polis Project (2020) notes, "As of 10 October 2020, the pandemic has killed 1,07,471 [sic] people in India while the lockdown has killed 971 people."

19 On the "ropes of solidarity" in the Sunderbans in the wake of the wreckage of the cyclone in the region, see Jalais (2020).

REFERENCES

Abu-Lughod, Lila. 1990. "The Romance of Resistance: Tracing Transformations of Power through Bedouin Women." *American Ethnologist* 17 (1): 41–55.

Aditya, Vqueeram. 2018. "In the Fight against 377, Queer Politics Needs to Move Beyond Privacy." The Wire, July 9, 2018. https://thewire.in/lgbtqia/in-the-fight -against-377-queer-politics-needs-to-move-beyond-privacy.

Adkins, Lisa. 2004. "Passing on Feminism: From Consciousness to Reflexivity?" *European Journal of Women's Studies* 11 (4): 427–44.

Agnes, Flavia. 2002. "Law, Ideology and Female Sexuality: Gender Neutrality in Rape Law." *Economic and Political Weekly* 37 (9): 844–47.

Agnes, Flavia. 2013. "Controversy over Age of Consent." *Economic and Political Weekly* 48 (29): 10–13.

Agrawal, Arun. 2005. *Environmentality: Technologies of Government and the Making of Subjects.* Durham, NC: Duke University Press.

Agustin, Laura Marie. 2007. *Sex at the Margins: Migration, Labour Markets and the Rescue Industry.* London: Zed Books.

Ahearn, Laura. 2001. *Invitations to Love: Literacy, Love Letters, and Social Change in Nepal.* Ann Arbor: University of Michigan Press.

Ahmed, Sara. 2000. "Whose Counting?" *Feminist Theory* 1 (1): 97–103.

Ahmed, Sara. 2006. *Queer Phenomenology: Orientations, Objects, Others.* Durham, NC: Duke University Press.

Ahmed, Sara. 2014a. *The Cultural Politics of Emotion.* 2nd ed. Edinburgh: Edinburgh University Press.

Ahmed, Sara. 2014b. "Feminist Critique." Feministkilljoys, May 26, 2014. https:// feministkilljoys.com/2014/05/26/feminist-critique/.

Ahmed, Sara. 2014c. "Selfcare as Warfare." Feministkilljoys, August 25, 2014. https:// feministkilljoys.com/2014/08/25/selfcare-as-warfare/.

Ahmed, Sara. 2017. *Living a Feminist Life.* Durham, NC: Duke University Press.

Akanksha. 2009. "The Politics of Lesbian Visibility in Indian Socio-cultural Context." *Swakanthey,* no. 6: 1–3.

Akanksha and Malobika. 2007. "Sappho: A Journey through Fire." In *The Phobic and the Erotic: The Politics of Sexualities in Contemporary India,* edited by Brinda Bose and Subhabrata Bhattacharyya, 363–68. Kolkata: Seagull Books.

Alam, Aftab. 2016. "Civil Society under Siege: A Slew of Actions by the Government Threatens Its Vibrancy." *Indian Express*, August 1, 2016. https://indianexpress .com/article/opinion/columns/ngos-barred-from-foreign-funds-pm-narendra -modi-un-human-rights-ngo-funding-2946735/.

Altman, Dennis. 1996. "On Global Queering." *Australian Humanities Review*, no. 2. http://australianhumanitiesreview.org/1996/07/01/on-global-queering/.

Alvarez, Sonia E. 1998. "Advocating Feminism: Latin American Feminist NGO 'Boom.'" *International Feminist Journal of Politics* 1 (2): 181–209.

Alvarez, Sonia E. 2014. "Beyond NGO-ization? Reflections from Latin America." In *Theorizing NGOs: States, Feminisms, and Neoliberalism*, edited by Victoria Bernal and Interpal Grewal, 285–300. Durham, NC: Duke University Press.

Anjaria, Jonathan Shapiro, and Ulka Anjaria. 2013. "The Fractured Spaces of Entrepreneurialism in Post-liberalization India." In *Enterprise Culture in Neoliberal India: Studies in Youth, Class, Work and Media*, edited by Nandini Gooptu, 190–205. London: Routledge.

Anjaria, Jonathan Shapiro, and Ulka Anjaria. 2020. "*Mazaa*: Rethinking Fun, Pleasure and Play." *South Asia: Journal of South Asian Studies* 43 (2): 232–42.

Armstrong, Elisabeth. 2004. "Globalization from Below: AIDWA, Foreign Funding, and Gendering Anti-violence Campaigns." *Journal of Developing Studies* 20 (1–2): 39–55.

Armstrong, Elisabeth. 2013. *Gender and Neoliberalism: The All India Democratic Women's Association and Globalization Politics.* London: Routledge.

Arondekar, Anjali R. 2010. "Time's Corpus: On Sexuality, Historiography, and the Indian Penal Code." In *Comparatively Queer: Interrogating Identities across Time and Cultures*, edited by Jarrod Hayes, Margaret R. Higonnet, and William J. Spurlin, 113–28. New York: Palgrave Macmillan.

Arondekar, Anjali R., and Geeta Patel. 2016. "Area Impossible: Notes toward an Introduction." *GLQ* 22 (2): 151–71.

Arya, Sunaina, and Aakash Singh Rathore, eds. 2020. *Dalit Feminist Theory: A Reader.* London: Routledge.

Bacchetta, Paola. 2002. "Rescaling Transnational 'Queerdom': Lesbian and 'Lesbian' Identitary-Positionalities in Delhi in the 1980s." *Antipode* 34 (5): 947–73.

Bacchetta, Paola. 2004. *Gender in the Hindu Nation: RSS Women as Ideologues.* New Delhi: Women Unlimited.

Bakshi, Asmita. 2020. "From Riot Relief to COVID-19, Spontaneous Solidarities Are Leading the Way." *Mint*, April 10, 2020. https://www.livemint.com/mint -lounge/features/from-riot-relief-to-covid-19-spontaneous-solidarities-are -leading-the-way-11586520804897.html.

Ballakrishnen, Swethaa S. 2021. *Accidental Feminism: Gender Parity and Selective Mobility Among India's Professional Elite.* Princeton, NJ: Princeton University Press.

Bandyopadhyay, Sekhar. 2011. *Caste, Protest and Identity in Colonial India: The Namasudras of Bengal, 1872–1947.* 2nd ed. New Delhi: Oxford University Press.

Bandyopadhyay, Sekhar. 2014. "Does Caste Matter in Bengal? Examining the Myth of Bengali Exceptionalism." In *Being Bengali: At Home and in the World*, edited by Mridula Nath Chakraborty, 32–47. London: Routledge.

Banerjea, Niharika. 2014. "Critical Urban Collaborative Ethnographies: Articulating Community with Sappho for Equality in Kolkata, India." *Gender, Place and Culture* 22 (8): 1058–72.

Banerjea, Niharika, Kath Browne, Eduarda Ferreira, Marta Olasik, and Julie Podmore. 2019. "Introduction: Transnational Ruminations on Lesbian Feminisms." In *Lesbian Feminism: Essays Opposing Global Heteropatriarchies*, edited by Niharika Banerjea, Kath Browne, Eduarda Ferreira, Marta Olasik, and Julie Podmore, 1–28. London: Zed Books.

Banet-Weiser, Sarah. 2018. *Empowered: Popular Feminism and Popular Misogyny.* Durham, NC: Duke University Press.

Basu, Amrita, ed. 1992. *Two Faces of Protest: Contrasting Modes of Women's Activism in India.* New Delhi: Oxford University Press.

Basu, Deepankar, and Debarshi Das. 2019. "Three Factors That Led to the BJP's Impressive Gains in West Bengal." The Wire, May 27, 2019. https://thewire.in /politics/election-results-2019-bjp-west-bengal.

Basu, Srimati. 2015. *The Trouble with Marriage: Feminists Confront Law and Violence in India.* Berkeley: University of California Press.

Batliwala, Srilatha. 2007. "Putting Power Back into Empowerment." Open Democracy, July 30, 2007. https://www.opendemocracy.net/en/putting_power_back _into_empowerment_o/.

Baudh, Sumit. 2007. "Reflections of a Queer Dalit." *Plainspeak*, no. 3: 32–37.

Baviskar, Amita, and Raka Ray. 2015. *Elite and Everyman: The Cultural Politics of the Indian Middle Classes.* New Delhi: Routledge.

Baxi, Pratiksha. 2012a. "Delhi Gang Rape Case: Death Penalty Won't Help Rape Survivors." *Economic Times*, December 24, 2012. https://economictimes .indiatimes.com/delhi-gang-rape-case-death-penalty-wont-help-rape-survivors /articleshow/17736285.cms?from=mdr.

Baxi, Pratiksha. 2012b. "Rape Cultures in India." Kafila, December 23, 2012. https:// web.archive.org/web/20130403051020/http://kafila.org/2012/12/23/rape -cultures-in-india-pratiksha-baxi/.

Baxi, Pratiksha. 2019. "Governing India's Daughters." In *Re-forming India: The Nation Today*, edited by Niraja Gopal Jayal, 383–403. Gurgaon, India: Penguin.

Bayat, Asef. 2009. *Life as Politics: How Ordinary People Change the Middle East.* Cairo: American University in Cairo Press.

Benedicto, Bobby. 2014. *Under Bright Lights: Gay Manila and the Global Scene.* Minneapolis: University of Minnesota Press.

Berlant, Lauren G. 2011. *Cruel Optimism.* Durham, NC: Duke University Press.

Bernal, Victoria, and Inderpal Grewal. 2014a. "Feminisms and the NGO Form." In *Theorizing NGOs: States, Feminisms, and Neoliberalism*, edited by Victoria Bernal and Inderpal Grewal, 301–10. Durham, NC: Duke University Press.

Bernal, Victoria, and Inderpal Grewal. 2014b. "The NGO Form: Feminist Struggles, States, and Neoliberalism." In *Theorizing NGOs: States, Feminisms, and Neoliberalism*, edited by Victoria Bernal and Inderpal Grewal, 1–18. Durham, NC: Duke University Press.

Bernal, Victoria, and Inderpal Grewal, eds. 2014c. *Theorizing NGOs: States, Feminisms, and Neoliberalism.* Durham, NC: Duke University Press.

Bernstein, Elizabeth. 2010. "Militarized Humanitarianism Meets Carceral Feminism: The Politics of Sex, Rights, and Freedom in Contemporary Antitrafficking Campaigns." *Signs* 36 (1): 45–71.

Berry, Kim. 2003. "Developing Women: The Traffic in Ideas about Women and Their Needs in Kangra, India." In *Regional Modernities: The Cultural Politics of Development in India,* edited by K. Sivaramakrishnan and Arun Agrawal, 75–98. Stanford, CA: Stanford University Press.

Bersani, Leo. 1995. *Homos.* Cambridge, MA: Harvard University Press.

Bhaskaran, Suparna. 2004. *Made in India: Decolonizations, Queer Sexualities, Transnational Projects.* New York: Palgrave Macmillan.

Bhattacharya, Sayan. 2013. "The Queer Market." *Kindle Magazine,* May 3, 2013. http://kindlemag.in/queer-market/.

Bhattacharya, Sayan. 2014. "In Her Voice." *Our Voices: The Orinam Blog,* May 17, 2014. http://orinam.net/malobika-in-her-voice/.

Bhattacharya, Sayan. 2015. "The Cool Queers." *Kindle Magazine,* June 23, 2015. http://kindlemag.in/cool-queers/.

Bhattacharya, Sayan. 2020. "'Their' Suicide Letter: An Exercise in Reading That Is Always Incomplete." In *Women Speak Nation: Gender, Culture, and Politics,* edited by Panchali Ray, 150–62. London: Routledge.

Bhog, Dipta. 2017. "Including to Contain: The Girl Child, Gender and Elementary Education in India." In *Feminist Subversion and Complicity: Governmentalities and Gender Knowledge in South Asia,* edited by Maitrayee Mukhopadhyay, 200–232. New Delhi: Zubaan Academic.

Biswas, Ranjita. 2007. "Am I that Sex? When our Lips Speak Gender Sexuality Together." *Swakanthey* 4 (1): 1–2, 10 (Kolkata: Sappho for Equality Publication).

Biswas, Ranjita, Sumita Beethi, and Subhagata Ghosh. 2019. "Maneuvering Feminisms through LGBTQ Movements in India." In *Lesbian Feminism: Essays Opposing Global Heteropatriarchies,* edited by Niharika Banerjea, Kath Browne, Eduarda Ferreira, Marta Olasik, and Julie Podmore, 103–48. London: Zed Books.

Borah, Rituparna, and Subhalakshmi Nandi. 2012. "Reclaiming the Feminist Politics of 'SlutWalk.'" *International Feminist Journal of Politics* 14 (3): 415–21.

Borthwick, Meredith. 1984. *The Changing Role of Women in Bengal, 1849–1905.* Princeton, NJ: Princeton University Press.

Bose, Brinda. 2017. *The Audacity of Pleasure: Sexualities, Literature and Cinema in India.* Gurgaon, India: Three Essays Collective.

Bose, Pradip Kumar. 1995. "Sons of the Nation: Child Rearing in the New Family." In *Texts of Power: Emerging Disciplines in Colonial Bengal,* edited by Partha Chatterjee, 118–44. Minneapolis: University of Minnesota Press.

Boyce, Paul. 2007. "'Conceiving *Kothis*': Men Who Have Sex with Men in India and the Cultural Subject of HIV Prevention." *Medical Anthropology* 26 (2): 175–203.

Boyce, Paul. 2014. "Desirable Rights: Same-Sex Sexual Subjectivities, Socioeconomic Transformations, Global Flows and Boundaries—in India and Beyond." *Culture, Health and Sexuality* 16 (10): 1201–15.

Boyce, Paul, and Rohit K. Dasgupta. 2017. "Utopia or Elsewhere: Queer Modernities in Small Town West Bengal." In *Urban Utopias: Excess and Expulsion in Neoliberal South Asia*, edited by Tereza Kuldova and Mathew A. Varghese, 209–25. Cham, Switzerland: Palgrave Macmillan.

Boyce, Paul, and Aniruddha Dutta. 2013. "Vulnerability of Gay and Transgender Indians Goes Way Beyond Section 377." The Conversation, December 15, 2013. https://theconversation.com/vulnerability-of-gay-and-transgender-indians-goes -way-beyond-section-377-21392.

Boyce, Paul, and akshay khanna. 2011. "Rights and Representations: Querying the Male-to-Male Sexual Subject in India." *Culture, Health and Sexuality* 13 (1): 89–100.

Brown, Michael. 2000. *Closet Space*. London: Routledge.

Brown, Wendy. 2003a. "Resisting Left Melancholia." In *Loss: The Politics of Mourning*, edited by David L. Eng and David Kazanjian, 458–66. Berkeley: University of California Press.

Brown, Wendy. 2003b. "Women's Studies Unbound: Revolution, Mourning, Politics." *Parallax* 9 (2): 3–16.

Brown, Wendy. 2015. *Undoing the Demos: Neoliberalism's Stealth Revolution*. New York: Zone Books.

Butler, Judith. 1993. "Critically Queer." *GLQ* 1 (1): 17–32.

Butler, Judith. 1998. "Merely Cultural." *New Left Review*, no. 227: 33–44.

Butler, Judith. 2002a. "Is Kinship Always Heterosexual?" *Differences* 13 (1): 14–44.

Butler, Judith. 2002b. "What Is Critique? An Essay on Foucault's Virtue." In *The Political: Blackwell Readings in Continental Philosophy*, edited by David Ingram, 212–28. Malden, MA: Blackwell.

Butler, Judith. 2004. *Undoing Gender*. New York: Routledge.

Calkin, Sydney. 2017. "Disrupting Disempowerment: Feminism, Co-optation, and the Privatised Governance of Gender and Development." *New Formations*, no. 91: 69–86.

Chacko, Priya. 2020. "Gender and Authoritarian Populism: Empowerment, Protection, and the Politics of Resentful Aspiration in India." *Critical Asian Studies* 52 (2): 204–25.

Chakrabarty, Dipesh. 2000. *Provincializing Europe: Postcolonial Thought and Historical Difference*. Princeton, NJ: Princeton University Press.

Chandra, Uday, Geir Heierstad, and Kenneth Bo Nielsen, eds. 2016. *The Politics of Caste in West Bengal*. New Delhi: Routledge.

Chandra, Uday, and Atreyee Majumder. 2013. "Introduction: Selves and Society in Postcolonial India." *South Asia Multidisciplinary Academic Journal*, no. 7: 1–17.

Chattaraj, Durba. 2010. "Roadscapes: Everyday Life along the Rural-Urban Continuum in 21st Century India." PhD diss., Yale University.

Chattaraj, Durba. 2015. "Globalization and Ambivalence: Rural Outsourcing in Southern Bengal." *International Labor and Working-Class History*, no. 87: 111–36.

Chatterjee, Partha. 1989. "The Nationalist Resolution of the Women's Question." In *Recasting Women: Essays in Indian Colonial History*, edited by Durba Sangari and Sudesh Vaid, 233–53. New Delhi: Kali for Women.

Chatterjee, Partha. 2004. *The Politics of the Governed: Reflections on Popular Politics in Most of the World*. New York: Columbia University Press.

Chatterjee, Shraddha. 2018. *Queer Politics in India: Towards Sexual Subaltern Subjects*. London: Routledge.

Chaudhuri, Maitrayee. 2004. "Introduction." In *Feminism in India*, edited by Maitrayee Chaudhuri, xi–xlvi. New Delhi: Kali for Women / Women Unlimited.

Chaudhuri, Runa Das. 2019. "Cultivating 'Beverage-hood': The Shaping of Tastes and Identities in Textured Spaces of a South Kolkata Locality." *Society and Culture in South Asia* 5 (1): 70–92.

Cheng, Sealing. 2010. *On the Move for Love: Migrant Entertainers and the U.S. Military in South Korea*. Philadelphia: University of Pennsylvania Press.

Choudhury Lahiri, Shoma, and Sarbani Bandyopadhyay. 2012. "Dressing the Feminine Body." *Economic and Political Weekly* 47 (46): 20–24.

Chowdhry, Prem. 2007. *Contentious Marriages, Eloping Couples: Gender, Caste, and Patriarchy in Northern India*. New Delhi: Oxford University Press.

Chowdhury, Elora Halim. 2011. *Transnationalism Reversed: Women Organizing against Gendered Violence in Bangladesh*. Albany: State University of New York Press.

Chowdhury, Elora Halim, and Liz Philipose, eds. 2016. *Dissident Friendships: Feminism, Imperialism, and Transnational Solidarity*. Urbana: University of Illinois Press.

Chu, Andrea Long, and Anastasia Berg. 2018. "Wanting Bad Things: Andrea Long Chu Responds to Amia Srinivasan." *The Point*, June 8, 2018. https://thepointmag .com/dialogue/wanting-bad-things-andrea-long-chu-responds-amia-srinivasan/.

Chua, Lynette J. 2018. *The Politics of Love in Myanmar: LGBT Mobilization and Human Rights as a Way of Life*. Stanford, CA: Stanford University Press.

Ciotti, Manuela. 2012. "Resurrecting *Seva* (Social Service): Dalit and Low-Caste Women Party Activists as Producers and Consumers of Political Culture and Practice in Urban North India." *Journal of Asian Studies* 71 (1): 149–70.

Clarke, John. 2008. "Living with/in and without Neo-liberalism." *Focaal*, no. 51: 135–47.

Clark-Parsons, Rosemary. 2019. "I See You, I Believe You, I Stand with You: #MeToo and the Performance of Networked Feminist Visibility." *Feminist Media Studies* 21 (3): 362–80.

Cody, Francis. 2013. *The Light of Knowledge: Literacy Activism and the Politics of Writing in South India*. Ithaca, NY: Cornell University Press.

Cohen, Lawrence. 2005. "The Kothi Wars: AIDS Cosmopolitanism and the Morality of Classification." In *Sex in Development: Science, Sexuality, and Morality in Global Perspective*, edited by Vincanne Adams and Stacy L. Pigg, 269–304. Durham, NC: Duke University Press.

Cooke, Bill, and Uma Kothari, eds. 2001. *Participation: The New Tyranny?* London: Zed Books.

Cornwall, Andrea, Jasmine Gideon, and Kalpana Wilson. 2008. "Reclaiming Feminism: Gender and Neoliberalism." *IDS Bulletin* 39 (6): 1–9.

Cornwall, Andrea, and Maxine Molyneux. 2006. "The Politics of Rights: Dilemmas for Feminist Praxis: An Introduction." *Third World Quarterly* 27 (7): 1175–91.

Cross, Jamie. 2014. *Dream Zones: Anticipating Capitalism and Development in India.* London: Pluto.

Cruikshank, Barbara. 1999. *The Will to Empower: Democratic Citizens and Other Subjects.* Ithaca, NY: Cornell University Press.

Cvetkovich, Ann. 2003. *An Archive of Feelings: Trauma, Sexuality, and Lesbian Public Cultures.* Durham, NC: Duke University Press.

Da Costa, Dia. 2010. *Development Dramas: Reimagining Rural Political Action in Eastern India.* New Delhi: Routledge.

Daniyal, Shoaib. 2019. "Between Mamata and Modi's Populism, the Bhadralok Is Now a Marginal Player in Bengal's Politics." *Scroll.in*, May 19, 2019. https://scroll.in/article/923875/between-mamatas-and-modis-populism-the-bhadralok-is-now-a-marginal-player-in-bengals-politics.

Das, Devaleena. 2020. "Body, Boundaries and *Sindoor* Feminism in India." *South Asia: Journal of South Asian Studies* 43 (6): 1019–40.

Dasgupta, Debanuj, and Niharika Banerjea. 2013. "States of Desire: Homonationalism and LGBT Activism in India." *Swakanthey* 10 (1): 1–2, 4.

Dasgupta, Rohit K. 2014. "Articulating Dissident Citizenship, Belonging, and Queerness on Cyberspace." *South Asia Review* 35 (3): 203–24.

Dasgupta, Rohit K. 2017. *Digital Queer Cultures in India: Politics, Intimacies and Belonging.* London: Routledge.

Dasgupta, Rohit K., and Debanuj Dasgupta. 2018a. "Introduction: Queering Digital India." In *Queering Digital India: Activisms, Identities, Subjectivities,* edited by Rohit K. Dasgupta and Debanuj Dasgupta, 1–26. Edinburgh: Edinburgh University Press.

Dasgupta, Rohit K., and Debanuj Dasgupta, eds. 2018b. *Queering Digital India: Activisms, Identities, Subjectivities.* Edinburgh: Edinburgh University Press.

Datta, Anisha. 2009. "Syncretic Socialism in Post-colonial West Bengal: Mobilizing and Disciplining Women for a 'Sustha' Nation-State." PhD diss., University of British Columbia.

Datta, Ayona, Nabeel Ahmed, and Rakhi Tripathi. 2018. "How Technology Brought the #MeToo Movement to India." *Independent*, November 4. https://www.independent.co.uk/news/world/asia/india-metoo-sexual-harassment-tech-mobile-phones-social-media-a8606756.html.

Dave, Naisargi. 2011. "Ordering Justice, Fixing Dreams: An Ethnography of Queer Legal Activism." In *Law Like Love: Queer Perspectives on Law in India,* edited by Arvind Narrain and Alok Gupta, 25–42. New Delhi: Yoda.

Dave, Naisargi N. 2012. *Queer Activism in India: A Story in the Anthropology of Ethics.* Durham, NC: Duke University Press.

De Alwis, Malathi. 2009. "Interrogating the 'Political': Feminist Peace Activism in Sri Lanka." *Feminist Review*, no. 91: 81–93.

Dean, Jonathan. 2010. *Rethinking Contemporary Feminist Politics.* London: Palgrave Macmillan.

Death, Carl. 2016. "Counter-conducts as a Mode of Resistance: Ways of 'Not Being Like That' in South Africa." *Global Society* 30 (2): 201–17.

De Jong, Sara, and Susanne Kimm. 2017. "The Co-optation of Feminisms: A Research Agenda." *International Feminist Journal of Politics* 19 (2): 185–200.

De la Dehesa, Rafael. 2010. *Queering the Public Sphere in Mexico and Brazil: Sexual Rights Movements in Emerging Democracies.* Durham, NC: Duke University Press.

Desai, Manisha. 2016. "Feminist Efforts to Democratize Democracy: Insights from Four Decades of Activism in India." In *Social Movements and the State in India: Deepening Democracy?*, edited by Kenneth Bo Nielsen and Alf Gunvald Nilsen, 93–114. London: Palgrave Macmillan.

Desai, Rajvi. 2019. "How the NRC-CAA Will Affect Women, Transgender People and People with Disabilities." The Swaddle, December 26, 2019. https://theswaddle .com/how-the-nrc-caa-will-affect-women-transgender-people-and-people-with -disabilities/.

Desai, Rajvi. 2020. "In Shaheen Bagh, Muslim Women Redefine Carework as Resistance." The Swaddle, January 6, 2020. https://theswaddle.com/in-shaheen-bagh -muslim-women-redefine-carework-as-resistance/.

Deshpande, Satish. 2003. *Contemporary India: A Sociological View.* New Delhi: Penguin.

Devika, J. 2016. "Feminism and Late Twentieth-Century Governmentality in Kerala, India: Towards a Critical History." In *Feminist Subversion and Complicity: Governmentalities and Gender Knowledge in South Asia*, edited by Maitrayee Mukhopadhyay, 79–99. New Delhi: Zubaan Academic.

Dhall, Pawan. 2020. *Out of Line and Offline: Queer Mobilizations in '90s Eastern India.* New York: Seagull Books.

Donner, Henrike. 2008. *Domestic Goddesses: Maternity, Globalisation and Middle-Class Identity in Contemporary India.* Aldershot, UK: Ashgate.

Donner, Henrike. 2016. "Doing It Our Way: Love and Marriage in Kolkata Middle-Class Families." *Modern Asian Studies* 50 (4): 1147–89.

Dosekun, Simidele. 2020. *Fashioning Postfeminism: Spectacular Femininity and Transnational Culture.* Urbana: University of Illinois Press.

Duggan, Lisa. 2003. *The Twilight of Equality? Neoliberalism, Cultural Politics, and the Attack on Democracy.* Boston: Beacon.

Dutt, Yashica. 2019. *Coming Out as Dalit: A Memoir.* New Delhi: Aleph.

Dutt, Yashica. 2020. "The Specter of Caste in Silicon Valley." *New York Times*, July 14, 2020. https://www.nytimes.com/2020/07/14/opinion/caste-cisco -indian-americans-discrimination.html.

Dutta, Aniruddha. 2012a. "Claiming Citizenship, Contesting Civility: The Institutional LGBT Movement and the Regulation of Gender/Sexual Dissidence in West Bengal, India." *Jindal Global Law Review* 4 (1): 110–41.

Dutta, Aniruddha. 2012b. "An Epistemology of Collusion: *Hijras, Kothis* and the Historical (Dis)continuity of Gender/Sexual Identities in Eastern India." *Gender and History* 24 (3): 825–49.

Dutta, Aniruddha. 2014. "Contradictory Tendencies: The Supreme Court's NALSA Judgment on Transgender Recognition and Rights." *Journal of Indian Law and Society*, no. 5: 225–36.

Dutta, Aniruddha. 2019. "Dissenting Differently: Solidarities and Tensions between Student Organizing and Trans-Kothi-Hijra Activism in Eastern India." *South Asia Multidisciplinary Academic Journal*, no. 20: 1–20.

Dutta, Debolina, and Oishik Sircar. 2013. "India's Winter of Discontent: Some Feminist Dilemmas in the Wake of a Rape." *Feminist Studies* 39 (1): 293–306.

Edelman, Lee. 2004. *No Future: Queer Theory and the Death Drive.* Durham, NC: Duke University Press.

Elyachar, Julia. 2005. *Markets of Dispossession: NGOs, Economic Development, and the State in Cairo.* Durham, NC: Duke University Press.

Eng, David L. 2010. *The Feeling of Kinship: Queer Liberalism and the Racialization of Intimacy.* Durham, NC: Duke University Press.

Eng, David L., Judith Halberstam, and José Estaban Muñoz. 2005. "What's Queer about Queer Studies Now?" *Social Text* 23 (3–4): 84–85.

Eschle, Catherine, and Bice Maiguashca. 2018. "Theorising Feminist Organising in and against Neoliberalism: Beyond Co-optation and Resistance?" *European Journal of Politics and Gender* 1 (1–2): 223–39.

Eves, Alison. 2004. "Queer Theory, Butch/Femme Identities and Lesbian Space." *Sexualities* 7 (4): 480–96.

Ferguson, James. 1990. *The Anti-politics Machine: "Development," Depoliticization, and Bureaucratic Power in Lesotho.* Cambridge: Cambridge University Press.

Ferguson, James. 2011. "Toward a Left Art of Government: From 'Foucauldian Critique' to Foucauldian Politics." *History of the Human Sciences* 24 (4): 61–68.

Ferguson, James. 2015. *Give a Man a Fish: Reflections on the New Politics of Distribution.* Durham, NC: Duke University Press.

Ferguson, James, and Akhil Gupta. 2002. "Spatializing States: Toward an Ethnography of Neoliberal Governmentality." *American Ethnologist* 29 (4): 981–1002.

Fernandes, Leela. 2000. "Restructuring the New Middle Class in Liberalizing India." *Comparative Studies of South Asia, Africa and the Middle East* 20 (1–2): 88–104.

Fernandes, Leela. 2006. *India's New Middle Class: Democratic Politics in an Era of Economic Reform.* Minneapolis: University of Minnesota Press.

Fernandes, Leela, and Patrick Heller. 2006. "Hegemonic Aspirations: New Middle Politics and India's Democracy in Comparative Perspective." *Critical Asian Studies* 38 (4): 495–522.

Fernando, Mayanthi. 2019. "Critique as Care." *Critical Times* 2 (1): 13–22.

Foucault, Michel. 1985. *The Use of Pleasure.* Vol. 2 of *The History of Sexuality*, translated by Robert Hurley. New York: Vintage Books.

Foucault, Michel. 1997a. "The Ethics of the Concern for Self as a Practice of Freedom." In *Ethics: Subjectivity and Truth*, edited by Paul Rabinow, 281–303. Vol. 1 of *The Essential Works of Foucault 1954–1984.* New York: New Press.

Foucault, Michel. 1997b. *The Politics of Truth.* Edited by Sylvère Lotringer. New York: Semiotext(e).

Foucault, Michel. 2008. *The Birth of Biopolitics: Lectures at the Collège de France, 1978–1979.* Edited by Michel Senellart. Translated by Graham Burchell. Basingstoke, UK: Palgrave Macmillan.

Fraser, Nancy. 2009. "Feminism, Capitalism and the Cunning of History." *New Left Review*, no. 56: 97–117.

Fraser, Nancy. 2013. *Fortunes of Feminism: From State-Managed Capitalism to Neoliberal Crisis.* London: Verso Books.

Freeman, Carla. 2014. *Entrepreneurial Selves: Neoliberal Respectability and the Making of a Caribbean Middle Class.* Durham, NC: Duke University Press.

Freeman, Carla. 2020. "Feeling Neoliberal." *Feminist Anthropology* 1 (1): 71–88.

Gairola, Rahul K. 2018. "From *Bombay Dost* to Global Host: Mobile Imaginings of Cybergaysians in Contemporary Queer India." In *New Feminisms in South Asia: Disrupting the Discourse through Social Media, Film, and Literature*, edited by Sonora Jha and Alka Kurian, 85–104. New York: Routledge.

Gajjala, Radhika. 2018. *Online Philanthropy in the Global North and South: Connecting Microfinancing, and Gaming for Change.* Lanham, MD: Lexington Books.

Gandhi, Nandita, and Nandita Shah. 1991. *The Issues at Stake: Theory and Practice in the Contemporary Women's Movement in India.* New Delhi: Kali for Women.

Gangoli, Geetanjali. 2007. *Indian Feminisms: Law, Patriarchies, and Violence in India.* Aldershot, UK: Ashgate.

Ganguly-Scrase, Ruchira. 2003. "Paradoxes of Globalization, Liberalization, and Gender Equality: The Worldviews of the Lower Middle Class in West Bengal, India." *Gender and Society* 17 (4): 544–66.

Ganguly-Scrase, Ruchira, and Timothy J. Scrase. 2009. *Globalization and the Middle Classes in India: The Social and Cultural Impact of Neoliberal Reforms.* London: Routledge.

Ghatak, Anchita. 2020. "At Kolkata's Park Circus, Another Women's Sit-In Protest Keeps the Struggle Going." The Wire, January 15, 2020. https://thewire.in/rights/kolkata-park-circus-anti-caa-protest-women.

Ghose, Toorjo. 2012. "Politicizing Political Society: Mobilization among Sex Workers in Sonagachi, India." In *South Asian Feminisms*, edited by Ania Loomba and Ritty A. Lukose, 285–305. Durham, NC: Duke University Press.

Ghosh, Amitav. 2005. *The Hungry Tide.* New Delhi: HarperCollins.

Ghosh, Apoorva. 2015. "LGBTQ Activist Organizations as 'Respectably Queer' in India: Contesting a Western View." *Gender, Work and Organization* 22 (1): 51–66.

Ghosh, Jayati. 2009. *Never Done and Poorly Paid: Women's Work in Globalizing India.* New Delhi: Women Unlimited.

Ghosh, Subhagata, ed. 2016. *We Speak.* Kolkata: Sappho for Equality.

Ghosh, Swati. 2017. *The Gendered Proletariat: Sex Work, Workers' Movement, and Agency.* Oxford: Oxford University Press.

Gilbertson, Amanda. 2017. *Within the Limits: Moral Boundaries of Class and Gender in Urban India.* New Delhi: Oxford University Press.

Gilbertson, Amanda. 2021. "The Changed and the Unchanged: Peer Learning for Gender and Development in Delhi." *Gender, Place and Culture* 28 (2): 176–91.

Gill, Rosalind, and Christina Scharff. 2011. "Introduction." In *New Femininities: Postfeminism, Neoliberalism and Subjectivity*, edited by Rosalind Gill and Christina Scharff, 1–17. Basingstoke, UK: Palgrave Macmillan.

Giraud, Eva. 2019. *What Comes after Entanglement? Activism, Anthropocentrism, and an Ethics of Exclusion.* Durham, NC: Duke University Press.

Gjøstein, Dagrun K. 2014. "A Veiled Change Agent: The 'Accredited Social Health Activist' in Rural Rajasthan." In *Women, Gender and Everyday Social Transformation in India*, edited by Kenneth B. Nielsen and Anne Waldrop, 139–56. London: Anthem.

Glover, Karima. 2021. *A Regarded Self: Caribbean Womanhood and the Ethics of Disorderly Being*. Durham, NC: Duke University Press.

Gooptu, Nandini. 2009. "Neoliberal Subjectivity, Enterprise Culture and New Workplaces: Organised Retail and Shopping Malls in India." *Economic and Political Weekly* 44 (22): 45–54.

Gooptu, Nandini, ed. 2013. *Enterprise Culture in Neoliberal India: Studies in Youth, Class, Work and Media*. London: Routledge.

Gooptu, Nandini. 2016. "New Spirituality, Politics of Self-Empowerment, Citizenship and Democracy in Contemporary India." *Modern Asian Studies* 50 (3): 934–74.

Gooptu, Nandini, and Rangan Chakravarty. 2013. "Reality TV in India and the Making of an Enterprising Housewife." In *Enterprise Culture in Neoliberal India: Studies in Youth, Class, Work and Media*, edited by Nandini Gooptu, 140–56. London: Routledge.

Gopinath, Gayatri. 2005. *Impossible Desires: Queer Diasporas and South Asian Public Cultures*. Durham, NC: Duke University Press.

Gordon, Avery F. 1997. *Ghostly Matters: Haunting and the Sociological Imagination*. Minneapolis: University of Minnesota Press.

Goswami, Diti. 2019. "Low and Declining Female Work Participation: The Case of Rural West Bengal." *Journal of Labor and Society* 22 (2): 325–43.

Gould, Deborah. 2009. *Moving Politics: Emotion and ACT UP's Fight against AIDS*. Chicago: University of Chicago Press.

Govinda, Radhika. 2009. "In the Name of 'Poor and Marginalized'? Politics of NGO Activism with Dalit Women in Rural North India." *Journal of South Asian Development* 4 (1): 45–64.

Gqola, Pumla Dineo. 2021. *Female Fear Factory*. Cape Town: Melinda Ferguson Books.

Grewal, Inderpal. 2005. *Transnational America: Feminisms, Diasporas, Neoliberalisms*. Durham, NC: Duke University Press.

Grewal, Inderpal. 2017. *Saving the Security State: Exceptional Citizens in Twenty-First-Century America*. Durham, NC: Duke University Press.

Grover, Shalini. 2011. *Marriage, Love, Caste and Kinship Support: Lived Experiences of the Urban Poor in India*. London: Routledge.

Gupta, Akhil. 2001. "Governing Population: The Integrated Child Development Services Program in India." In *States of Imagination: Ethnographic Explorations of the Postcolonial State*, edited by Thomas Blom Hansen and Finn Stepputat, 65–96. Durham, NC: Duke University Press.

Gupta, Akhil. 2012. *Red Tape: Bureaucracy, Structural Violence, and Poverty in India*. Durham, NC: Duke University Press.

Gupta, Charu. 2009. "Hindu Women, Muslim Men: Love Jihad and Conversions." *Economic and Political Weekly* 44 (51): 13–15.

Gupta, Hemangini. 2016. "Taking Action: The Desiring Subjects of Neoliberal Feminism in India." *Journal of International Women's Studies* 17 (1): 152–68.

Guru, Gopal. 1995. "Dalit Women Talk Differently." *Economic and Political Weekly* 30 (41–42): 2548–50.

Halberstam, Judith. 1998. "Transgender Butch: Butch/FTM Border Wars and the Masculine Continuum." *GLQ* 4 (2): 287–310.

Halberstam, Judith. 2003. "What's That Smell? Queer Temporalities and Subcultural Lives." *Scholar and Feminist Online* 2 (1). http://sfonline.barnard.edu/ps/printjha.htm.

Halberstam, Judith. 2005. *In a Queer Time and Place: Transgender Bodies, Subcultural Lives*. New York: New York University Press.

Halberstam, Judith. 2011. *The Queer Art of Failure*. Durham, NC: Duke University Press.

Halperin, David M. 1997. *Saint Foucault: Towards a Gay Hagiography*. New York: Oxford University Press.

Hansen, Thomas Blom. 1999. *The Saffron Wave: Democracy and Hindu Nationalism in Modern India*. New Delhi: Oxford University Press.

Harris, Anita. 2004. *Future Girl: Young Women in the Twenty-First Century*. New York: Routledge.

Hartman, Saidiya. 2019. *Wayward Lives, Beautiful Experiments: Intimate Histories of Social Upheaval*. New York: W. W. Norton.

Hebbar, Prajakta. 2015. "Viral 'Bold Is Beautiful' Ad Supporting LGBT Rights Is Simply Beautiful, but It Isn't the First One." *Huffpost*, June 11, 2015. https://www.huffingtonpost.in/2015/06/11/lesbian-ad-india_n_7558378.html.

Hemmings, Clare. 2011. *Why Stories Matter: The Political Grammar of Feminist Theory*. Durham, NC: Duke University Press.

Hemmings, Clare. 2018. *Considering Emma Goldman: Feminist Political Ambivalence and the Imaginative Archive*. Durham, NC: Duke University Press.

Hemmings, Clare, and Ilana Eliot. 2019. "Lesbian Ghosts Feminism: An Introduction." *Feminist Theory* 20 (4): 351–60.

Henry, Todd A. 2020. "Introduction: Queer Korea; Toward a Field of Engagement." In *Queer Korea*, edited by Todd A. Henry, 1–53. Durham, NC: Duke University Press.

Hesford, Victoria. 2005. "Feminism and Its Ghosts: The Spectre of the Feminist-as-Lesbian." *Feminist Theory* 6 (3): 227–50.

Heyes, Cressida J. 2007. *Self-Transformations: Foucault, Ethics, and Normalized Bodies*. Oxford: Oxford University Press.

Heyes, Cressida J. 2020. *Anaesthetics of Existence: Essays on Experience at the Edge*. Durham, NC: Duke University Press.

Hickel, Jason. 2014. "The 'Girl Effect': Liberalism, Empowerment and the Contradictions of Development." *Third World Quarterly* 35 (8): 1355–73.

Hinchy, Jessica. 2019. *Governing Gender and Sexuality in Colonial India: The Hijra, c. 1850–1900*. Cambridge: Cambridge University Press.

Hodžić, Saida. 2014. "Feminist Bastards: Toward a Post-humanist Critique of NGOization." In *Theorizing NGOs: States, Feminisms, and Neoliberalism*, edited by Victoria Bernal and Inderpal Grewal, 221–47. Durham, NC: Duke University Press.

Hodžić, Saida. 2016. *Twilight of Cutting: African Activism and Life after NGOs*. Berkeley: University of California Press.

hooks, bell. 2014. "Are You Still a Slave? Liberating the Black Female Body." Panel discussion featuring bell hooks, Eugene Lang College, the New School for Liberal Arts, streamed live on May 6, 2014. YouTube video, 1:55:32. https://www .youtube.com/watch?v=rJkohNROvzs.

Horton, Brian A. 2018. "What's So 'Queer' about Coming Out? Silent Queers and Theorizing Kinship Agonistically in Mumbai." *Sexualities* 21 (7): 1059–74.

Human Rights Watch. 2019. *Violent Cow Protection in India: Vigilante Groups Attack Minorities*. New York: Human Rights Watch. https://www.hrw.org/report/2019 /02/18/violent-cow-protection-india/vigilante-groups-attack-minorities.

Hussein, Nazia, ed. 2017. *Rethinking New Womanhood: Practices of Gender, Class, Culture and Religion in South Asia*. Cham, Switzerland: Palgrave Macmillan.

Hutnyk, John. 1996. *The Rumour of Calcutta: Tourism, Charity and the Poverty of Representation*. London: Zed Books.

Iqani, Mehita. 2016. *Consumption, Media and the Global South Aspiration Contested*. Basingstoke, UK: Palgrave.

Iqani, Mehita, and Caio Simões de Araújo, eds. 2021. "Research Topic: Post-feminist Practices, Subjectivities and Intimacies in Global Context." Frontiers. https:// www.frontiersin.org/research-topics/15493/post-feminist-practices-subjectivities -and-intimacies-in-global-context.

Jaffe, Sarah. 2020. "Social Reproduction and the Pandemic, with Tithi Bhattacharya." *Dissent*, April 2, 2020. https://www.dissentmagazine.org/online_articles/social -reproduction-and-the-pandemic-with-tithi-bhattacharya.

Jaffrelot, Christophe. 2003. *India's Silent Revolution: The Rise of the Lower Castes in North India*. London: Hurst.

Jaising, Indira. 2005. *Men's Laws, Women's Lives: A Constitutional Perspective on Religion, Common Law and Culture in South India*. New Delhi: Women Unlimited.

Jakimow, Tanya. 2013. "Spoiling the Situation: Reflections on the Development and Research Field." *Development in Practice* 23 (1): 21–32.

Jakimow, Tanya. 2015. *Decentering Development: Understanding Change in Agrarian Societies*. New York: Palgrave Macmillan.

Jakimow, Tanya. 2018. "Being Harmed While Doing Good: Affective Injuries in a Community Development Programme, Medan, Indonesia." *Journal of the Royal Anthropological Institute* 24 (3): 550–67.

Jakobsen, Jostein, and Kenneth Bo Nielsen. 2020. "Compounding Aspirations: Grounding Hegemonic Processes in India's Rural Transformations." *Revue canadienne d'études du développement* 41 (1): 144–60.

Jalais, Annu. 2010. *Forest Tigers: People, Politics and Environment in the Sundarbans*. London: Routledge.

Jalais, Annu. 2020. "Amidst the Wreckage of Amphran, a Heartwarming Reminder from Sundarbans of What It Means to Be Human." *Scroll.in*, June 9,

2020. https://scroll.in/article/964166/amidst-the-wreckage-of-amphan-a -heartwarming-reminder-from-sundarbans-of-what-it-means-to-be-human.

Jeffrey, Craig. 2010. *Timepass: Youth, Class, and the Politics of Waiting in India*. Stanford, CA: Stanford University Press.

Jenkins, Katy. 2009. "'We Have a Lot of Goodwill, but We Still Need to Eat …': Valuing Women's Long-Term Voluntarism in Community Development in Lima." *Voluntas* 20 (1): 15–34.

Jenkins, Rob. 1999. *Democratic Politics and Economic Reform in India*. Cambridge: Cambridge University Press.

Jha, Sonora, and Alka Kurian, eds. 2018. *New Feminisms in South Asia: Disrupting the Discourse through Social Media, Film, and Literature*. New York: Routledge.

Jodkha, Surinder, and Aseem Prakash. 2016. *The Indian Middle Class*. New Delhi: Oxford University Press.

John, Mary E. 1996. *Discrepant Dislocations: Feminism, Theory, and Postcolonial Histories*. Berkeley: University of California Press.

John, Mary E. 1999. "Gender, Development and the Women's Movement: Problems for a History of the Present." In *Signposts: Gender Issues in Post-independence India*, edited by Rajeswari Sunder Rajan, 100–124. New Delhi: Kali.

John, Mary E. 2002. "Women's Studies: Legacies and Futures." In *Between Tradition, Counter Tradition and Heresy: Contributions in Honour of Vina Mazumdar*, edited by Lotika Sarkar, Kumud Sharma, and Leela Kasturi, 47–62. Noida, India: Rainbow.

John, Mary E. 2009. "Reframing Globalization: Perspectives from the Women's Movement." *Economic and Political Weekly* 44 (10): 47–48.

John, Mary E. 2013. "The Problem of Women's Labour: Some Autobiographical Perspectives." *Indian Journal of Gender Studies* 20 (2): 177–212.

John, Mary E. 2014. "Feminist Vocabularies in Time and Space: Perspectives from India." *Economic and Political Weekly* 49 (22): 121–30.

John, Mary E. 2020. "Feminism, Sexual Violence and the Times of #MeToo in India." *Asian Journal of Women's Studies* 26 (2): 137–58.

Joshi, Yuvraj. 2012. "Respectable Queerness." *Columbia Human Rights Law Review* 43 (2): 415–68.

Jyoti, Dhrubo. 2017. "Dalit, Queer, Proud—Liberation Lies at the Margins of Our Intersections." Velivada, April 17, 2017. https://velivada.com/2017/04/17 /dalit-queer-proud-liberation-lies-at-the-margins-of-our-intersections-dhrubo -jyoti/.

Kabeer, Naila. 1994. *Reversed Realities: Gender Hierarchies in Development Thought*. London: Verso Books.

Kalpagam, U. 2019. *Neoliberalism and Women in India: Governmentality Perspectives*. Lanham, MD: Rowman and Littlefield.

Kamat, Sangeeta. 2002. *Development Hegemony: NGOs and the State in India*. New Delhi: Oxford University Press.

Kang, Akhil. 2016. "Queering Dalit." *Tanqueed*, October 2016. https://www.tanqeed .org/2016/10/queering-dalit-tq-salon/.

Kannabiran, Kalpana. 2018. "In the Footprints of Bhanwari Devi: Feminist Cascades and #MeToo in India." Prajnya Grit Working Paper, Prajnya Trust, Chennai, India, November 2018. http://www.csdhyd.org/gritwp18kk.pdf.

Kapur, Ratna. 2005. *Erotic Justice: Law and the New Politics of Postcolonialism*. London: Glass House.

Kapur, Ratna. 2012. "Theorising SlutWalk: Critical Feminist Perspectives." *Feminist Legal Studies*, no. 20: 63–64.

Kapur, Ratna. 2013. "Gender, Sovereignty and the Rise of a Sexual Security Regime in International Law and Postcolonial India." *Melbourne Journal of International Law* 14 (2): 317–45.

Kapur, Ratna, and Brenda Cossman. 1996. *Subversive Sites: Feminist Engagements with Law in India*. Thousand Oaks, CA: Sage.

Kar, Sohini. 2018. *Financializing Poverty: Labour and Risk in Indian Microfinance*. Stanford, CA: Stanford University Press.

Kar, Sohini, and James Bradbury. 2020. "Buddha and Nilima: The City after Communism." *Contemporary South Asia* 28 (4): 485–97.

Karim, Lamia. 2001. "Politics of the Poor? NGOs and Grass-Roots Political Mobilization in Bangladesh." *Political and Legal Anthropology Review* 24 (1): 92–107.

Karim, Lamia. 2011. *Microfinance and Its Discontents: Women in Debt in Bangladesh*. Minneapolis: University of Minnesota Press.

Karnad, Raghu. 2020. "Farewell to Shaheen Bagh, as Political Togetherness Yields to Social Distance." The Wire, March 24, 2020. https://thewire.in/politics/farewell -to-shaheen-bagh-as-political-togetherness-yields-to-social-distance.

Katyal, Akhil. 2016. *The Doubleness of Sexuality: Idioms of Same-Sex Desire in Modern India*. New Delhi: New Text.

Kaur, Ravinder. 2020. *Brand New Nation: India in the Global Economy*. Stanford, CA: Stanford University Press.

Kaur, Ravinder, and Nandini Sundar. 2016. "Snakes and Ladders: Rethinking Social Mobility in Post-reform India." *Contemporary South Asia* 24 (3): 229–41.

Kaviraj, Sudipta. 1997. "Filth and the Public Sphere: Concepts and Practices about Space in Calcutta." *Public Culture* 10 (1): 83–113.

Kaviraj, Sudipta. 2014. "Remembering P. C. Joshi." In *People's "Warrior": Words and Worlds of P. C. Joshi*, edited by Gargi Chakravartty, 378–84. New Delhi: Tulika Books.

Keating, Christine, Claire Rasmussen, and Pooja Rishi. 2010. "The Rationality of Empowerment: Microcredit, Accumulation by Dispossession, and the Gendered Economy." *Signs* 36 (1): 153–76.

Kenny, Bridget. 2019. *Retail Worker Politics, Race and Consumption in South Africa: Shelved in the Service Economy*. Cham, Switzerland: Palgrave Macmillan.

Khalili, Laleh. 2016. "The Politics of Pleasure: Promenading on the Corniche and Beachgoing." *Environment and Planning D: Society and Space* 34 (4): 583–600.

khanna, akshay. 2005. "Beyond 'Sexuality'(?)." In *Because I Have a Voice: Queer Politics in India*, edited by Arvind Narrain and Gautam Bhan, 89–103. New Delhi: Yoda.

khanna, akshay. 2009. "Taming of the Shrewd Meyeli Chhele: A Political Economy of Development's Sexual Subject." *Development*, no. 52: 43–51.

Khoja-Moolji, Shenila. 2018. *Forging the Ideal Educated Girl: The Production of Desirable Subjects in Muslim South Asia.* Berkeley: University of California Press.

Khubchandani, Kareem. 2020. *Ishtyle: Accenting Gay Indian Nightlife.* Ann Arbor: University of Michigan Press.

Kirmani, Nida. 2020. "Can Fun Be Feminist? Gender, Space and Mobility in Lyari, Karachi." *South Asia: Journal of South Asian Studies* 43 (2): 319–31.

Koffman, Ofra, and Rosalind Gill. 2013. "'The Revolution Will Be Led by a 12-Year-Old Girl': Girl Power and Global Biopolitics." *Feminist Review* 105 (1): 83–102.

Kotiswaran, Prabha. 2011. *Dangerous Sex, Invisible Labor: Sex Work and the Law in India.* Princeton, NJ: Princeton University Press.

Kotiswaran, Prabha. 2017. "A Bittersweet Moment: Indian Governance Feminism and the 2013 Rape Law Reforms." *Economic and Political Weekly* 52 (25–26): 78–87.

Krishnan, Kavita. 2020. *Fearless Freedom.* New Delhi: Penguin.

Krishnan, Sneha. 2018. "Bitch, Don't Be a Lesbian: Selfies and Same-Sex Desire." In *Queering Digital India: Activisms, Identities, and Subjectivities*, edited by Rohit K. Dasgupta and Debanuj Dasgupta, 151–64. Edinburgh: Edinburgh University Press.

Krishnan, Sneha. 2020. "Where Do Good Girls Have Sex? Space, Risk and Respectability in Chennai." *Gender, Place and Culture* 28 (7): 1–20.

Kumar, Radha. 1993. *The History of Doing: An Illustrated Account of Movements for Women's Rights and Feminism in India, 1800–1990.* New Delhi: Kali for Women.

Lahiri, Ishadrita. 2020. "Corona Crisis: Kolkata's Park Circus Protestors 'Work' from Home." The Quint, March 24, 2020. https://www.thequint.com/news/india/kolkata-news-coronavirus-caa-protestors-at-park-circus-keep-shoes-at-venue-during-quarantine.

Lakkimsetti, Chaitanya. 2020. *Legalizing Sex: Sexual Minorities, AIDS, and Citizenship in India.* New York: New York University Press.

Lalwani, Vijayta. 2020. "'Got Your Azaadi?': Investigation into Delhi Violence Sparks Concerns about Bias against Muslims." *Scroll.in*, May 24, 2020. https://scroll.in/article/962567/got-your-azaadi-investigation-into-delhi-violence-sparks-concerns-about-bias-against-muslims.

Lamb, Sarah. 2000. *White Saris and Sweet Mangoes: Aging, Gender, and Body in North India.* Berkeley: University of California Press.

Lang, Sabine. 1997. "The NGOization of Feminism." In *Transitions, Environments, Translations: Feminisms in International Politics*, edited by Joan W. Scott, Cora Kaplan, and Debra Keates, 101–20. New York: Routledge.

Lefebvre, Alexandre. 2017. "The End of a Line: Care of the Self in Modern Political Thought." *Genealogy* 1 (2): 1–14.

Lefebvre, Alexandre. 2018. *Human Rights and the Care of the Self.* Durham, NC: Duke University Press.

Legg, Stephen. 2007. *Spaces of Colonialism: Delhi's Urban Governmentalities.* Oxford: Blackwell.

Legg, Stephen. 2014. *Prostitution and the Ends of Empire: Scale, Governmentalities and Interwar India.* Durham, NC: Duke University Press.

Legg, Stephen, and Deana Heath, eds. 2018. *South Asian Governmentalities: Michel Foucault and the Question of Postcolonial Orderings*. Cambridge: Cambridge University Press.

Legg, Stephen, and Srila Roy. 2013. "Neoliberalism, Postcolonialism and Hetero-Sovereignties." *Interventions* 15 (4): 461–73.

Lemke, Thomas. 2001. "'The Birth of Bio-politics': Michel Foucault's Lecture at the Collège de France on Neo-liberal Governmentality." *Economy and Society* 30 (2): 190–207.

Lemke, Thomas. 2011. "Critique and Experience in Foucault." *Theory, Culture and Society* 28 (4): 26–48.

Leve, Lauren. 2014. "Failed Development and Rural Revolution in Nepal: Rethinking Subaltern Consciousness and Women's Empowerment." In *Theorizing NGOs: States, Feminisms, and Neoliberalism*, edited by Victoria Bernal and Inderpal Grewal, 50–92. Durham, NC: Duke University Press.

Li, Tania Murray. 1999. "Compromising Power: Development, Culture, and Rule in Indonesia." *Cultural Anthropology* 14 (3): 295–322.

Li, Tania Murray. 2007. *The Will to Improve: Governmentality, Development, and the Practice of Politics*. Durham, NC: Duke University Press.

Lieder, K. Frances. 2018. "Performing Loitering: Feminist Protest in the Indian City." *TDR* 62 (3): 145–61.

Livermon, Xavier. 2020. *Kwaito Bodies: Remastering Space and Subjectivity in Post-apartheid South Africa*. Durham, NC: Duke University Press.

Loh, Jennifer Ung. 2018. "Transgender Identity, Sexual Versus Gender 'Rights' and the Tools of the Indian State." *Feminist Review*, no. 119: 39–55.

Lorenzini, Daniele. 2016. "From Counter-conduct to Critical Attitude: Michel Foucault and the Art of Not Being Governed Quite So Much." *Foucault Studies*, no. 21: 7–21.

Lorenzini, Daniele. 2018. "Governmentality, Subjectivity, and the Neoliberal Form of Life." *Journal for Cultural Research* 22 (2): 154–66.

Love, Heather. 2007. *Feeling Backward: Loss and the Politics of Queer History*. Cambridge, MA: Harvard University Press.

Lukose, Ritty A. 2009. *Liberalization's Children: Gender, Youth, and Consumer Citizenship in Globalizing India*. Durham, NC: Duke University Press.

Lukose, Ritty A. 2018. "Decolonizing Feminism in the #MeToo Era." *Cambridge Journal of Anthropology* 36 (2): 34–52.

Macharia, Keguro. 2016. "On Being Area-Studied: A Litany of Complaint." *GLQ* 22 (2): 183–89.

Madhok, Sumi. 2010. "Rights Talk and the Feminist Movement in India." In *Women's Movements in Asia: Feminisms and Transnational Activism*, edited by Mina Roces and Louise P. Edwards, 224–42. London: Routledge.

Madhok, Sumi. 2012. *Rethinking Agency: Developmentalism, Gender, and Rights*. London: Routledge.

Madhok, Sumi, and Shirin M. Rai. 2012. "Agency, Injury, and Transgressive Politics in Neoliberal Times." *Signs* 37 (3): 645–69.

Mahmood, Saba. 2005. *The Politics of Piety: The Islamic Revival and the Feminist Subject*. Princeton, NJ: Princeton University Press.

Majumder, Atreyee. 2018. *Time, Space and Capital in India: Longing and Belonging in an Urban-Industrial Hinterland*. New Delhi: Routledge.

Majumder, Sarasij. 2018. *People's Car: Industrial India and the Riddles of Populism.* New York: Fordham University Press.

Majumder, Sarasij. 2021. "The Gift of Solidarity: Women Navigating Jewelry Work and Patriarchal Norms in Rural West Bengal, India." *Journal of South Asian Development* 15 (3): 335–51.

Malkki, Liisa H. 2015. *The Need to Help: The Domestic Arts of International Humanitarianism*. Durham, NC: Duke University Press.

Mani, Lata. 2014. "Sex and the Signal-Free Corridor." *Economic and Political Weekly* 49 (6): 26–29.

Mankekar, Purnima. 2013. "'We Are Like This Only': Aspiration, *Jugaad*, and Love in Enterprise Culture." In *Enterprise Culture in Neoliberal India: Studies in Youth, Class, Work and Media*, edited by Nandini Gooptu, 27–41. London: Routledge.

Martin, Luther H., Huck Gutman, and Patrick H. Hutton, eds. 1988. *Technologies of the Self: A Seminar with Michel Foucault*. Amherst: University of Massachusetts Press.

Massad, Joseph A. 2002. "Re-orienting Desire: The Gay International and the Arab World." *Public Culture* 14 (2): 361–85.

Matebeni, Zethu. 2011. "Exploring Black Lesbian Sexualities and Identities in Johannesburg." PhD diss., University of the Witwatersrand.

Mazzarella, William. 2005. "Middle Class." In *Keywords in South Asian Studies* (online encyclopedia), edited by Rachel Dwyer. London: University of London School of Oriental and African Studies. https://www.soas.ac.uk/south-asia -institute/keywords/file24808.pdf.

McGuire, Meredith Lindsay. 2011. "'How to Sit, How to Stand': Bodily Practice and the New Urban Middle Class." In *A Companion to the Anthropology of India*, edited by Isabelle Clark-Decès, 117–36. Malden, MA: Blackwell.

McLaren, Margaret A. 2002. *Feminism, Foucault, and Embodied Subjectivity*. Albany: State University of New York Press.

McLaren, Margaret A. 2004. "Foucault and Feminism: Power, Resistance, Freedom." In *Feminism and the Final Foucault*, edited by Dianna Taylor and Karen Vintges, 214–34. Urbana: University of Illinois Press.

McRobbie, Angela. 2009. *The Aftermath of Feminism: Gender, Culture and Social Change*. London: Sage.

Menon, Nivedita. 2004. *Recovering Subversion: Feminist Politics beyond the Law*. New Delhi: Permanent Black.

Menon, Nivedita. 2007a. "Outing Heteronormativity: Nation, Citizen, Feminist Disruptions." In *Sexualities*, edited by Nivedita Menon, 3–51. New Delhi: Women Unlimited.

Menon, Nivedita, ed. 2007b. *Sexualities*. New Delhi: Women Unlimited.

Menon, Nivedita. 2009. "Sexuality, Caste, Governmentality: Contests over 'Gender' in India." *Feminist Review* 91 (1): 94–112.

Menon, Nivedita. 2010. "Introduction." In *Empire and Nation: Selected Essays*, edited by Partha Chatterjee, 1–22. New York: Columbia University Press.

Menon, Nivedita. 2012. *Seeing like a Feminist*. New Delhi: Penguin.

Menon, Nivedita. 2019. "Sexual Violence and the Law in India." In *Research Handbook on Feminist Jurisprudence*, edited by Robin West and Cynthia G. Brown, 184–212. Cheltenham, UK: Edward Elgar.

Menon, Nivedita, and Aditya Nigam. 2007. *Power and Contestation: India since 1989*. London: Zed Books.

Mindry, Deborah. 2001. "Nongovernmental Organizations, 'Grassroots,' and the Politics of Virtue." *Signs* 26 (4): 1187–211.

Mitcheson, Katrina. 2012. "Foucault's Technologies of the Self: Between Control and Creativity." *Journal of the British Society for Phenomenology* 43 (1): 59–75.

Mitra, Durba. 2020. *Indian Sex Life: Sexuality and the Colonial Origins of Modern Social Thought*. Princeton, NJ: Princeton University Press.

Mitra-Kahn, Trishima. 2012. "Offline Issues, Online Lives? The Emerging Cyberlife of Feminist Politics in Urban India." In *New South Asian Feminisms: Paradoxes and Possibilities*, edited by Srila Roy, 108–30. London: Zed Books.

Moeller, Kathryn. 2018. *The Gender Effect: Capitalism, Feminism, and the Corporate Politics of Development*. Berkeley: University of California Press.

Mokkil, Navaneetha. 2019. *Unruly Figures: Queerness, Sex Work, and the Politics of Sexuality in Kerala*. Seattle: University of Washington Press.

Moodie, Megan. 2015. *We Were Adivasis: Aspiration in an Indian Scheduled Tribe*. Chicago: University of Chicago Press.

Mosse, David. 2019. *Cultivating Development: An Ethnography of Aid Policy and Practice*. Ann Arbor, MI: Pluto.

Mourad, Sara. 2016. "The Boundaries of the Public: Mediating Sex in Postwar Lebanon." PhD diss., American University of Beirut.

Mukherjee, Ishan. 2019. "Battle for the Bhadralok: The Historical Roots of Hindu Majoritarianism in West Bengal." *Caravan*, November 29, 2019. https://caravanmagazine.in/politics/historical-roots-of-hindu-majoritarianism-in-west-bengal.

Mukhopadhyay, Maitrayee, ed. 2016. *Feminist Subversion and Complicity: Governmentalities and Gender Knowledge in South Asia*. New Delhi: Zubaan Academic.

Muñoz, José Esteban. 2009. *Cruising Utopia: The Then and There of Queer Futurity*. New York: New York University Press.

Munshi, Vidya. 2005. "Political Participation." In *The Changing Status of Women in West Bengal, 1970–2000: The Challenge Ahead*, edited by Jasodhara Bagchi, 81–96. New Delhi: Sage.

Nagar, Ila. 2018. "Digitally Untouched: Janana (In) Visibility and the Digital Divide." In *Queering Digital India: Activisms, Identities, Subjectivities*, edited by Rohit K. Dasgupta and Debanuj Dasgupta, 97–111. Edinburgh: Edinburgh University Press.

Najmabadi, Afsaneh. 2008. "Transing and Transpassing across Sex-Gender Walls in Iran." *Women's Studies Quarterly* 36 (3–4): 23–42.

Najmabadi, Afsaneh. 2014. *Professing Selves: Transsexuality and Same-Sex Desire in Contemporary Iran*. Durham, NC: Duke University Press.

Narrain, Arvind. 2012. "The Criminal Law (Amendment) Bill 2012: Sexual Assault as a Gender Neutral Offence." *Economic and Political Weekly* 47 (35). https://www

.epw.in/journal/2012/35/web-exclusives/criminal-law-amendment-bill-2012
-sexual-assault-gender-neutral.

Narrain, Arvind, and Gautam Bhan. 2005. "Introduction." In *Because I Have a Voice: Queer Politics in India*, edited by Arvind Narrain and Gautam Bhan, 1–30. New Delhi: Yoda.

Narrain, Arvind, and Alok Gupta. 2011. "Introduction." In *Law Like Love: Queer Perspectives on Law*, edited by Arvind Narrain and Alok Gupta, xi–lvi. New Delhi: Yoda.

Nash, Jennifer. 2011. "Black Feminism, Love-Politics, and Post-intersectionality." *Meridians* 11 (2): 1–24.

Nash. Jennifer. 2019. *Black Feminism Reimagined*. Durham, NC: Duke University Press.

Nielsen, Kenneth Bo. 2016. "Mamata Banerjee: Redefining Female Leadership." In *India's Democracies: Diversity, Co-optation, Resistance*, edited by Arild Engelsen Ruud and Geir Heierstad, 101–34. Oslo: Universitetsforlaget.

Nielsen, Kenneth Bo. 2018. *Land Dispossession and Everyday Politics in Rural Eastern India*. London: Anthem.

Nielsen, Kenneth Bo, and Anne Waldrop. 2014. "Women and Gender in a Changing India." In *Women, Gender and Everyday Transformation in India*, edited by Kenneth Bo Nielsen and Anne Waldrop, 1–18. London: Anthem.

Nilsen, Alf Gunvald. 2018. *Adivasis and the State*. New Delhi: Cambridge University Press.

Nilsen, Alf Gunvald. 2020. "India's Breaking Point." Polis Project, January 11, 2020. Accessed August 3, 2020. https://thepolisproject.com/indias-breaking-point/.

Nilsen, Alf Gunvald, and Srila Roy. 2015. "Reconceptualizing Subaltern Politics in Contemporary India." In *New Subaltern Politics: Reconceptualizing Hegemony and Resistance in Contemporary India*, edited by Alf Gunvald Nilsen and Srila Roy, 1–27. New Delhi: Oxford University Press.

Nirantar Trust. 2015. *Early and Child Marriage: A Landscape Analysis*. New Delhi: Nirantar Trust.

Nuttall, Sarah. 2009. *Entanglement: Literary and Cultural Reflections on Post-apartheid*. Johannesburg: Wits University Press.

O'Connell Davidson, Julia. 2005. *Children in the Global Sex Trade*. Cambridge: Polity.

O'Grady, Helen. 2004. "An Ethics of the Self." In *Feminism and the Final Foucault*, edited by Dianna Taylor and Karen Vintges, 91–117. Urbana: University of Illinois Press.

Oksala, Johanna. 2013. "Neoliberalism and Biopolitical Governmentality." In *Foucault, Biopolitics and Governmentality*, edited by Jakob Nilsson and Sven-Olov Wallenstein, 53–72. Huddinge, Sweden: Södertörn University.

Omvedt, Gail. 1993. *Reinventing Revolution: New Social Movements and the Socialist Tradition in India*. Armonk, NY: M. E. Sharpe.

Ong, Aihwa. 2006. *Neoliberalism as Exception: Mutations in Citizenship and Sovereignty*. Durham, NC: Duke University Press.

O'Reilly, Kathleen. 2006. "Women Fieldworkers and the Politics of Participation." *Signs* 31 (4): 1075–98.

Oza, Rupal. 2006. *The Making of Neoliberal India: Nationalism, Gender, and the Paradoxes of Globalization.* New York: Routledge.

Panjabi, Kavita. 2015. "Hokkolorob: A Hashtag Movement." *Seminar*, no. 674, October 2015. http://www.india-seminar.com/2015/674/674_kavita_panjabi.htm.

Patel, Geeta. 2004. "Homely Housewives Run Amok: Lesbians in Marital Fixes." *Public Culture* 16 (1): 131–57.

Paul, Cithara. 2010. "Sachar Figures Reveal Bengal Apathy." *Telegraph India*, February 9, 2010. https://www.telegraphindia.com/india/sachar-figures-reveal-bengal-apathy/cid/547125.

Pearce, Ruth, Deborah L. Steinberg, and Igi Moon. 2019. "Introduction: The Emergence of 'Trans.'" *Sexualities* 22 (1–2): 3–12.

Peck, Jamie. 2013. "Explaining (with) Neoliberalism." *Territory, Politics, Governance* 1 (2): 132–57.

Phadke, Shilpa. 2020. "Defending Frivolous Fun: Feminist Acts of Claiming Public Spaces in South Asia." *South Asia: Journal of South Asian Studies* 43 (2): 281–93.

Phadke, Shilpa, Sameera Khan, and Shilpa Ranade. 2011. *Why Loiter? Women and Risk on Mumbai Streets.* New Delhi: Penguin.

Phipps, Alison. 2020. *Me, Not You: The Trouble with Mainstream Feminism.* Manchester, UK: Manchester University Press.

Pigg, Stacy Leigh. 1992. "Inventing Social Categories through Place: Social Representations and Development in Nepal." *Comparative Studies in Society and History* 34 (3): 491–513.

Polis Project. 2020. "Pandemic and the State's Response: Understanding Lockdown Deaths in India." Polis Project, June 13, 2020, last updated October 10, 2020. https://www.thepolisproject.com/read/pandemic-and-the-states-response-understanding-lockdown-deaths-in-india/.

Poonam, Snigdha. 2018. *Dreamers: How Young Indians Are Changing the World.* London: C. Hurst.

Pratt, Geraldine. 2008. "Book Reviews: Authors Meet Critics; A Set of Reviews and Response." *Social and Cultural Geography* 9 (2): 213–36.

Puar, Jasbir. 2007. *Terrorist Assemblages.* Durham, NC: Duke University Press.

Puar, Jasbir. 2013. "Homonationalism as Assemblage: Viral Travels, Affective Sexualities." *Jindal Global Legal Studies* 4 (2): 23–43.

Puri, Jyoti. 2016. *Sexual States: Governance and the Struggle over the Antisodomy Law in India.* Durham, NC: Duke University Press.

Puwar, Nirmal. 2004. *Space Invaders: Race, Gender and Bodies out of Place.* Oxford: Berg.

Radhakrishnan, Smitha. 2011. *Appropriately Indian: Gender and Culture in a New Transnational Class.* Durham, NC: Duke University Press.

Radhakrishnan, Smitha. 2018. "Empowerment, Declined: Paradoxes of Microfinances and Gendered Subjectivity in Urban India." *Signs* 44 (1): 83–105.

Rai, Shirin. 2002. *Class, Caste, and Gender: Women in Parliament in India.* Stockholm: International IDEA.

Rallin, Aneil. 2019. "Queer and Now: A Roundtable Forum with Dipika Jain, Akhil Kang, Sheena Malhotra, Hoshang Merchant, Shakthi Nataraj, Chayanika Shah,

Nishant Shahani, Oishik Sircar and Ruth Vanita." In *Women's and Gender Studies in India: Crossings*, edited by Anu Aneja, 356–74. London: Routledge.

Ram, Kalpana. 2008. "'A New Consciousness Must Come': Affectivity and Movement in Tamil Dalit Women's Activist Engagement with Cosmopolitan Modernity." In *Anthropology and the New Cosmopolitanism: Rooted, Feminist and Vernacular Perspectives*, edited by Pnina Werbner, 135–55. Oxford: Berg.

Ramamurthy, Priti. 2004. "Why Is Buying a 'Madras' Cotton Shirt a Political Act? A Feminist Commodity Chain Analysis." *Feminist Studies* 30 (3): 734–69.

Ramberg, Lucinda. 2016. "Backward Futures and Pasts Forward: Queer Time, Sexual Politics, and Dalit Religiosity in South India." *GLQ* 22 (2): 223–48.

Rankin, Katharine N. 2001. "Governing Development: Neoliberalism, Microcredit, and Rational Economic Woman." *Economy and Society* 30 (1): 18–37.

Rankin, Katharine N. 2010. "Reflexivity and Post-colonial Critique: Toward an Ethics of Accountability in Planning Praxis." *Planning Theory* 9 (3): 181–99.

Rao, Rahul. 2014. "Queer Questions." *International Feminist Journal of Politics* 16 (2): 199–217.

Rao, Rahul. 2015. "Global Homocapitalism." *Radical Philosophy*, no. 194: 38–49.

Rao, Rahul. 2020a. "Nationalisms by, against and beyond the Indian State." *Radical Philosophy* 2 (7): 17–26. https://www.radicalphilosophy.com/commentary /nationalisms-by-against-and-beyond-the-indian-state.

Rao, Rahul. 2020b. *Out of Time: The Queer Politics of Postcoloniality*. Oxford: Oxford University Press.

Ray, Panchali. 2019. "Women in/and Trade Unions: Consciousness, Agency, and (Im)possibilities of Alliances amongst Nurses and Attendants in Kolkata." *Contemporary South Asia* 27 (4): 502–15.

Ray, Raka. 1999. *Fields of Protest: Women's Movements in India*. New Delhi: Kali for Women.

Ray, Raka. 2000. "Masculinity, Femininity and Servitude: Domestic Workers in Calcutta in the Late Twentieth Century." *Feminist Studies* 26 (3): 691–718.

Ray, Raka, and Mary F. Katzenstein, eds. 2005. *Social Movements in India: Poverty, Power and Politics*. Lanham, MD: Rowman and Littlefield.

Ray, Raka, and Seemin Qayum. 2009. *Cultures of Servitude: Modernity, Domesticity and Class in India*. Stanford, CA: Stanford University Press.

Ray Chaudhury, Proma. 2020. "Welfarist Dilemma? The Politics of Gender in West Bengal's Cash Transfer Schemes." *Engenderings* (blog), London School of Economics and Political Science, February 13, 2020. Accessed August 3, 2020. https://blogs.lse.ac.uk/gender/2020/02/13/welfarist-dilemma-the-politics-of -gender-in-west-bengals-cash-transfer-schemes/.

Reddy, Gayatri. 2005. *With Respect to Sex: Negotiating Hijra Identity in South India*. Chicago: University of Chicago Press.

Rege, Sharmila. 1998. "Dalit Women Talk Differently: A Critique of 'Difference' and towards a Dalit Feminist Standpoint Position." *Economic and Political Weekly* 33 (44): WS39– WS46.

Roberts, Nathaniel. 2016. *To Be Cared For: The Power of Conversion and Foreignness of Belonging in an Indian Slum*. Berkeley: University of California Press.

Romani, Sahar. 2014. "Generation NGO: Youth and Development in Urban India." PhD diss., University of Oxford.

Romani, Sahar. 2015. "Being NGO Girls: Gender, Subjectivities and Everyday Life in Kolkata." *Gender, Place and Culture* 23 (3): 365–80.

Rose, Nikolas. 1999. *Power of Freedom: Reframing Political Thought.* Cambridge: Cambridge University Press.

Rottenberg, Catherine. 2018. *The Rise of Neoliberal Feminism.* New York: Oxford University Press.

Rottenberg, Catherine. 2019. "#MeToo and the Prospects of Political Change." *Soundings: A Journal of Politics and Culture* 71 (71): 40–49.

Roy, Ananya. 2003. *City Requiem, Calcutta: Gender and the Politics of Poverty.* Minneapolis: University of Minnesota Press.

Roy, Ananya. 2010. *Poverty Capital: Microfinance and the Making of Development.* London: Routledge.

Roy, Anupama. 2014. "Critical Events, Incremental Memories and Gendered Violence: The 'Delhi Gang Rape.'" *Australian Feminist Studies* 29 (81): 238–54.

Roy, Arundhati. 2020. "The Graveyard Talks Back: Fiction in the Time of Fake News." *Caravan*, February 12, 2020. https://caravanmagazine.in/literature/arundhati-roy-the-graveyard-talks-back.

Roy, Dayabati. 2014. *Rural Politics in India: Political Stratification and Governance in West Bengal.* New Delhi: Cambridge University Press.

Roy, Srila. 2009. "Melancholic Politics and the Politics of Melancholia: The Indian Women's Movement." *Feminist Theory* 10 (3): 341–57.

Roy, Srila. 2011. "Politics, Passion and Professionalization in Contemporary Indian Feminism." *Sociology* 45 (4): 587–602.

Roy, Srila. 2012a. "Introduction." In *New South Asian Feminisms: Paradoxes and Possibilities*, edited by Srila Roy, 1–26. London: Zed Books.

Roy, Srila, ed. 2012b. *New South Asian Feminisms: Paradoxes and Possibilities.* London: Zed Books.

Roy, Srila. 2012c. *Remembering Revolution: Gender, Violence, and Subjectivity in India's Naxalbari Movement.* New Delhi: Oxford University Press.

Roy, Srila. 2014. "New Activist Subjects: The Changing Feminist Field of Kolkata, India." *Feminist Studies* 40 (3): 628–56.

Roy, Srila. 2015. "The Indian Women's Movement: Within and beyond NGOization." *Journal of South Asian Development* 10 (1): 96–117.

Roy, Srila. 2016a. "Breaking the Cage." *Dissent* 63 (4): 74–83. https://www.dissentmagazine.org/article/breaking-cage-india-feminism-sexual-violence-public-space.

Roy, Srila. 2016b. "Women's Movements in the Global South: Towards a Scalar Analysis." *International Journal of Politics, Culture, and Society* 29 (2): 289–306.

Roy, Srila. 2017a. "Enacting/Disrupting the Will to Empower: Feminist Governance of 'Child Marriage' in Eastern India." *Signs: Journal of Women in Culture and Society* 42 (4): 867–91.

Roy, Srila. 2017b. "The Positive Side of Co-optation? Intersectionality: A Conversation between Inderpal Grewal and Srila Roy." *International Feminist Journal of Politics* 19 (2): 254–62.

Roy, Srila. 2017c. "Whose Feminism Is It Anyway?" The Wire, November 1, 2017. https://thewire.in/gender/whose-feminism-anyway.

Roy, Srila. 2019. "Precarity, Aspiration and Neoliberal Development: Women Empowerment Workers in West Bengal." *Contributions to Indian Sociology* 53 (3): 392–421.

Roychowdhury, Poulami. 2013. "'The Delhi Gang Rape': The Making of International Causes." *Feminist Studies* 39 (1): 282–92.

Roychowdhury, Poulami. 2015. "Victims to Saviors: Governmentality and the Regendering of Citizenship in India." *Gender and Society* 29 (6): 792–816.

Roychowdhury, Poulami. 2016. "Desire, Rights, Entitlements: Organizational Strategies in the War on Violence." *Signs* 41 (4): 793–820.

Rubin, Gayle. 2011. *Deviations: A Gayle Rubin Reader.* Durham, NC: Duke University Press.

Ruud, Arild. 2003. *Poetics of Village Politics: The Making of West Bengal's Rural Communism.* New Delhi: Oxford University Press.

Salem, Sara. 2019. "Haunted Histories: Nasserism and the Promises of the Past." *Middle East Critique* 28 (3): 261–77.

Samaddar, Ranabir. 2014. "Elitist Protest in Jadavpur: Students' Movements the World Over Are Now Led by the Chattering Classes." *DNA*, October 22, 2014. https://www.dnaindia.com/analysis/column-elitist-protest-in-jadavpur-2028218.

Samaddar, Ranabir. 2016. *Neo-liberal Strategies of Governing India.* London: Routledge.

Sangari, Kumkum. 2007. "Shaping Pressures and Symbolic Horizons: The Women's Movement in India." In *At the Cutting Edge: Essays in Honour of Kumari Jayawardena,* edited by Neloufer de Mel and Selvy Thiruchandran, 36–67. New Delhi: Women Unlimited.

Sangari, Kumkum, and Sudesh Vaid, eds. 1989. *Recasting Women: Essays in Indian Colonial History.* New Delhi: Kali for Women.

Sangtin Writers and Richa Nagar. 2006. *Playing with Fire: Feminist Thought and Activism through Seven Lives in India.* Minneapolis: University of Minnesota Press.

Sanyal, Paromita. 2014. *Credit to Capabilities: A Sociological Study of Microcredit Groups in India.* New York: Cambridge University Press.

Sarkar, Tanika. 1991. "Reflections on Birati Rape Cases: Gender Ideology in Bengal." *Economic and Political Weekly* 26 (5): 215–18.

Sarkar, Tanika. 1993. "A Book of Her Own, A Life of Her Own: Autobiography of a Nineteenth-Century Woman." *History Workshop,* no. 36: 35–65.

Sarkar, Tanika. 2001. *Hindu Wife, Hindu Nation: Community, Religion, and Cultural Nationalism.* Bloomington: Indiana University Press.

Sarkar, Tanika. 2018. "Special Guest Contribution: Is Love without Borders Possible?" *Feminist Review* 119 (1): 7–19.

Sarkar, Tanika, and Urvashi Butalia, eds. 1995. *Women and the Hindu Right: A Collection of Essays.* New Delhi: Kali for Women.

Schalk, Sami. 2018. *Bodyminds Reimagined: (Dis)ability, Race, and Gender in Black Women's Speculative Fiction.* Durham, NC: Duke University Press.

Scharff, Christina. 2014. "Gender and Neoliberalism: Exploring the Exclusions and Contours of Neoliberal Subjectivities." Theory, Culture and Society, April 1, 2014. https://www.theoryculturesociety.org/christina-scharff-on-gender-and -neoliberalism/.

Scott, Joan W. 2004. "Feminism's History." *Journal of Women's History* 16 (2): 10–29.

Sedgwick, Eve. 1990. *Epistemology of the Closet.* Berkeley: University of California Press.

Semmalar, Gee Imaam. 2014. "Gender Outlawed: The Supreme Court Judgment on Third Gender and Its Implications." Round Table India, April 19, 2014. Accessed August 3, 2020. https://www.roundtableindia.co.in/because-we-have-a-voice-too -the-supreme-court-judgment-on-third-gender-and-its-implications/.

Sen, Debarati. 2017. *Everyday Sustainability: Gender Justice and Fair Trade Tea in Darjeeling.* Albany: State University of New York Press.

Sen, Debarati, and Sarasij Majumder. 2015. "Narratives of Risk and Poor Rural Women's (Dis)-engagements with Microcredit-Based Development in Eastern India." *Critique of Anthropology* 35 (2): 121–41.

Sen, Priyadarshini. 2013. "Waxing Sapphic Gently." *Outlook India*, April 15, 2013. https://www.outlookindia.com/magazine/story/waxing-sapphic-gently/284806.

Sen, Samita. 2000. "Toward a Feminist Politics? The Indian Women's Movement in Historical Perspective." Working Paper Series No. 9, Policy Research Report on Gender and Development, World Bank Development Research Group / Poverty Reduction and Economic Management Network, Washington, DC, April 2000. http://documents.worldbank.org/curated/en/205981468752698664/pdf/multi -page.pdf.

Sen, Samita. 2001. "Gender and Domesticity: Liberalisation in Historical Perspective." *UNEAC Asia Papers*, no. 4: 1–20.

Sen, Samita, and Nilanjana Sengupta. 2012. "Marriage, Work and Education among Domestic Workers in Kolkata." *Economic and Political Weekly* 47 (43): 67–77.

Sen, Uditi. 2018. "Choukathe Danriye (Standing at the Threshold): Queer Negotiations of Kolkata's Archives and Society." *QED* 5 (3): 84–99.

Sengupta, Nilanjana. 2013. "Poor Women's Empowerment: The Discursive Space of Microfinance." *Indian Journal of Gender Studies* 20 (2): 279–304.

Sengupta, Parna. 2005. "Teaching Gender in the Colony: The Education of 'Outsider' Teachers in Late-Nineteenth-Century Bengal." *Journal of Women's History* 17 (4): 32–55.

Shah, Chayanika. 2005. "The Roads That E/merged: Feminist Activism and Queer Understanding." In *Because I Have a Voice: Queer Politics in India*, edited by Arvind Narrain and Gautam Bhan, 158–70. New Delhi: Yoda.

Shah, Svati P. 2012. "Sex Workers' Rights and Women's Movements in India: A Very Brief Genealogy." In *New South Asian Feminisms*, edited by Srila Roy, 27–43. London: Zed Books.

Shah, Svati P. 2015. "Queering Critiques of Neoliberalism in India: Urbanism and Inequality in the Era of Transnational 'LGBTQ' Rights." *Antipode* 47 (3): 635–51.

Shahani, Nishant. 2017. "Patently Queer: Late Effects and the Sexual Economies of India." *GLQ* 23 (2): 195–220.

Shandilya, Krupa. 2015. "Nirbhaya's Body: The Politics of Protest in the Aftermath of the 2012 Delhi Gang Rape." *Gender and History* 27 (2): 465–86.

Sharma, Aradhana. 2008. *Logics of Empowerment: Development, Gender, and Governance in Neoliberal India*. Minneapolis: University of Minnesota Press.

Sharma, Jaya, and Soma K. Parthasarathy. 2007. *Examining Self-Help Groups: Empowerment, Poverty Alleviation, Education; A Qualitative Study*. New Delhi: Nirantar.

Sharma, Maya. 2006. *Loving Women: Being Lesbian in Underprivileged India*. New Delhi: Yoda.

Sharma, Shubhra. 2011. *"Neoliberalization" as Betrayal: State, Feminism, and a Women's Education Program in India*. New York: Palgrave Macmillan.

Singh, Pawan. 2017. "At Home with Their Queerness: Same-Sex Relationality and the Indian Family in Advertising Media." *Feminist Media Studies* 17 (5): 721–36.

Singh, Radhika. 2011. *The Fabric of Our Lives: The Story of Fabinida*. New Delhi: Viking.

Sinha Roy, Mallarika. 2011. *Gender and Radical Politics in India: Magic Moments of Naxalbari (1967–1975)*. London: Routledge.

Sinha Roy, Mallarika. 2020. "Inside/Out: Women's Movement and Women in Movements." In *Women Speak Nation: Gender, Culture, and Politics*, edited by Panchali Ray, 163–84. London: Routledge.

Sircar, Oishik. 2012. "Spectacles of Emancipation: Reading Rights Differently in India's Legal Discourse." *Osgoode Hall Law Journal* 49 (3): 527–75.

Sircar, Oishik. 2017. "New Queer Politics in the New India: Notes on Failure and Stuckness in a Negative Moment." *Unbound: Harvard Journal of the Legal Left* 11 (1): 1–36.

Sircar, Oishik, and Dipika Jain. 2017a. "Introduction: Of Powerful Feelings and Facile Gestures." In *New Intimacies, Old Desires: Law, Culture and Queer Politics in Neoliberal Times*, edited by Oishik Sircar and Dipika Jain, xiii–lxi. New Delhi: Zubaan.

Sircar, Oishik, and Dipika Jain, eds. 2017b. *New Intimacies, Old Desires: Law, Culture and Queer Politics in Neoliberal Times*. New Delhi: Zubaan.

Soderlund, Gretchen. 2005. "Running from the Rescuers: New U.S. Crusades against Sex Trafficking and the Rhetoric of Abolition." *NWSA Journal* 17 (3): 64–87.

Sperring, Sam, and Zahra Stardust. 2020. "Engorged: Fucking (with) the Maternal—An Analysis of Antinormativity, Cultural Legitimacy, and Queer Authenticity." In *Mothers, Sex, and Sexuality*, edited by Michelle Walks, Joani Mortenson, and Holly Zwalf, 213–39. Bradford, ON: Demeter.

Spivak, Gayatri Chakravorty. 1988. "Can the Subaltern Speak?" In *Marxism and the Interpretation of Culture*, edited by Cary Nelson and Lawrence Grossberg, 271–313. Basingstoke, UK: Macmillan Education.

Spivak, Gayatri Chakravorty. 2012. *An Aesthetic Education in the Era of Globalization*. Cambridge, MA: Harvard University Press.

Still, Clarinda. 2017. *Dalit Women: Honour and Patriarchy in South India*. London: Routledge.

Strey, Jacquelyn P. 2017. "Queerness's Domain? Queer Negotiations, Utopian Visions and the Failures of Heterotopias in Bangalore." In *Urban Utopias: Excess and*

Expulsion in Neoliberal South Asia, edited by Tereza Kuldova and Mathew A. Varghese, 247–67. Cham, Switzerland: Palgrave Macmillan.

Subramanian, Ajantha. 2015. "Recovering Caste Privilege: The Politics of Meritocracy at the Indian Institutes of Technology." In *New Subaltern Politics: Reconceptualizing Hegemony and Resistance in Contemporary India*, edited by Alf Gunvald Nilsen and Srila Roy, 76–102. Oxford: Oxford University Press.

Subramanian, Ajantha. 2019. *The Caste of Merit: Engineering Education in India*. Cambridge, MA: Harvard University Press.

Sukthankar, Ashwini. 1999. "Introduction." In *Facing the Mirror: Lesbian Writing from India*, edited by Ashwini Sukthankar, xii–xli. New Delhi: Penguin.

Sukthankar, Ashwini. 2007. "Complicating Gender: Rights of Transsexuals in India." In *Sexualities*, edited by Nivedita Menon, 91–102. New Delhi: Women Unlimited.

Sukthankar, Ashwini. 2012. "Queering Approaches to Sex, Gender, and Labor in India: Examining Paths to Sex Worker Unionism." In *South Asian Feminisms*, edited by Ania Loomba and Ritty A. Lukose, 306–32. Durham, NC: Duke University Press.

Sunder Rajan, Rajeswari. 2003. *The Scandal of the State: Women, Law and Citizenship in India*. New Delhi: Permanent Black.

Sutanuka. 2007. "Queering Justice: Polymorphously Yours." *Swakanthey* 4 (1): 8–10.

Tambe, Ashwini. 2019. *Defining Girlhood in India*. Urbana: University of Illinois Press.

Taylor, Dianna, and Karen Vintges, eds. 2004. *Feminism and the Final Foucault*. Urbana: University of Illinois Press.

Tellis, Ashley. 2012. "Wanted: A New Feminist Movement in India." Sify, last updated December 31, 2012. https://www.sify.com/news/wanted-a-new-feminist-movement-in-india-news-topnews-mm5lMlgcabfsi.html.

Tenhunen, Sirpa. 2009. *Means of Awakening: Gender, Politics and Practice in Rural India*. Kolkata: Stree.

Tenhunen, Sirpa. 2018. *A Village Goes Mobile: Telephony, Mediation, and Social Change in Rural India*. Oxford: Oxford University Press.

Tenhunen, Sirpa, and Minna Säävälä. 2012. *An Introduction to Changing India: Culture, Politics and Development*. London: Anthem.

Thangarajah, Priyadarshini, and Ponni Arasu. 2011. "Queen Women and the Law in India." In *Law Like Love: Queer Perspectives on Law*, edited by Arvind Narrain and Alok Gupta, 325–37. New Delhi: Yoda.

Thapan, Meenakshi. 2004. "Embodiment and Identity in Contemporary Society: Femina and the 'New' Indian Woman." *Contributions to Indian Sociology* 38 (3): 411–44.

Tharu, Susie, and Tejaswini Niranjana. 1994. "Problems for a Contemporary Theory of Gender." *Social Scientist* 22 (3–4): 93–117.

Thayer, Millie. 2010. *Making Transnational Feminism: Rural Women, NGO Activists, and Northern Donors in Brazil*. London: Routledge.

Vijayakumar, Gowri. 2021. *At Risk: Indian Sexual Politics and the Global AIDS Crisis*. Stanford, CA: Stanford University Press.

Von Schnitzler, Antina. 2016. *Democracy's Infrastructure: Techno-politics and Citizenship after Apartheid*. Princeton, NJ: Princeton University Press.

Walters, William. 2012. *Governmentality: Critical Encounters*. London: Routledge.

Ward, Jane. 2008. *Respectably Queer: Diversity Culture in LGBT Activist Organizations*. Nashville, TN: Vanderbilt University Press.

Warner, Michael, ed. 1993. *Fear of a Queer Planet: Queer Politics and Social Theory*. Minneapolis: University of Minnesota Press.

Wiegman, Robyn. 1999. "Feminism, Institutionalism, and the Idiom of Failure." *Differences* 11 (3): 107–36.

Wiegman, Robyn. 2000. "Feminism's Apocalyptic Futures." *New Literary History* 31 (4): 805–25.

Wiegman, Robyn. 2002. "Academic Feminism against Itself." *NWSA Journal* 14 (2): 18–37.

Wiegman, Robyn, and Elizabeth A. Wilson. 2015. "Introduction: Antinormativity's Queer Conventions." *Differences* 26 (1): 1–25.

Williams, Raymond. 1977. *Marxism and Literature*. New York: Oxford University Press.

Williamson, Terrion. 2019. "In Defense of Ourselves." In "Black Feminism Reimagined, by Jennifer C. Nash" (symposium). Syndicate, November 21, 2019. https://syndicate.network/symposia/literature/black-feminism-reimagined/.

Wilson, Kalpana. 2008. "Reclaiming 'Agency', Reasserting Resistance." *IDS Bulletin* 39 (6): 83–91.

Wilson, Kalpana. 2015. "Towards a Radical Re-appropriation: Gender, Development and Neoliberal Feminism." *Development and Change* 46 (4): 803–32.

Zaidi, Sarover, and Samprati Pani. 2020. "If on a Winter's Night, Azadi…." Indian Cultural Forum, February 24, 2020. Accessed August 3, 2020. https://indianculturalforum.in/2020/02/24/if-on-a-winters-night-azadi/.

INDEX

raising age of, 204n23, 205n25; rural women's defense of, 127–30

Citizenship Amendment Act (CAA), 171–74, 199n21, 213n9, 213n12, 214n13

clothing and jewelry: queer aesthetics and caste closet and, 90–94; rural women and, 109–11, 137–40, 209n15; self-care and, 148–49; self-fashioning and, 137–40

coercion, microfinance and role of, 123–26, 128–30

collective identity, self-transformation *vs.*, 11–12, 136–37, 180nn21–22, 208n11

colonialism: child marriage and, 117–19; Indian feminism and, 12–16, 177n4, 180n24

coming out: antinormativity and intersectionality in, 99–100; caste and class and, 90–94; Global North framing of, 197n7; queer domesticities and, 81–84, 197n8, 198n10; queer self-fashioning and, 77–80; self-fashioning and, 95–99; transmasculinity and homelessness and, 85–90, 197nn8–9, 199nn16–17; Western master narrative of, 197n7

Communist Party of India (CPM), 18–23, 182n39

communist politics, SFE activism and, 96–99

consciousness-raising: Indian women's movement and, 6, 45–46, 204n16; Janam's focus on, 104–6, 111–16, 205n30; SFE focus on, 56–62

consumption: microfinance and, 203n12; queer aesthetics and caste closet and, 90–94, 200n23, 200n25; self-care and, 146–49, 210n26, 210n27

co-optation: development and, 32–36; Indian feminism and, 26–28, 166–70; indoor toilet campaign as symbol of, 35–36, 141–45; queer feminist governmentality and, 72–76; queer politics in India and, 48–49

Counsel Club (Kolkata), 50

counter-heteronormative movements, 38–40

COVID-19 pandemic and impact of, 173–76

critical feminism, neoliberalism and, 9–12

critique of feminism, co-optation and, 166–70

Cross, Jamie, 212n38

cruel optimism, 156–59

cyberfeminism, in India, 40–41. *See also* activism: digital activism

Cyclone Amphan, 174

Da Costa, Dia, 206n35

Dalit Bahujan parties, 18–23, 179n13

Dalit feminism: coming out and, 77–80; digital activism and, 189n42, 190n44; growth of, 208n6; human rights and, 171, 201n32; millennials and, 42, 44–45, 189n38; queer aesthetics and, 93–94

Das Theke Das Hajar network, 189n37

Dave, Naisargi, xx, 38, 51, 57, 67, 83, 190n5, 197n8

Debi, Rashsundari, 132–33, 135, 207n1, 210n24

decriminalization of homosexuality, 28–31, 44, 67, 184n4, 184n6, 200n28

Defense of Muslim Women's Act of 1986 (Shah Bano Act), 181n29

dependency, women's support groups and circuits of, 51–55

Desai, Manisha, 187n25

Devi, Bhanwari, 35, 186n21

digital technology: crowdsourced list of sexual predators, 189n43; Dalit activism and, 189n43, 190n44; Indian feminist activism and, 188n34, 189nn40–41; millennial feminism and, 43–45; subcultural formation and belonging and, 63–67, 194n29

dol (self-help group), difference and hierarchy of NGO staff in interaction with, 122–23, 127–30, 207n44

domestic respectability: clothing and jewelry as symbols of, 137–40; control of women through, 141–45, 208n4; rural women's political activism and, 150–52; self-care and, 147–49; workforce participation and, 135–37, 208nn6–7

Donner, Henrike, 144

dowry, Janam/Vigil Group's focus on, 113, 211n31

Durbar Mahila Samanwaya Committee, 188n30

Dutt, Yashica, 77, 93, 191n12, 201n32

Dutta, Aniruddha, 77, 93, 188n30, 191n12, 201n32, 202n40

Ebang Bewarish (*. . . And the Unclaimed*) (documentary), 60–61

economic development: feminist critiques of, 207n43; human rights and, 103–6; Indian special economic zones, 212n38; microfinance and, 113–16; millennial feminism and, 40–45; social norms approach in, 204n17; women's co-optation and resistance and, 32–36, 209n12

Edelman, Lee, 197n5

education: ambivalent benefits of, 206n35; child marriage activism and, 119–23, 205n32; compromised freedom in, 135–37; girl effect and, 117–19, 205n33; neoliberal development and, 33–36; women's aspirations and, 153–56

elopement: agency through, 122, 129–31; consent and coercion and, 211n35; Janam's focus on, 116, 144; social media and, 110, 152

empowerment: girl effect and, 117–19; microfinance linked to, 103–6; pleasure and, 161–66; self-care and, 145–49; self-government and, 9–12

Eng, David, 198n10

entanglement: development and women's co-optation and resistance, 32–36; Indian feminism and, 26–31; of lesbian and feminist activism, 51–55; neoliberalism and girl effect and, 116–19; of pleasure and power, 161–66

entrepreneurialism, globalization of, 10–12

Eschle, Catherine, 179n16

Fabindia retail chain, 92, 200n26

family and kin: caste and class and coming out, 94; child marriage and, 118–19;

microfinance institutions and, 106; power structures within, 149–52, 211n33, 211n34; queer antinormativity and, 196n2, 197nn4–5; queer domesticities and, 79–84, 198n10; queer homelessness and rejection and, 85–90, 198n14

fasting, by Hindu Bengali women, 146–47

Fearless Freedom (Krishnan), 134

feminist failure, governmentality and, 24–25, 130–31, 207n45

feminist governmentality: in Bengal, 24, 48–49, 60–62; colonialism and, 177n4; critique of microfinance and, 33–34; cruel optimism and, 156–59; digital technology and, 63–67; entanglement in states and law of, 26–31; evolution of, 47–76; failure of, 130–31; history of Indian liberalization and, 12–16; homonormativity and, 69–72; identity politics and, 56–57; limits of, 123–30; millennial feminism and, 42–45; NGO-ization paradigm and, 36–40; principles of, 5–8; productive capacity of, 133–34; queer/lesbian dichotomy, 56–58; reorganization of, 62–67; self-fashioning and, 9–12, 80; sex workers and, 14–16, 185n9; SFE regulation and conduct of lesbian life and, 67–72; transgender groups and, 30–31, 72–76

feminist scholarship: as "imperial gift," xi–xii; in India, 4–5; self-government and, 9–12

FeministsIndia, 214n17

Feminist Theory (journal), 160–61

Ferguson, James, 115–16, 204n20

Fernando, Mayanthi, 161

financial stability: Janam's discussion of, 113–16; lesbian and feminist advocacy for, 51–52; queer domesticities and, 81–84; rural women's political activism and, 150–52, 211n32

Fire (film), 21, 30, 39, 50, 183n43

Floyd, George, 214n17

Foucault, Michel, 77, 179n14, 179nn17–18

Fraser, Nancy, 33

Freeman, Carla, 5, 10
friendship (*bondhura*), 141–45, 210n22
funding politics: Leftist suspicion of, 183n41; Indian feminism and, 2–3; NGO-ization paradigm and, 37–40

Gandhi, Rajiv, 181n29
gang rape cases: Indian feminism and, 1, 7, 19, 182n38, 186n21, 187n25; limits of legalism in, 35; millennial feminist protests against, 41–45
gay male activism, lesbian Indian women and, 50–51
gender: ambiguity and homelessness of, 85–90; Bengali culture and, 17–23; femininity and, 82–84; Indian liberalization and issues of, 14–16; Janam's focus on, 111–16; neoliberal development and, 32–36
Ghatak, Anchita, 172
Ghose, Toorjo, 188n30
Ghosh, Amitav, 200n27
Ghosh, Apoorva, 53–54
Ghosh, Subhagata, 28, 191n8, 192n18, 196n42
Gilbertson, Amanda, 204n17
Giraud, Eva, 27, 184n2
globalization, NGO-ization and, 39–40
Global South: gender and sexual violence in, xi; philanthrocapitalism in, 33–36; queer feminist governmentality in, 5–8; racialization and feminism in, 10–12; subaltern women in, 33–36
going out (*ghora*), 141–45
Gooptu, Nandini, 180n22
Gopinath, Gayatri, 197n9
Gordon, Avery, 178n12, 212n3
governmentality: development and, 32–36; Indian feminism and, 23; neoliberal logic and, 5–8; racialization and, 10–12; self-government and, 161–66; subaltern politics and, 24
Gqola, Pumla, 212n4
graamer meye (subaltern lesbian of rural Bengal), 49, 57–58, 60–62, 72, 163–64, 167, 212n3

grassroots activism, NGO-ization paradigm and, 36–40
Grewal, Inderpal, xix, 26–27

Halberstam, Judith, 199n20, 207n45
Halperin, David, 77
Hartman, Saidiya, 132, 134, 207n3
hashtag feminism, 44–46, 190n46
Hemmings, Clare, 160, 175, 178n12, 212n5
heteronormativity: Indian institutionalization of, 28–31, 184n5; Indian liberalization and challenges to, 14–16; moral policing of, 83–84; ruptures with, xv
hijras, 30–31, 186n13, 186n16; transgender politics and, 74–76, 196n44
Hindu nationalism: gender and sexuality in, 35–36, 41–45, 171–76; Muslim masculinity stereotype in, 129–30; neoliberalism and, 7–8; postindependence liberalization and, 14–16
Hindu Right: autonomous women's groups and, 209n13; Ayodhya dispute, 171; caste politics and, 96–99, 202n39; child marriage and, 118–19; economic liberalization and rise of, 15, 26; millennial feminist challenges to, 42–43
HIV/AIDS epidemic: biopolitics of, 38–39; Indian sexual politics and, 28–31, 186n18; NGO-ization and, 39–40; queer movement in India and, 21–23, 184n6; subaltern politics and, 14–16
Hodžić, Sadia, 36
#Hokkolorob, 45–46, 64
home-based labor: respectability of, 135–37; for rural women, 206n34
homelessness, coming out and, 85–90, 197nn8–9
homonationalism, 97–99, 190n2, 192n17
homosexuality: decriminalization in India of, 28–31, 44, 67, 184n4, 184n6, 200n28; media sensationalization of, 67
hooks, bell, 183n45
Horton, Brian, 79
household (*ghare*): Indian women's confinement to, 133–37, 208n4; self-care and burden of, 145–49

human rights: Janam's advocacy based on, 103–6, 112–16; queer politics and, 53–54, 191nn11–12

Hungry Tide, The (Ghosh), 200n27

identity politics: SFE and, 56; transphobia and, 74–76

indebtedness from microfinance: burden of, 33–36, 206n40; neoliberal perspective on, 114–15; power relations and, 124–26, 206n41

Indian feminism: autonomy and co-optation in, 3–4; Bengal politics and, 18–23; care ethics and, 170–76; class and caste issues in, xiii–xv; Communist Party of India and, 182n39; co-optation and intersectionality in, 26–28, 166–70; evolution of, 1–5; generational divides in, 201n37; governmentality and, 23; Hindu Right and, 209n13; history of Indian liberalization and, 12–16; millennial feminisms and, 40–45; pleasure and fun sought by young feminists, 141–45; political activism and, 172–76; public-private divide and, 30–31; queer to transgender in, 72–76; self-government and, 161–66; state relations with, 28–36

Indian National Trinamool Trade Union Congress, 19

Indian Penal Code, Section 377: reinstatement of, 77–80; repeal of, 28–31, 44, 184n4, 185n9

Indian women's movement (IWM): changes in, 4–5, 178n10; co-optation and intersectionality in, 8, 26–28; emergence of, 1–2, 177n2; globalization and, 187n26; legal engagement in, 185n7; lesbian activism and, 29–31; millennial feminism and, 42–45; neoliberal development and, 32–36; NGO-ization paradigm and, 36–40; otherness in, 11–12; postindependence development of, 13, 180nn25–26; suspicion of Western politics in, 45–46

"India Shining" campaign, 15

individual transformation, Janam's ideology of, 114–16, 122–23

indoor toilets, protection of women and, 35–36

Integrated Child Protection Scheme, 205n28

Internet: hegemony of English on, 194n32; lesbian dating and, 64–67, 194n31; millennial feminism and, 43–45, 189n42; subcultural formation and belonging and, 63–67

intersectionality: antinormativity and, 99–100; caste and class and coming out and, 90–94; co-optation and, 168–70; feminist governmentality and, 126–30; hashtag feminism and, 46; queerness and, 79–80

Iran, transsexuality in, 198n14, 199n18

Jakobsen, Jostein, 153, 211n36, 212n38

Janam (pseudonym), 4–5; in Bengal, 21–23; child marriage activism and, 104, 116–30; compromise and limits of work by, 126–30; COVID-19 pandemic and work of, 174–76; evolution of, 102–6; feminist failure and, 131; gender training and consciousness-raising and, 111–16; gender violence focus of, 104–6; governmental techniques of, 6–8; microcredit plus rights activism of, 102–6, 119–23, 207n44; millennial feminism and, 101–2; peer education model of, 112, 204n17; political activism and, 150–52; self-government and development of, 9–12; SFE collaboration with, 162–66; translocal logic and practices and, 123–26; Vigil Group (VG) established by, 104, 110, 119–23; women's aspirations and role of, 154–56

jewelry, as marriage symbol, 139–40

John, Mary, xiii, 8, 13–14, 38, 135, 184n1, 187n26, 208n5

Joshi, Yuvraj, 197n6

Karim, Lamia, 206n41

Karnad, Raghu, 173

Karwa Chauth festival, 69–70
Kaur, Ravinder, 92, 200–201n30
Kaviraj, Sudipta, 98–99, 101–2
Khadi Bhandar company, 92–93, 200n29
Khalili, Laleh, 149
Khubchandani, Kareem, 193n26
Kirmani, Nida, 209n19
Kiss of Love campaign, 42
Kolkata, India: cafe culture in, 193n23; caste and class issues in, 201n35; culture and politics in, 50; leftist hegemony in, 95–99; queer activism in, 47–48; queer domesticities and, 81–84; queer life and politics in, 62–67; queer self-fashioning in, 79–80; radical feminism in, 45–46, 107, 181n32, 183n40; transgender politics in, 73–76
Kolkata Book Fair, 201n36
kothis, 30–31, 186n13
Krishnan, Kavita, 40, 42, 134–35, 141, 207n1
Krishnan, Sneha, 194n29, 206n38
Kumar, Radha, 207n42

labor of women: caste and class and, 34–36, 186n19; home-based labor, 206n34
Lall, Jessica, 188n33
Lamb, Sarah, 140–41
law, Indian feminism and role of, 28–31, 185n7
Lefebvre, Alexandre, 179n14, 210n23
Left Front government (Bengal), 17–20, 111–12, 182n33, 182n37
Legg, Stephen, 184n5
LGBTQ politics: in Bengal, 20–23; cast and class in India and, 47–49; critiques of, 56–57; entanglement in state and law of, 28–31; evolution in India of, 50–55; human rights and, 53–54; Indian decriminalization of homosexuality and, 28–31, 200n28; lesbian hauntings in India and, 178n12; millennial feminism and, 42–45; NGO-ization and, 39–40; queer domesticities

and, 81–84; respectability in, 197n6; SFE activism and, 96–99; shifting assemblages in, 202n40; transgender minorities and, 72–76, 99–100, 199nn18–20; transnational aspects of, 188n31
liberalization of India: feminism and, 12; history of, 12–16; queer culture in, 77–80
limited intersectionality, 94
loitering, pleasures of, 44–46, 141, 190n44, 209n20
Love, Heather, "feeling backward", 54, 75, 178n11, 191n13
love jihad campaigns, 118, 129
Lukose, Ritty, 16, 209n16

Maguishca, Bice, 179n16
Mahila Samakhya program, 32–33, 211n30, 212n37
Maitree (Friendship) feminist conglomerate, 20–23, 29–30, 52, 102–3, 189n37
Majumder, Sarasij, 61, 136
makeover paradigm, self-care and, 149
Mandal Commission, 15, 181n28, 186n15
Manjuben Truckdriver (film), 199n16
market ideology: microfinance institutions and, 103–6, 112–16; queer marketization and, 67–72; women's empowerment linked to, 33–36
marriage: clothing aesthetics and, 139–40; contestation and reconfiguration in, 151–52; queer feminist contestation about, 69–72, 195n39, 198n11; transgender politics and, 74–76. See also child marriage
masculinity, transgender identity and, 85–90
matte aesthetic in Indian women's clothing, 92, 140
media coverage: of Indian feminism, 35–36; Indian feminism and, 7; of lesbian Indian women, 50; sensationalization of homosexuality in, 67
Menon, Nivedita, xiii, 19, 37, 56–57, 181n29, 188n30, 201n31
#MeToo movement, 44–46, 190n46

feminism and perspectives on, 29–31; Indian liberalization and issues of, 14–16; leftist politics in Bengal and, 96–99; in millennial Bengal, 20–23; NGO-ization and politics of, 38–40; sexual identity and, 183n45; taboos in Indian concerning, 52; women's agency concerning, 150–52

sexual minorities: state and, 29–31; subordination and marginalization of, 73–76

sexual violence: digital technology and mobilization against, 44–45; Indian lesbian experience of, 51–55; IWM hierarchy of, 29–30; Janam's focus on, 104–6, 202n2, 204n22; laws involving, 14–16, 30–31, 202n2; marriage and, 124–26; millennial feminist protests of, 41–45; women's mobilization against, 102–3. *See also* gang rape cases

sex work: Indian feminism and, 14–16, 185n9; NGO-ization and struggles of, 39–40; organization in Bengal of, 20–23, 183n42, 188n30; police targeting of, 30–31; transgender politics and, 73–76

Shah, Amit, 213n9

Shah, Chayanika, 185n10

Shah, Svati P., 193n21

Shahani, Nishant, 190n2

Shah Bano, 181n29

Shaheen Bagh (Muslim women's sit-in), 172–76

Shakti (power), 113, 204n18

Sharma, Aradhana, 35, 155, 211n30, 212n37

Sharma, Manu, 188n33

Shiv Sena, 177n1

sindoor, 70–72, 139–40, 195n38

Singh, Pawan, 80

Singh, V. P., 181n28

Sinha Roy, Mallarika, 101, 180n27, 183n41

Sircar, Oishik, 30, 186n14, 190n2

SlutWalk marches, 41, 43, 189n39

smart phones, women's rights and, 109–11, 148–49

social media: elopement and, 110, 152; Indian feminist activism and, 188n34, 190n46, 209n21; queer activism and,

48; rural women and, 209n15, 209n21; SFE's use of, 64–67, 69–72

social norms approach in development, 204n17

social transformation: cruel optimism and, 156–59; marketization of, 38; postindependence Indian women's movement and, 13–16; self-governance *vs.* collective identity and, 11–12, 180n21

Sonar Bangla (Golden Bengal), 107, 181n32

South Africa, space and sexuality in postapartheid era, 193n27

sovereignty, NGOs and, 6–8, 183n41

Spivak, Gayatri Chakravorty, 60–61

state: child marriage and, 117–19, 125–26, 205n28; gendered labor segregation and, 34–36, 186n19; governmentality and, 5–8; Indian feminism and role of, 14–16, 28–36; millennial feminist rejection of, 41–45; neoliberal development and, 32–36; NGOs and, 37–40, 186n20, 212n40; sexual minorities and role of, 29–31; transgender politics and, 87–90, 200n21

Still, Clarinda, 208n6

Strey, Jacquelyn, 63

subaltern subjects: communism and, 98–99; disobedience framing of, 127–30; feminist failure and, 130–31; feminist governmentality and, 5–8, 24, 177n4; marginal sexual groups and, 30–31; microfinance coercion and, 124–26; neoliberalism's impact on, 165–66; NGO-ization and, 37–40; peer education model and, 112, 204n17; postindependence Indian women's movement and, 13–16, 178nn8–9, 180n27; queer feminist governmentality and, 49; transgender identity and, 72–76; women's agency and, 33–36; women's aspirations and, 155

subjectivity: feminist theory and, 9–12, 180n22; microfinance institutions and, 112–16

Subramanian, Ajantha, 202n41

suicide, SFE and issues of, 59–62, 192n18, 192n20

CPSIA information can be obtained
at www.ICGtesting.com
Printed in the USA
BVHW051021211222
654758BV00015B/126

9 781478 018889